A Way to Be Free
Volume II

PULPLESS.ᴄᴏᴍ, ɪɴᴄ. Books by Robert LeFevre

A Way to Be Free, Volumes I and II
Slander (forthcoming)
Cosmo (forthcoming)
Death Valley Johnny (forthcoming)
The Fundamentals of Liberty (forthcoming)
This Bread is Mine (forthcoming)
Raising Children for Fun and Profit (forthcoming)

A Way to Be Free

The Autobiography of Robert LeFevre

Volume II
The Making of a Modern American Revolution

PULPLESS.COM, INC.
10736 Jefferson Blvd., Suite 775
Culver City, CA 90230-4969, USA.
Voice & Fax: (500) 367-7353
Home Page: http://www.pulpless.com/
Business inquiries to info@pulpless.com
Editorial inquiries & submissions to
editors@pulpless.com

Copyright © 1999 by Loy LeFevre
All rights reserved. Published by arrangement with Loy LeFevre. Printed in the United States of America. The rights to all previously published materials by Robert LeFevre are owned by the Loy LeFevre, and are claimed both under existing copyright laws and natural logorights. All other materials taken from published sources without specific permission are either in the public domain or are quoted and/or excerpted under the Fair Use Doctrine. Except for attributed quotations embedded in critical articles or reviews, no part of this book may be reproduced or utilized in any form or by any means, electronic or mechanical, including photocopying, recording, or by any information storage and retrieval system, without written permission from the publisher.

First Pulpless.Com™, Inc. Edition September, 1999.
Library of Congress Catalog Card Number: 99-62898
ISBN: 1-58445-144-0

Book and Cover designed by CaliPer, Inc.
Cover Photograph courtesy of Loy LeFevre
© 1999 by Loy LeFevre

Paperless Book™ digital editions of this and all other Pulpless.Com™ books are available worldwide for immediate download 24-hours-a-day every day from the Pulpless.Com, Inc., web site, either for a small charge, or *free* with commercial messages. Please visit our Catalog on the World Wide Web at
www.pulpless.com

A Note from the Publisher

After my first encounter with Bob LeFevre, listening to a speech he gave at the Hunter College Libertarian Conference in New York City, in September, 1972, I braved my first and only ride on the back of a motorcycle, holding on for dear life through mid-Manhattan traffic, to meet him at his hotel room. We immediately hit it off, talking until two a.m., after which I was convinced that I seriously needed to rethink some of my most cherished notions about the nature of justice. Bob was incredibly generous with his time to this first-year college student.

Soon afterwards, we entered into extensive correspondence, resulting in his inviting me out to his and Loy's home in Santa Ana, California, in February, 1973. During that visit, I did a short taped interview with Bob that was published in *New Libertarian Notes*, in June 1973.

Two years later, in May, 1975, I invited Bob to be the keynote speaker at the second CounterCon conference on libertarian economics, which I organized off-season at a summer camp owned by relatives of mine. Three months later I moved to Southern California, and Bob's presence there was undoubtedly one of the attractions.

Bob LeFevre was one of my best friends until the day he left us. This was no exclusive honor since you'd have to work overtime *not* to be one of Bob LeFevre's friends. My aunt Henri, an ideological socialist for her entire life, was charmed by Bob's two presentations at the CounterCon conference, despite Bob's arguing the opposite of just about everything she believed.

I am delighted not only to be able to publish the life of Robert LeFevre, in his own words, for the first time anywhere, but also, to be able to publish in upcoming months, in addition to his classic nonfiction works, previously squirreled-away manuscripts including two novels and a short story collection.

I thank Loy LeFevre for trusting me with the honor of bringing the major life's work of Robert LeFevre to a world sorely in need of both his ideas and his kindness.

I also thank Victor, Veronica, and Vanessa Koman for the arduous task of OCR scanning in the photocopy of a 2096 page typescript of uneven quality.

Finally, I extend my gratitude to Wendy McElroy, an accomplished author in her own right, for the marvelous feat of editing this massive work to the high standards that Bob LeFevre required during his career as a writer, editor, and publisher. Wendy started with often-hashed text files, from a manuscript which was dictated in large part by Bob LeFevre to his secretary, Ruth Dazey, and Wendy polished this diamond-in-the-rough into a Hope Diamond.

—J. Neil Schulman, June 9, 1999

To Loy LeFevre,
Ruth Dazey
Edith Shank
and Marji Llewellyn

Table of Contents

CHAPTER	PAGE
LXII	11
LXIII	21
LXIV	33
LXV	45
LXVI	59
LXVII	69
LXVIII	81
LXIX	89
LXX	101
LXXI	115
LXXII	127
LXXIII	135
LXXIV	145
LXXV	159
LXXVI	173
LXXVII	187
LXXVIII	197
LXXIX	207
LXXX	217
LXXXI	229
LXXXII	239
LXXXIII	249
LXXXIV	259
LXXXV	269
LXXXVI	279
LXXXVII	291
LXXXVIII	299
LXXXIX	311
XC	321

CHAPTER	PAGE
XCI	333
XCII	345
XCIII	353
XCIV	367
XCV	379
XCVI	389
XCVII	403
XCVIII	413
XCIX	425
C	437
CI	451
CII	461
CIII	471
Epilogue	485

Chapter LXII

I had to make up for lost time. My four years in the service seemed like four years of suspended animation. I had made the assumption that my country came first. My personal affairs had been in a mess at the time I enlisted, but I was entirely sincere in my patriotic devotion.

I would be out of the Army for good in a few months. During the transition, I wanted to place myself in line for a good income. I had experienced enough of poverty and lack. My obligations to my children, my wife, my former wife, and my various creditors had at last created a spirit of rebellion in me. I wanted money, big bucks, fast!

Before the hostilities, I had earned a good income while in the real estate and business opportunity fields. The earnings were irregular, but the commissions were generous. And the way to make up for lost time was to throw myself into the real estate business once more.

Back at Inter-City Company, nothing worked fast enough for me. To increase my earnings, I must become a property owner as well as an agent. That way I could get the best out of both worlds.

The difficulty with becoming a property owner, particularly with income property, is that a person needs some money of his own with which to get started. While it may not take a great deal, a few hundred dollars seemed as far away from my grasp as a million.

Undeterred, I began looking around for some kind of income property I could acquire with little or no down payment.

As anyone knows, when it comes to income property, if the seller takes back the mortgage himself all he ever receives from the buyer is a down payment. The differential between purchase price and selling price—the interest on the unpaid balance and the full price paid—is all generated by the property itself.

Because sellers know this, it is difficult to find one who doesn't want a good-sized down payment or independent financing so that he can turn his investment capital around.

In this case, luck was with me. I had been fully informed of market conditions prior to the war. Now, as I brought myself up to date, I ran across an apartment house building with no vacancies. It was in such bad condition, I figured the owner might be happy to unload it. And with little or nothing in the way of cash up front.

This building was located on the Great Highway, a few blocks north of the Fleishacker Zoo. It fronted the Pacific Ocean and was buffeted by wind, salt spray, and fog virtually every day of the year.

When I drove Loy out to see it, she was dismayed. I could hardly blame her. The building was the tallest one south of the Cliff House. It jutted, stark and ugly, with salt spray dimming its windows, which stared with cataract myopia across the western billows.

Her first reaction was: "I'd rather be caught dead than live in that thing."

I had to admit that the building was not a thing of beauty. I explained that, while our sense of aesthetics coincided, my interest was occasioned by its income potential. What we needed was money. The building could produce it. We would buy it for an investment, not for pleasure. Because it was in bad condition, we might be able to buy it without any down payment, if I could talk fast enough.

Presuming this to be utter nonsense, Loy went along with the idea.

The exterior was gray stucco. It loomed above the one-and-two story residences in the vicinity like a snaggle tooth in the lower jaw of a broom-riding witch. Everything about it was rectangular. The windows were rectangle, the front door a rectangle, the facade a rectangle.

The property was owned by an elderly widow, who was known to her tenants as "Old Lady Grant." To my delight, I discovered that this poor widow woman was a millionaire several times over. She had made a fortune owning buildings just like this one. I didn't want to be a party to talking a poor widow out of needed dollars. A rich widow was different.

I called on Mrs. Grant one evening. She was as gaunt and rectangular in her person as her property. She made money on this apartment building and on everything else she owned, by operating frugally. If the roof sprang a leak, she repaired it herself by daubing tar in likely looking places. It often leaked. Just as often she daubed. She refused to repaint or to fix up. She explained that the tenants could do that if they pleased. She was eighty years of age and the gleam in her eye for the dollar was as clear as a schoolgirl's complexion.

Why had she let the building deteriorate to its present condition? She explained that government price and rent controls had tied her hands. She couldn't afford to make improvements or repairs. She couldn't raise rents. So as inflation occurred and costs for various services zoomed, she saw to it that services declined, leaving her in the profit column. Otherwise, she explained, she'd be better off to burn the place and forget it.

She gave one of the tenants a discount for managing the place for her and netted between $200 and $250 a month, depending on the number of vacancies she had. She furnished heat and hot water. Each tenant paid for his own lights, gas, and telephone.

There was one four-room apartment, six three-room, six two-room, and one single—for a total of fourteen units. Additionally, there was a sleeping room with zero amenities, which rented for $10.00 per month. All the apartments were furnished in v-e-r-y early turn-of-the-century stuff. Some had made the turn too sharply; some hadn't quite made it.

The rents throughout the building were unbelievably low. They ranged from $10.00 per month for the sleeping room to $45.00 per month for the four-room apartment. The two and three-room apartments ranged from $22.50 to $37.50.

When the building was full, it netted about $250 per month. It had an excellent record for occupancy. There is a certain type of person who is so enchanted by the ocean that he will do almost anything to live in sight of it.

Mrs. Grant wanted $50,000 for the whole package and she owned it clear of any encumbrances. Further, as it turned out, she didn't want the cash. She was willing to carry back a first mortgage. Thus, she would finance it herself. But she wanted $5,000 as a down payment.

I permitted her to believe that I could readily put up the $5,000 if, after a close examination, I still liked the building. The important fact related to income and the ability of income property to pay for its own purchase. I could own the building for a few years, pay off the encumbrances, whatever they turned out to be, and then sell my equity for cash. Thus, I could make something out of nothing. All I risked was my time and energy, presuming I could raise the money elsewhere.

I went with Mrs. Grant to survey the property. It was as badly cared for inside as the exterior foreshadowed. The furnace room contained two furnaces that burned oil. One of the chores of the in-resident manager was to turn on the furnaces each day and to turn them off as well. Hot water was provided from four to eight p.m. only. Heat in the building was provided from five to eight p.m. Never mind the weather.

The furnace room was a filthy hole covered with soot and grease. However, it met all legal requirements and was inspected at least once a year.

What was truly appalling to me was a fairly large area in the rear of, and under, the building. The structure was classed as a three-story, frame and stucco apartment house. In theory, that meant three stories above ground and a full basement under the ground.

Because of its proximity to the ocean, the basement was entirely above ground. Excavation would probably have produced seawater. So, in reality, the basement was on the ground floor and there were three full stories above it. However, the basement (first floor) contained three ground-level apartments. Where the fourth apartment should have been was nothing but an open space. The structure had been erected on vertical beams that stood naked and unproductive. Into that vacant area, junk was piled from the cement slab to the floor joists above. One quick look and I realized that section posed a fire hazard. It also provided a great opportunity. In the market place, what appears to be a problem is, in fact, an opportunity.

That unproductive, unfinished eyesore was large enough for a two-room apartment. If I owned the building, I could finish that off and rent it out for $50 or $60 per month, furnished.

That would enhance the profit picture, making the building more valuable, thus increasing a future selling price. By clearing up the furnace room, adding a touch of paint and doing a bit of fixing, the place could shine. It would never be beautiful. The architects had seen to that. But it was functional, and it could be made more so. In the process, it could earn more money.

A further advantage of the building was the garage. There was room for twelve cars. Unfortunately, the garage had been built with only six doors. Six cars would have to be parked behind the first six. And the garage building was so close to the apartment house, there was inadequate turning room. By removing half of the garage spaces, there would be turning room and at least adequate parking for six. Nothing would be lost in terms of potential income, and space would be gained for all.

I told Mrs. Grant I wanted a few days to think it over, and then closeted myself with Mr. Weiss. Did he any ideas where I could find $5,000 for a down payment?

He had an idea. A woman named Caroline Gray was a good friend of his who was often called upon to help with financing business opportunities. She was known affectionately as "Ma" Gray. She didn't put up the money herself, because her word was good. She made a business of co-signing notes, primarily with the Morris Plan Company.

The Morris Plan would lend money on furniture and fixtures but, in addition, wanted a co-signer. Mrs. Gray would receive a fee, usually $1,000, for signing the note with the Morris Plan. Her fee was paid up front. Thus, if $5,000 were wanted, $6,000 would be borrowed. It was up to the buyer to operate the business he had purchased in such a way so as to pay off the loan. Meanwhile, Mrs. Gray got what she lovingly referred to as her "pound of flesh."

The reason Weiss relied on her, the reason the Morris Plan tended to accept her almost without question was because, in the event of default, Mrs. Gray, herself would take over the faltering business and make it pay. Mentally and physically, she was the counterpart of Old Lady Grant. And then some.

In respect to the transaction under consideration, we were talking about real estate rather than a business opportunity that usually entailed nothing more durable than a lease. So Weiss suggested that Mrs. Gray borrow the money herself from the Morris Plan and take back a second mortgage on the apartment house.

She would receive $1,000 up front. I would make her payments for her at the Morris Plan. During the term of the loan, I would arrange to give "Ma Gray" an additional $1,000 from time to time until she received a total of $5,000 for herself. Thus, I would actually be paying an extra $5,000 for the building. Of course, I would have to pay the interest as well.

This appeared to me to be a splendid beginning with no money of my own. The transaction was completed. Loy and I became the owners of record of an apartment house building on the Great Highway in San Francisco.

Laws prevented us from evicting any tenant unless there was legal cause. Legal cause consisted only of a failure to pay the rent, creating a public nuisance, or any other kind of illegal activity conducted by a tenant. Rents were frozen absolutely, under the OPA.

Once more, luck came our way. The tenant who occupied the single unit gave notice. I decided, and Loy agreed under pressure, that it would be to our best interests to move into that single unit. It wasn't large enough for us but we could put up with it until something larger in the building opened.

When we moved in, we found our circumstances little less than appalling. The single was on the ground floor (basement) and had been one of the rooms of a three-room apartment. It had been redesigned as a kitchenette apartment. But the only barrier separating us from the remaining two-room apartment on that floor was a large double door, comprised of multiple panes of glass masked by drapes.

Every noise in the two-room apartment came to our ears with ease. Indeed, there was no way to shut it out.

Had the tenant been conducting her affairs in a normal way this might have been tolerable. But the very first night we discovered that our neighbor was engaged in some behavior that was contrary to our expectations.

The two-roof was occupied by a married woman whose husband was a sailor. He was at sea and she was, at least in theory, alone.

The first night in our new quarters, we were awakened by a male voice coming through the double door. Following those bass tones came other sounds, indicating that some of the furniture was doing double duty. Then came haggling over the price.

Loy and I stared at each other, astonishment and disgust filling our thoughts. Then it got worse.

The two-room apartment, being on the first floor, happened to have both a front and a back door. The front door opened from the lobby. The back door opened directly to the driveway on the south side of the building.

The male voice we had heard turned out to belong to the first customer of the evening. There were others. They came in the front way and exited out the back.

Loy pounded on the door and demanded that the noise stop. For her pains, she received a string of profanity from an outraged soprano who told us to mind our own business.

I took a crack at communication, explaining that what went on in that apartment was our business since we were the new owners.

This claim had no effect whatever and business continued as usual.

The next day I confronted our tenant and explained that what was happening in her apartment was illegal. If it continued, I said, she would be evicted.

I was laughed at and told I was powerless to throw anyone out. She was the tenant. As Lon as she paid her rent, she could do as she pleased in her own apartment. The law protected her.

After a few days, or rather nights, in which, with variations, the same scene repeated, I decided to take legal steps to bring that enterprise to a close. I brought a legal action. The tenant was served notice to appear in court on a specific date to show cause why she should not be evicted.

Acting as my own attorney, I stood before the judge in the appropriate courtroom and demanded eviction. I alleged that my tenant was engaged in illegal sexual acts and, under the law, should be thrown out.

The woman was called to the bench, where, with tears running down her cheeks, she said that I was a mean, vicious person; that she was an honest, moral, God-fearing, married woman. She always paid her rent. The rent was cheap. She didn't have any money. I was one of those greedy, wealthy people who were out to take advantage of a poor lonely woman who had nowhere to turn. I was the owner, and, therefore, rich.

The judge turned to me. Did the woman pay her rent? She did. Did she pay on time? She did. How did I know what went on inside her apartment? Was I an eyewitness to any illegal activity?

I was not. However, I explained that various males came into the lobby and waited their turn. By this time I had actually witnessed that part of the operation. Then, they went into the apartment and went out the back door. I was also a witness to that. I admitted I didn't know what went on inside the apartment.

What did go on, the judge asked the tenant? She was doing the laundry of these various men, most of them sailors and friends of her husband, she explained. That was it. Laundry. As a favor. That was what the haggling over prices was about. She charged very little, but some of the men for whom she was only doing a favor wanted to cheat her out of their "laundry bills."

With a show of restraint both marvelous and ironic, the judge ruled in favor of the tenant. He told me to back off and content myself with minding my own business. When I tried to rebut that he shut me off. I had exhausted "legal recourse."

About a week after this, while Loy and I were making plans to rent another apartment somewhere, the problem was solved, and in the middle of the night.

We were awakened from a sound sleep by the sound of riot behind the closed doors. Things were bouncing off the walls. There was the crunch and shatter of breaking furniture. Blows were being exchanged. There were screams and moans and shouts occurring in more combat.

Loy called the police and they arrived, with moderate alacrity. By the time they got there, the tumult had subsided. They knocked at the tenant's door. It was opened by a huge sailor with a gash on his face and a grim set to his jaw. The woman cowered on the far side of the room. A mouse was beginning to form over one eye, her hair was disheveled, and her clothing torn. The room was a shambles.

The sailor introduced himself. "I'm the bitch's husband," he began. "I've been on a two-year hitch and just came home tonight. That dirty whore was spreading herself for a bunch of jacks. I've kicked them out."

"Well, you never sent me no money, you bastard!" the woman shrilled.

"Shut your goddamn mouth, honey," he said. "If I ever catch you doin' that kind of thing again I'm gonna kick your ass so hard you'll be riding on your own shoulders."

The woman winced and shuddered. The mental image his threat contained caused me to shudder in turn.

"I believe I have grounds to evict these people, don't I?" I asked the police.

"Don't bother," the sailor said. "She's going. We've got a home. She just came down here thinking I wouldn't find her. But I knew where to look. She's done it before."

"That seems to take care of things," the policeman said. "However, you could press charges for damage if this is your furniture."

"No charges, officer. Just see that they're out of here."

"Give me thirty minutes," the husband said. "Get your stuff together, sweetie face, or I'll give you another shiner."

Back in our single unit, we heard the departure.

"At last," I said to Loy, "we'll have a good night's sleep. I hope we don't have to go through anymore of this kind of thing to take possession of our own building." Loy said nothing. But she gave me a look that said, in effect, "Is this what it means to be a landlord?"

Chapter LXIII

While acquiring title and ultimate control of the apartment house, I continued in the Army's rehabilitation program. This entailed a drive to Southern California at least once a month so I could be examined and be given a small dose of physical therapy.

On one such visit to Santa Ana, I witnessed an event that remained in my memory. I had located a short cut by means of which I could reach the Army hospital by driving along a dirt road between two large orange groves. The way was narrow and dusty, but the saving in time and gasoline was significant enough so that I used it.

While driving along this little used lane one day, I heard the sound of a siren behind me and saw a police car closing fast in a cloud of dust. I knew I was not guilty of the slightest infraction, as I was operating at reduced speed. But, due to the narrowness of the right of way, I veered to the side and the police car roared past. Before I could regain the full use of the lane, a second car brushed by me on the left, driven by a civilian at a rate of speed exceeding that of the black and white.

A quarter of a mile further I came upon both vehicles. The civilian driver had forced the police vehicle to the side and both officers were still inside. The civilian was standing beside the official car. I stopped and rolled down the window to inquire as to the reason for the breakneck pursuit. I didn't have to ask.

The civilian, an ordinary businessman, by his attire, was in a towering rage. As his voice reached my ears, he was roaring, "...and at such a speed! You offered a threat to life and limb. I could have been killed."

I heard the officer at the wheel say, "Just who are you, anyway?"

I had instant anticipation. The civilian would reveal that he was a friend or a relative of someone in power. That was certainly the answer the officer expected. But the civilian's response came sharp and clear.

"Who am I?" he bellowed. "I'm a taxpayer, that's who! And don't you ever forget it!"

Both officers sat dumbly, nodding, acquiescing, the very picture of meek docility. I thought they'd clap handcuffs on their verbal assailant. But they didn't. They cowered like small boys caught too near the chocolate frosting.

I needed no questions answered, and drove on. But the phrase haunted me. "I'm a taxpayer, that's who! And don't you forget it!" Apparently, in Santa Ana at least one civilian was putting into practice the letter of the law. Probably, he was an attorney. But whoever he was, he was chastising the police and they were taking it. I decided that if one had courage, he could and really should speak up in his own favor.

So I decided with finality that I wanted nothing more to do with the Army. When the time came for me to be mustered out, I was given the option of entering the reserves. I ruled against it, although I was urged repeatedly to reconsider. Remaining in reserve status would bring me a bit of extra pay, and the obligations didn't amount to much. I could have used the money. There is a kind of tenuous security found in getting something for nothing. But I wanted *out*.

Also, I was told that I could apply for partial disability as a result of my injury. I wanted none of that, either. I had been a burden on the taxpayers long enough. I'd make it on my own, or I'd fail trying.

I received my honorable discharge, with a good conduct ribbon and two battle stars. In December, I had been in service just one month short of four years. The battle stars were awarded because I happened to be in territory classed as a "war zone" during hostilities. Nobody ever shot at me directly. But it was quite true that bombs fell in London and shells fell on the countryside to the east of Dijon while I was in those areas.

Ethel called for another meeting of the faithful. Loy and I attended. This time, Pearl and Jerry were present. As before, the major interest expressed by everyone there related to a "dictation." Could such an event occur? The requirement of having Pearl on hand had been met.

I should have refused absolutely. I didn't. Pearl's presence was as persuasive, subtle, and nearly as profound as it had been before the war. The truth was that I didn't know if I could regain the mental state of detachment necessary to these mysterious dictations. I was curious.

After considerable importuning, I agreed to make the attempt. I asked my friends to bear with me and to understand if, as a result of all that had transpired, I failed to "make contact."

With this agreed upon, I again sat facing Pearl. With no difficulty whatever, I climbed the stairs of my mind and blanked out. When I "came back," a dictation had occurred and I had no recollection of it whatever.

Loy was fascinated by what had occurred, but she was extremely uneasy. Her anxiety increased when it became apparent that Pearl's interest in me was meeting with a response. Who could blame her? Pearl danced attendance on me to Jerry's and Loy's mutual unhappiness.

Later, Ethel asked Loy to sing again. Neither Loy nor I recall the ballad that she sang, but the words were pertinent and poignant. The song let everyone know that her claim to me was not only final, but also one of equity. She would not consent to playing a secondary role.

After the gathering, Loy reinforced the ballad lyrics in private. I did my best to assure her that my interest in Pearl was purely within the metaphysical realm. I wanted nothing to do with her personally. I believed it, while at the same time hoping I was being entirely honest. Who of us knows himself totally?

The situation that developed made it easy for me to ignore Pearl. She and Jerry resided in Santa Rosa. Loy and I lived at the beach in San Francisco. The big challenge to us related to earning a living and turning the apartment house into a real "money maker." Theology and philosophy would have to wait.

Good luck came my way again. The one really fine apartment in the building became available, and Loy and I moved into it. Meanwhile, we had joined the single apartment to the adjacent two-room, converting it to its original size. We worked to encourage the tenant of the sleeping room to leave, so we could add it to the four and make it a five-room luxury suite. This took time, but finally we succeeded.

Loy acted as manager of the apartment house, which included tending the furnaces. We christened them "David" and "Goliath." David was relatively tractable and Loy would light it in the afternoon. We improved our service at an increased cost to us, but we wanted hot water and gave the tenants the benefit.

Goliath was another story. For those unfamiliar with the oil furnaces of that era, something of an explanation is due.

The furnace room was a filthy, oil-smelling cube I dubbed "the black hole." There the two furnaces sat, each connected to the oil tank outside and underground. Neither furnace had a pilot light. To light either one, the blower was first turned on. That produced a jet of air, which blew past the oil intake nozzle. Next, the oil valve was turned. That produced a flow of viscous fuel that oozed into the presence of the air stream, where it was picked up and sprayed all over the combustion chamber.

Now, one lit a roll of newspaper and threw it into the chamber. The spraying oil quickly soaked the burning paper. If all went well, ignition ensued and the furnace roared its approval in life-threatening fury.

Sometimes the oil would put out the fire, and a second or third attempt had to be made. After three or four attempts, if ignition had failed each time, one had to wait half an hour while the oil dried out. If the chamber got too oil-soaked, nothing worked.

David was a pussycat and obeyed Loy quite well, although it frightened her. Goliath was another story. This monstrous creature had a malignant personality. Even when it was turned off, it glowered and sneered. I confess to being intimidated myself on more than one occasion. It never worked the first time.

I was reassured, supposedly, by "Old Lady Grant," who confided that only rarely did an oil furnace blow up. Somehow, it seemed to me that no furnace would ever blow up more than once. And once was too many.

Whenever Goliath ignited, a blast of orange flame would billow out in the general direction of the furnace operator. You had to get close to make it work at all; but you had to keep your distance or become part of the heating process.

I came home one day to find Loy in tears, standing before Goliath, and literally scared to death. After that I usually managed to get home in time to light Goliath myself, and then try to look unconcerned while I quieted my jumping nerves.

I vowed that, as soon as we could afford it, I'd get rid of David and Goliath and put in some new gas furnaces that would be both clean and automatic. At the moment, my purse was too thin even though my business at Inter-City Company was doing well.

I had purchased a fifteen-unit apartment house, but thanks to changes I had wrought, it now had only thirteen units with twelve rentals. The single and the sleeping room were gone, and we occupied five rooms taking up the entire north side of the first floor above ground. Thus, income was down and expenses were up.

We decorated our commodious quarters, which cost us still more. But, at last, we did have a lovely place to live. Gradually, we replaced the furniture until we could be proud of our abode.

Now that we were settled in San Francisco, another dimension was added to my life. My former wife, Peggy, and Pearl's former husband, Sidney, were living in San Rafael in Marin County, only a few miles north of the Golden Gate Bridge. My two sons, Robbie and Dave, now got to visit us with some regularity. This was a delight to both Loy and me. So far as I could tell, the arrangement pleased both boys, too.

While we were busy adjusting to all these changes and taking on one responsibility after another, Loy became pregnant. We had talked of having children and had actually wanted a little more time before such a momentous responsibility was undertaken. Pregnancy, however, is an imperative. Once it occurs, destiny holds the reins. Our thinking now had to include a newcomer who would arrive in only a matter of months.

About this time I managed an exceptionally large deal and earned a magnificent commission. Weiss insisted as he paid me, that I retire the debt I owned Ma Gray since he wanted her indebtedness at Morris Plan reduced so she could sign notes in future transactions.

I could see the logic, and although the money wasn't yet due, I cleaned up that obligation and still had some funds left over. This act made me the Ace at the Company and A-one in Ma Gray's eyes.

Now I drew up plans for the apartment that I hoped to add on the ground floor. I found a draftsman who converted my crude sketches into an acceptable blueprint. With this in hand, I went to the San Francisco City Hall to obtain a building permit so that construction could begin.

When I stood at the counter where building permits were issued and explained what I proposed doing, I was greeted with every courtesy. The clerk looked at my plans, admitted there was nothing wrong with them, and then got out a Platt book to check on the location to make sure that no zoning regulation would be violated.

He checked few other points of reference and finally returned to where I still stood. "I can't issue you a permit, LeFevre."

I was astonished. "Why not?" I asked.

"You have misrepresented the building you are in. Your building is a three-story building. The area is zoned for three stories. You're trying to add a fourth story. That is against the law."

"That's not so. The building I have is four stories. I'm just trying to clean up a fire-hazard and provide some scarce housing."

"No. Your building is three stories high. It says so right here."

He showed me a copy of an earlier permit granting permission to build a three-story, frame and stucco apartment house.

"I assure you," I said, "I am quite capable of counting to four. I can even do it on my fingers." I demonstrated. "One, two, three, and when I add this finger, that makes four."

"I appreciate that, but your building is only three stories high."

"Look," I said. "I have two apartments on the fourth story already. And a vacant space that is dangerous and filthy. I'm not trying to change the height of the building. Not by so much as an eighth of an inch."

The clerk didn't lose his calm. "I see why you're confused," he said. "The building permit allows a three-story building with a full basement. You are counting the basement as though it is a full story."

"What you are calling a full basement is entirely above ground," I said.

"I don't care where it is, it's the basement."

"Very well. Then I want to put an apartment in the basement."

"That is not permitted. It must be above ground."

"It is above ground. "

This was an impasse. "Would it help if I took you out there and showed you the place? I assure you it is a four...no, check that. It's a three-story frame and stucco apartment house with a full basement above ground. I'll be glad to show it to you."

"I'm sorry. I can't give you a permit."

I remembered that courageous man in Santa Ana who had given the police a dressing down. "Now, just one minute," I said with finality. "I am doing nothing wrong. The papers are full of the information that there's a housing shortage. Of course there is. The price controls on everything have prevented the building of new units so there is a desperate need."

"I'm doing what I can to help take care of that need. It's patriotic. It's what is needed. Also, if the fire marshal went out there he'd probably condemn the place because of its potential danger as a fire hazard.

"I don't know who I have to see or what I have to do, but I'm going to put in that apartment. What do you think of that?"

The clerk laughed. Then he leaned in my direction and lowered his voice. "I don't blame you a damn bit. These laws are silly, but rules are rules."

I stared at him.

"Tell you what," he said, still sotto voce. "Why don't you go ahead and build it without a permit? Nobody has to know. Nobody's going to interfere. I agree with you. But I'd get into trouble if I issued a permit."

"So, why don't you go ahead? We'll just look the other way."

I brightened at once. "Hey. That's great. I really don't give a darn about the permit. I just want to be allowed to do the right thing in respect to my own property."

"Then, go ahead," he said.

We shook hands, both smiling. I rolled up my plans and went out looking for help. I hired a carpenter and the work progressed nicely. The junk was removed and carted away. I took out the non-productive parts of the garage, doing some of the work myself. The new apartment was framed in, the plumbing installed, the windows and doors put in place.

All that was needed was plastering and some cabinet work, and, of course, the painting. There would be no rent control on the new apartment. I could charge whatever the market would allow. With this addition, I could put the building back into the same income bracket it had once enjoyed.

Loy phoned me at work. Something had gone wrong. A strange man had appeared and posted a red sign on the door to the new apartment. The carpenter had immediately packed up his tools and departed. I'd best come home at once.

Loy was so upset I feared something might go wrong with her pregnancy. I dashed home and found the forbidding sign. All workmen were forbidden to enter the premises. I was in violation building code on thirteen counts.

The next day I presented myself to the building inspector's office to learn the extent of my wrongdoing. Sure enough, lack of a building permit was number one. But there was more. Much more. The building, itself, was a non-conforming building. That would have to be corrected. The new apartment didn't have the prescribed ceiling height. It was short by exactly one inch. The building would have to be raised by one inch. The wrong kind of windows had been used. The wrong insulated wiring had been used. The new door was hinged on the wrong side, some of the fixtures already installed were not recommended, and would have to come out.

But now the big problems. The building could only have three floors above ground. A basement must be below ground. The roof of the building—and most particularly the skylight that illumined the central stairwell—were old and dangerous. Replacement with improved materials was required. The furnaces were on the brink of exploding and would have to be replaced. And, finally, the building did not have a "dry stand-pipe."

I checked out my situation. Excavation below eight feet was forbidden at the point the apartment house stood. By order of the building department, the building must be lowered by ten feet, while at the same time elevated by one inch. Various particulars must be altered—a new roof and skylight provided, new furnaces put in, and a dry standpipe installed. The building could not be where it was because of zoning. However, it was forbidden to take it down because of the housing shortage. I could not add an apartment, but I was forbidden to close an apartment. The building could not remain the way it was, but no permit could be issued so I could effect changes. Without a permit I could do nothing.

I returned to City Hall. A review board met each week I learned, and I decided to attend these board meetings to explain the dilemma the City's intrusion into my private affairs had created.

For six weeks I was present at these meetings. Again and again, I protested the situation into which I had been put. I stated I had tried to get a permit, but that the clerk had assured me he couldn't issue one. At the same time, he had urged me to proceed without a permit.

The clerk was called on the carpet. To no one's surprise but mine, denied the whole thing. He had never seen me before. How could he, a mere clerk, give assurances to anyone? I must be some kind of nut to make such an allegation.

At the end of six weeks, one official took me aside. When no one was looking he said, "I figure you've had your lesson, LeFevre."

"What does that mean?"

"It means that, in this city, if you want to get ahead, you have to play the game."

"Look, I'm a peaceful citizen and a war veteran. I'm not trying to hurt anyone. What I'm trying to do is constructive. I'm doing it with my own money. What game am I missing?"

"We won't talk about that any more. If you agree to do certain things with your building, I think the board will grant you a permit."

"I've told you from the beginning that I'm willing to do anything in reason. Taking the building down, or elevating it aren't reasonable. But I'll be happy to do whatever I can do, in reason."

"Of course, Here's what's required. First, tear out the new apartment and lower the cement slab by one full inch. Never mind the rest of the building."

"Why don't you require me to vacate all the ground floor or basement apartments and lower their floors, too?"

"You're not responsible for those so we're skipping them. But the ceiling height of your new apartment is dangerous."

"I see. The same height in the other apartments isn't dangerous!"

"You got it."

"Whatever you say."

"Now, you're getting the picture. And there's no dodging the furnace or the roof issues, LeFevre. And the skylight that you have is dangerous; it must be replaced."

"I've agreed to that from the beginning," I reminded him. "In fact, I was planning all that anyhow. One of the reasons I bought the place was because it could be improved."

"And if you improve it, you can charge higher rents, right? "

"Naturally. Of course, the OPA won't let me. "

He winked. "That won't last. No problem. You've got to make a buck here or there."

That was a surprise. "If I couldn't profit what's the point of being in business and taking all this hassle?"

"We understand that. I'm glad to see you understand it, too."

He was becoming tiresome. "So? What else?"

"The building must have a dry standpipe."

"Do you mind telling me what that is?"

"You don't know?"

"Never heard of it."

"It's a requirement of all buildings above three stories in height. We are declaring your building to be three stories high, but because it actually is four stories, and non-conforming, you must meet requirements for the four story building."

"Okay. If I must, I must. But what is a dry standpipe?"

He grinned. "You've seen 'em lots of times and probably didn't know what you were looking at. It's an empty pipe strapped to the outside of the building, running from ground level to the roof with outlets on each floor. In the event of fire, the fire department can attach a hose at the bottom and immediately have water pressure on all floors and the roof, regardless of what has happened to water pipes inside the building."

I had seen pipes like that and nodded. "Okay," I said. "I'm stuck. I happen to have a three-story building that is four stories in height so I must put on a dry pipe that hopefully will never be used."

"You got it, Charley."

"Anything else?"

"Well, the other things aren't big. Just rebuild your apartment with approved insulation, fixtures, and so on. Put in the windows we approve and hang your door correctly. Got that?"

The cash register in my mind was shifting into high gear. "And if I agree to do all those things, what happens? "

"Well, then there's a fine for operating without a permit. "

"Ye Gods," I said. "What you're asking for is going to cost me at least $10,000. And now you're going to fine me on top of that? How much?"

"Well." For the first time the official seemed a trifle unsure of himself. "I can't really say how much the fine would be. But, it's just possible, you being a veteran and all, that we could waive the fine."

"I'd sure be happy about that," I admitted.

He leaped on the remark. "Would you say that we had," he hesitated... "done you a favor?"

"Well, yes. If there's to be a fine and it could be set aside that certainly would be a favor."

"Now, if people do you a favor, LeFevre, don't you usually try to do them a favor?"

What could he mean? I nodded. "Well, sure. I try to show my gratitude. Doesn't everyone? What are you getting at? "

"If you agree to do what I've outlined, you'll get your permit. And the fine will be waived."

"That," I said, "would be great."

"You'd consider that a favor? "

"Yes, I would."

A benign smile settled on his face.

"What kind of a favor do you want in return? We you asking for money?"

The smile converted to horror. "No. No. Not for a minute. That would constitute a bribe."

I was catching on. "Not if you don't define it that way."

He considered that remark and nodded. "I suppose you're right. But nothing like that. No. No. Not at all."

"What then?"

"Well, I was thinking that sometimes good friends, who do favors for each other exchange little gifts."

"That's true."

"Well, LeFevre, I figure about two cases of scotch would be about right. You see, I'm not alone in this and we'd have to cover all the bases."

"I see."

"Very well." He sighed with a show of relief and the smile returned. "We'll say nothing more. Your permit will arrive in the mail in a day or so."

"Beautiful," I said.

He offered his hand and although I loathed the sight of him, I took it. I hadn't been asked to sign anything and wasn't at all sure that I'd ever get the permit. However, true to his word, the permit did arrive.

The carpenter was recalled and asked to tear out what he had put in. A jackhammer operator was brought to the site. He smashed the concrete slab under the apartment and men with shovels gouged out the dirt until a new level for a new slab was reached.

When the apartment was completed, the result created an on-going hazard. One had to step down to enter the apartment, and step up to leave. More than once, people tripped over it. But that hazard was legal and complaints were impossible.

With permit in hand, I found it relatively easy to borrow the necessary funds to effect all the changes needed. The dry standpipe cost $850.00. I remember that, particularly. The roof and skylight ran a couple of thousand. The furnace room and the new furnaces fully installed ran just under $4,000. To top everything off, I now had the entire building re-painted inside and out.

It was still a monstrosity. But it was a clean, white monstrosity.

I made one mistake. In all the excitement, I completely forgot the cases of scotch. By the time I remembered, it was too late.

Chapter LXIV

Three strands of endeavor had finally formed. Each of them shared my time and my thoughts in the developing tapestry of events. The year was 1946 and I was obsessed with a desire for money and business success. This was the major thrust. I dreamed about making big money. I planned and schemed on how to get it. No matter how much I made, it was never enough.

The second strand, not so obsessive as the first, was interest in my family. I had neglected my first opportunity to be a good father. I didn't wish to be guilty of a second round of neglect. At the same time, I viewed the task of being fatherly as of providing dollars, before much else could be done. Therefore, in wishing to come close to my boys, to my wife, and to the new life that would soon join us, my obsession to earn was reinforced.

The third strand was my interest in theology, philosophy, and the persistent mystery surrounding some of my own behavior. What was that really all about? The unanswered questions ebbed and flowed in my consciousness. Was there a God? Was God's name "I Am?" If so, was the Ballard description of God's function accurate? Were there Masters? Was I in touch with them? Was I, perhaps, hallucinating? Or was I, in reality, nothing more than a con man, taking advantage of others?

If the latter were true, why had I never exploited that advantage? I was revolted by the idea of living at the expense of others. But, in fact, I had done so to some degree in the years immediately preceding the war. Even then I had insisted, to Pearl's dismay, on earning my own way and on being the biggest contributor to the financial obligations our little group assumed.

This metaphysical strand faded from view as I busied myself with work and moneymaking. But it was being braided into the very warp and woof of my life, sometimes without my awareness. Most especially was this true whenever Pearl put in an appearance. She never let me forget that I'd had certain unique experiences. Nor did she let me overlook the fact that she and I had been a party to many of them together. Therefore, I would not be allowed to abandon or forget that part of my life.

Strand one dominated everything. How could I make more money faster?

Two ideas formed. I was doing well with the apartment house. Why not buy a second business? Then, possibly, a third, fourth, and fifth. Additionally, instead of working as a salesman with licenses at Inter-City, why not become a broker with my own office?

Brokers obviously made more money than salesmen did. True, their obligations were much larger, their expenses greater. But the more units of business one could acquire, the better one's chances for profit. As a broker, I could write my own ticket.

The broader one's base, the greater one's security. If a person had one business and it failed, he was through. If he had a number, one could fail; he could stride across the loss, relying on his successes elsewhere.

My specialty was multiple housing. The key procedure, at least for me, was the one I had followed on the Great Highway. Find a building in distress; buy it cheap, with little or none of my own money involved. Then, let the building pay for itself.

In multiple housing, the biggest profits were to be found in hotels. Very well, I would shop around for listings and hopefully find a hotel where the owners wished to leave. They would help finance—and I could enjoy the privilege of improving—the property, enhancing the cash flow and, then, ultimately, selling at a good profit.

I researched the smaller hotels in San Francisco, primarily those located in the central business district, the triangle occupying the space between Market and Van Ness, bounded on the north by Fisherman's Wharf and on the east by the Embarkadero.

Luck was with me. The Ormond Hotel on Eddy Street, in the heart of the Tenderloin (so-called for various reasons) appeared to be what I wanted. I obtained a listing on the lease. In checking with the owners of the building, I learned they didn't wish to renew. Rather, they wished to sell out entirely.

This hotel was a six-story red brick edifice with a large lobby, 120 rooms—60 with private baths. It was badly worn, having been built shortly after the great fire of 1906. The listing by the owner showed him paying $1,000 per month rent and making about $1,000 per month above operational costs. Obviously, if I purchased both the lease and the building, it should produce a net of close to $2,000 per month, as the rent payment would be internalized in my favor.

When I asked what price the owners wanted, I was given a figure so low, in terms of the size of the hotel and competitive prices, that I marveled. It was a mere $90,000. That came down to only $750 per room. The man with the lease wanted $5,000 for his interests, including the furniture and good will. That was less than $50 per room additional for furniture, linens, and everything else. I could buy the package for less than $100,000.

Without letting the owners know that their price was below market, I asked whether they would be satisfied with the price and if they would be willing to pay a commission from that sum. No problem. They would be delighted to sell for $90,000.

Often a building will have some hidden flaw, which can only be revealed by a close personal inspection. I had found that true with the apartment, so I asked the owners for a close eyeballing with them on hand to answer to questions. Something must be wrong with the building, which accounted for their price. Hotels of similar vintage and size were $20,000 to $50,000 higher.

The inspection of the hotel proper produced no surprises. When we went into the basement I found the flaw I had expected. The area immediately below the lobby was a wreck. At one time, obviously, there had been a restaurant in that space. Now it was a shambles. It looked as if a bomb had exploded. Bits of smashed furniture were strewn about. What had been a lunch counter, canted crazily on top of a pile or rubble consisting of broken concrete, floor tile and other debris.

A large kitchen area adjoined. The equipment it had once contained had been ripped away and the whole place reeked of wet plaster from leaky pipes, decay and neglect. The furnace room had been maintained in good order and the familiar oil burning monsters were in place. Contrary to the apartment house, these furnaces worked, were clean, and in good order. But there was that non-productive space approximately 60 feet by 100 feet that could certainly be used for something.

The lobby elevator and the lobby stairs descended to the basement. In addition, a stairway rose to street level where the separate entrance had been boarded up.

Better yet, from my view, just off the lobby on the main floor, were a pair of rooms, comprising a two-room suite with a bath. One room fronted the street and had a large plate glass window.

That room could serve as my office when I became a broker. The smaller room could serve as office for a secretary.

With visions of the enormous amount of lucre I could make with this property, I asked the owners if they would deal with me as a buyer, rather than as a broker. Would they discount the price to me to the extent of the commission and permit me to purchase?

The owners, a pair of elderly retired gentlemen, agreed. No problem at all. They wanted to sell and were willing to pay the commission. The deal was looking better and better.

They wanted $20,000 down payment and would happily carry back the differential. They, like "Old Lady Grant," owned the building clear of encumbrances.

I made an offer, contingent upon my ability to finance and also upon my ability to obtain the leasehold interests in a satisfactory manner. They accepted and the transaction was underway.

Anyone with experience will at once realize that my precipitous behavior at this point was rash. Obvious questions never passed my lips. I had leaped to the conclusion that the reason for the low price related to the basement in shambles. So, I didn't inquire. Thirty minutes of research would have made me far less eager. I look back at this decision today with a feeling of embarrassment, even after all these years. It is one thing to be ignorant; it is quite another to be stupid. To be ignorant is unavoidable in facing anything new. To be stupid is to refrain from seeking answers when information is available.

My instant decision in this case was a matter of stupidity. All I had to do was ask the sellers why they hadn't cleaned up the basement and done something with all that space. I didn't ask because I presumed I knew the answer without asking. Actually, I was fearful of asking because I anticipated that a probe on my part might have convinced them to raise the price.

I'll make the escrow story brief. I managed to secure a loan from an insurance company that was larger than the sum the brothers were willing to tale back on a first deed of trust. I saved out about $5,000 of my own money. I managed to convince Ma Gray that she should do again for me what she had done once already to her considerable profit. She put up $10,000. She received a second deed of trust and the assurances of a large bonus.

With my own funds, I bought the lease and furniture. With Grays' borrowed funds as earnest money, and with the insurance loan, the sellers were paid off in full. I became the owner of record of the Ormond Hotel on Eddy Street in the Tenderloin of San Francisco.

While these negotiations proceeded, other events were shaping up, too. I passed the state examinations and obtained a broker's license, both for real estate and business opportunities. I failed the exam for the insurance broker's license and had to take the exam again before I passed it.

A woman who had bought and sold a number of guesthouses through the Inter-City Company owned leasehold on Clay Street in the Pacific Heights district. She was wearing herself out with the work involved because her husband, who usually did much of the work, had become an invalid. She wanted to sell fast and needed no cash at all.

That's my kind of deal, so I took over the guesthouse business as well.

At this juncture, Pearl emerged again as a mainstay. She and Jerry, and the rest of "our gang," had been meeting occasionally on weekends for outings and study sessions.

When it came to managing the guesthouse on Clay Street, I found it far easier to obtain the property than to run it. But Pearl said she would be glad to undertake it for me. Pearl could do anything. I had complete confidence in her ability.

So it happened that Pearl was installed as guesthouse manager of a very upbeat enterprise, called the "Henry Clay." She got some help from Blanche and Edy—two other women in our group—and made that guest house sing. It showed a profit right from the first.

Meanwhile, 1947 dawned and Loy's time came. We learned it one weekend. Both boys had been visiting us in our apartment on the Great Highway. As was our custom, on Sunday evening we drove to San Rafael to return the two to their mother. The road leading to the Deihl home had some rough spots in it, and we hit one of those bumps quite hard.

Loy grabbed my arm. "Something's happened," she said, looking apprehensive "I think the baby is coming."

We delivered the boys and raced to the hospital in San Francisco where arrangements had been made. The matron in charge of the ward looked at me with compassion. She understood that giving birth is often very hard on fathers.

"Why don't you go home and get a good night's sleep?" she asked.

"It's your wife's first and this may be a false alarm. In any case, it will take a good deal of time and you are no help."

I wasn't convinced. "I'll wait around for a while," I said. "There's no way I could get any sleep."

I joined a pair of expectant fathers in carpet scuffing. One of them had been there so long he was bleary-eyed and in need of a shave. But I figured I'd make certain before I left.

It wasn't long at all before a nurse showed up with a baby cradled in her arms. I was overjoyed to learn that it was mine. While I had anticipated a girl, the little squirming package of life was all-male. He was red and wizened, gave me a look as though he recognized me, and then tried to yell and eat his fist at the same time. Could he have had a premonition of the kind of world he was getting into?

Loy had come through with flying colors and I visited with her briefly. With a happy heart I returned to the apartment. Everything seemed to be working in my favor at last. I was bridging the gap between my first two sons and me. I was earning good money and soon it could be big money. My newest son would have every advantage. No one could have had more reasons for rejoicing than I.

At last I was handling considerable sums of money. Indeed, I had to make a bank deposit once a day instead of two or three times a month. I'd raced from the Great Highway to the hotel. Then, I'd dash out to the guesthouse on Clay Street. Then back to the hotel. Meanwhile, I'd be setting up appointments to show other properties to prospective clients.

Loy loved the beach, but she was alone and far away much of the time. What she didn't like, even with all the improvements at the apartment, were the tenants. They were constantly asking for more service, re-decoration, and better furniture. But there was no way we could do half of the things they demanded without losing money, and that I was determined to avoid.

The law specified that if a landlord improved his property substantially, the OPA—recently re-christened the OPS—would review the facts and sometimes grant a landlord some price relief.

I prepared a case, showing the thousands of dollars I had spent on improvements to the building, and presented it. When I went to the office of the OPS for the decision, I was abruptly turned down. I hadn't proved that I had spent any money in improvements.

I asked to see the local head of the OPS. When that was denied, I was so angry I ignored the secretary and stormed into the big man's sanctum. I confronted him just as he was about to leave for a game of golf.

I don't remember exactly what I said to him, but it went something like this: "When I was in the Army, you and the rest of your ilk seized power and are now engaged in trying to ride rough shod over every businessman in the city. I'm going to get a price increase on my rents or bring a legal action against your office for incompetence." There was more but I have forgotten.

I produced my receipts, each marked paid in full. The total was more than $10,000. What did his office mean when it said I hadn't spent any money? What kind of proof did they want?

I created a minor furor and was told that the big man, in person, would now take an interest. It seems he knew nothing about my case. His underlings had handled it.

A couple of weeks later a letter came which granted me permission to raise every rent in the apartment building by $2.00 per month! $28 more per month. A $336 per year increase, assuming no vacancies and no occupancy by the owner. At that rate, it would take more than thirty years to get back what I had spent! How kind and benevolent the government is.

The reason my request had been turned down was now explained. In trying to determine how much money had been spent, the investigators had ignored my receipts. Instead, they had asked each of my tenants. With a single exception, every tenant had testified in the most solemn manner that I had spent nothing at all. Nothing had been done. The property was being neglected and they were suffering because of my greed.

Loy was now completely fed up with the tenants, and who could blame her? Couldn't we have a home of our own? By now I had one honest tenant and he was delighted to manage the building for a few dollars discounted from his rent. Surely, as the owners of an apartment house and a hotel, we could afford a house of our own.

Marvelously, we found a large house on Clay Street about a mile from the guesthouse, purchased it, and moved in.

Another event occurred that must be included in this recitation. A special election was being held for the City of San Francisco. I considered voting a sacred privilege, but my schedule was such that I had to be out of town on a hotel deal in Monterey on Election

Day.

The newspapers explained that absentee ballots were available for people such as myself. All I had to do was go to City Hall and vote in advance, explaining the reason for one's absenteeism.

Grabbing a few minutes from my busy schedule, I drove to City Hall and went into the office of the Registrar. An elderly civil service employee was on duty. When I explained my anticipated predicament, he produced the ballot, laid it on the counter and told me to proceed with my markings.

I explained that I was a broker and would have to be away. Also, I remarked that I was a veteran and the last time I had voted had been by absentee ballot when I was in France.

He nodded in understanding. Then he said, "I presume you are now living at the same address."

"No," I said. "I've moved to a new address. We might as well make that change while I'm here."

In sudden anger, the clerk snatched away my ballot and crumpled it up. "You were about to commit a felony'" he shouted at me.

Others in the office, some would-be voters like myself, recoiled from me as though I were waving a gun.

"What do you mean, I'm about to commit a felony?" I demanded. "Since when is voting a felony?"

"You aren't eligible to vote'" the clerk shouted. "It's a felony to pose as the resident at an address that has been vacated. "

In the stillness that followed that outburst I got hold of myself. "Listen to what I have to say," I said between clenched teeth. "I have done nothing wrong. Don't you dare refer to me as a felon? When I went into the Army, I gave up that address. I spent four years away from home and voted whenever an election came along. I'm going to do it now."

"No, you're not!" the clerk growled.

"I'm going over your head," I said with finality. "Whether you like it or not, I intend to vote!"

I stormed out of the Registrar 's office and went to the office of the Mayor. The Mayor's administrative assistant sat at his desk, nattily dressed, a smile on his handsome face. I stood before him.

"My name is Robert LeFevre," I began. "I have just come from the Registrar's office where I was denied my rights as a voter. I wish to see the Mayor."

The smile remained. "Of course. Let me see." He consulted a ledger. "I can arrange an appointment for a few minutes Tuesday morning next week."

"That won't do at all. My expression was grim. "I want to see the Mayor. I want to see him now. I am a peaceful man and a law-abiding citizen. Your clerk in the Registrar's office has called me a felon and that is something I will not tolerate. I am going to see the Mayor. Now! Or I am going to kick in the door to the Mayor's office, starting at once. Do you understand that?"

The smile fled. "Yes. Yes, of course. I can see that you're upset. Just wait a minute."

The assistant leaped from his desk, vanishing into an adjacent room. I looked around. I had created something of a sensation. The richly decorated room was lined with chairs and perhaps a dozen or so people were seated, obviously waiting to see His Honor. They gaped at me as though I had lost my senses.

Presently, the assistant returned. He eyed me as though he expected me to pounce. "If you'll just have a chair, sir," he said, "His Honor will see you in a few minutes." Then in a whisper he added, "We don't want any trouble now, do we?"

"No trouble at all," I assured him. "I am an absentee voter for the coming election. I simply insist on voting. That's all there is to it."

I sat, and my wait was brief. I was ushered into the adjoining room and there, at his Louis XIVth desk, sat the leading politician of San Francisco.

"My name is Robert LeFevre," I said. "I'm a veteran. I came here to vote. The clerk in the Registrar's office tore up my ballot. He said I was about to commit a felony because I've changed my address.

"It is not a felony to change one's address or to vote. I intend to vote. I understand that a person becomes ineligible to vote when he moves. Now, get my picture. I gave up my address when I enlisted in the Army. Overseas I didn't have any address but an APO. But I voted. Every time.

"I intend voting today. I hope to do it peacefully. I want you to see to it that I can do that. Now, if you can't, let me spell out what I propose to do.

"First, I shall call the newspapers and explain the situation to them. I will give them time to get their reporters and cameramen over here. Then I 'm going to go back to the Registrar's office. There

I will vote. If the clerk doesn't permit it, I shall manhandle him if I have to. If I must, I will make a shambles out of the Registrar's office. You have my word on it. I will vote! Is that understood?"

A smile came over the Mayor's face, while a wary light crept into the back of his eyes. "You appear to be a determined Man."

"Appearances are not deceiving you," I said. "I am angry. I intend to vote. I prefer to be peaceful about it. But you can put money on it. Vote, I shall!"

The Mayor didn't flinch. He leaned back in his chair and gnawed his lip. "It's a technicality, of course. We just don't want people voting more than once. You understand that."

"I am not trying to vote more than once. Once will be enough."

"Well, it so happens, Mr. LeFevre, that the City Council is meeting and I'm scheduled to be with them. Why don't you come along? I'd like them to hear directly from you. Perhaps we can resolve this difficulty."

"I hope you can," I said. "But you do understand my position."

The two of us moved through more doors and came into a large room occupied by about a dozen or so men, all well dressed, all seated in expectation of hearing from the Mayor.

"Gentlemen," the Mayor began, "I have brought one of our citizens to this meeting because I want you to hear from him in person. He has a complaint. He's been overseas during the late hostilities. but managed in every election to cast a ballot.

"Of course, when he entered the Army he vacated his address. Technically, he isn't eligible. But, why don't you tell them yourself, Mr. LeFevre?"

I repeated my story, ending it with the threat to bring in the press to watch me vote.

A few of the Councilmen exchanged smiles. One said, "I wish all the voters took elections this seriously."

There was a bit of whispering and consultation among them. The Mayor took a chair and tossed me a grin.

Finally, one of the Councilmen said, "I don't see any way out of it. LeFevre isn't eligible. We don't have the power to make an exception in his case."

"Now, just a minute," the Mayor said. "I'm not so sure we can't resolve the difficulty." He turned to me.

"How long were you away from San Francisco during the war,

Mr. LeFevre?"

"Approximately four years."

"During that time did you take up permanent residence anywhere else?"

"I was in the Army. I lived in various places. My orders always read that each change was permanent."

"Yes, yes, I know," said His Honor. "But I want to get at this problem from a deeper level. Did you ever really *wish* to live somewhere else? "

I thought about that. "No, sir. In all my movements, I planned to return here as soon as my tour of duty ended."

"Could it be fair to say," the Mayor continued, "that your heart was always here in San Francisco?"

I hadn't thought of it quite that way. "Well, I guess you could say that. Actually, I think that's an honest appraisal. I always expected to come back to California and to San Francisco. So, I guess my heart was here."

His Honor beamed in triumph. "You see, gentlemen, here we have a classic case. It has long been understood that where a man's heart is, there is his home. Wouldn't you agree?"

There was some chuckling and nodding among the Council. No voice was raised in opposition.

"I see we are of one mind. The gist of the matter is that Mr. LeFevre never really left our city. His heart was here all the time, gentlemen. He hasn't moved. Oh, I know," he waived a hand. "He's at a different address within the city. But we don't have to take note of that detail at this juncture. Mr. LeFevre doesn't want to vote twice; he's going to be out of town."

"So, here's what you do," he said to me. "Wait another fifteen minutes. The clerk in the Registrar's office will go out to lunch and someone else will be on duty. You go back there and don't say anything about your address. Just cast your ballot as you intended all along. You can provide your latest resident address at another time. Will that be all right?"

"It's fine with me if it's all right with you," I said. "I'm not interested in the technicalities. I simply intend to vote."

"Then do it." He stood and I was dismissed.

I waited the prescribed quarter hour and voted, saying nothing about my changed location. Of course, there was no further difficulty.

Chapter LXV

Handling an apartment house with a dozen or so units doesn't require much more than patience, a willingness to work long hours, and skill in doing odd jobs. I tended to be short on patience and lacking in skill. But I was willing and eager to work, which helped offset the deficiencies.

The tenant at the beach in whom Loy and I both reposed trust and the management of affairs appeared well endowed with all three qualities. His name was Jim Laughlin. He, his wife, and a brand new baby occupied the apartment I had built.

Now, with a hotel and guesthouse business—both flourishing, and a brand new real estate business throw in—I found myself meeting a payroll. I first hired Jim as the manager of the beach property, and then I hired him as my hotel manager and general assistant. It was a good decision. Jim earned his pay. In our association, he never gave me reason to wish for a better man. He was one of the best.

Pearl was already on my payroll at the guesthouse. She hired some help there and managed everything well.

I needed a secretary. Ruth Dazey, the youngest of Ethel's daughters, had obtained a job with the San Francisco Chamber of Commerce in that capacity. A very serious and studious girl, with a passion for making everything perfect, she was also a devout student of metaphysics. I hired her for my real estate office that now took the name "LeFevre Investments." Other businesses I acquired went under the heading of "LeFevre Enterprises."

Ruth was a dandy, with a single flaw. She was unnecessarily harsh on herself for any shortcoming. She invariably sought the ideal. She insisted on top performance from me as well as herself, and was as harsh with me for shortcomings as she was skillful in her own. She was surely one of the world's most consistent perfectionists. She would become emotionally distraught whenever anyone behaved in a manner she felt was less than the best in them. This made her at times an uncomfortable person to be with. But why complain? Ruth was splendid. She was one of the finest typists I have ever met. She could take dictation as rapidly as I could speak. I don't recall a single instance in which she lied about anything. Her honesty and loyalty were of a caliber most businessmen dream of finding, but rarely do.

In buying the hotel I had acquired the entire hotel staff: four clerks, five maids, a housekeeper, and an engineer—all of whom had to be paid.

In my real estate business, I needed salesmen. I started with three, all working on commission, and expanded until I had six. One of them was a complete surprise and a harking back to my days with the "I Am."

The man I had replaced when I joined the Ballard staff, Jim Rogers, showed up at my office one day. He was out of work, divorced, and down on his luck. He was a gifted communicator, as I well knew, and I helped him get his license. Then, I took him on as a salesman.

Ethel had a real estate license, but she worked at her affairs as they had been. I was unable to hire any other "I Am" people at this time, although I had good reason to do so, if any could be found. The mental and physical discipline demanded of a devout student of the Ballard teachings made them ideal employees.

Another man out of my past showed up—my old roommate from the ETO, Captain Chuck Steinberg. I offered to take him on as a salesman provided he would follow instructions, get a license, and work hard on commissions. He was looking for something less demanding, with a guaranteed paycheck. We didn't click, and he went his way.

Now that I had these various businesses with profits coming along nicely, the time had arrived to improve the Ormond Hotel. I began by re-naming it the Jefferson. I bought an enormous outside sign three stories high and hung it on the building.

Next, I conducted a minor survey. There wasn't a restaurant in the block on Eddy Street where I was located. Looking beyond that block, I learned that the nearest restaurant was two and a half blocks away. In that space, there were dozens of hotels, apartment houses, and rooming establishments.

My principle place of business was in the center of a desert so far as eating was concerned. If I could start a restaurant, serve a general menu, and offer good food at reasonable prices in a clean and modern surrounding, I should do well.

Despite the prohibition against liquor under the metaphysical rules, I realized that a successful restaurant in San Francisco would have to serve at least wine and beer. My survey showed no such establishment within a four-block geographic area. The Jefferson could become an oasis.

I found a skilled craftsman who specialized in designing restaurants. San Francisco is justly famous for some of its wining and dining establishments. The man I was fortunate enough to hire had designed several of the better places.

My belief was that the ordinary working man and woman would appreciate a truly nice place at modest prices. That was the kind of eating place I wanted. And I got it. I borrowed funds when needed, as my credit by now was excellent. I cleaned up the basement, brought in the best equipment, and finished it off with bright and modern decor.

I built a fireplace to add a touch of cheer, took care of all fire requirements, and then some. I asked both Jim and my restaurant specialist to spare no expense in that department. A brick exterior with a wooden interior could become a furnace if anything went wrong. The health department and the fire marshal's office had certain requirements; we met them all. The construction and installation were checked and re-checked, with permits issued all along the route.

At last, it was completed. I named it "The Patriots" and crowned the effort with a colorful sign depicting the flag raising at Iwo Jima. This was hung outside above the entrance to the stairway from the street. To make use of that famous photograph, I contacted the photographer and, for a fee, obtained his permission to reproduce it.

I had said nothing to anyone about my intention to serve alcoholic beverages. My reason had to do with Pearl, Ruth, and others with an "I Am" background. Pearl was operating the Henry Clay without liquor. She would have been shocked if she had known my plans. My intention was to obtain the license at the last minute, and then shrug off objections by indicating its lack of importance. In fact, the sale of liquor can make an establishment. Failure to provide it can break it.

Thus, I laid out as much money to improve the property as I had paid for the investment originally. Strike one! At last, I went to the Board of Equalization (a government euphemism) to obtain an "on sale" license.

I was denied. Flatly, finally, and no appeal. The absence of bars and cafes in that particular part of the tenderloin was not a matter of happenstance. The four hundred block on Eddy Street was a rough part of town. Years earlier, there had apparently been a business in that location which had served as a nucleus for undesirables. By design, no licenses for liquor would be issued under any circumstances.

Strike two!

I spent a useless week trying to find someone at City Hall who would sympathize and lend a hand. It finally dawned on me. In all probability, the wreckage in the hotel basement told the story. It was the Jefferson (nee Ormond) which had been the focal point of festering bad behavior. Had I asked questions of the sellers at the time I made the transaction, I could have found that out. Certainly, if I had inquired at City Hall about obtaining a license, I would have learned what I needed to know before making the offer.

Now it was too late. I had a great deal of money tied up in a lovely restaurant in a part of town where drinking at mealtime is a way of life. I tried to hide my disappointment, explaining to Jim and others that there was no reason why we couldn't succeed if we offered good food at low prices.

I rationalized by adding up the advantages. First, I had my own tenants who numerically came to about 140 persons, all with appetites. There would be a natural tendency for them to go to the nearest eating-place if prices and food favored them. Additionally, in the vicinity, there would have been at least another 2,000 residents. That's not a bad beginning, I reasoned.

I let it be known that I was hiring, and began to take applications, beginning with a chef. I found a man with good credentials and took him on. Then, one day as I sat in the dining room, ready to interview other applicants, a man walked up to me and introduced himself. He was the agent of the Union, handling waiters and culinary personnel.

"I understand you're hiring," was his opening.

"That's right."

"You'll be taking all Union people, of course."

I was doing my best to keep a low profile as far as the Union was concerned. I responded, truthfully, "Of course." I don't like being dictated to.

"What do you figure your minimum staff during off hours?"

This was a crucial point. Anyone in the restaurant business knows that there are times in the day when virtually no customers are on hand. Then, at meal times, you can be overrun. If you plan your working schedules correctly, you stagger duty tours so that as few people as possible are working during slack hours and as many as needed are on hand for busy periods.

The specialist who had created the design for "The Patriots" had counseled on this very point. We had arranged the kitchen, the counter, the booths and tables, the pantries and everything else, so that a minimum of three people could operate everything.

"Our minimum is three," I told the Union man. "Our maximum doesn't exist. That remains to be learned once we find what business we can attract."

"We don't see it that way."

"Oh? How do you see it?"

"This is a damn fine restaurant."

"Thanks. We planned it that way."

"The Union council has made a determination. Your minimum is eleven."

"Eleven!" I came out of my chair. That's...that's not reasonable. We can't afford that—not during off-hours. We don't know yet what we can bring in."

"I said eleven, LeFevre."

"I heard you. But we can't do it."

"Then hear this. If you try to hire less than that as your regular on-duty people, you're going to have a picket line out front. We don't play around. You'll hire eleven or you won't get your doors open."

My heart sank. Thoughts of hiring non-union or paying less than Union scale caused me to turn ashen. But having eleven people on the payroll didn't bring the color back to my face. Profits in a restaurant are marginal at best. You've got to peddle a lot of coffee and sandwiches to meet even a modest payroll.

The Union was demanding $1500 per week in payroll, (the chef alone drew $600, even in those days). Even without sharpening my pencil, I knew I was in big trouble.

Were I to buck this demand, thanks to the character of the Unions, my earlier run-ins in Minnesota would become common knowledge in San Francisco. And some of those people wanted me dead.

I knuckled under. "We can try it," I said. "I don't think we can make it."

"You'd better."

"You might consider this," I said. "If we can't make it, nobody will have a job here. Isn't it better to have some people with jobs than nobody with jobs?"

"Frankly, LeFevre, we don't give a shit about your place. If you take a dive that's your problem. If you do operate, you'll do it our way. Is that clear?"

"I won't even be able to pay back the money I borrowed."

"Ho ho and ha ha! You're making it big. We're gonna get a cut. Maybe some of your other businesses will have to bail this one out. So who cares? Eleven." He pushed his face close to mime. "Got it?"

"I hear you," I said.

Strike three!

We opened the restaurant. It took no time at all to learn that I had a white elephant. I had to raise prices above the line I wanted to establish. Immediately, a great deal of the business vanished.

We did our best. We planned and scrimped, and the Union help I hired turned in good performances. But we started in the red and stayed there.

One mid-morning I was sitting in a booth talking to the chef. We were planning the menu for the following day, trying to arrange for good food and to make frugal use of everything we had.

Out of the corner of my eye I watched a man eating a late breakfast at the counter. My attention was with the chef and the menu. However, the man at the counter finished eating, got up, said something to the waitress, and walked out. I didn't see him stop to pay his check. Indeed, I didn't see him receive a check.

When the chef returned to the kitchen, I sauntered over to the counter. "That man who just ate," I said. "I wasn't watching closely and may have missed it. But I didn't see him pay for his breakfast. "

The waitress smiled. "I didn't give him a check."

"You didn't?" I was astonished.

"I never give him a check."

"You don't? Is he your father?"

"Of course not. My father would pay like everyone else."

"Look, Miss," I said. "Perhaps you have the wrong impression. This is supposed to be a restaurant where we sell food and service.

It isn't the Salvation Army. This means that you have to give every customer a check and insist that it be paid."

"Yes, sir. That's what I do."

"But not in this case?"

"Mr. LeFevre, I don't think you know who that man is."

"You're right. I don't. And, frankly, Miss, I don't care. The truth is, we aren't making it here in 'The Patriots.' We're going under. But there's a slim chance that business will reverse itself and take an upturn. In that case, just maybe, we might be able to see it through. That means we must collect every thin dime owed us. That way you get paid, I keep my business and your friend does his share."

"But you don't know who that man is."

"That's right."

"Mr. LeFevre, I'm a professional waitress. I've been doing this work for years. I never give that man a check."

"Why not?"

"He's the health inspector."

"So?"

"So, if he gets down on you for any reason, he could take away your license."

"He wouldn't do that. His job is to see that we keep the place clean and that a health hazard doesn't exist here. You and I will have to see to that. Now, when he decides to eat here, he's going to have to pay for his food like anyone else. And you're the one who's going to see to that, aren't you?"

The waitress nodded but she wore a dubious expression. "I'll do whatever you ask me to. Mr. LeFevre. But do you think that's a wise decision?"

"I don't think it's wise to fail in meeting the payroll. So, you let me make the policy decisions and I'll keep giving you a check each payday. How does that sound?"

"Okay," she laughed. "I hope you know what you're doing."

A week or so after this incident, I went out the main entrance of the hotel one morning, planning on walking in the direction of Market Street to seek some new listings. The separate entrance leading to The Patriots was immediately on my left as I turned. Standing in front of it was a workman. He was doing something to the door.

I positioned myself next to him and watched. He was attaching a hasp.

"What are you doing?" I asked, when his objective became clear.

"I'm closing this joint."

"Is that so? Can you tell me why?"

"I don't know. They're violating some health regulation or something, is all I know. So, I'm shutting them down."

"This happens to be my 'joint,'" I said. "Can you be more specific? Just which regulation have I violated?"

"Geez, Mister. Sorry. I didn't know who you was. I got no idea what's wrong. That ain't my business. I just shut the places they send me to, that's all."

"I don't believe you can close my place of business without giving me a reason."

The workman's jaw jutted. "I told you the reason. It's some health regulation. You'll have to go to the Health Department to find out."

"I most certainly will do just that. Meanwhile, I'm asking you in a nice way: stop defacing my property."

"Don't you go hassling me, Mister. I got my orders."

"I'm sure you have. But they didn't give you a deadline, did they? They didn't tell you to close the dining room at 9:00 a.m. or 10:30 or any other specific time, did they?"

The workman relaxed a trifle. "You're right about that. They just said to close it up. So that's what I'm doing."

"Look. I had no idea this was going to happen." I tried to think of some delaying tactic. "Why don't you come with me down to the dining room for a cup of coffee to give me time to call your boss and see what I'm doing wrong? I think a mistake has been made. You wouldn't want to make a mistake like that, would you? Shutting up the wrong place?"

He picked up a clipboard from the sidewalk and peered at the top page. "No, I got it right. See. That's the right address, ain't it?"

"I didn't think you'd make the mistake," I said. "I think your boss may have gotten his papers mixed up. It's an easy thing to do, you know. And I'll stand you to some pie or doughnuts along with the coffee. How's that? I'm not asking you not to do your job. I'm just asking you to give me a bit of time so I can find out. Okay?"

"Sure, that's okay by me." The workman smiled. "You're an all-right G. And you're right. There ain't no particular time, so long as I do it today."

"Then come with me."

At the counter I said to the girl, "I'll pay this man's check. Give him some coffee and something to go with it. Give me some time. I want to make a couple of phone calls."

I raced up to my office and called the Health Department, asking to speak to the inspector in charge of the district in which the restaurant was located. He was "in the field" and couldn't be reached until after 4:00 PM.

Then I phoned an attorney who did an occasional legal chore for me.

Fortunately, he was in his office. "Did you get a legal notice of intent to close?" was his first question.

"No, " I said. "Nothing. Of course, today's mail hasn't come yet. But I've had no notice."

"Then I'll get them to back off. No problem. But whatever is wrong, you're going to have to fix. You must be violating some ordinance."

"I can't imagine which one. But any kind of a delay will give me a chance. Frankly, I think they've got their wires crossed, somehow. We're doing everything by the book."

"I'11 call you back. Sit tight."

Fifteen minutes later, the call came. I was instructed to have the workman call his office. He was on his second or third cup when I returned to the dining room. He made the call from the cashier's phone, looked pleased and said with admiration in his eyes, "You must have some kind of pull, buddy." With that, he made his exit.

At four o'clock I was in the Health Department. The inspector came in shortly after my arrival, cast a quick look in my direction, refusing to meet my eyes. He went into a private office. Presently he came out to the counter and called my name.

After identifying myself as the owner of The Patriots, I said: "Could you let me know what particular offense we're guilty of?"

"I sure can," he said. His tone was nasty. "You're maintaining a health hazard in your place of business."

"Could you be more specific? I know I'm in the wrong. But I can't correct a problem unless I know exactly what it is. Believe me, I don't intend being responsible for a health problem."

The inspector glared. "On my last inspection," he gave the time and date, "I found a waitress wading in the food!"

"Wading! In the food? My God!" This had to be some trumped up accusation. "Give me the woman's name," I said, "and I'll let her go at once. I can assure you, sir, that wading in the food is against our policy."

"I don't know her name."

His look of hostility remained so I went on. "I can certainly see that you people do a marvelous job. Obviously, I can't watch everything all the time. Isn't it fortunate that we have people like you who catch errors like this? Please accept my apology on behalf of all my employees as well as myself. I'll see that nothing of that sort ever happens again."

The inspector's face thawed. "I'll have to put you on probation. But as long as you take this attitude I think we can avoid closing you altogether."

"Thank you very much," I said.

Back at the Patriots, I called a meeting of all the waitresses on duty. I explained what had occurred. When I used the phrase "wading in the food," their looks of consternation and dismay were all that I could have hoped. Clearly, nothing of that sort could have happened.

Then one of the waitresses spoke up. "I think I may be the guilty one," Mr. LeFevre."

"Really? Tell me about it."

"I did have my foot on some food when the inspector was here last time."

"For a fact?"

"It was like this. I was in the pantry getting some dinner salads ready when the inspector showed up. The pantry has swinging doors and he opened one so that it bumped me, and I had to turn around. My foot was on a piece of lettuce. I must have dropped it without noticing. I threw it away at once and he saw me do it. But it's true. My foot was on that lettuce. I guess that's wading."

I nodded. "Could be. Something like that, of course. You didn't put that piece of lettuce back on a plate, did you?"

"Certainly not"'

"Well," I said. "It's just possible that our friendly government inspector has a chip on his shoulder. Will all of you please be exceptionally careful? We're on probation for a bit, it seems. But at least we can stay open."

Events went smoothly for a few days. Then, again one morning, I turned in the direction of Market Street as I was leaving the main entrance, and there was the workman diddling with my door once more.

"Hi," I said pleasantly. "What is it this time?"

"I'm shutting you down this time for sure," he said. He wasn't happy about it. "And don't ask me. It ain't the Health Department. I don't know what it is. You see, I don't really work for the Health Department. I'm..."

I interrupted. "I really don't have to know about the internal organization of City Hall," I said. "Just tell me what I'm doing that's wrong."

"I don't know. Honest. But it ain't Health this time. I asked about that. Cause I figgered you'd have pull. And there's no point coming over here for nothing."

"How's about some coffee?"

"I'm kind of busy." He was hesitant.

"What's the harm? I just need some time."

"Is pie included?"

"Surest thing you know."

"It's really good pie."

"Fine. It's on me. Let me make some calls."

I wasted no time and called my attorney at once.

I got his full attention when I told him I had received no advance notice on this occasion, either.

"Sounds like harassment to me," he said. "Sit tight. I'm going to call a judge I happen to know."

This time nearly half an hour passed and the workman was growing restless when the return call came. The workman was ordered to call his employer, and I was ordered to meet my attorney at City Hall.

After a bit of snooping, we found that the complaint against the Patriots had come from the Fire Marshal's office. The attorney and I went there to find out about it.

The Fire Marshal was present and I asked what I was doing wrong. It turned out that I was in violation of a city fire ordinance. I protested. In putting in the restaurant, we had met all fire requirements and had been inspected repeatedly with permits to proceed issued at intervals. I was particularly concerned about fire. What had I failed to do?

"You don't have the sign posted."

"What sign?"

"Every restaurant open to the public must display a sign that shows the total number of persons allowed in the establishment at one time."

"I never heard of the sign," I said.

I was informed that "ignorance of the law" is no excuse.

Again, I apologized. I was wrong. I freely admitted it. I didn't know. I was wrong about that, too. I should have known. Mea culpa. But could I please be informed as to what the sign should say; where it should be posted; the size of the sign; the size and nature of its lettering; and, how many persons would be agreeable to the powers that be?

The Fire Marshal wasn't mollified, but my attorney made an observation including a threat to sue on the basis of harassment. So it was agreed; if I posted the sign at once, I could continue. But not a moment was to be lost.

I was given the dimensions of the sign and its lettering. I was given a wording that I carefully wrote down. I was told where it was to be posted.

I swore by all that was holy that I would comply at once. I raced to a sign painter, paid a premium to get him to drop other chores and paint me a sign at once. With it, I returned to the Patriots and supervised the engineer's placement of it. The sign went up, still damp.

The attorney was breathing fire and brimstone when I said goodbye to him. I wanted no more trouble. I just wanted to operate in peace.

The episode hadn't ended. In a few days my friendly, cooperative workman was back again. This time he was specific. There was a sign relating to fire prevention that I hadn't posted; ergo I must be closed. For failure to comply.

I offered to show him the sign. That wasn't his department. He was not to see or to speak. He was to shut me up.

I had already run up quite a bill with my attorney and I didn't waste time on phone calls. I dashed to the Marshal's office to protest, this time ready for a toe-to-toe confrontation.

The Marshal explained that there was an ordinance, passed immediately after the great fire of 1906, It had been determined that all signs relating to fire and fire prevention must be made out of fireproof materials. I had made my sign of cardboard. It was flammable. Probably, it hadn't even been treated.

Why hadn't I been advised of this on my previous trip? I hadn't asked. And, again, ignorance of the law was no excuse.

Very well. I was in the wrong again. But surely, my good faith must have been in evidence. I would immediately have a new sign made—this one of sheet metal.

Not good enough, I was told. Sheet metal is only fire resistant. The sign must be fire proof.

Very well. What material was I to use?

A most interesting event followed that question. The Fire Marshal retired to his office. The upper portion of the door was glass and I could see in, although he closed the door. I moved until I could watch him at his desk.

The Marshal made use of the telephone and after a few minutes returned to the counter. "We have decided," he said, "That if you'll make your sign of bronze, that it will answer all specifications."

I agreed to do so at once. "We" had decided. I didn't ask questions.

I could find only one firm that made bronze signs. I commissioned the job. It took six months and cost over five hundred dollars. But I furnished the Marshal's office with proof that the sign was on order so we remained in business.

A few days later, I entered the Patriots feeling about as blue as one can feel. Things were not as I had planned. The local government and the Union were putting me through the wringer. I'm sure my dejection was evident.

The waitress at the counter came up to me with a big smile. "I've got some good news for you," she said.

"I could use some," I admitted.

"There's a new health inspector," she said. "They've moved the regular man to another territory."

A light dawned. "Miss," I said, "You are now a witness to a change in policy at the Patriots. The next time the Health Inspector shows up, feed him. No check. Got it? None. And if he comes in with friends and family, feed them, too. Keep track, and send me the check. From here on, the inspector is on the house."

"Yes, sir," she said with delight. "It's the only way to go."

From that day forward we had no further difficulties. The new inspector was jovial, friendly, and non-observant. So much so, in fact, that when someone stole our bronze sign, and I replaced it with the earlier cardboard placard, nothing was said. Later on, the attorney let re know that the firm which made bronze signs in the city had as its principle factotum, a relative of the mayor.

Chapter LXVI

One of the most difficult lessons I needed to learn was willingness to admit my own error. I should have closed the Patriot. That would have meant waving goodbye to about $100,000, the cost of the improvements, and I couldn't see it. I kept insisting that somehow I'd make the Patriots work.

Had I exercised reasonable judgment, I could have seen that it is adding foolishness to folly to throw good money after bad. The best advice would have been to admit the mistake, forget about it, and turn to other things, taking care to be more cautious in the future.

Instead, I reasoned this way. The restaurant was draining all the profits from the Jefferson. I had built a loser and hung it around my own neck like an albatross. There are two ways to rectify an unbalanced budget: 1. Increase income, or 2. Cut costs. If you can do both at once, you'll probably succeed. But either one of the procedures at least opens up a possibility for success. The reasoning is sound and my spirit was willing. But my tools were inadequate for the job.

The newspapers and radio stations were cranking out propaganda against businessmen on a daily basis. It seems businessmen were callused, indifferent, greedy monsters. They were unwilling to take any social responsibility. All businessmen ever thought about was a profit. These were the accusations. If I closed the Patriots, I'd be throwing a dozen people out of work. Wasn't that the very thing businessmen were accused of doing? They had no feelings, no sensitivity for the worker. They fired workers from purely selfish reasons.

I wasn't going to be guilty of conduct that could justify criticism of that kind. I did care about my employees. Of course, I realized that if I didn't make it, we'd all be out of work. But certainly, the answer to the problem wasn't a wholesale reduction in staff. Reducing expenses wasn't going to be my method. I'd pursue the other avenue of increasing income.

I'd ask everyone to work harder and I'd redouble my own efforts. Perhaps we could pull it out. Once all the borrowed sums and accumulated unpaid balances on time purchases were handled, we'd make it. The debt was unmanageable. With that out of the way, the daily cash flow from the restaurant would pay for its operation, although never for its replacement.

A number of business opportunities now opened that I pursued for increased income.

I had spoken so frequently to the "I Am" group about the advantages of being in business for one's self that Edith Shank now came forward. I earned a reasonable commission by getting her into a guesthouse of her own in the city of Pittsburgh, California. Pearl was doing well at the Henry Clay and I put that property up for sale.

The apartment house at the beach was doing well, so I put that on the market. Both properties sold swiftly, and at a good profit. The earning from both I now used to pay off bills at the Jefferson and Patriot.

I heard of a second hotel only a few blocks from the Jefferson and went to examine it. It proved to be the Glenburn on McAllister Street, just a block from the civic center. It had been a very fine, small hotel when it had first been built. It contained sixty rooms with one hundred percent baths, and designed for operation by a minimum staff. Like everything else, it had been allowed to run down during the war.

The owner of the building was a crotchety old Scot, appropriately named Bruce. He was the male counterpart of "Old Lady Grant." Two doors from the Glenburn was a second Bruce property, the Motel Astor. Bruce ran both hotels, but he was in his sixties and the two places were proving too much for him. He was willing to put a lease on the Glenburn. In addition to these properties, he owned half a dozen apartment houses, duplexes and fourplexes, and a dozen private residences. He had accounts in every bank in town. He was so frugal; he would never buy a hat. In the gusty San Francisco breezes, he wore a brown paper bag over his thinning white hair.

He didn't trust the banks so he spread his money around, depositing only $10,000 in each. He chose that figure because it was the sum supposedly insured by the Federal Deposit Insurance Corporation.

I approached him with the idea of buying more real estate. He was afraid real estate values might go down so he didn't wish to purchase. I suggested that he sell some of the real estate he had. He was afraid that the purchasing power of the money was deteriorating, and he didn't want that kind of money.

We did strike a bargain with the Glenburn. He would give me a one-year lease at no cost whatever. I had to pay $1,200 per month rent and agree to replace any furniture or furnishings. I would return the hotel to him with inventory intact. To insure my performance, I would post a $5,000 bond, refundable to me at the end of the year.

Rents were frozen at $2.00 per night for each room. That is, if the OPA had classified the room for transients. However, there were a number of permanent residents in the house, with rents of $1.00 per night, or $30,00 per month, including daily maid service, heat, lights, and telephone. The OPA said they weren't transient unless the present tenant vacated.

I figured I could net about $500 or $600 per month in spite of the high monthly figure on the lease. And, of course, if any of the permanent residents departed, I could double their room rate from $1.00 to $2.00 per night.

The lease transaction was completed and now, instead of worrying about the Henry Clay and the apartment house, I worried about the Glenburn.

A few weeks later, a third hotel came to me. A couple I had dealt with since 1940 operated a rather good American Plan Hotel on & Sutter and Gough. It was called the Majestic. They had done well, but they were tired—it was so easy to wear one's self out in multiple housing activities—and they wanted a quick deal. They didn't need the cash; they wanted out. I took over the Majestic with no money down and agreed to pay them the same price they had paid, but over a period of months. Again, Pearl and my "I Am" friends came to manage and direct the property.

Meanwhile, Loy's mother had run into difficulties. She had done well in her Jackson Street guesthouse. She had sold that at a profit and moved into a more lucrative operation just off the Berkeley campus of the University of California.

In great distress she phone, one day to advise that her house was "full of communists." There was a young student who prided himself on being a Marxist, who had organized her tenants against her. They were refusing to pay their rents because they had it in for landlords in general. They wanted the government to step in and confiscate her property.

Meanwhile, to justify their refusal to pay rent, they were claiming all manner of neglect and lack of service. Because of the OPA, she couldn't evict without extensive legal procedures for which she had neither the time nor the money. They expected her to feed them at her expense, house them at her expense, redecorate and repair their rooms at her expense. If she refused any of their demands they created an uproar, marched in the street, discouraged new people from filling vacancies, and made her life miserable. They accused her of being part of the idle rich. Neither word described her in the least.

I had to do something about this. An attorney friend managed to get an eviction of the ringleader, after which the place settled down somewhat. But Mama's interest—we always called her Ma-mah, stressing the last syllable—in guesthouses was waning. If people could do things like this to her and the government sided with the tenants, then who could blame her?

I had managed to augment my income with the new hotels. Now I convinced Loy that financially we were still in difficulty and I prevailed on her to give up our home, renting it to Mama as a new guesthouse. The Clay Street residence was large and would accommodate about fifteen guests. I had followed the same procedure with our "I Am" group on Vallejo Street before the war and it had worked out well.

Where would we live, Loy wanted to know. We'd live at the Jefferson, I told her. I took four rooms out of circulation and had them converted into a rather fine, if diminutive four-room suite. I couldn't blame her for not being enthusiastic. The Clay Street house was so lovely. The Jefferson was anything but. However, the rental paid by Mama covered the payments on Clay Street. Again, we took a step toward a balanced budget.

By this time I was working nearly around the clock. I opened a new branch in my real estate activities and began selling houses as well as multiple housing units. Anything and everything I could conceive of that would turn a dollar, I leaped at.

Pearl and Ethel approached me with an idea. I was so occupied with my various endeavors that the "gang" rarely saw me. This was not satisfactory. Both felt that my concepts and my "inner contacts" were essential. However, they did understand my priorities and had demonstrated their willingness to help me. Now I could help them.

They wished to organize a center for metaphysical studies. This would entail establishing a specific location as a meeting place that they would lease as a permanent headquarters. This would give them an opportunity of attracting new people to the ideas we all felt were important.

I agreed with the concept, but explained that I was too busy to take any role that would require specific performance at stated times. I would work with them and, when I had the time, I would be happy to meet with them so we could discuss ideas. Also, I would be entirely willing to lecture on occasion. I would back the idea from time to time with a small gift. But, again, I couldn't commit myself to anything of consequence.

Apparently, having my approval was meaningful, and they went ahead with it. In choosing a name for their corporation, they decided to omit any identifying words that might class it as "I Am" or metaphysical or even religious. They chose the name "The San Francisco Group," and under that cognomen formal incorporation occurred.

The Mama's experience in Berkeley, and similar reports from other people, convinced me that something was very wrong in the Bay Area. I, myself, had been thwarted and put into a bind by both government and Union intrusion.

If the government had not turned down my plea for a liquor license, and if the Union (government backed) hadn't forced me to have a featherbedded payroll, I would be the owner of an outstanding success. It was my naivete that had put me into my predicament. I hadn't really believed that the government could take a position against me simply because I was trying to run a business. But both government and Union had, in fact, cost me several thousand dollars in expenditures, some of them totally nonsensical. They were preventing me from running my business in an intelligent manner. Yet I was loyal, patriotic, a veteran and a taxpayer.

When I spoke to various people about the possibility of a communist threat, such as Mama had run into, I was looked at furtively. Then, in whispers and "off the record," I was told that this nation was suffering from this problem from coast to coast. It wasn't just in San Francisco. Communists, I was told, had infiltrated the government. They were casting a malevolent spell on the American way of life. I was given a few books to read and—warned that communists were everywhere.

My secretary, Ruth, assured me that her father had been engaged in ferreting out some of these subversives and had prepared a basic list. But it was and had to be kept secret. If it became known that a person was anticommunist, he could lose his job or become persona non grata in his own circle of friends.

On checking with the authors of some of these books, I was told they had all had difficulties of enormous size in getting published. It had all begun, I was told, with FDR. While there were may fine Democrats, they were, in general, rather favorable to communist theory. However, if you called a person a communist you could be sued.

Frankly, I knew little or nothing about communism. I hadn't as yet read the *Communist Manifesto* or *Das Kapital*. But there was one thing I did know about. I knew about my own business. I knew that the government had created the OPA, as a "war measure" with the promise that, once the war ended, it would be disbanded.

The war had ended. The OPA was now the OPS. But it certainly hadn't been disbanded.

I decided to write a letter to my Congressman. Clearly, he represented me. At least, that's what I had been taught to believe. I was an honest man. Honest, perhaps, to the point of being naive. But I had several businesses. I was providing an item in short supply called housing. The rents then in vogue were far below the break-even point if a person wanted to put his buildings into good condition or build new ones.

I drew up the letter. Ruth and I worked it over together making sure that I stated the situation as I saw it with accuracy and brevity. I reminded my federal representative that the OPS was a holdover that should be eliminated, as the government had promised to do. Would he move as quickly as possible to get it done, if you please?

A few weeks later I got a personal letter from my Congressman. I could hardly believe what it said. In it, the Congressman let me understand that there was no intention whatever of getting rid of the OPS. The reason, as he stated it, were people just like me. I was a landlord. Never before that letter had I seen that word used with the connotation he employed. As a landlord, I was a member of the idle, privileged class. Obviously, I couldn't be a landlord unless I was rich, greedy, and a slob.

If the OPS were disbarred, my Congressman advised, people like me would turn around and "gouge" the little people who were completely helpless. Rather than working to get rid of the agency, my "representative" was working to broaden and extend its powers. Taxes on land should be increased. Anyone in business was "bad" by definition. The worst of the lot were the landlords who did no work but fattened themselves at the expense of the poor.

I showed this letter to a few people. They assured me that my Congressman, a Democrat, was one of hundreds who were loyal to Russia and doing their best to destroy this country.

In whatever spare time I had, I now took to reading. Everything I read seemed to confirm the allegation that some kind of infiltration had taken place. This wasn't the America I had volunteered to defend against any and all foreign foes. It was a strange land and it was alien to it.

How was it possible for all this to occur? Ah, the answer from books and from acquaintances was prompt. Most of our difficulties came from the Democrats under FDR, who were taking from those who had to divvy it up among those who hadn't produced it. The nation was becoming a welfare state.

What we needed to do was to get back to the Constitution, the Bill of Rights, and the Declaration of Independence. Under those documents, each American had the right to try; success wasn't guaranteed and many would fail. But, at least, they could try. What they made was theirs. And if they didn't make it, tough. I had been raised in a household where this was believed, and I believed it, too.

Since FDR, taxation had been introduced, not as a device to pay the costs of government, but as a device to redistribute income. And this was the core of the Marxist position.

All of the anti-capitalist thinking was pretty scary. I didn't know enough about economic theory to have one of my own. But I did know that my Congressman didn't represent me, although he pretended to do. His policies were inimical to my best interests.

The San Francisco Group had been organized; it seemed a good time to organize something else. I ran an ad in the papers setting up a general meeting for people who realized that something had gone wrong. If enough people came, we'd organize some kind of a group to study the issues, and then write letters to our Congressmen urging them to vote for the "American way" of life.

About forty people convened in the lobby of the Jefferson. Half of them were from the San Francisco Group; the other half were newcomers.

The upshot was that we organized under the name, "The People's Unofficial Committee." Every one of the people present was fed up with officialdom, and for cause. So we didn't want anyone to think we were "officials." Ours was an unofficial group and would derive its importance by that very fact.

Now I had two extracurricular groups to work—with my metaphysical friends and my unofficial friends. To make things even more interesting, I acquired still another business, a retail store that sold recordings and musical equipment.

No matter how busy I became I was always ready to launch a new project or go out of my way to get something done. I had maintained contact by mail with my two European friends, Marjorie Llewellin, in London, and Daisy Pallier, in Paris.

During the post-war stringency imposed upon England and France, it seemed to me that the smart people would naturally come to America. I could see no way for Daisy to manage such a shift in location. With her small son and her lack of a readily salable commercial skill, she would have difficulties in the United States.

Marjorie Llewellin, as a trained physical therapist, could manage well. Indeed, it seemed to me that life in America would be far more rewarding than what she could reasonably expect in Britain. Her skills were in demand anywhere. I urged her to consider a move to San Francisco.

Marjorie thought about it, contacted the emigration authorities in London. They advised that she would move to the United State if I would act as her sponsor. Of course, I agreed. By so, doing I ran into another one of these governmental labyrinths, the full exposition of which would take a complete volume in itself.

To reduce a ponderous and frustrating story, let me summarize. I had to sign for Margie. First, I had to agree that she would not become a welfare burden. Then, I had to swear by my sacred honor that she would not have a job. (The reason for this contradiction was a move by the unions, which wanted all jobs in this country to be reserved for "natives.") Also, I mustn't hire her myself. I wasn't to support her. But her own government wouldn't permit her to take more than a pittance out of England.

How she was to survive didn't seem to concern anyone.

Somehow Margie managed and, despite these confusions, arrived in America and at last in San Francisco. I consoled myself with the rationale that there must be some "pinkos" in the Immigration Department. I should not pay too much attention to anything they said.

Upon arrival stateside, Margie discovered that her license to practice in London—won by better than six years of advanced education and training, combined with years of experience—meant nothing.

She would have to pass several examinations here before she could be accepted. Hospitals everywhere were crying for people with her skills. But she was compelled to stay outside the work force both by the licensing requirement and because of the Immigration and Labor Departments.

She persevered and readily found employment. Meanwhile, she lived with us on Clay Street and was quickly adopted by the San Francisco Group.

All of these excursions and alarms took their toll on me. I was becoming short of temper as I operated under growing pressure from all directions.

Chapter LXVII

One of my less endearing traits from earliest youth has been a tendency to take everyone with great seriousness. I was now desperate for money to meet my various obligations. I presented a grim visage to Loy and my familiars. I told them the truth. We were strapped for funds. If we pressured every penny, we might just pull through.

Accompanying my sober and even somber mood I had another trait. This one was very attractive. When I explained that I was having a difficult time no one believed me. Apparently, I am a person who radiates opulence. So, when I explained that I hadn't so much as a thin dime to squander, everyone laughed, nodded like an insider, and urged me to spend money.

My various enterprises in San Francisco were, in the main, successful. I had created a pressure cooker to keep them all running, and I was the principle item under pressure. It took awhile, but finally I began to see the funny side. The "I Am" teachings had probably helped me accept the fact that every problem I had was one of my own making. I had heaped obstacles and traps in the direction I was to go, and then expected people to sympathize when I became short of breath while trying to get around, over or through them.

I had worked myself to the brink of a nervous breakdown. I suspect it was the hotel business that opened my eyes, made it possible for me to laugh at myself, and thus avoid the men with the straight jackets.

People aren't what we think they are. We have impressions gleaned from books, articles, newspapers, and teachers. And, today, from the electronic media. Most of us develop a set of six or eight stereotypes and we try to fit everyone into this or that mold. (He's that kind of a guy. She's that sort. Etc.)

If you have three hotels, some guesthouses, and any kind of social life, then you begin to realize that no two persons fall into the same category. You begin to suspect that those who are mentally lethargic have invented the very concept of categorizing. Dealing with a few hundred people, many of them, is an education in itself.

People are funny.

Let me tell you about some of my employees at the Jefferson. First, there was Bert. He was a fine-looking, soft-spoken man in his fifties when he first showed up asking for a job as a clerk. He had worked at some good establishments and, on checking his references, I found him highly recommended with only one problem. Once in a while, he would get drunk. Otherwise, he was as good a clerk as could be found.

He assured me he had given up liquor absolutely and forever, so I gave him the night shift. He was splendid for about four months. Then one morning when I showed up Bert was gone. It took me two days to find him. He was in a neighboring hotel, soaked to the gills and without the slightest recollection of what had happened. It took about three weeks to dry him out.

Since he had misplaced all the collections he had made on the night he fell from the wagon, I fired him. But I regretted it later, for he was the best night clerk I ever had...when he was sober.

I hired him back and worked out an arrangement.

I found that he could stay sober for about four months. So after four months of work I laid him off, while he was still in good shape. He would disappear, get himself absolutely stinking, and I'd see nothing of him for two or three weeks. Then, he'd come back to the Jefferson, a five-day growth of beard on his face, reeking of cheap booze, and wearing clothes that looked and smelled like mop-up rags at a racing stable. Again, with the most sober and pathetic assurances, he would tell me he was off the stuff. For good. I learned one thing out of this experience. Never believe an alcoholic. They are among the world's most convincing liars.

Over at the Glenburn on MacAllister Street, I hired a clerk whose visage that made Jack Pallance look like a baby sitter. His name was Clarence Virgil. His hands were pudgy; his body was short and twisted. He limped seriously, having been born with a flat wheel. His face was the very map of villainy. He had thick, black beetle-brows, a hooknose, and hair that tended to hang like a pair of ram's horns on each side of his swarthy face. One ear was large, the other smaller; one eye was larger than the other, and they were not at the same degree of latitude. This was not the face or the figure of someone to inspire confidence. I never knew a gentler, more honest and more persevering worker.

What may have provided the triggering mechanism for my belated emergence of a sense of humor could have been some of my tenants. Let me tell you about one of them.

Mrs. Dayton was a pleasant-appearing woman, probably in her late forties or early fifties. She lived at the Glenburn as a permanent guest for $30.00 per month, with everything furnished. She tended to dress well, kept her hair in good condition, and paid her rent on time.

Like many others, her weakness seemed to be the demon rum. For days at a time, she would leave the hotel in the morning, returning in the evening, the very picture of nine-to-five rectitude. And then she'd get paid.

On those bi-monthly occasions, she would be late entering the lobby of the Glenburn. The door had a recoil device intended to close it after someone had entered. It usually exerted far more resistance than was necessary, but the engineer was apparently unable to adjust it correctly. Using the door was akin to taking on an arm wrestling champion.

When Mrs. Dayton was in her cups she had unusual difficulty with the door. She would lean against it trying to swing it open and would invariably lose at least one shoe and sometimes both. She would carefully, lugubriously, retrieve her footwear, simper a bit, and try to appear charming in her stocking feet.

Then holding her offending pumps in one hand, she drew a bead on the desk, which she had to reach before getting to the elevator. Her passage across the lobby, following the calculations of her mental astrolabe, was marvelous to behold. Once at the desk, she would shift her sights to the elevator door. Somehow, by dead reckoning, she would swing her way to the milestone in-transit.

One Saturday afternoon, Mrs. Dayton entered the lobby in barroom mint condition. After tacking into the wind and out again, she finally got to the elevator and disappeared behind its clanging door.

Perhaps twenty minutes later, a stranger entered the lobby and came up to the desk. "There's a woman out on the fire escape," he said. "Third or fourth floor, I think."

"What about it?" I asked.

"Well, I thought you'd want to at least take a look. She's taking off her clothing."

It was Mrs. Dayton. She wasn't hurting anyone but she was delightfully conspicuous. Someone nearby had already called the police. Presently, an officer showed up to restore neighborhood decorum. Policemen learn to take events of this sort in stride. He didn't give her a ticket. He persuaded her to go back in her room and get dressed.

In any event, perhaps thirty minutes later, a properly attired Mrs. Dayton reappeared at the elevator. Leaning to starboard, she navigated the narrows until she stood before me at the counter. She was like a little girl who had been spanked and was now reporting to "Daddy" to apologize for her behavior.

She managed to get both eyes on my face simultaneously. "I'm not a bad woman, Mr. LeFevre!" she said. "I was hot."

Two brothers rented an apartment from us at the Great Highway. We took a special interest in them when the tenant just below their third floor unit complained repeatedly that the lads were maintaining some kind of nuisance in their room. It was a nuisance because it made a lot of noise.

I checked on the report one day when the boys were away. The nature of the "nuisance" was easy to identify. The lads were toy train enthusiasts. They must have had about sixty feet of track laid out in their relatively small quarters. Every night, they got down on the floor and played with their trains.

I think I envied them. I had never been able to afford the kind of layout they had obtained. These boys were young men in their late twenties or early thirties. We became good friends. I gave them a room at the Glenburn where they could make a layout on a carpeted floor and, thus, avoid complaints from tenants underneath.

The one oddity of these two chaps, besides their addiction to trains, was their unwillingness to seek or hold a job commensurate with their abilities. The reason was explained to me. They were heirs to a considerable fortune. One of these days, they were going to come up with several millions of dollars each. Thus, these young men, of more than average ability and education, drifted through all the years I knew them. They never applied themselves, but lived in expectation of that great day when they'd have millions fall on them.

Last I heard they were still living in expectation. I profoundly doubt that they inherited much of anything. At the time, it struck me as almost incomprehensible. The real fun in living wasn't in having a lot of money; the real fun was in doing something successfully, which paid off as you did it. Like happiness, money has to be earned to be appreciated.

Whenever possible, I registered transients, instead of permanent guests. The rule of the Office of Price Stabilization (OPS) was that a hotel room housing 8 permanent guest had a fixed rate. But if the permanent guest departed, then the hotel could re-classify that room as a transient and immediately double or treble the rates. (From $1.00 per night to $2.00 or even $3.00.)

At the Glenburn, I took note of a room I thought would serve nicely as a transient, if I could manage to get rid of the permanent guest. I chose this particular room to work on because I had never seen the tenant.

Upon inspecting the room, I found it full of bills, receipts, and memoranda of all sorts, but nothing in the way of a guest. There were stacks of bills on the bed. The dresser drawers had been pulled out, boards put across the bathtub and that, too, was covered with bills. The table, the john, any and every flat surface in the room was covered with paper.

All I had to go on was the name of the tenant. Once a month his check came through the mail, paying his room rent far in advance. Obviously, this man didn't need a room for sleeping. He needed additional space for filing pieces of paper he wanted to keep. Meanwhile, there was a shortage of sleeping rooms in the city. So I made inquiries with the OPS concerning my chances. Could I oust this tenant who never used his room and never needed it for a night's sleep?

There were only two legally acceptable grounds. Failure to pay rent, or proof that the occupant was breaking the law in some manner. There was no chance with the first. He was, perhaps, the most prompt tenant in the hotel, so far as paying his rent was concerned.

What about all those bits and pieces of paper? Aha, my suspicious mind suggested. Perhaps these were slips of paper relating to some illegal activity that he was keeping from the prying eyes of workers at his office, wherever he might work.

Suddenly, I had a great idea. Surely, all that paper in the room was dangerous. A spark, a flaring match, an electric short...and a fire would rage out of control in a moment, fueled by half a ton of used paper. I'd take it up with the Fire Marshal. I had been a "good boy" at the Jefferson. I wasn't in any trouble. Perhaps I could enlist the Fire Marshal's assistance. If the Marshal thought a cardboard sign was a fire hazard, surely all this waste paper would fall into the same category.

Then I did a double take. The bills and receipts in the room carried the name of the tenant, as did the hotel directory at the desk. It hadn't dawned on me before. The tenant was the Fire Marshal. This was confirmed when the man himself, breaking his rule of mailing in the check, happened to stop by to pay his rent. He looked at me, puzzled, trying to remember my face. I didn't help him out. I abandoned any notion of evicting the Fire Marshal for creating a fire hazard.

Perhaps the strangest adventures I ever had were at the Glenburn. While the Jefferson was in the tenderloin, the Glenburn was almost on skid row. Of course, it was on the "right" side of Market and not to be compared to a Mission Street or Howard Street establishment. But we had many transients at the Glenburn who were in such a state of fluidity that they could have been poured back into the wine bottle from whence they had vaporized.

The lobby was small and at street level, with the desk much too close to the front door. Those wishing to operate hotels, take note. The closer to the front door the registration counter is located, the more your establishment will be attractive to hold-up men. A crook likes to come in, pull his job, and then get away without running across a big lobby.

Just behind the desk was the elevator serving all floors. Behind the elevator were fire doors that effectively shut the lobby off from the rest of the hotel.

There was one additional unique feature. Beyond the elevator, the height of the basement's ceiling was about a story and a half, but it was normal height under the lobby. Thus, the first floor of rooms was actually half a floor above the lobby. A stairway led to that floor. A second stairway, starting almost at the front door, went all the way up to the second story, which was a story and a half high.

On New Year's Eve, a tenant who had imbibed far too much, came through the fire door on the second floor. He paused a story and a half above the lobby floor, and then came down that straight and narrow set of treads with a single step. If he'd been sober, he'd have been killed, or at least maimed. As it was, he picked himself up from the ruins of a grandfather clock we kept at the base of the flight. He grinned and wondered aloud if there was anything left to drink. He was uninjured.

Thanks to the registration desk's proximity to the street, a thug confronted my night clerk, just as he was sealing $80.00 into an envelope. The clerk had collected from a tenant nearly three months in arrears, and the rule for handling cash at night was simple. Get rid of it fast.

Only ten dollars in small bills was kept at the desk to make change. If a tenant paid a bill, the money was sealed into a Glenburn envelope and dropped down the chute. I had caused the engineer to cut a mail slot in the desk, which connected with a huge two-ton safe in the basement, through a corresponding slot in the top of the safe. The money was identified by writing the name of the tenant on the envelope and, of course, entering the figure in the hotel ledger. That way, the most a robber could pick up was $10.00.

The clerk had just completed tucking the money into the envelope and had written the payer's name, when he saw a man with a revolver in his hand entering the lobby from the street. Foolishly, the clerk tried to push the envelope into the slot where it would have been safe. But the desk was close enough to the front door, so he was pistol-whipped for his effort. The crook got the envelope with the money in it.

Curiously, the police were on hand almost at once.

The Glenburn was the second hit for this particular crook that night and his first victim, a block away, had already phoned. As the robber ran from the hotel with the Glenburn envelope in a coat pocket, the cops swooped down and arrested him.

An officer brought the envelope back to the desk so the clerk could identify it as hotel property. Without opening the envelope, he did so, attesting there was $80.00 inside, and signing his name as night clerk.

I knew nothing about all this until I came in the following morning. I immediately contacted the police department and attempted to get my hands on the $80.00. After all, we had already waited a long time for those dollars and we needed them badly.

I was told that the $80.00 was "evidence." I was assured that it would be kept safely and returned to me after the trial. I wanted to know why the envelope with the clerk's signature wouldn't suffice and was told that the envelope had to be kept sealed until the trial when it would be opened to prove the actual nature of the theft.

The robbery occurred in 1947. I'm still waiting for the money. And without taking the time to sketch the details, I can report that I wasn't passive about my various attempts to retrieve it.

But I must tell about my prize guests at the Glenburn. I'll call them Mr. and Mrs. John Smith. They both had jobs and were model tenants at least five days out of every week. They paid their rent promptly, were quiet, and courteous.

Saturday was payday. Mrs. Smith would arrive before her husband. She would "make certain" respecting mail and messages, see that any sums owing were paid and then would go to her room.

Presently, Mr. Smith would come in. On Saturdays he was invariably drunk and invariably angry. With body language that clearly said, "Don't anyone try to interfere," he'd work his way up the short flight of steps, wrestle the fire door open, and disappear down the corridor of the first floor.

There would be an on-going interlude of quiet lasting anywhere from five to ten minutes. Then, without warning, the riot would begin. There would be pounding on doors and walls. Sometimes, the sound of splintering furniture would reach the lobby. There would be shouts and a woman would scream several times. Sometimes it seemed the whole building shook as fists pounded into flesh and one or another body met with the floor. The uproar would rise to a crescendo and there would be the sound of breaking glass. Then quiet would descend once more.

Five minutes later, Mrs. Smith would reappear. She'd come into the lobby from the street. Painfully, she'd push open the door with the heavy recoil. Painfully, she would limp past the desk and drag herself up that short flight of steps. Her clothing would be torn. Often there would be a welt over an eye or bruises on a cheek. Her hair would be disheveled and, on occasion, a trace of blood would show at the corner of her mouth.

But she always smiled, it seemed almost in relief. And she said nothing whatever. Favoring whatever portion of her anatomy had been most recently battered, she'd disappear in the direction of her room.

That was all there was to it. It occurred nearly every Saturday night for the full year that I held the lease at the Glenburn.

Mr. Smith would accuse his wife of infidelity, beat her up, and then, invariably, throw her out the window. She would fall the half story to the paved alley. Sometimes he'd break furniture. Sometimes he'd batter in the door. Always he'd break the window. But she never broke.

One time, I tried to persuade him to leave the window open when he left for work on Saturday. It would save us replacing the glass and might prevent a serious cut to his wife.

Apparently, breaking the glass was half the fun. Mrs. Smith took the beating with a happy countenance. The two of them always paid for any damage. They didn't object to the costs. They immediately settled. They got on well together except for these outbursts.

When I first began calling a glazier for a replacement pane, I was very careful to get the measurements with precision. After that it didn't matter. I'd simply announce that it was the Glenburn calling and the man on duty would say: "We have it all cut. We'll bring it over about ten."

LeFevre Enterprises and LeFevre Investments were in motion. My headquarters were at the Jefferson but I was in and out, and all around town. Everywhere I went I made money, except in the Patriot's dining room.

The San Francisco Group was busy; the People's Unofficial Committee was busy. And my own energy was wearing thin.

One morning at the Jefferson, my hotel clerk, Margie, (not to be confused with Marjorie Llewellin), went to the dining room for coffee. Ruth Dazey, my secretary, who supervised just about everything with surpassing skill, filled in behind the counter.

The Jefferson had a large, attractive lobby with the registration desk well inside the building, about thirty-five feet from the front entrance. At the right, as one entered, were the two rooms I used for my real estate business. Then came the desk with space behind it about the size of a sleeping room.

Ruth used one of the two rooms for her office. She could enter my office or, by using a rear door, she could enter the space behind the counter and serve as a hotel clerk.

It was about ten in the morning. I was out on some errand. The engineer was in the furnace room. The maids were making up the rooms. The Patriot's dining room had its sparse contingent of paying customers but that was in the basement. Ruth Dazey was in her office with the door ajar so she could keep an eye on the hotel switchboard and the registration desk. She was the only person on the first floor when a man, wearing a yellow oilskin slicker, came to the registration desk.

She slid from her desk and moved to the counter. She smiled and said, "Good morning. May I help you?" The counter was elbow height.

Just below where Ruth positioned herself was a drawer containing registration forms, receipts, and other stationary supplies. There was also a loaded 45.

The drawer was slightly open and Ruth had a glimpse of the gleaming black revolver. With her mid-section she pushed it shut. She didn't like guns. The stranger had said nothing, so Ruth spoke again. "Would you like a room?"

With a sudden sweeping motion, the man in the oilskin raised his hand and arm to counter level. His hand was in his slicker pocket and he didn't remove it. Ruth's eyes dilated in horror. His fingers were closed around a blunt object in the pocket. She couldn't be sure. It looked like a pistol, very much like the one in the drawer.

"Don't try nothing funny," the man hissed. "Open the safe and give me the money. All of it!"

The Glenburn safe may have been in the basement, but the Jefferson safe, a full six feet in height was in plain sight behind the counter. We didn't keep money in it. We used it so that guests could check their valuables. Few Jefferson guests had valuables and the safe dated to an earlier time. It was rarely used for any purpose.

"Sir," Ruth said, "I'm not the hotel clerk and I don't have the combination. If I had it, I'd do as you ask. Unfortunately, I can't."

"Please don't be upset. The hotel clerk has gone down to the dining room for coffee and will be back in just a few minutes. She has the combination."

The man seemed to steel himself. "I ain't kidding, lady. Open that safe or I'll plug you. "

"You're frightening me," Ruth said. "But I'm unable to do as you ask. You see, I'm really Mr. LeFevre's secretary. I'm not the hotel clerk. See. My office is in there." She gestured. "If I could, I'd open the safe at once. But I don't have the combination."

"Lady, I mean business."

"So do I, sir." The man began to shake. Ruth grew more fearful.

"Please, Mister. Don't be scared. No one will hurt you. Why don't you Just sit over there in one of those easy chairs? The clerk will be back very soon, I promise. And then she'll open the safe."

"You're trying to pull something. You're gonna call the cops."

Ruth put up her hands, "Not me, sir, Oh, no. I really wish I could open the safe, but I can't. I really can't. Please believe me. But don't be nervous. Everyone will do as you ask. Just have a chair and be patient."

The man glared, then suddenly turned and ran from the lobby. Ruth grabbed the counter as relief swept over her.

Later, when she reported the incident, I asked her about the revolver, "Why didn't you reach for the gun?" I asked.

"It never occurred to me," she said. "I knew it was there, but I've never even picked up one of those things. I wouldn't have known what to do."

"Then, let me congratulate you. You did the right thing, and always remember it in the future. When a crook confronts you, don't try to see which of you is the best shot. We can always get more money. We can't replace you. "

"I was terrified," Ruth said.

"Let me ask you. What if Margie had come back from coffee, while the man with the gun was standing there? Would you have opened the safe then?"

"Of course. I said I would. And I would."

"Again, you get an 'A,'" I said. "Bear in mind that your own fear is no greater than that of the crook. He's bound to be frightened. He knows he's doing something he shouldn't do. And he's not thinking too clearly or he wouldn't be doing it. Folding up in front of a threat isn't guaranteed to protect you. But it is the best thing to do to remove the fear of the assailant. You are safer with a brave crook than you are with one who's scared to death."

Chapter LXVIII

I had performed wonders with the Jefferson. My efforts at that location had probably enhanced property values up and down Eddy Street. I had cleaned up the operation, invested about $125,000 over and above the price I had paid, and had managed to improve the hotel's clientele generally. These developments had not gone unnoticed.

An occasional businessman from a better part of San Francisco, dropped in to congratulate me on the progress shown and to wonder, aloud, if I hadn't put more money into the property than the neighborhood warranted. I stoutly insisted that slums and other areas showing decay and decline could be brought back if the owners would spend the money. These gentlemen, while revealing admiration, would walk off shaking their heads. They were wise to remain skeptical.

I was rewarded for all I had done by a substantial boost in my real estate taxes. I protested that if property owners were penalized for improvements, then there would be small incentive to improve. I was told that the hotel was now worth more and, in consequence, I had to pay my increasingly large "fair" share.

There was one further step I could take to bring the Jefferson into the black ink with the Patriot's dining room still functioning. I could sell everything else I had, use the money to reduce the debts, and put all my eggs into the Jefferson basket. That would mean selling our lovely home on Clay Street. It would also mean that Loy and I and our new son would have to move into the Jefferson. The tenderloin district is not the ideal location in which to raise a family. But I had to make every effort to make the restaurant and hotel a financial success.

On the second floor, immediately above my real estate office and the lobby desk, I took four rooms out of service and converted them into a four-room apartment. The rooms weren't large. But we managed two bedrooms, a living room, a kitchen, and two baths. One of the baths was converted into a utility area. I anticipated eating in the hotel dining room much of the time, but I relished the idea of seclusion and privacy with my own little family. So the kitchen was provided with a small nook for food service. My "own little family" frequently included Rob and Dave, whom we picked up at their mother's home in Marin County, and then returned later.

I managed to unload the Glenburn, the record shop, the apartment building, and the Majestic. Naturally, I kept my real estate and insurance business operational and continued with the Jefferson. At last the Clay Street home sold; we moved into the hotel.

Whatever bills might have been outstanding in other locations, I converted to accounts due and payable at the Jefferson. The building and its operations included all my assets and covered all my liabilities. Thanks to the losses accruing at the dining room, my total net came to about $50,000. This was a decided shrinkage. I consoled myself by recalling that I had begun with no money of my own.

By this time my concern for business profits had faded into second position. Increasingly—thanks to my reading and to the San Francisco Group and the People's Unofficial Committee—my interests burgeoned into concern for my country. Politically, the nation was in difficulty. There was no question that the principles of private property, private business management, and reward or failure for individual effort were on the wane.

Government at all levels was intruding. The economic theories of Karl Marx, wherein Government became a giant holding company of all productive property, were in the ascendancy. By 1948, we entered a business recession and my efforts to recoup my losses were further hampered.

My mind was a morass of confusion. I needed a period of time, of personal tranquility in which I could assimilate all of the strange, new ideas that I had picked up. I needed time to organize my thoughts and regain perspective. Then, I would know what to do.

My nerves were frayed. I was hard to live with. My temper was short and my decisions not always as sharp as they had once been.

Reluctantly, I came to the only conclusion I could.

I must sell out totally. My assets were larger than my liabilities. If I could bring in a party with more resources, he could bring the Jefferson into fruition as a real moneymaker.

At long last, I ran an ad in an effort to sell my one remaining package. I could survive nicely on my net from such a sale, until I had managed to re-think my position. Then, rather than concentrating on real estate or on multiple housing, perhaps I could raise my voice across the nation. I could try to awaken the unwary to the perils of socialism, which were now attaching themselves like barnacles to the American economy.

I even dreamed of getting into politics. However, when I would practice my decrees in solo or with the group, I invariably came up with negative feedback.

My ad for the Jefferson awakened little or no interest. I had a few nibbles, mostly from persons far less capable than me when it came to riding herd on so fractious a critter as I bestrode.

I changed the ad, offering to trade the Jefferson's equity and potential for some smaller property with a corresponding equity, but without the potential. Again, I came up empty.

One Sunday, Loy looked up from reading The Examiner. She had spotted an ad put in by a party in Southern California. They had a Beverly Hills home, formerly owned by a famous moving picture star. They wanted to trade their equity for equity in a San Francisco business.

That seemed made to order. It was up to me to take the initiative. Jerry Dorris, Pearl's husband, agreed to go with me, so the two of us could look over the property in Beverly Hills.

The San Francisco Group, mostly under Pearl's management, had done well. It was not an outstanding success, yet she had brought a few new people into the group. By now, this religious study unit rented a meeting place and conducted weekly services.

While I didn't particularly want a piece of Los Angeles real estate, I did want to dispose of the hotel. It occurred to me that the group might have use for some such asset. Perhaps, the building could serve as a focal point for Group activities. Meanwhile, Loy and I could live in it while we became more active in public affairs. Perhaps, between metaphysical studies on the one hand, and the People's Unofficial Committee on the other, a trade might be warranted. In any case, I wanted someone with me. I no longer trusted my own decisions and Jerry was a hard working, sober realist. His judgment should be sound.

I telephoned the Beverly Hills number listed in the ad and talked with a Mrs. "Gypsy" Buys. The property they proposed trading was the famous Falcon Lair, a residence constructed by Rudolph

Valentino as a love token to his wife, Natasha Rambova. "Gypsy" sang the praises of the property insisting it was worth great sums of money. It consisted of a mansion in Benedict Canyon situated on three acres and with a view commanding Catalina Island on a clear day.

Following the phone call, Jerry and I went to Southern California and drove up Benedict Canyon to the address, #2 Bella Drive. To reach the property, we took Sunset Boulevard, then headed into the hills on Benedict Canyon. We turned sharply left onto Bella Drive. The road looped, and then climbed at a thirty-degree angle. On our right we passed the "stables," a building constructed by Valentino to house his fine Arabians, and now converted into a small dwelling. That property was not included in the deal.

Just beyond the stables, a narrow asphalt track zigged sharply right and made a looping, dizzying ascent that seemed at least a forty-percent rise. After about a hundred yards, we reached the top of the incline and found a walled estate—the main building set some fifty yards back from the road. A circular gravel track admitted us to the grounds and, if followed, would have returned us to the road again by a second gate. A five-car garage with a guesthouse of some six rooms surmounting it, fitted into the estate wall at that juncture.

The mansion immediately captured all attention. Constructed in typical Spanish motif, complete with white stucco and a red tile roof, it seemed to be a lovely, graceful building of only one story. Actually, the house was a full two stories in height but because it had been constructed on the brow of the hill, the second floor was below the first and not visible from the front. The wall, also of stucco, ran from the house to the guesthouse garage, creating an element of concealment. One could imagine all manner of things behind the wall. It appeared, in fact, to be an extension of the main building. Actually, it was merely a wall, blocking out a view of the precipitous drop that plunged from the small mesa to Benedict Canyon Boulevard far below. Thus, a portion of the estate was outside that protecting curve of masonry.

We parked in front of massive hand-carved doors, set in a turret at ground level. Behind us, a large circular fountain sent an uncertain spray into the air, splashing back into the pool containing some white and red spotted carp, intending to be identified as gold fish.

Jerry shook his head. "I can't see how we'd ever make use of this,

Bob," he said.

I was intrigued in spite of myself. "I'm inclined to agree," I said. "But we've come all this way. We certainly ought to look around."

"Sure."

I rang the bell and Mrs. Buys opened the door in person. She was a fairly large woman of middle age who gave every indication of conveying a favor by letting us view this precious landmark. She and her husband, Gerald, had purchased the place in order to open it as a nightclub. The difficulty, she explained, was the narrow-mindedness of the City Council, which refused to let them sell booze at this address.

I confess to experiencing a twinge of sympathy.

She conducted us through the building. I had been in many homes much larger. Some of the houses in the Pacific Heights District in San Francisco really were mansions with huge rooms and accommodations for many people. Falcon Lair was actually a gracious three-bedroom home, designed for beauty and comfort. I had been anticipating something at least as large as the St. Paul property. This wasn't it. But I have never seen a floor plan lending so much beauty to a graceful and gentle life style. The home had not been planned for ostentation or show. It was a very private and intimate retreat for an actor who, even half a century after death, is remembered as one of the silver screen's great lovers.

When Jerry and I entered The Lair, we first found ourselves in a tiled foyer, with a small powder room and coat closet on the right and the living room directly ahead. As we walked into the living room, the effect was breath taking.

The floor was carpeted in white plush. At the far side, a series of windows overlooked all of Beverly Hills. The furniture was Louis XIV, gracefully French, finished in white and gold. A fireplace was on our right hand. A large archway on our left led into the dining room, dominated by a lovely chandelier. The plush carpet extended throughout both rooms and the dining room, too, had an abundance of windows with a continuation of the living room view. The entire effect was cheerful, bright, and warm.

One of the principal architectural effects became evident. The whole building was formed in a crescent, around the top of the mesa. Thus, the dining room angled from the living room with a sixty rather than ninety-degree turn.

Moving left from the dining room, we entered the butler's pantry, and then the kitchen and breakfast nook. Sunshine and happiness spilled over everywhere. Reversing direction, we were led back across the living room to a passage that took us to the library. Here the carpet was a dark, lustrous blue setting off the magnificent shelves and cabinets in oak or walnut.

Between the living room and library was a room Gypsy identified as the Valentino dressing room. It was probably just that. The entire room was tiled with mirrors, each about eight inches square. This tiling included the ceiling. Gypsy explained that it was important for moving picture stars to know how they looked from up above.

Back in the living room, we came to the stairway. This was a flight of steps, carpeted in white plush, which went down, not up. An ornamental iron railing guarded the stairwell. The descending wall was one large mirror.

The three bedrooms were below the main floor, yet each had a view. One of the bedrooms contained a huge four-poster bed that Gypsy identified as the original Valentino furniture. She may have been right. The posts were Arabian in curving, painted splendor and might readily have decorated a set for the filming of "The Sheik."

There were two large bathrooms, tiled and gleaming. The stall shower in one might well have suggested that bathing with a friend could conserve energy. It contained a tiled alcove, large enough to accommodate a slender accomplice, should concealment have been deemed advisable.

Outside we discovered that the property on which the house sat provided a good deal of its charm. The bedroom floor opened to a large flagstone terrace. It was only the first of three, each one set below the other, each one surrounded by a concrete balustrade that, from a distance, would appear to be marble. Perhaps at one time marble had been used.

Beyond the lowest terrace came the precipice again, covered by a rank growth of willows, manzanita, and gardenias. There were gardenias everywhere. I roamed the grounds. Along the slopes below the kitchen were paths leading to a tiny gazebo that Gypsy entitled the "Valentino Shrine." A dark red rose, almost black it was so dark, grew amidst the gardenias.

The place was a tiny jewel set in a wilderness of shale, shrubs, and sky. Across the canyon in one direction was the visible tower of what Gypsy identified as the estate of the late John Barrymore. In the other direction and across the arroyo created by Bella Drive, was another huge place. She identified it as the one-time home of that other great screen lover, John Gilbert.

I wondered if the homes of these three (at one time) eligible bachelors could have provided the name Benedict Canyon. To this day, I don't know. It would have been appropriate.

By the time we had explored the guesthouse and the five-car garage, Mr. Gerald Buys pulled into the graveled drive. Jerry and I shook hands with him.

He was tall, urbane, and handsome. He and Gypsy made a striking pair.

I discussed the merits of the hotel. I explained that the hotel made money and that the restaurant did not. However, since the Buys were nightclub people, they would know better than I would how to make the place pay. The Jefferson had been, and could be again, a real moneymaker.

The Falcon Lair property was obviously not a moneymaker, nor was it represented as such. The Buys did not own it free and clear; there was a loan at the bank. Allegedly, it had a $50,000 equity that matched the $50,000 equity I had at the Jefferson. Actually, at that time, $50,000 was the market value of the property against which was a $35,000 encumbrance. But that small a sum was one I believed I could manage.

The Buys agreed that the next step was up to them. They held out the hope that if I had the Falcon Lair property, then I could sell it later for a great deal of money.

Jerry and I returned to San Francisco. Jerry hadn't been impressed with the place, but I was eager for anything that might conceivably give me some time to think and reorganize my life. I was also convinced that if the Buys took an interest in the Jefferson, they would know how to make it sing.

In my office, I drew up an offer to exchange equities, basing it on the information disclosed. Because of the miles between us, I gave the Buys two full weeks to examine the San Francisco property and to approve of the trade. The offer would expire at the end of two weeks.

I signed this offer and sent two copies to the Buys by mail.

Without warning, a couple of days later, Gerald and Gypsy Buys appeared at the Jefferson. I showed them everything and they said I would hear from them soon.

Within another day or so, Gerald Buys phoned. The deal was off. He didn't return the copies of the offer and I committed a serious breach of the responsibilities of agency. I should have asked for the return of that signed agreement. Doubtless it would have been sent had I requested it. But I viewed their verbal rejection as final, and neglected the obvious. I was, it seemed, back to square one, insofar as the Jefferson was concerned.

An idea had been in my mind and I approached Pearl with it. Perhaps the San Francisco Group would be willing to accept the $50,000 equity in the Jefferson as an endowment. I would be willing to assign all my right, title and interest in the property to the Group. The Group would assume all the bills, without which, of course, the property would have been worth a great deal more. In time, it would be paid off and the Group would have a very valuable asset.

Pearl could step in, exercise her considerable managerial skills, and possibly bring in some members of the Group as employees. Together they could pull the Jefferson out of its skid. I wanted nothing for myself. I merely wanted the bills paid. I also wanted everything good for my friends in the Group.

Pearl was dubious. This was a far larger proposition than she had ever attempted to manage. Without any doubt, she had a sincere concern for me and for my own wishes. Jerry wasn't impressed, and the Group split over the question. Some favored it and some didn't. Still, a $50,000 equity wasn't to be sneezed at.

In the end, my wishes—and perhaps they were Pearl's too, (I am not sure)—prevailed. In gratitude, I gave the equity to the Group, drew up the necessary papers, and the property passed from my hands into those of the San Francisco Group, Inc.

By this time, I was facing a complete nervous collapse. With Sunny and other Group members in charge of the property, Pearl invited Loy, Tommy, and me to come up to Santa Rosa to the Dorris Ranch for a few days of rest and recuperation. Gratefully, we accepted the invitation.

We drove north to the peaceful environs of Jerry's orchards. At last, I was able to pause in my mad pace, take stock of my affairs, and reassess my own assets and liabilities whatever they might be.

Chapter LXIX

The complete change afforded by country schedules brought a much-needed sense of peace. I was truly exhausted. It had become virtually impossible for me to concentrate on anything.

Jerry raised prunes. In terms of acreage, his ranch was small. In terms of production, he did well. I spent the first day at the ranch working in tandem with Jerry. There were drying racks where prunes were placed in the sun and there were trees to be pruned...any number of chores to perform.

I presented Jerry with my old Army carbine. I have never liked guns and Jerry, at one time, had enjoyed hunting. He had an appreciation for firearms, but as an "I Am" student had put hunting aside. His eyes lit up when he saw the fine weapon furnished by the Army Air Corps and I thought that Jerry and I reached a kind of unspoken comradeship when his fingers caressed the barrel and stock. There had always been something of tension between us. After all, I had loved Pearl and he had married her. His hospitality to Loy and me, coupled with my gift, seemed to bring us closer.

The next day, Pearl and I had opportunity for a more relaxed and hence, a more philosophic discussion. Dullard I had been. Pearl had brought the San Francisco Group into the picture at the Jefferson Hotel in order to further her plans for the future. If I would stop being a businessman and concentrate on the "I Am" teachings and the dictations, then perhaps she and I would be working more closely together. This was her hope, and it had been visible to all but me.

What did I want to do? Truthfully, I didn't know. I wanted to do what was right and best, whatever that meant. Pearl's suggestion appeared to have merit and I promised to think about it. Meanwhile, I needed the rest and the change in scenery and procedure, a conclusion no one challenged. I spent our second day at the ranch helping Jerry to some degree, thinking about my future moves, and sleeping a good deal. The old fashioned ranch house was conducive to a far more tranquil life than I had been leading for the prior two years.

The third morning I arose late. Loy and Pearl were in the big ranch kitchen while I ate breakfast. Jerry was already off on some errand.

The telephone rang and Pearl surrendered the instrument to me with reluctance. It was about the real estate business and she wanted to shield me from any more involvement.

The caller was an attorney named Mays. I had made his acquaintance during some real estate transaction, so we were not altogether strangers. He began by letting me know that he was acting for his clients, Mr. and Mrs. Gerald Buys.

I wasn't even on guard. Splendid. What did his clients wish?

They had changed their minds about the Jefferson, Mr. Mays said. They now wanted to trade their property in Beverly Hills for the Jefferson equity.

"I'm surprised to hear that," I said. "Gerald Buys telephoned me from Beverly Hills to tell me there was no deal."

"Well, they've changed their minds, Mr. LeFevre," attorney Mays answered. "And they plan to hold you to your contract. They have signed and accepted the offer you made. They have instructed me to demand delivery of the Jefferson property."

"If they want the hotel, then I'll see they get it," I said. "No problem."

Mays laughed. "What do you mean, 'no problem?' You've already sold the hotel."

I was so sluggish mentally that I still didn't get the drift. "I didn't sell it," I said.

"Oh, yes you did. I have the record of the transaction right here before me. It's in the daily abstract. It shows that you transferred the Jefferson to an investment holding company called the San Francisco Group." He named the date and time of transfer.

I laughed. "The San Francisco Group isn't a holding company; it's a group of my friends who study philosophy."

"I don't know anything about that," Mays admitted. "But you don't own that hotel anymore. And we are demanding specific performance on your signed contract.

"You're in big trouble, LeFevre. It's illegal to contract with two parties for the same property at the same time."

I began to comprehend at last. "Mr. Buys put me on notice that he didn't want the hotel."

"Do you have any record of that, LeFevre?"

"No, I do not. But I'm telling you the truth."

"Well, I'll tell you what I have. I have a contract signed by you and my clients, in which you offer to trade the equity in your hotel, the Jefferson, for their equity in the Beverly Hills property, known as 'Falcon Lair.' That contract still has a week to run. The Buys have accepted that offer. They demand specific performance. What do you want me to tell my clients?"

"Tell them I'm very pleased. I will be happy to receive the Beverly Hills property and they may have the hotel."

"But you can't do that if you don't own the Jefferson."

"You'd be surprised what I can do, Mr. Mays. The contract will be honored, I assure you."

I hung up the receiver, and turned to Pearl. "The Group really wasn't enthusiastic about the Jefferson as I recall," I said.

"That's true," she confirmed. "Actually, they acted...we acted, out of love and respect for you. That hotel was doing you no good. It's a big pain trying to run it and make everything work. We can do it, but I don't think anyone really wants to."

"How would the Group take to the idea of trading the Jefferson for the Beverly Hills property? I know Jerry didn't think too highly of Falcon Lair, but I don't think he likes the hotel either. The big advantage of the Beverly Hills property relates to the relative indebtedness. There's a $35,000 first trust deed against Beverly Hills. There's something close to S200,000 worth of indebtedness from all sources against the Jefferson.

"The sellers in Beverly Hills, Gerald and Gypsy Buys, are demanding specific performance on an existing contract. And they can enforce it. My personal view is that the Buys don't really want the hotel, they simply want to take advantage. They think I sold the hotel at a good price and they want to compel me to pay that price to them since they don't think I can deliver the Jefferson."

"You really did put yourself in a bad position, didn't you?" Pearl said.

"Yes, I really did. I should have asked for the return of the contract. Probably the Buys would have mailed me their copy had I asked for it. But then, when they thought I had sold the hotel profitably, they saw themselves in the position of being the owner of a property I had sold. If they had thought there was a chance of selling the Jefferson, they would have taken it."

"They don't sound like very nice people," Pearl observed.

"I can see their side of it," I admitted. "They are on sound legal grounds unless I can figure out how to let them have the hotel."

"That part's easy," Pearl said. "Sonny has been reporting to me on the hotel and it's a real bear-cat to operate. She doesn't like it. It's in a bad part of town. If the Buys want it, then the Group will see that they get it. The only problem then becomes the Beverly Hills property. What would we do with that?"

"Sell it, of course," I said. "Or perhaps you'd like to use it as a kind of southern headquarters for the Group. The Group is renting space in San Francisco, and you could let that go."

"Come on, Bob. We don't want to live in Los Angeles. Nobody in the Group would think of going there."

"Since it's my neck that's on the line," I said, "Loy and I could go there to serve as caretakers and to see that it gets sold. Meanwhile, if a handful of students would move south temporarily and take up residence there at Falcon Lair, we could all get jobs. Our rent paid to the Group would cover monthly payments readily, and we could then put the property on the market and dispose of it. After all, whatever can be made would belong to the Group. That might well be the quickest method that could be devised to provide the Group with some funds so it could really get off the ground."

"Let me think about that," Pearl said. "I wish you'd ask Saint Germain what to do. In any case, I think the property still belongs to you. If there were anything to be made out of it, which I doubt, it would be yours. The hotel is still yours, too, the way I see it. We only stepped in to help you. And if it helps you to transfer the property to someone else, I know the Group will want to do it."

"It would certainly help me," I said. "It might even keep me out of jail. I should have demanded that contract back. I didn't. I'm at fault. Are you sure the Group won't mind getting rid of the hotel?"

Pearl laughed. "They hate the place. But we'll do whatever needs to be done. You know that. What we want is your undivided interest in the philosophy."

"That's absolutely wonderful. So, here's what happens. I'll have to go back to town right away. I'll get some papers from the attorney, which the Group leaders will have to sign since the property is technically and legally a property of the Group. Then we'll set up a date for closing. After that, Loy and I will go to Beverly Hills to act for the Group as caretakers and spokesmen when we put it on the market. It will be a great deal easier to handle than the Jefferson."

"I hope you're right."

"So do I."

The program Pearl and I quickly outlined was the one we followed. The technicalities were quickly handled to the discomfiture of Mr. Mays. He had been positive about my inability to act. Without friends such as I had found in the "I Am," he would have been entirely correct. As it was, the Group accepted Falcon Lair in exchange for the Jefferson. Meanwhile, Group personnel continued to manage the property.

Edith Shank, Marjorie Llewellin, and Ruth Dazey were all willing to move to Beverly Hills on a temporary basis to become mainstays in providing income for the property. Nora Laidlaw also wished to participate, at least part of the time. Additionally, Claire and Betty Henderson, mother and daughter, who had joined our Group while we were still living at 1300 Jones decided that a move to Los Angeles could be beneficial. Still others indicated that they would be happy to do what they could, from time to time, and would visit on occasion.

At last, all was in readiness. Leaving Tommy in the care of one of our "I Am" friends, Loy and I flew to Los Angeles, planning on taking a cab from the airport up to Falcon Lair. Once in physical possession, the Buys would be at liberty to move to San Francisco. This procedure had been agreed upon between us by means of the telephone.

When we debarked from the plane, newsboys were crying "extra...extra."

I glimpsed the headline and bought a paper. The Los Angeles Times had a front page banner which read: "Love Cult Buys Falcon Lair."

Loy and I gaped at each other. "What's happened?" Loy asked. "I guess we didn't get the property after all."

"Oh, no!" I said. "Don't you see? The press got word of this transaction and they have twisted it all out of shape. You and I are the 'love cult.'"

Loy sputtered. "A love cult' How could you and I be a love cult?"

"Remember, Hon. The property isn't ours, it belongs to the San Francisco Group. The Buys thought the Group was a holding company. So did their attorney. The San Francisco Group, as a title, doesn't tell anyone anything. And remember, this is the former home of Valentino. The press has put that together and come up with a bomb."

"A bomb is right."

We'll straighten it out right away."

"How can we?"

"I don't know. Obviously, it's ridiculous!" I was thinking of some of our staid and conservative friends in the Group. They would be so embarrassed by that headline that their facial expressions would rival the faces painted by Dore in Dante's Inferno.

We sped out to Falcon Lair.

Gypsy came to the door to welcome us. She was bustling about making last minute preparations to leave. I asked her what she knew about the story in the Times. She took credit for inventing it and without hesitation.

"You know perfectly well the San Francisco Group isn't any 'love cult' or anything close to it," I said. "It's a study group and that's all. I told you that. Why did you tell reporters what you did?"

She goggled at me as though finding it difficult to believe I was as stupid as I appeared. "I've done you a big favor!" She said, "You're getting a million dollars worth of publicity. I wish I could have done it for myself, but the reporters wouldn't listen. When I told them about your Group they bought it. It's great isn't it?"

"It's not true!" I insisted.

"So what? It's a great yarn. I've given you a big boost. You'll probably be able to sell this place for a big price because of that publicity."

"Mrs. Buys, all my life I've tried to tell the truth. I don't think anything good comes from saying things that aren't so."

Gypsy shook her head sadly. "Where have you been?" She gave a short laugh. "You just can't be that naive. The way to make money in this world is to tell people what they want to hear. Nearly everyone would like this place to be a love cult, a location where the lovelorn could come to have their problems resolved for them. If you haven't got a love cult, you might think of starting one.

Gypsy provided me with an over-the-shoulder leer. "I'm not so sure your group isn't a love cult already. You aren't so bad looking you know...and all those women!"

Loy was standing with me and I could feel her stiffen. "I'm a married man, Mrs. Buys," I said. "I can assure you..."

"God, Mr. LeFevre, you are dense! If you don't see it yet, you will. Nobody's trying to break up your marriage. I'm talking about business. I've given you one hell of a big boost. I only wish you could do the same for us with that crummy hotel in Frisco."

"If you thought the hotel was crummy, why did you insist on getting it?"

"Kee-rist, LeFevre. Are you for real?" Then Gypsy shook her head. "Don't bother to answer. I'm busy. Gerald will be back soon and we're almost ready to leave. Just look around and we'll surrender the keys in about an hour." She hurried off.

I showed Loy the famous Lair. The furnishings were luxurious, far better than anything either of us had ever experienced. The place, itself, was a disappointment in respect to its size. But as a beautiful and well-planned house, it was unsurpassed.

Loy is something of an artist, both musically and in regard to decor. She was as embarrassed as I was concerning the publicity. But she was captivated with the surroundings. Since the exchange of equities entailed a turnkey procedure, the Buys were leaving furniture and furnishings behind, just as we were at the Jefferson. On that basis, Loy's pleasure was visible. She was radiant. Living at Falcon Lair was going to be light years above our meager advantages in the tiny apartment we had at the hotel.

Gerald Buys appeared before long at the wheel of a new station wagon. He and Gypsy loaded their personal possessions aboard and took off, leaving Loy and me alone at the Lair.

Loy was still mentally planning who would be billeted in which room, when a crunch on the gravel in the driveway heralded the arrival of another vehicle. It was Jerry Dorris—good scout that he always was—driving with Edith and Margie, who were to be tenants until we could dispose of the property.

The precise chronology of events escapes me at this point. Others from the north arrived, as well. I believe Tom Laidlaw showed up driving his mother, Nora, and Carol Dazey. Ruth was still at the hotel helping to operate the place.

As I recall, the first newcomers managed to straighten things out so that we all spent the night. The next morning, Jerry and I drove off in his car, leaving Loy and some members of the Group in possession. I would be returning in a few days, bringing Tommy, probably Ruth, and perhaps others as well. On that occasion, I would be driving my own car.

Back in San Francisco, I met an outraged Ethel Dazey. The publicity had upset her more than anyone else in the group. Ethel was socially prominent. She was already confronting the astonished stares and comments of her peers. Of course, I did what I could to placate her, explaining that Gypsy had apparently concocted the story out of pique over the transaction. I was quite sure the Buys didn't really want the Jefferson. They simply wanted to get rich at my expense. I had, in fact, forced their hand.

Ethel was neither amused nor calmed. She had already called the San Francisco Examiner. As one of the officers of the Group, she had explained that the entire "love cult" story had been made up out of the nonexistent clothes of the Emperor.

"Ethel," I said. "I agree with you. The story was a dirty trick. And the reporters who accepted it in LA without checking with us betrayed one of the principles of good reporting. But you know, it might just work to our advantage. If we handle ourselves correctly.

"In any case, the story is out. We can't prevent it. The damage has been done. We must roll with the punches and capitalize on it if we can. Gypsy says the publicity may enhance the value of the place. If so, we might be able to get a better price for it than otherwise."

"It's no such thing," Ethel flared. "We'll be lucky to sell it at all. We ought to sue the Buys. And if I didn't know you had nothing to do with it, I'd be in favor of suing you, too."

"I know how you feel," I said.

"No, you don't' I've already had to face suggestions of this sort anyway. You and Pearl did represent a kind of focal point for love...in a divine sense. This is a travesty! Anyway, the Examiner is going to print a retraction although there is no way we can overcome the harm that has been done."

"What do you want me to do?"

She glared. "I really don't have any idea. But I'll tell you something. I'm mad as hell."

Ethel never used words like that. The depth of her anger can be readily appreciated.

I did my best to counter. "Ethel, we had some dreadful publicity at the time the Ballards were sued. We lived that down. We'll live this down, too. Somehow.

She stamped off but my final impression was that she had been mollified to a degree.

The next morning, I had reporters waiting to see me. The first came from the Examiner. "That's quite a story about Falcon Lair," the newsman said. "However, one of your Group," he consulted his notes, "one Ethel Dazey, has released a story that there's nothing to it. She says it's a pack of lies. What do you say?"

"Ethel Dazey has told you the truth," I said. "The story's been a total fabrication. Not a word of truth in it."

He asked other questions concerning the origin and purpose of the Group, and I supplied the information. He nodded. "Just as I thought. Probably a slow news day. And anything about love, sex, or Valentino is good copy when nothing else works. But, man, you got coverage. The AP picked up the story. It's even been carried by Reuters, UP, and other services. It's worldwide."

"It's hooey!"

"I'll quote you."

"Thanks."

A bit later, a man showed up from the Chronicle. He was so pleased with himself that he couldn't stop snickering. We met in the Patriot's dining room.

"This Valentino caper is the best story I've seen in years!" he chortled. "Absolutely marvelous! Wow! It's a real winner."

"You know it's not true."

"Sure. I know that. Anyone will know that. But it sure is one hell of a story. I've written a follow-up but I had to see you first."

"How could you write a follow-up before you talked to me?"

He laughed. "Wait 'til I read it to you. It's a gasser."

We sat there. Between laughter and snorts, he produced his notebook and read. What he had written was so hilarious that I couldn't help laughing, too. I was depicted as the "old professor." According to his yarn, I was concerned about the great disappointments in love that so many experienced. So the San Francisco Group was going to do something about it. Valentino had always been the love idol of American women, so at great cost, our Group had managed to get hold of Falcon Lair.

Those disappointed in their respective romances were urged to report to Falcon Lair. The ghost of Valentino would be summoned, and that specter would provide advice on how to handle one's love affairs.

We had planned to shoot red, white and blue rockets at sunset, blazing out over Beverly Hills. However, the Beverly Hills City Council had ruled against it as too large a fire hazard. A big disappointment. In any case, we had a fountain and the lovelorn could throw coins in it. Successful romances would invariably ensue from those who made a wish at the time the coin was tossed.

The story went on and on. When he finished we were both laughing.

"You know," I said, "I deny the whole thing. There's nothing to it. It's funny, all right. You made the whole thing up."

"Of course I did," he admitted gleefully. "You'd never have thought of that stuff."

"How right you are. Therefore, you can't publish it."

"Oh, yes, I can. In fact, I'm going to."

"I'll simply deny it."

"Of course you will. But what a story!"

"You've missed your calling," I said. "You should be writing fantasy. In fact, that's what this is."

"You know it. I know it. But it'll be in this evening's paper. I'll expect you to deny it."

"You can be sure I will."

"Fine. No problem." He put away his scrawlings.

"What happens if you and the Chronicle are sued?"

He grinned in my face. "It's your word against mine, isn't it? Frankly, LeFevre, I've done my homework. Your reputation isn't so hot. Mine is pretty damn good. Guess which one of us will appear best before his honor?"

"You can't do that."

"Just be sure you get this evening's Chronicle."

When he had gone, I contacted Ethel. "We're going to have another blast of publicity," I warned her. A reporter from the Chronicle came over with a previously written cock and bull story. It'll be in tonight's paper."

"Didn't you deny it?" she demanded.

"You know I did," I told her. "But it did no good. This man had looked up my past in respect to the "I Am" mail fraud suit. It's his word against mine and I'm afraid, based on what has occurred before, that his credibility is better than mine."

Ethel had herself under far better control. "Then we'll just have to grin and bear it," she said. "I've been talking with Pearl. The Masters will see to it that our real work isn't injured. In fact, this may be turned around to our advantage."

"I surely do hope so," I said. "It's a sad state of things when a man who is asked for his position can give it and still be ignored."

"What about the *Examiner*?" Ethel asked

"I denied it with him, too. However, he accepted what I had to say. The *Examiner* will print a retraction."

"That will help a great deal," she said. There was music in her voice again.

Chapter LXX

Before I made my final exit from San Francisco, the San Francisco Group held an executive meeting. I was not an officer of the Group and was not present. However, the decision reached by the directors granted exclusive and plenipotentiary powers to me as the Group's spokesman and decision-maker in Los Angeles.

Acting as the agent for the Group, I was authorized to get rid of the Beverly Hills property as rapidly as possible. Those who were going to Beverly Hills, as well as those already in residence, wanted to spend a minimum amount of time in the Southland. Getting a good price for the property was secondary. Getting speedy action was foremost. The reason was officially spelled out. The view of the Group was that the property belonged to me. My transfer of the hotel to the Group was seen as an act in good faith, but the property had been accepted as a convenience to me. The Group had never wanted the property and didn't want it now. A decision had been made. Get rid of it.

Privately, I reasoned that this determination would not prevent me from seeing that the Group was the beneficiary. Whatever the dollar return on the property, I could always give it to the Group.

Meanwhile, Pearl and her marvelous co-workers would stay on, handling everything for me. I was instructed to forget about the Jefferson. Instead, I was to move the Beverly Hills real estate and concentrate on my own studies. Hopefully, I could and would become the Group leader most of the members seemed to feel I was destined to become.

As it worked out, the Buys refused to assume some of the debts with which I had saddled the hotel. Apparently, there were legal loopholes I had not foreseen. Thus, even though I accepted the indebtedness in Beverly Hills as I had agreed, they did not accept the indebtedness of the Jefferson as the contract had specified.

I had one or two small real estate transactions to wind up, the commissions for which I turned over to Pearl, who promptly paid bills with them. Finally, after only a few days, all was in readiness. I drove south with Tommy and Victoria Howe. Tommy called her "Toria" and she became his "nana." The two were the best of friends.

Tommy was only two and Toria was probably in her late seventies. I never did know her correct age. She was an ideal choice when it came to looking after the lad. She was nearly deaf and when his importuning would rise above the level of static, she could and would turn off her hearing aid.

By the time I got back to Falcon Lair, the publicity occasioned by the arrival of a "love cult" was beginning to taper off. But curiosity about the people who were staying at Falcon Lair was building.

As tourists know, every weekend all along Sunset Boulevard, hawkers congregate at intersections, selling maps to "the homes of the stars." Even though Valentino had been dead for twenty years, Falcon Lair was still identified on these maps. Thanks to the publicity, tourists wanted to see Falcon Lair.

Day after day, people from far off places came painfully up that steep approach from Bella Drive. They would park, get out, peer around, and enter the grounds. As often as not, they would ring the bell and ask to be shown through the house. Sometimes they would come by the busload, most especially on weekends.

We were never alone. In order to deal intelligently with their questions, I obtained a book about the life of Valentino and read up on the subject. According to the version with which I became familiar, Valentino had built Falcon Lair as a surprise for his wife, Natasha Rambova. When the place was completed he took her up to proffer it as a token of his love.

The story had it that Natasha entered, looked around, decided she didn't like the place, and refused to spend even one night. There are plenty of other versions circulating. Indeed, I began to learn a most interesting fact relating to the life and times of those who live in "Hollywood." The truth isn't necessarily sought or even respected. "What matters is "hype." If you can come up with a good story, it will probably be accepted. If the truth doesn't scan well, forget it.

"Beverly Hills is a community of truly remarkable people. Many of them are wealthy. Virtually all of them act as if they are.

My first thought, once I had unpacked and joined the household, was to get some action going in respect to a sale of the property. I called on one real estate firm after another. I found one company that would list the property, but refused to promote it. Thanks to the publicity, I was told, there was no chance whatever of finding a buyer. Most refused to even take a listing. This surprised me. I had always been willing to list; but in Beverly Hills, the Lair and its publicity weren't acceptable.

I managed to get one realtor involved enough to promote it with an ad, provided I'd pay for it. The arrangement didn't produce a single qualified client. Curiosity seekers by the score. But when a sale was suggested, I was met with shaking heads and a look that seemed to say: "Nobody will ever buy. Why would you even think of selling?"

Instead of boosting the value of the property by publicity, Gypsy had destroyed whatever value the market might have found in it. Was there any avenue by which to turn the publicity to favorable account and restore our good name?

An idea finally jelled. I put together all the pieces at my disposal. The country was experiencing distinct and decided erosion of the personal freedom of everyone. This was brought about by the expansion of government during the war. There was now a visible communist influence. You didn't dare call anyone a communist because it could result in a slander suit, so it became prudent to talk of socialist influences.

But what was worse, I had a disquieting, growing apprehension. I had become a fairly close reader of the daily press. The factors were all present. A new war was looming. When and where I had no idea. Thus, not only was freedom being lost, but there was a mounting possibility that war would break out again. I had good reason for dread in that direction.

The eyes of the world were focused in our direction because we appeared to be kooks. Why not make use of the publicity and turn it in our favor?

I held an informal meeting with my peers. Most of them had gotten outside employment and were providing the funds to keep the Beverly Hills enterprise afloat. That put a strain on everyone and kept us all strapped. However, we managed. Selling the place appeared to be impossible for an indefinite period.

What about this idea? Why shouldn't we offer our equity in Falcon Lair as a prize to the individual or group that could come up with the best means by which peace and freedom could be maintained? The equity, whether $50,000, as the contract alleged, or $15,000 as reality dictated, was real enough.

If we offered the Lair as a prize, we'd run a contest for about ninety days, and then turn over the property. We'd make it clear that the property had a first mortgage against it, which the winner would have to assume. Hopefully, we'd find someone better fixed financially than we were.

Some in the Group expressed doubts, but most were intrigued with the possibility. They were in the Southland because of me. I had the authority to do whatever I deemed advisable. And the idea of bringing this entire episode to as speedy a conclusion as possible seemed commendable, particularly if we could erase our image as a love cult.

We debated the question of timing. My own feeling, after getting feedback from so many realtors, was that the Lair would he unwanted real estate for at least a year or more. The Group finally agreed with the proposal.

At this juncture, I thought of my old Army buddy, Vern Hansen. His experience in Special Services, together with my own, might be utilized in planning a real program. At my invitation, Vern came to stay with us briefly at the Lair and we worked out a program.

The first thing we would do would he to conduct a pilgrimage...that is to say...we would march for peace and freedom. Those wishing to participate in the contest would comprise the body of marchers.

Marching for causes became a popular device during the sixties, but this was the forties. The only people marching for anything were Union workers with the universal cry of "gimmee more!" How about a march to cry "give us less government, more freedom to behave constructively, and let's not have another war!"

We wouldn't intrude on anyone. Instead, we'd hold our march from the bottom of Bella drive, moving up in twilight as a candle-lit procession. Arriving at the Lair, everyone would sign a pledge that Vern would prepare. Each signer would agree to support American principles, agree to oppose communism, and accept the ideas of peace and freedom. Vern saw our situation as the rest of us did. Communism was bringing about both war and a loss of freedom.

Our march would be on a public street for a very short while, and it would end on private property. We would not trespass. Trespass was a method used by many to obtain coverage by the media. We didn't need it. Reporters were phoning us daily as to what our plans were in respect to the love cult. Denials were laughed at. The newsmen "knew" the score.

What would happen after the pilgrimage?

Vern and I worked that out. Vern would produce a document that would be bound into a large book. It would contain all the signatures. Once we had it in our possession, and with the contest ended, the property would be award. I would go to New York and present the book to Billy Rose. He had demonstrated his remarkable talents as an impresario in designing the water ballet and bringing the first aquacade to the San Francisco World's Fair. His reputation was established and he would know what to do. He was "big time."

We would ask Mr. Rose to undertake a similar extravaganza for America on behalf of American peace and freedom. With all those signatures and with a chance to add to his already abundant fame, perhaps he'd undertake this chore as well. He might be impressed by the hundreds of people whom we hoped would sign the petition.

Again, I had one of my strange seizures. First my back went out. I hobbled about on a cane. Then—call it a dream, if you like—I had a dreadful vision. It happened during the night and it probably was no more than a nightmare. But I fantasized a terrible battle raging with Americans and strange-looking foreigners engaged in deadly, hand-to-hand struggle. It was very real.

I told my associates, including Vern, that I had a premonition of the beginning of another war. I was asked if this was the Battle of Armageddon. I said I didn't know, but I was sure a war was on the way.

I was also asked if Saint Germain had told me. I denied it. I admitted that it was possible, but this was different from other inner promptings or visions I'd had previously.

After my first report, I refused to discuss the matter further. I was still in a state of confusion about the inexplicable bits of information and/or guidance that I picked up from time to time. But I accepted the vision, if that's what it was, as accurate. I simply "knew." That is to say, I was emotionally certain I was correct. War was coming. Perhaps, if we were able to put this pilgrimage together in favor of peace and freedom, it might have some ameliorating influence and stall or prevent another national bloodletting.

Vern departed to work on the document and the book that was to house it. I called the press to announce the contest. The Los Angeles Daily News gave us the best coverage, but all the papers and radio stations got in on the act. The News gave us a five-column, front-page spread, together with a fine picture of the Lair as seen from Bella Drive.

So, just as the publicity was flagging, a new burst of front-page interest was engendered.

This time the reaction was favorable. Although we could no longer consider a sale, at least we could get rid of the burden. The earlier story was now seen as a "gimmick" to attract attention so that the "real" story of Falcon Lair could be told. In the supercharged atmosphere of "Hollywood," I was deemed "shrewd" to have planned the whole thing.

Now important people augmented the curious. The Mayor of Beverly Hills, a few prominent socialites, and many social climbers called and made us feel welcome. About a dozen persons, some acting for themselves, some acting as representatives of organizations, signed up as contestants.

The first Sunday following the contest announcement, the telephone rang. When Loy answered, a rich tenor voice said: "I am Pietro Gentile." Do you like spaghetti?"

Loy can be quick on the up-take. "Hi, Pietro. Sure, I love spaghetti. Who doesn't?" Who in the world was Pietro Gentile? She'd never heard of him.

"How many people are there right now?"

Loy looked around. I was explaining the contest to a group of visitors in the living room. Counting residents eighteen were present. She gave the number to the voice.

"Don't worry about a thing," came Pietro's merry tones. "I will provide the dinner for all." The telephone clicked off.

Perhaps an hour later, the front doorbell rang for the umpteenth time that day. Loy went to answer. She swung open the huge hand-carved panel. All she could see was the lower extremities of a man, a portion of the lower extremities of a second man, and a huge corrugated carton that was held at chest level by both men. It was so long that it couldn't get through the door. From the top of the box jutted stalks of celery, clusters of spaghetti, and other goodies. Her vision of their faces was blocked.

Loy opened the second panel of the door. A third person, a woman, held up one third of the carton, which must have been the better part of five feet long.

Loy admitted the trio. As a quartet they all moved to the kitchen. There for the balance of the morning, they all made dinner. It must have been a jolly occasion. Sounds of operatic arias—solos and duets—poured from that wing of the Lair, accompanied by the most enticing of odors. By the time the meal was ready, forty people were present. Pietro had brought enough to feed them all.

Some were actors and actresses. Some were singers, dancers or would-be contestants. It was a jolly occasion and we were ready for it. It seemed that this time the publicity had hit a nerve. The American people were worried about their loss of freedom and concerned about the chances of another war.

When all had eaten, I made a brief statement about the contest. I was cheered and applauded. I was called a "great philanthropist," which I most certainly wasn't.

This was only the beginning. Ditra Flame, the famed and mysterious "woman in black" who still visits Rudolph Valentino's grave on Rudy's birthday, came up to see us several times. So did others who remembered Rudy, or who were concerned with the current political and economic situation.

One of our more interesting visitors called on us in the following way. One morning, as I was about to leave the property on some errand, I started out but stepped back inside. I recognized the woman who was walking up the gravel drive, toward the house.

I called to Loy, "Hon, guess who's coming to see us. Mae Murray!"

Loy raced to the front door, peered out, and then confirmed. "That's Mae Murray." I have found that wives often do this. Whenever a fact is reported, they check it out. Rarely do they accept what their husband says. A husband fact isn't really a fact until confirmed.

"I wonder what she wants?" Loy said.

"Probably a tour of the property," I suggested.

Loy looked at me curiously. "What makes you think so? I'll bet she's coming to hit us up for a contribution to her favorite charity. You're a philanthropist, remember."

"That's one whale of a sharp guess," I said. "You're probably right. We haven't any money. Maybe I can settle the matter by giving her a tour instead."

"Why don't you just say we haven't any money?"

The Hollywood posture is contagious. "Hey," I said. "Don't undermine us. We're giving away $50,000 aren't we?"

The doorbell rang and together we opened and confronted Miss Murray. I greeted her by name. I had seen many a moving picture in which she had starred. I readily knew her, although she wouldn't have identified me from Adam's ox.

Miss Murray was wearing graceful chiffon of bright pattern and had on a large, floppy hat. "Welcome to Falcon Lair," I said. And without waiting for her to explain why she had come, I sought to establish priorities.

"I suspect you've come to look over the former Valentino property," I suggested.

She smiled, instantly receptive. "That's a splendid idea. You know, I knew Rudy. Back in the old "silent" days, of course. I'd love a tour of the place."

Loy and I did our best. We conducted the star throughout the property and ended in the living room, sitting back on the divan with that magnificent vista of Beverly Hills stretching before us.

Miss Murray picked up the conversational initiative and talked about the "old days." She was completely charming and we listened with rapt attention. Time passed. Mentally, I dismissed the errand I had been about to run. It would have to wait. Miss Murray still wore her hat.

Twelve o'clock came. I anticipated that any moment Miss Murray would say that she had a luncheon appointment. She didn't say it. One o'clock came and the conversational flow surged on like a river.

Loy began to fidget. Finally, she excused herself, went into the dining room. Then turning back, she signaled for my attendance. I excused myself and went out of sight around the corner.

"Why doesn't she leave?" Loy asked. "It's lunch time."

"Maybe she's not hungry."

"Well, I am," she said. "I'll bet you are, too."

"You got that right. So, why not invite Mae to have lunch with us?

"I haven't anything decent in the house, that's why. I can't invite her. Not without warning."

"What are you planning to feed me?" I asked.

"You know what I mean. I was going to heat up some soup and make some sandwiches. But I can't invite a moving picture star to a lunch of soup and sandwiches."

"Look," I said. "She's human. She probably eats the same kind of things the rest of us eat. You go out and invite her to share our meager fare. If she doesn't like the menu she can go. After all, we didn't invite her."

"I hate it."

"Do it anyway. Consider it an exercise in humility."

A couple of daggers came from Loy's brown eyes and she marched out to Miss Murray. I followed. It turned out that Miss Murray would like nothing better than soup and sandwiches. Ideal fare for this lovely day, as she saw it.

So, Miss Murray stayed for lunch and more conversation. She kept her hat on.

Afterwards we returned to the living room. The words continued to flow. Presently, the others began to show up. Loy absented herself following the repast, and I heard the grocery boy arrive with some fresh supplies. This was at a time when grocery stores were happy to make deliveries.

I introduced each one of our group as they appeared on the scene. Finally, Loy made something of a grand entrance. She now invited Miss Murray to have dinner with us so Loy could make amends for a very meager lunch. She had planned this and that. Would Miss Murray please give Loy a chance to make amends?

Miss Murray was most gracious. Nothing would please her more. She had found our company stimulating and was ecstatic about the way she was being treated. I found her opinion entirely reasonable. So, we all gathered in the dining room where we fared very well indeed. The hat still shaded Mae's still lovely features.

We all assembled in the living room. Some of what Miss Murray had said to Loy and me earlier, was now repeated for the benefit of others. But it was a weekday and work was on the agenda for the morrow. One by one, members of our small group separated from the river of recollection, and retired. Nine o'clock came. No suggestion that it was time for her to go. Finally, Loy and I were all that were left and the floodgates were at full. I looked at my watch, and then put it to my ear. It was after ten.

What does one do? I was beginning to feel trapped. Yet, I could hardly stand up and start to undress. I managed to catch Loy's eye. There was a hidden, yet frantic, appeal. How could we get rid of this woman?

"Miss Murray," I said, thrusting through the torrent like a stubborn snag, "I've been thinking of something that just might be a means of making you very happy. As you know, we still have the bed that is reported to be Valentine's. It's the one Mrs. LeFevre and I use.

"But we do have a spare. And we could use it for one night. How would you like to spend a night in Valentino's bed? Obviously, Valentino isn't present. I can't even guarantee that his ghost will show up, although this has often been rumored."

I hoped I wasn't coming off too heavy. I laughed. "Actually, despite reports to the contrary, we've never seen Rudy's ghost nor anything resembling it. But if you'd like to, you'd be welcome to stay. Then you can tell your friends that you spent a night in Valentino's bed. You won't have to tell people what year it was, you know."

I don't know which of my comments did the trick but as it turned out, nothing would please Miss Murray more than to spend a night under our roof.

She retired behind the closed door still wearing her hat.

Next morning, after most had gone, Miss Murray reappeared, the hat still in place. Loy had the hat figured. Miss Murray had lost her hair and the hat with its wisps of stray locks was her transformation.

We had a belated breakfast, after which our guest sighed, thanked us for our hospitality, and said that—although loath to do it—she would have to go. Silently, we thanked our lucky stars.

We ushered her to the front door. Out she went. I was about to depart myself on that long-delayed errand but suddenly I remembered. I hadn't seen a car in the driveway. How had Mae managed to get up that steep and perilous drive without one?

Using a side door I circled the property to a point where I could look down on Bella Drive. The road was steep and curved. Many feared to trust their cars on it. I readily made out the dainty form of Miss Murray, carefully picking her way down the precipitous asphalt. But there was no car in evidence anywhere. She had walked a long way to reach our door.

I postponed my own departure. After all, if I came up to this woman and she was still afoot, I'd have difficulty in just sailing past as though she didn't exist. She had been with us nearly 24 hours.

From my vantage point, I watched. She arrived at Bella Drive and, although I lost sight of her from time to time, she continued walking. She would reappear in my line of sight further down hill. There are many homes of Hollywood notables in Benedict Canyon. I knew of some of them. It was likely Miss Murray knew of many more.

Finally, I saw her, a tiny figure far away. She went up the steps of another home and presently was admitted there. Only then did I go on my errand.

I asked around about Mae Murray. She was fondly remembered by many. And the information was universal. Mae Murray was broke. She didn't have a dime to her name. She had earned mountains of money, running well into seven figures. But she had never invested in anything. She had apparently believed that a new picture would be planned one day, and she would again be asked to star. It wasn't, and she didn't.

Mae Murray is dead now, buried with other members of the Hollywood community who died without a penny to their names. But there was one thing about Mae Murray I always remembered. She had pride. Self-esteem.

The ploy she had used with us was the method she depended on to keep herself alive in her last years. She cadged on the people of Beverly Hills. She was still an enchanting guest and a good communicator. She knew things about all the people and buildings in the old Hollywood. She lived out her years as the lady who came to lunch, and dinner.

She refused to become a recipient of charity whether offered by government welfare or private institutions. People like Miss Murray are worth knowing.

One of the more unusual visitors at the Lair provided us with an experience none present will ever forget.

One day a man appeared at the door who was a well-known spiritualist from Great Britain named Flint. He had read about the love cult in the London papers and had traveled all the way to Beverly Hills in hopes of conducting a seance at the Lair. He told us that his "control" had advised him that if he were to undertake that journey, the ghost of Valentino would appear.

We were trying to live down the image of "Love Cult" and I was reluctant to permit such a procedure. The Ballards had always voiced contempt for Spiritualism and condemned the seance that, as they saw it, opened the participants to dangerous and destructive spiritual forces and entities. I echoed those views.

However, other members of the Group pleaded with me to reconsider. Reluctantly, I changed my mind and granted permission for Mr. Flint to hold a seance in the house. A date was set and Mr. Flint selected one of the downstairs bedrooms for his session. He chose the room identified to us by several as the one in which Valentino had slept during his brief stays at the Lair. It was adjacent to our bedroom, which contained the famous bed.

To cooperate with Mr. Flint, all other furniture was taken from the room. Instead, it was furnished with a circle of chairs in which those participating were to sit. To my surprise, Mr. Flint didn't want a table. In my limited understanding of Spiritualism, I had presumed that a table was an essential. Perhaps British ghosts were less fussy. Anyway, there was no table.

I was pleased by this variation. I had heard many reports and, of course, seen movies where people gathered around a table, touched hands, and put out the lights. Then table raps and other things transpired.

Next, Mr. Flint announced that he didn't believe in dousing the lights. His seance would be conducted with the lights full up. I was truly intrigued by this news.

I began to wonder if Mr. Flint might have the same ability (or affliction) I had. In view of these departures from what I presumed to be the norm, I decided at the last minute to make myself a part of the circle.

Everyone except Victoria wanted to participate. Victoria was happy to take Loy to the guesthouse for the evening, so the Lair itself was vacant of people except in the seance room where we gathered.

We didn't have to hold hands. Mr. Flint requested that we sit still and close our eyes. That was the limit of his instructions to us. We were to be as receptive as possible. He and his "control" would see what could be done.

Mr. Flint went into a trance state at which point a voice, distinctly differing from his own, came from Flint's vocal chords. This voice had a cockney accent and was identified as "Mickey."

Mickey's first observation was apparently addressed to all of us. "Plush 'ouse yer got 'ere, mattes," he said.

He and Flint had a dialogue in which Mickey seemed to be encouraging Valentino to come forward and make himself known.

Finally, the voice changed again, this time varying only slightly from Flint's normal tones. We were advised that the great silent screen lover would deliver a message.

The "message" brought by Valentino was completely ordinary and mundane. I was disappointed then, and I can remember nothing worthwhile about it now.

Following, there was a period of questions from those participating. The answers were in such vague generalities that I found it easy to catalogue Flint as a fake and one who hadn't even done his homework well.

But, no harm had been done and everyone behaved with decorum and courtesy. As we stood around chatting after it had all ended, a sound came to everyone's ears. The toilet in the powder room just off the main entry hall, flushed.

There was no mistaking the sound. It had been a source of some embarrassment before this. Any sound in that little room was readily heard by everyone below.

Several of us raced upstairs; believing that some intruder had entered the house unhidden. But no one was there.

The only conclusion any of us could draw was that if the ghost of Valentino had really arrived, then he hadn't cared much for the seance either. He had indicated his displeasure in an extremely earthy and practical manner. To this day that strange sound from the plumbing remains unexplained.

Chapter LXXI

Plans for the pilgrimage were implemented. A kiosk was constructed and placed at the bottom of the hill where the marchers were to assemble. Each would be provided with a candle and a printed pamphlet explaining the purpose of the march and the objective we sought to dramatize. We were pro-America, anti-Communist. We were for freedom and against war. We identified America with freedom and peace. We identified communism with slavery and war.

Meanwhile, contestants appeared and signed up. Some were splendidly concerned, each convinced that his own particular approach to the problem of maintaining freedom in a climate of peace, was the best available.

Some were simply posers—people having no particular insights or contributions to make but who wanted to be around the action.

We scheduled the pilgrimage for Easter Sunday evening. One of the contestants loaned us some stereo equipment and Loy organized a program of music, which we put on loudspeakers all during the day. We started with a sunrise service on the terrace and ended right after dusk as the last of the "pilgrims" came up the hill and signed the petition.

Leading or organizing the march was out of character for me. I had seen enough Union picketing and marching to last me a lifetime. But I had made a discovery that undoubtedly is the same discovery many others have also made.

The press is unwilling to report ideas. If the government sets a policy, the matter will be reported. If a person outside of government challenges that policy and argues against it, that person can whistle for a breeze. The press will brush him off. I cannot come down harshly on the media for this.

Most of us are eager for attention. If the media had a policy of publicizing every notion dreamed up by private citizens, every newspaper would be a swamp and every media event a morass. The press has, in this case, taken a position that it had to take. It will report an event. But if nothing happens, there is no news.

When government sets a policy, something has happened. Subsequent events have become mandatory to some degree. When a private citizen expresses a contrary opinion, nothing has happened. Subsequent events are not necessarily influenced.

In my own experience, I had seen how it worked. Had Gypsy gone to the newspapers and proposed to set up a "love cult" in the Falcon Lair residence, the reporters would probably have said: "Go ahead, Gypsy. We'll attend the grand opening to see what's going on when it's happening." As a matter of fact, she might have done just that. It wouldn't have bought a line of copy.

The reason she was able to attract worldwide attention was because an event had happened. The property had been sold to an organization calling itself "The San Francisco Group." Except in political (and occasionally now in scientific) circles, the same rule still applies, The press accepts a governmental (or a scientific) statement as credible. The statement of a private person isn't credible until action of one kind or another takes place.

While I must approve the discretion exercised by the press, it is conceivable that this same discretion is part of the motivational package today employed by terrorists. Many of the bomb planters, political or industrial kidnappers, and crackpots running around with lethal hardware have an idea they want the public to learn. They have discovered that no one will pay the slightest attention to what they think. But they can get immediate attention if they blow up a building, hijack a plane, kidnap a prominent figure, or commit mayhem.

Or, in a less strident manner, if they stage a big march, and get out a few thousand people. If, inn the process, they stop traffic, trample on a few lawns, or get a few people arrested for refusing to obey a police order, the media will duly make a report.

Vern had convinced me that public attention was needed. The ideas we shared about keeping this country out of war and returning it to a climate of private enterprise, sans governmental intrusion, had to be promoted in a big way.

But neither Vern nor I could foresee the kind of turmoil that public demonstration can engender, as the 1960's were to unveil. After all, this was 1949. We were concerned with getting press coverage. But at the same time we took pains to guard against a traffic tie-up, trespass on private property, or any kind of civil disobedience. We wanted peace. As we saw it, the methods employed to achieve peace had to be consistent with the thing itself. We were not of the ilk who favored peace to the point where we would violate the rights of others in an effort to attain it.

Nor did we favor peace as a device to take pressure off communists, who were apparently engendering war. We hoped that if we approached the question of peace or war, freedom or slavery, and managed a good press, then thousands of discerning persons would join with us.

There were fewer participants than we had hoped. The numbers of persons and organizations entering the contest were disappointing also. But, at least, we were launched on a program that would transfer the property into hands with a better financial grasp than my own. And, in process, who could tell? Perhaps someone would come up with a break-through in the realm of geo-politics and world tranquility.

Vern returned to the Lair with the product of his efforts. It was impressive. He had designed and, at his own expense, created a huge tome about three feet high by two and a half feet wide. In magnificent handcrafted letters, he had spelled out the problem and written a stirring appeal. The sheets of signatures could be affixed and made a part of the book on the final pages.

For several months after the pilgrimage, people came to the Lair with the intention of signing that petition. Once in a while, after reading what Vern had written, a given individual would refuse to sign. In each case, when we queried them as to their reason, they said they were reluctant to go on record against communism. Everything else was fine. This was an eye-opener. I had presumed that being for America and against its enemies wasn't controversial.

During these first months at the Lair, the Jefferson creditors, supposedly to be paid from Hotel Jefferson income, came after me. It did me no good to explain that the Buys had undertaken to handle the debts; I had been the one who contracted them. They looked to me.

They saw me as a person about to donate $50,000. In vain, I explained that I no longer was a property owner. The San Francisco Group owned the Lair and they were making the payments. I was merely their agent, a spokesman acting for them. I was disposing of the Lair because the Group had no long-range ability to finance the property or to pay my debts. Certainly, they had no obligation to do so. I hadn't brought the Group into the picture as a method of avoiding payment. Rather, I had done it to assure payment.

Pearl, with her marvelous ability to deal with people, managed to pay off some of the more pressing obligations by working something out with the Buys. I was never completely clear on what she did. Whatever it was, it worked.

Finally, and acting on the advice of Ethel and others in the Group, I filed for bankruptcy under Chapter 13. This made it possible for me to get the least worthy and most obstreperous creditors off my back. Yet I could pay back at least some of the debt over a period of time. At last, the pressure was dissipated.

While the contestants labored to prepare their respective programs in support of Peace and Freedom, Ruth Dazey was sent across the country to book me as a speaker in front of every receptive group she could find. She traveled under what we called, "The Falcon Lair Foundation." We felt this a better term than "The San Francisco Group" which had proved so misleading. If anyone asked for further information, we explained that the Foundation owned the Falcon Lair. Legally it was known as the San Francisco Group. The SFG was the FLF.

While the foregoing events were transpiring, I was carrying out other instructions given me by the Group. I was supposed to study, meditate, and reflect in the hope that I would once more assume leadership of the metaphysical activities in which Pearl and I had been involved.

I began by reading up on communism, studying some early American history, and cracking a few books on philosophy. The more I studied, the less enthusiastic I became about the metaphysical approach. I broadened my studies, getting into religion on a comparative basis. My findings alienated me from the metaphysical.

The people I read were reasonable and intelligent men and women who had sought to approach the great mysteries of life in as detached and objective a manner as possible. My approach had always been through my emotions. Theirs was through reason. I had become involved with the "I Am" because of an inner experience. They were involved because they were seeking to know rather than to do.

After announcing the prize contest, I was called upon to speak in front of various service clubs in Beverly Hills and elsewhere in Los Angeles. Pietro Gentile, our uninvited tenor of that first Sunday, introduced me at one of the clubs in Beverly Hills. He was so impressed with me that his introduction elevated me to sainthood on the instant. I thanked him for his excessive praise. Then, I added that the only possible way I could demonstrate his eulogy was warranted would be to have lightning flash from my brow, and then to rise through the ceiling. Since I was incapable of these things, I hoped they would listen to my concerns without the aura that Pietro had provided.

Thanks to my earlier experiences as an actor and announcer, I could give a good account of myself from a public platform.

Ruth Dazey wrote to us that she had booked me in Salt Lake City before a most prestigious club. She would now travel to Omaha and continue eastward, trying to arrange a series of talks in each city so that I could spend about a week in each one.

I had planned on traveling alone because of cost factors, but Ethel interposed. Because of that "love cult" episode, and the preponderance of women in the Group, she deemed it advisable for Loy to travel with me.

This was most satisfactory to both of us, especially since the Group agreed to underwrite the added expense. And Victoria would love to stay on at the Lair, looking after Tommy.

Then, Loy came up with an added dimension that made our speaking tour far more impressive. She agreed to sing at the meetings where I spoke. Her golden voice was added to the presentation. If my talk was, on occasion, abrasive, her lovely person offered a soothing and inspiring contrast.

Neither Loy nor I played the piano and this precluded melodies from her on some occasions. But Loy often overcame this lack, when no accompanist could be found. She had perfect pitch and would sometimes sing a capella. Nearly always, she would conclude her repertoire with a rendition of The Lord's Prayer.

I didn't know it at the time—I only learned of it recently—that one of Ethel's reasons for insisting on Loy's presence had to do with the FBI. Unbeknownst to me, an agent called on at least one of the Group members in San Francisco. An FBI agent wanted to know what was going on. He called upon Kathleen Blamey, a cousin of the Dazey sisters, and an associate member of the Group at Rudy's

Lair in Beverly Hills.

Despairing of explaining the complexities of "I Am," Kathleen had simply shrugged, and said to the agent: "Well, what do you suppose? There's a handsome, healthy man down there. And all those women!"

The agent nodded knowingly and accepted that as an explanation. No problem. Ethel knew of this inquiry, but I did not. It is, however, quite characteristic. Everyone expects to find sex at the base of every relationship involving men and women. Had Kathleen endeavored to explain that in the "I Am" sex was proscribed except for procreation, she would have been looked at as "weird." Her statement would have been discredited. As it was, I didn't even know I had been a subject of investigation until Kathleen told me of it during the Christmas season of 1980.

One bit of news arrived that upset us. Gerald Buys committed suicide. The reasons were never explained in the brief newspaper article that was forwarded to me from one of the Group in San Francisco. Standing in the little apartment Loy and I had occupied at the Jefferson, he had pulled a revolver and put a bullet into his brain.

The time came for us to leave for Utah. Ruth had done well, not only arranging for my speech in Salt Lake City, but also half a dozen other appearances booked in or nearby Ogden. Further, she had managed to arrange a place for us to stay as honored guests.

Mariner Eccles, a prominent banker and financier, was a well known figure in Washington politics. Mr. and Mrs. Eccles owned the Hotel Ogden. Mrs. Eccles, finding us interested in peace and freedom, asked for the pleasure of entertaining Loy and me in her penthouse atop the building. Mariner was away so much of the time that she would enjoy having company.

We could hardly have improved on the prestige and comfort Ruth had managed to obtain for us. Mrs. Eccles was not only charming, but also she was also interested in metaphysical matters. We were royally treated. We had several splendid visits with her during the week to ten days we spent in the "Inter-Mountain Empire." During our stay, we met Mariner briefly. Then, he was on his way back to Washington again.

While I had been booked at a number of knife and fork organizations prior to my appearance at the Salt Lake City Club, I prepared diligently for that evening. It was to be a major address.

Daily study of the newspapers revealed a number of facts. The Mormons were very patriotic. They were hard working, dedicated people. I found it easy to like them and to communicate with them. This wasn't surprising. Peggy and I had spent a happy in Utah earlier.

But I detected something new to me. Some of the most prestigious and important people in the region were on record, daily, in the press, as being favorable to this or that governmental ukase. Each government endeavor undermined free enterprise and the right of a person to own and manage his own property without government interference. This was precisely what Karl Marx had called for in his turgid and stodgy "Das Kapital," through which I had managed to wade.

How could these people protest their patriotism while publicly favoring ideas that I viewed as "un-American?"

Upon inquiry, I learned that I was to have a full hour for my talk. However, I was urged to leave some time at the end of my presentation for questions. An hour and a half would be mine.

With so much time at my disposal, I decided to begin in as non-controversial a manner as possible. I would, gradually, by citing chapter and verse, show what the communist ideas were. Then I would show that some of these ideas had already become American policy. Finally, I would reveal that many of the people in Salt Lake and environs—despite their protestations of loyalty to everything American—had, in fact, been promoting and favoring a philosophy alien to our founding fathers.

I would wind up by calling for a new pledge of loyalty to the Constitution, the Bill of Rights, and the Declaration of Independence. Hopefully, by this process, I would awaken at least some of them to the dangers to our traditions. The pilgrimage of peace and freedom would he augmented.

It was a grand meeting. More than three hundred people filled the huge ballroom on the top floor of the hotel where the banquet was held. When the multiple courses had been consumed, the program chairman, sitting next to me, took over.

Some reports were given. Then various people were called upon to come to the podium for brief speeches. Without exception, these people were witty, informed, and worth hearing. Again and again, I looked at my watch.. Time was passing swiftly and in a most enjoyable manner. My talk was becoming less and less important.

During the remarks of the final celebrity, the MC looked at his watch, raised his brows and whispered: "The time got away from us, I'm afraid, Mr. LeFevre. We do have to quit on time. Sorry. Please limit your remarks to about fifteen minutes, leaving about five for questions and answers. That's all the time we have."

Before I could protest, he was on his feet beginning his introduction.

I nearly panicked. This was to be my major effort. I had planned a full hour during which I would present a reasonable if impassioned case history. With only twenty minutes altogether, I had no time for that.

I knew that within that room were some of the very people who were engaged in this strange political and economic dichotomy. They ostensibly favored America and the free enterprise system, yet they appeared to be following some of the dicta in the Communist Manifesto.

I cut out all of my talk except the closing. I began by stating in a ringing voice, "I am here because I am wholly in favor of the American system of Free Enterprise!"

I expected a feeling of opposition, probably accompanied by a shocked and disbelieving silenced. Instead, I was applauded to the echo.

Perhaps they didn't quite understand what I meant. I took another tack and said the same thing again in another way. "This means, that I favor the right of every person in the country to own his own property, to manage it as best he can, an to win or lose on the basis of his own judgment."

Thundering applause.

I mentioned the Constitution. More applause. I cited the Declaration and the Bill of Rights. The clapping was nearly continuous. I came up with nearly every cliche in the books. In that brief interlude, I must have been applauded forty times. Apparently I could do no wrong.

I found myself in the position of a man who charges a door, which he believes to be locked only to find that it wasn't even latched. I had hurled myself through an opening I could have walked through with ease.

There were no questions. Everything I had said escaped controversy. I was congratulated again and again. I felt cheated and dismayed. In fact, I had accomplished nothing whatever.

I am a slow learner. But I do learn. By the time Loy and I arrived in Omaha, I was getting myself better organized. I prepared a short quiz that was to become a mainstay of mine for a number of years. It consisted of twenty-five questions, all of which could be typed on a single sheet of paper using both sides. I had it copied, so I could distribute it to my audiences.

The questions were all phrased so that each could he answered with a simple "yes" or "no." The first question was this: "Do you know and understand the purposes and methods of Communism and/or Socialism?"

The second question was: "Do you favor either Communism or Socialism?" The remaining twenty-three questions were all taken from the Manifesto or Das Kapital by Marx, or from some of the writings of other well-known socialists.

Nearly without exception, I was being booked at gatherings where a meal would first he served, after which, the talk would be given. Most of these were luncheon groups. But even the morning and evening meetings usually began with breaking bread. Starting in Omaha, I circulated these sheets of questions asking the attendees to respond while they ate. The questions weren't difficult and would take only a few minutes to answer.

I would have someone collect them and bring them to the head table where I usually ate but little anyway due to my diet. I would look over the answers and thus have a "feel" for the opinions held by the people to whom I was to speak.

It is customary for instructors to look down on "true and false" (yes or no) quizzes, for one justifiable and understandable reason. Instructors teach what they believe to be facts. If a participant has a good ear, takes good notes, or can remember one way or another—and thus play back to the instructor some of the information he has communicated—a good grade will usually follow. The instructor doesn't want his student's opinions. He wants to be assured that what he has taught has been received.

But I wanted opinion. I wanted to know where my audience was before I spoke. For that purpose I strongly recommend the true-false approach.

As a matter of experience, I found something else to be important about the use of true-false questions. The common procedure—to lecture, and then to require playback—tends to stimulate the memory. Memory is important. It is a marvelous tools we all need.

However, the true-false approach tends to stimulate thinking, rather than memory. I found that many people hadn't bothered to think about the issues I was raising. The only opinions they expressed were those of others from whom they had acquired their responses.

The yes and no technique jolted some of them into trying to formulate their own points of view.

My own experience produced what to me was an astonishing pattern. I used this quiz perhaps twenty or thirty times before the year was over. I had total agreement in respect to the first two questions. Did the participant know what communism and socialism were all about? Answer 100% of the time: yes. Did the participant favor either communism or socialism? Answer 100% of the time: No.

However, in the twenty-three remaining questions, where I got down to specifics, I never found agreement in any group before which I appeared. Sometimes an audience would be divided right down the middle. Sometimes, the preponderant number favored the position I would have recommended. They really didn't want communism or socialism. But to my growing alarm, when it came to certain areas being debated in the public media at the time, the larger number often stood squarely in favor of communism or socialism, while stoutly maintaining they did not.

The rank and file of Americans to whom I spoke were either seeking to deceive, or they really didn't understand the issues. They were responding to what are now called: "Buzzwords." America, was a buzzword (good). so were the words Constitution, Bill of Rights, Declaration of Independence, freedom, peace, love, motherhood, free enterprise, etc., etc. Communism was a buzzword (bad). So were the words, Socialism, slavery, war, taxation, intrusion, oppression, aggression, dishonesty, and so on.

Interestingly, democracy was a buzzword (good) while dictatorship was a buzzword (bad).

From Omaha eastward, I fancy that I made a few fairly telling statements. I received a relatively favorable press, awakened a hit of antagonism, and met some marvelous people who wanted to do the right thing but were often confused about what it might he.

Ruth did a fantastic job. She had never attempted anything of the kind before. She came through with flying colors and without having taken a college course to learn how.

I told my story in major locations such as Minneapolis, St. Paul, Milwaukee, Chicago, Columbus and finally New York City. I told the same story in some small, out of the way places, as well.

In New York, I sought out Billy Rose, obtained an audience with him, turned over the tome with the signatures attached, and pleaded with him to consider the proposition. He thought I was a crackpot, probably out of my mind. Or, at least, he let me accept this as his evaluation of the idea. I still think it was pretty good. Rose was clearly the wrong man for the job when I explained he'd have to raise all the funds himself.

When Loy and I had left San Francisco to move to Falcon Lair, her mother and sister had pulled up their San Francisco roots and had returned to New York City. We found them living in a basement apartment in Brooklyn, just keeping afloat. At the moment I had nothing to offer, but I urged them to believe that before long I'd be back on my feet. They should consider a return to the West Coast. They had been disappointed in their New York sojourn and were excited about what Loy and I had been doing. They agreed to think about it.

Also, we overtook Ruth in New York. Our own personal pilgrimage had ended. So the three of us headed back where we took up residence again in Falcon Lair.

Chapter LXXII

The time arrived for us to award the San Francisco Group's equity in Falcon Lair.

There were nine finalists. Each had made a more or less formal presentation ranging from excellent to very poor. There was nothing new. Various members or the group, acting as judges, went over the offerings.

It took little time, in fact, to arrive at a realization that only three of the nine had produced an argument worthy of serious attention. We dropped the other six and concentrated on the three remaining.

San Francisco Group decided that before making the award, we should first ascertain the financial ability of the recipient. The winner would have to be accepted by the bank in the assumption of the trust deed.

One by one, I interviewed the three top contestants. None was in a financial position that even compared with our own. I asked specifically, what each would do with the Lair if the award went to him and his organization.

The answer was the same in each case. None had the financial ability necessary. What an enormous oversight on my part' I hadn't even inquired. I had presumed that full disclosure on our part, which had been made, would cull out any individual or organization lacking a financial footing.

At last, I called the three finalists to the Lair for a joint meeting. The time had come, I explained, for us to award the property. Could all three of them, working together in peace and freedom, join forces at least temporarily and jointly accept the property?

Not a chance! It turned out that their mutual disagreements precluded any possibility of a working truce. One of them summed it up for all. "Frankly, Mr. LeFevre, none of us really want Falcon Lair. We were hoping to expand our own special approach to the problems by the publicity the award might bring. We want the publicity. You keep the property."

The irony was conspicuous. Here were people dedicated to peace who couldn't cooperate long enough to accept an award jointly.

But we had announced a contest. We had conducted it according to the rules. We had formally made the awards, divesting ourselves of the property and bestowing it upon the three, none of whom—individually or jointly—accepted.

We gave the story to the papers. Mercifully, they did little with it, although it did appear.

Now what? The bank didn't want the property either, and wouldn't accept it voluntarily. There would first have to be a foreclosure. But there was no reason for such drastic measures. Our monthly payments were up to date. We would have to be in arrears by at least six months before legal steps would be taken. Perhaps, during that time, something would occur to change our financial picture and we'd be happy to keep the property.

There were no dissenting voices in our group. We were honor bound to let the property go. Some who had been in Beverly Hills wanted to return to San Francisco. Others were willing to stay on to see what would happen next.

The Lair was the kind of place where the unexpected turned up frequently. Members of the Group weren't even disappointed with the outcome of the contest. They had always felt the place belonged to me, even if they were the real owners. The errors were mine; the mistakes in judgment, mine. If anything could be salvaged, it was mine—good or bad. I cashed in on the benefits. Six months' expense-free occupancy of the Lair.

I had already started a program of reading and reflection. I went back to the books, patronizing the local library. I studied history and philosophy while concentrating on political theory.

Slowly an idea formed. I would get into politics myself. In my efforts to comprehend the occult and to work with Pearl at the metaphysical level, I had been warned repeatedly to stay away from politics. Now, with strong inner conviction, I believed that that prohibition had been removed.

I was naturally attracted to the Republican Party. The Democrats seemed to confuse "liberal'—a word originally serving to identify a supporter of liberty—with generosity. They were willingly generous with the taxpayers' money. Thus, liberal Democrats were generous Democrats. They rarely gave away their own funds. They scooped in dollars from the public, and then distributed it as largesse.

I knew the difficulties first-hand when it came to meeting a payroll. I had also learned what occurs when it isn't met. So it was natural for me to put on my best suit one evening and attend a meeting of Republican Party workers. They were getting organized for the 1950 elections. A story in the LA Times suggested that persons interested in becoming active in politics should show up to be counted.

When I had registered to vote in San Francisco, I had signed in as a Republican. I advised the various members of the GOP I met that evening that I was one of them and was thinking of running for office. I was "sized up" by some of the party pros as "presentable," and I got to meet a number of people who were already prominent in political circles in California.

Among those I shook hands with during one or another meeting, included Earl Warren, Governor of the state, Goodwin ("Goody") Knight, Lieutenant Governor, Richard Nixon, Congressman, and a number of "young Turks" who, like myself, had become interested in politics. These included Evelle Younger, Pat Paulson, and Pat McGee. I liked them all and was particularly fond of Goody Knight.

At one of these sessions, I met Ronald Reagan. He was thinking of bolting the Democratic Party and putting on the dress of the GOP. I recall one meeting in particular when, running short of folding chairs, Reagan was asked to help enlarge the seating capacity. The two of us worked in tandem, snapping the chairs open and lining them up.

I admired Reagan as a fine actor. His presence, together with his cooperative attitude, helped to convince me that there were some very fine people attracted to the Republican organization.

At this particular time, the most praiseworthy remarks were reserved for Nixon. It seemed that the Republicans in the Congressional District, which included Whittier at that time, had run a want ad for someone to become their standard bearer. Richard had applied and managed to get GOP backing. With it, he had gone on to victory. He was in Congress and he was considering abandoning his seat in the lower House in order to make a run for the Senate.

The more I thought about politics, the less the ordinary business activity appealed to me. I had become concerned with policy and with foreign affairs. I viewed communism and free enterprise as conflicting doctrines. Business had become banal.

Having made a number of speeches where I had done well, my

course of future action was clearly before me. I would probably be able to run a good, effective campaign. I was anything but tongue-tied. I would not stoop to modesty. I was increasingly concerned about the possibility of a new war. It seemed to me that one was being deftly arranged. And the economic policies of the government under the presidency of Harry Truman appalled me.

I made myself available for various public speeches in the Los Angeles area and was soon in demand in a minor way. But before I threw my hat in the ring, I decided to get Goody's personal recommendation.

I made an appointment to meet him in offices he temporarily occupied in the new Los Angeles City Hall. As Lieutenant Governor, Goody traveled a good deal and I was fortunate enough to catch him in the Southland.

He and I were now on a first name basis. Alone with him, I laid it out. I had learned that many people found my name and my appearance familiar to them. It was because of the publicity accompanying the Falcon Lair episode. But the public memory is short. Few could place me, but many seemed to think they knew me.

The initial publicity concerning the Lair hadn't been particularly savory. Further, I had just filed under Chapter 13. Could a person with these events in his immediate background hope to win GOP support?

Goody wasn't the least bit hesitant. I would be doing the right thing if I made a try. Almost any office. What particular one did I have in mind?

I knew nothing whatever about California politics. My ignorance seemed to qualify me for something far more grand. Besides, there was a Congresswoman representing the 14th Congressional District named Helen Gahagan Douglas, star of the moving picture, *She,* the great Rider Haggard novel.

I was dismayed at her record. She was the number one absentee in Congress. And when she did show up, she almost invariably cast her vote in favor of more controls and more taxes levied against business. I suspected that she was sympathetic to socialism, if not communism. My thought was to run for Congress from the 14th, because it appeared to me that the lady was vulnerable.

Goody was all for it. I should consider the matter with great seriousness. However, the first thing I would have to do would be to move into the 14th. The opposition would have a field day at my expense if I tried to represent the 14th while residing in Beverly Hills. Further, it would be incumbent upon me to move prior to filing, so that my address, as I filed, would be in the proper district.

Goody also assured me that he couldn't take part in my campaign nor risk endorsing me. He always followed Warren's lead. But so far as he knew, the 14th didn't have a suitable Republican hopeful anyway. There was no reason in the world why I couldn't be the candidate. The district was overwhelmingly Democratic. Few Republicans would want to make an attempt there.

We were still in the closing months of 1949 and I couldn't file until 1950. However, I could continue to keep my name and face on public view by giving talks.

About this time, I received a real baptism of fire.

One of the old pros in the GOP, a woman named Betty Carlson, who often reminded me of Ma Gray in San Francisco, asked me to debate a certain radio personality at the South Bay Community Center.

Betty had a gravely voice and a heart of gold. She was certain I was the man to take on this particular celebrity. "Off the record," Betty said to me, "we think the man's a Commie." Jack Tenney, one of California's State Senators, had created a State unAmerican Activities Committee at Sacramento. He had published a book that listed communists and "communist sympathizers."

This State committee echoed the House UnAmerican Committee at Federal level, and the use of this book in the hands of Republicans was widespread.

I accepted Betty's invitation and prepared myself for the debate by using the Tenney publication. I found my adversary listed in the book with better than a dozen citations. He had endorsed one socialist measure after another. He had been identified at any number of communist or socialist meetings. He was "bad!" And he was apparently skillful and effective.

I virtually licked my lips in anticipation of the trap I was going to spring on this "pinko" when we began our debate.

The meeting house in South Bay was packed. My opponent arrived, dressed informally. I arrived proud and proper with tie, white shirt, and three-piece suit. It was at once apparent that in this particular audience my opponent was the favorite. He was applauded when he came into view. I was greeted with a splattering of applause from my friends at Falcon Lair, whom I had talked into attending, and two or three Republicans including Mr. and Mrs. Carlson. My well wishers were outnumbered thirty-to-one.

The debate was formal. The question: Resolved: "That the Steel Worker's Union has too much power." I was affirmative, of course.

My opening remarks consisted of a run down on the background of my opponent. I waved the Tenney book at the audience and showed that the man I was taking on was favorable to Karl Marx. Both publicly and privately, he was carrying forward the Marxist Revolution. He and his cause were unAmerican.

My adversary talked about the Steel Worker's Union, about the low wages workers had received before the Union, and about the gains made once they received a better wage. Additionally, he showed that steel production had increased after the Unions had done their job. He had a wealth of statistics at his disposal and made a solid presentation.

In rebuttal, I went back to my "trap." How could anyone accept anything this man had to say? His statements were right out of the Socialist textbook. Etc. Etc.

In the final summation, my opponent turned to me with an arch smile. "I remind the judges," he said, "that the question for this debate has to do with the Steel Workers Union. My opponent has concentrated his attack on me. What if everything he says is true? So what? That has nothing to do with the debate."

The man was right. The three judges and the audience poured out approval of his position. Surrounded by my supporters, I hastily retired.

On the way back to the Lair, I said to Loy and others in the car: "Boy, did I get a lesson! I didn't talk on the subject. I believed I could win by discrediting my adversary. I didn't even phase him."

"Well, at least you showed them what a Red he is," Ruth insisted.

"Sure, I did. But who cares? Obviously, love of country was absent from that group. I'm not going to get myself into that kind of a pickle again.

Loy nodded. "You were terrible."

I silently agreed. I had blown that one for certain. And I had wished so desperately to show the Republicans how well I could handle myself. I was thankful so few of them were present.

Our plans were now made. We would stay on at the Lair until after the first of the year. Then, Loy, Tommy, and I—together with Ruth, Edith and Margie—would move into the 14th district. Victoria would come, too.

We'd find a large apartment with plenty of sleeping space, and rent it so we could stay together during the campaign. All of us could participate in putting the campaign together.

About this time we heard again from Lorna, Loy's sister, who was still in New York. She felt trapped there. She had a job that brought in just enough to keep her and Mama alive. But it was a kind of blind-alley employment

That could continue for the balance of her life. She wanted out.

Lorna wanted to come west again, but Mama had had her fill of California. If I would return as escort, Lorna could come to stay with us and get started again in California. Meanwhile, Mama would return to Baltimore, live with her sister and, thus, be close to her roots.

Short of funds, the costs of going back to Gotham and returning seemed out of the question. But I recalled crossing most of the country years before with only $10.00 to spend. Why not employ the same method this time?

I took to reading the ads and finally located a driver who was going to New York City. He would provide a ride for a co-driver, along with a few dollars. The arrangement was made. Again, I traversed the United States at top speed for bottom dollar.

I spent a night or two in the Brooklyn apartment with Mama and Lorna. In the process, I lined up another return trip. This time, my employer wanted someone to deliver a new car to the West Coast. The principle end to be achieved was the transfer of his "girlfriend" to Los Angeles, where she would be taking up residence. He would provide the vehicle. His girlfriend would be a passenger. She would buy the gas.

He decided on me because another woman, my sister-in-law, would be a passenger. The arrangement seemed to he satisfactory all around. So, after only a brief respite, I was off again. This time, I took a southern route and drove slowly because of the new engine I was breaking in.

Our passenger was tall and dark. She wore her long hair in a "bun" and turned out to be a good companion. The trip was one of the more enjoyable cross-country treks of my experience.

Back in Los Angeles, we delivered the car and passenger to an agreed upon destination. Ruth met us to whisk us out to Falcon Lair.

During my absence, Edith had located an apartment that seemed suitable for our combined occupancy. It was in the Asbury Apartments near MacArthur Park and right smack in the middle of the 14th.

Shortly after the first of the year, we moved. Then I filed for Congress and prepared for the campaign.

Chapter LXXIII

When I appeared at City Hall to accomplish the formality of filing for office, I discovered that I had to qualify. The clerk explained.

My name, age, nation of origin, and other specifics could be readily accepted because they were matters of public record "somewhere." But I had to "prove" that a significant number of voters in the district I proposed to represent "favored" my candidacy.

The voters of the 14th Congressional District would have no discernable reason for "favoring" me. They didn't know me. Perhaps that was the one thing going for me.

Not so. "Proof" could readily be obtained. I must present signed petitions from x number of voters in my district that agreed to support me.

The 14th Congressional was composed of four State Assembly Districts. According to the laws of 1950, I must have 200 signatures of bona fide registered voters from each Assembly District, 800 in all.

Dismayed, I said: "You mean I've got to go out, meet at least 800 registered voters throughout the 14th District and convince them that I'm the man they want?"

The clerk nodded. "You can see the reason for this, Mr. LeFevre. You'll have to obtain a great many more votes than that. If you can't demonstrate a following of at least 800, why should anyone take your candidacy seriously?"

She had a point.

"I thought that was what my campaign was supposed to do."

"It is. But you have to prove backing before you begin." She smiled sweetly. It was clear she had a Willie fresh off a banana boat. "Go to window ___ and the man there will give you the appropriate petitions. They must be signed and returned here by day ___ so we have time to check and verify the signatures. Then your filing can be accepted."

It seemed to me that the system was putting the cart before the horse, but who was I to challenge the law while seeking a position where I would swear to uphold it?

I picked up the petitions. The places for signatures seemed endless.

As I made my way from the office, a lounger of shifty stance with gimlet eyes sidled up to me.

"Got your petitions, I see," he said.

"Pretty aren't they?"

"Gonna get the names yourself?"

"Shouldn't I?"

"Nothing' to stop you. Go ahead, if you wanna."

"Apparently you have some ideas on the subject."

"Yep." He hitched his trousers. "Some, as has nothing better to do, go out and ring doorbells. You? Well, you look like a busy guy. You probably got a lot to do. Right?"

At the moment I could think of all manner of business.

"If you've got a few bucks, I'll get the sigs. No problem. And I'll guarantee the minimum number to qualify. How about that?"

"Sounds good," I said. "But how can you find 800 people in four assembly districts who know me well enough to vote for me? I doubt if I could put my hands on 20."

"Never run before, I take it." He smirked. "Mister, you need me."

"There's a good possibility you're right."

He was my boon, life-long companion on the instant. "There ain't nothing' in the law says that the signers has to vote for what they signed. "Tell, they don't even have to vote. They just sign."

"And you can get 800 signatures just like that?" I snapped my fingers to indicate brevity. "How much?"

He named a figure. Considering the work involved it was reasonable.

"How do I know the names you get will be valid?"

"Hell, you don't have to pay me 'til you qualify. Okay?"

"You trust me?"

"Why not? You try welchin' and you'll be disqualified." He snapped his fingers. "Like that, see."

"It seems I have no choice."

"Sure you do." He started to turn away. "Go get 'em yourself."

"Hold it," I said. I You've made me a fair offer. I accept."

He grinned and took the petitions from my hand. "Give me your phone number. I'll give you a jingle when they're ready."

I told Betty Carlson about what had occurred. She immediately approved. That was the simple way to get the job done.

It didn't take long for my beady-eyed friend to round up the names.

In process I learned something that bothered me. It turned out that the people who sign petitions would and do sign almost anything. They don't know or care what they sign. Signing makes them feel important. But they often must attest or swear that what they sign is important.

With my filing behind me, Betty came up with some sage advice. As soon as possible, I must win the endorsement of the Republican Party. In California, in 1950, a candidate in a general election cross-filed. That is, I signed in as both a Republican and a Democrat. If I could poll a majority of votes in the primary, including a Democratic total larger than any Democratic hopeful, I would be the elected candidate and wouldn't face a challenge in November. But I needed the public backing of my own party to achieve anything.

I had no chance whatever of democratic support. With my openly expressed opinions about "limiting" government, it was doubtful if any democrat would touch me.

In the first hectic weeks, as I "ran" to first one club and then another, making my pitch, Betty was my constant mentor. I was as green as an alligator pear. She told me what to do and where to go. It turned out that a total of eight people had "qualified" to run for Congress from the 14th District. Just before filing closed, I was handed a surprise. Helen Douglas had decided not to run for re-election. Instead, the handpicked Democrat, who was to "inherit" the Democratic organization and presumably the office, was Sam Yorty.

I was tremendously disappointed. I had chosen the 14th District because of my dislike for Helen's policies. But Yorty was "clean" in that he did not hold any federal office. At the same time, he was well known locally as having already "paid his dues" in various minor roles for the Democrats.

There were various "public" meetings and a couple of "fact-finding" meetings staged by GOP party polls. I attended all of them, listened to Betty, and did pretty much what she asked. She and I got along famously, probably because she liked my willingness to state my position frankly. Fortunately, she approved or appeared to approve of my ideas respecting the reduction of the federal government's role.

I don't know how or why it happened. I think I am being frank when I say that it was probably Betty's doing, rather than anything I did myself. There was one final, crucial meeting at which I apparently gave a good account of myself. The next bit of news was a front-page story in the *LA Times*, that I had won Republican endorsement in the 14th.

This was an important step and I had taken it.

Next, Betty advised, I must raise as much money as possible. I must get out at least one general mailing to all the voters in the 14th and, if possible, win some financial assistance from the Central Committee. Then, I must hire a campaign manager.

I pursued the Chairman of the GOP Central Committee for days. He was a busy man and it took a lot of doing to corner him. I needed money now, during the primaries. At the Biltmore Hotel I buttonholed him between meetings, and laid it out. Could I get some help? And could I get it now? I believed I was doing a good job and would be a credit to the party.

The Chairman was equivocal. It wasn't policy to intrude into primary campaigns. If the Republican voters in the primaries chose me, there would be assistance.

I wouldn't let him go. I pulled out all the stops and played the Star Spangled Banner with vibrato. His mood softened and he capitulated. If I kept my nose clean, won personal endorsements from certain key people whom Betty Carlson could identify for me, there would be $10,000 in my primary war chest. And possibly more during the finals, of course.

I had no intention of operating with a dirty nose and assured him that I was deeply grateful for his consideration.

Fortunately, a little money began to come in from private sources. Careful account was kept of every dime. Then, by good fortune, my campaign attracted the savings and loan industry. Word apparently went out from somewhere that I was "okay."

Ed Crane of Coast Federal offered me a campaign headquarters in a vacant office in his bank building free of rent. We got enough dollars together to pay for printing my platform and to cover one general mailing. Out it went.

Meanwhile, my speech making had brought me into some measure of the public limelight. I was interviewed on the radio, and cracked the pages of the *Times* and some of the other papers. I was at least making ripples, even if there was no indication of a tidal wave.

No money arrived from the Central Committee, but surely the promise would be kept. I won a few of the important endorsements from various individuals who were influential, including a "God bless" from the Reverend Fifield at First Congregational Church, one of the more prestigious churches in the 14th.

A group of blacks from Watts (part of my district) endorsed me. This was surprising since one of my planks was the elimination of the Social Security system as well as public welfare. I argued that this system made the recipients appear to be second class citizens. The argument was greeted with a show of hostility at the talks with primarily black audiences.

However, there were some marvelous people of color in the 14th. They went against popular trends among their own people by recognizing that blacks really needed economic stability, procured by their own efforts, rather than support from others.

Even then there were some outstandingly successful black businessmen. There are many, many more of them today—a fact rarely noticed. I was even blessed with a bit of financial help from a large and successful insurance firm, headed by a black.

At last, I obtained a "professional" campaign manager. His contribution to my efforts was to insist on getting some billboards. The cost was prohibitive unless those dollars came from the Central Committee. And they didn't come. But we did manage some "one sheets" that were fairly large. We plastered them on blank walls—the political graffiti of the day.

My little "staff" worked at the Asbury at night and sometimes at campaign headquarters by day. They folded, stamped, and mailed. Edith kept the books with absolute accuracy.

Then, one day as I went out on my "run," the climate changed. I had made a great many "friends." At least, I thought I had. Now, people, who had always waved or shouted a cheery "hi," began to avoid me.

After a day or two of being shunned, it became evident that this was not merely coincidental or a "bad" day. My public talks continued, but private endorsements ceased abruptly.

I asked Betty to explain it. She was as concerned as I, but could shed no light on it. Apparently, she knew something was going on, but because of her obvious friendship for me, she was on the outside looking in.

In about a week, the answer came. Without contacting me or offering any kind of explanation, the *Times* ran a story that the Republicans had endorsed Jack Hardy for the 14th congressional race for Congress.

I tried to reach the Chairman of the Central Committee. He successfully avoided me. Other members of the Committee I had met before, and who had looked on my efforts with a kindly eye, were now "out" to me.

I promoted a "monster rally," my last important effort. Aside from my personal friends from the Asbury, and a handful of others, no one showed.

I called on the political editor of the *Times* and asked point blank to learn the origin of the story that endorsed Hardy. He was tight-lipped.

Then came a freshet of publicity for Hardy. Billboards appeared with his picture on them. A number of stories promoted him in the newspapers. One of them revealed that $10,000 (presumably promised to my campaign) had gone to him. I had been knifed in the back by my own party. Years were to pass before I learned the reason.

The primary elections were held in June. My ship had received a lethal torpedo long before. The vote counting was a mere formality, so far as my chances were concerned. Hardy won the primary for the Republicans, Yorty for the Democrats. I was one of the "also rans."

Within hours after the final returns were in, President Truman declared a "police action" in Korea. My fears were realized, for a "police action" was nothing more than a declaration of war without the consent of Congress.

The Constitution, I thought, prohibited such an act, and I was furious.

I sent a telegram to Bob Taft, "Mr. Republican," urging him to protest "such treason." He did so, using some of the wording from my telegram and making me feel that he at least had read it.

But the die had been cast. America was at war and I was a "nobody."

It wasn't the defeat that bothered me. It was the secrecy. I couldn't get a straight story from anyone. I had become persona non grata. To a degree, much the same climate was created for Betty and those few others who had been close.

Again, I visited the political editor of the *Times*. He wasn't exactly a fountain of information but there was one virtue I could be sure of. If he said anything, it would be true. I could rely on the accuracy of his words.

"All I want," I said to him, "is to have someone who knows tell me what dreadful wrong I performed. I feel betrayed."

He nodded. "Agreed. They stabbed you in the back."

"But why? I did have their endorsement. If they were going to revoke it, you'd think they'd at least have been open enough to tell me so to my face."

He stared fixedly at me but said nothing.

"Do you know why?" I asked.

"Yes."

"Then tell me."

"I'm not at liberty to do so. But don't worry about it. It's not the end of the world."

"It feels like it to me. Look, I'm no angel. Back in 1938 and '39, I was involved with the "I Am" and was included in a blanket lawsuit for mail fraud that was immediately dropped once I had explained my chores with the organization. I didn't appear at the trial. I wasn't even called as a witness. In fact, I had done nothing wrong."

"I know about that," he said calmly. "Nothing to it."

"The only other questionable event was my filing under Chapter 13. I'm still paying off my creditors, a little at a time. But I cleared both points with Goodie before I filed for the race. He said there was nothing to either of those things to disqualify me."

"There wasn't."

"There's something else?"

He stared at me, giving no sign.

I sighed. "Okay. I'm in Coventry and I don't know why."

"Want some advice?"

"Does it include hanging or the firing squad?"

He ignored the sally. "You're a newcomer in the Los Angeles area. There are lots of people who matter whom you don't yet know. You haven't paid your dues. Why don't you go to work to help get Nixon into the Senate? Helen Douglas' strongest district is the 14th. Your help there could be pivotal. Stop trying to walk off with a top prize until you've earned the backing you need by working your way up."

"Is that what this is all about?"

"Not really." He paused. "No, I'm not sure. It could be a factor. But it isn't the important one. However, there will be future elections. Play your cards slowly, one at a time. There's lots of time ahead of you."

"I'll think about it," I said. "Thanks for the advice."

I gave Betty an account of this verbal exchange and she leaped happily in approval. "It's a good idea, Bob. You could open a campaign headquarters for Nixon in the 14th, man it with volunteers and help distribute his literature."

"I'm having a bit of a problem liking Republicans right now," I said. "Except you. I don't think of you as a Republican, I think of you as a friend."

"Don't be like that," she rasped. "You've made a lot of friends in the party besides me. But this is what politics is all about. You've got to expect a bit of cloak and dagger work."

"Okay, chief," I said. "Though, to tell the truth, I thought we'd be cloaking and daggering Democrats. But what do I do now?"

"Well," she said. "You might begin this way. There's going to be an important meeting at the Biltmore where party workers can get to meet Nixon. Why don't you attend? You've surely got the time."

"Okay, Betty, I'll give it a shot."

A few days later I was one of perhaps fifty more or less enthusiastic supporters of Nixon who showed up at the big hotel for a luncheon. The others appeared more and I felt very much less.

After the bread breaking and gravy sopping had ended, Nixon spoke. His talk opened my eyes. One of the reasons I had gone was because Nixon had been and was being touted as a man "of principle." I really hadn't worked my way into a place where the party was "obligated" to me. And this was how it was done. The whole business of politics from grass roots to flowering power was built on doing favors. Back scratching. You did things for others. Then they were obligated to do things for you.

Nixon didn't mince words. He was the Republican nominee. And we all knew he stood foursquare for private enterprise. But California was predominantly Democratic. To win, he'd need the support of lots of people from the opposing party.

What did that mean? It meant that before he could do anything effectively in support of his principles, he first had to be elected. What did that mean? It meant that he would do anything necessary to get elected. First things first.

Spelled out it went this way: If, to get elected, he had to abide by Union rules and support some strike, he'd do it. If, to get elected, he had to cross picket lines, he'd do that.

He would be doing his best to tell people what they wanted to hear. We had to do the same. He was for free enterprise. But he was also for regulating those businesses that "needed" to be regulated.

He was against high taxation. But he was certainly in favor of reasonable and just taxation.

He was for America. That meant he had to be opposed to Communism. But we should understand that America stands for whatever the people want And he was for what the people wanted...at least, as he campaigned.

I had viewed my own campaign as a chance to state the truth as I saw it. Let the chips fall where they would. That was the fun of it. I knew there was small chance of winning a GOP post in a district as heavily Democratic as the 14th. But I felt it proper and honest to lay it on the line.

Now an office holder who was a real pro was educating me. The job of a campaigner is to win. To win, you do and say what is calculated to bring about the win. That's the whole ball of wax.

I left feeling betrayed again. But I had not been betrayed by Betty and the few stalwarts from my district who had helped raise money and who had come up with some dollars of their own. Perhaps I owed them something, despite the rout I had experience.

I set up the Nixon headquarters in the 14th. I did what Betty asked me to do. But my heart went out of the effort. The time had surely arrived for me to stop parading around as a political savant with answers to major problems.

I needed a job. It was time I started at the bottom all over again.

Chapter LXXIV

The experiences shared by most of the Group that had lived at Falcon Lair had created a most delightful and rewarding type of camaraderie. There had been something in the way of preparation for it, I suppose, because of our guesthouse experiences during the "I Am" days. At that time, too, a few of us had lived in the same house, eaten at one table, and been in constant, close communication.

Insensibly, we were now family. We worked together, concerned with one another's well being. We were acquainted with each other's strengths as well as weaknesses. So it was the most natural thing in the world that when the campaign ended there was no apparent wish to break up the coterie.

Edith was, without a doubt, the best financial mind we had among us. She was a professional bookkeeper, probably qualified to be a CPA. Edith always handled the money, the accounts, the bills; she scolded us if any of us wasted anything and gave us sparse approval when we did things right.

Ruth was probably the sharpest of all. She typed my letters and probably could have written them better than I did. She was a woman with ideas. The crusade we had undertaken in favor of freedom and peace reached her innermost self. She discussed ideas with me endlessly, demanding strict honesty, always striving for perfection. Ruth was dedicated to the same degree I was, perhaps even more so.

Margie, my Welsh friend from London, was another extremely intelligent lady. She brought to our group a sense of refinement and good breeding. Not that the others were lacking. But Margie was a gentle-lady in all things. And I had reason to discover how capable she was, later on.

Up to this time, Margie had served as a physical therapist, and as a matter of fact, had been of inestimable help to me professionally. The intense physical effort of conducting a campaign took its toll and I would sometimes return home with some of my back muscles in spasm. I didn't want to campaign on a cane or with crutches. Margie saw to it that it wasn't necessary.

She watched me like a hawk and when I showed signs of pain or began to list as my back went out, she would command me to lie down. Her knowledge of where my muscles were and which ones needed help was masterful. Her fingers and hands were like electro-magnets putting strained tendons to rights.

Now, as our campaign terminated, it became clear that Margie was ill. She was slender of build, frail in appearance. The amount of work she had cheerfully performed had been too much for her. She came down with tuberculosis. The only cure for this dreadful malady is plenty of rest, good food, quiet, loving care, and a stay in bed for months. Hospitalization was indicated. None of us would hear of it. We didn't have the funds. Further, we all loved Margie and wanted to take care of her.

Lorna was now a part of our household. She was six years junior to Loy and, hence, part of a younger generation. But Lorna is about as sharp a piece of work as one could find. Even at this formative period in her life, she had gained a maturity of view beyond her age. She fitted into our circle with ease, bringing vivacity and a great sense of fun.

Tommy of course was growing fast. He was still too young for school. No longer a toddler, he needed a great deal of attention. We were grateful to have Victoria with us. She helped in many ways and was marvelous with the child.

Loy was the center of everything that transpired. She handled the bulk of the household chores, including meal preparation, although the others pitched in when they could. Additionally, when cash was short, she would take a job to ease dollar pressure. When it comes to disposition, I am happy to say that Loy is the finest person I have ever known. She is invariably sunny and bright; the word "invariably" was not idly chosen. She is a happy, cheerful person no matter what.

If news came that the world was coming to an end tomorrow, she would probably laugh and say: "Que Serra Serra." Oh, look at that beautiful rose. See the lovely sunset. Listen to those marvelous notes from Verdi.

When other men complain of their wives, who are "always griping" and "always late," I confess to a feeling of good fortune. Loy is the epitome of being on time and she doesn't "gripe" about anything.

As a matter of fact, her cheerful outlook in the face of everything was disconcerting. During our first days of married life, I wondered if she really appreciated the magnitude of some of the problems I seemed to be confronting alone. From this uncertainty I deduced that either she didn't care. or didn't quite understand

I learned that neither was true. She's as smart as they come. She was actually one step ahead of me. She cared and she understood, but she had something to add. Whatever it was, it wouldn't get her down.

I am prone to worry. I often look on the dark side, not because I am attracted to negativity but because I am trying to overcome it. With me, it's an effort. With Loy, it's a breeze.

Loy is a natural individualist. She's a doer and a goer. Beauty and appreciation for what is lovely cloak her like a mantle. I doubt profoundly if I could have carried off the various enterprises I launched with a person other than Loy.

If I sing her praises, it is because it is deserved. She gave me complete latitude. She understood that each of the others brought something we needed to our efforts. If she resented their presence, which would have been a natural reaction, it never showed. The sun came up every day when she got up. It set when she went to bed.

The rest of us had our arguments and disagreements. Without being intrusive, Loy gathered us figuratively in her arms and, somehow, peace returned. In sum, we were a family. These ladies were Bob's Angels, long before "Charlie" was ever heard of.

We held a council of "peace" (not war) at the Asbury. What would we do, now that the campaign was over? Ruth summed it up as well as any of us could.

"Do we believe in this crusade we've been conducting? Is freedom in jeopardy? Obviously, war has already come and there's nothing we can do about that right now. But what of freedom? Do we mean what was said during the race? Or were we just posing in an effort to win a political victory?"

I looked around the living room at the expressions on the various faces. "I've learned one thing as a result of this campaign," I said. Naturally, I feel had. Even though I knew I had no chance I really, deep down, wanted a victory, But freedom can't be achieved this way. There is too much ambition and too much willingness to compromise in politics.

"I was stabbed in the back. I still don't know why, although I suspect it had something to do with the 'I Am.'" Everyone was listening with respect.

"What I'm trying to get at is this: If we mean business about freedom, then it's going to he a life-long effort. There's no quick and easy solution. Socialist and Communist influences are in the ascendancy. They have taken over already. If they are not total, it's no credit to our efforts.

"I don't know what really goes on at the inner levels. I've had some experiences I've seen some things. But I'm less and less certain about them. So I'm not looking for any help from the Masters. I don't expect any divine intervention."

"Do you mean to tell us that the Ballards and the "I Am" teachings were false?" Edith asked.

"No, Edy. I'm not saying that. There are great truths that we know and have shared in our individual experiences. But there's a lot of nonsense there, too. For instance, remember that dictation 'Daddy' gave back in Cleveland right after I'd joined their staff? Nazi submarines trapped by the Masters under water, which would be brought to the surface after the war ended, thus demonstrating the power of the Masters! Now that's poppycock. I sensed it at the time and I'll bet many of the students did, too."

Edith gave a knowing look in the direction of Ruth, who now spoke up.

"Then what about those dictations coming through you, Bob? Was some of that nonsense, too? Or maybe all of it?"

"I'm quite sure some of it was. Maybe all of it. I really don't know. And I admit I don't understand. I really don't know what was in most of those dictations. You took them down, in shorthand, and typed them up. Somehow, I was never interested in reading them—to your disgust, as I recall. I've looked at a few, of course. But by no means have I made it a point to read them. Some of what was said was true. I'm reasonably certain now that a lot of it was contradictory and confusing. And probably nonsensical.

"We're at a crossroads right now. And whatever happened in the past, whether reasonable or unreasonable, is over. From this point on there's no assurance that we're doing 'what the Masters wish.' I think all of us have used that thought from time to time to carry us over some rough spots.

"If any of you decide to continue this crusade for freedom, it's your own decision exclusively. As for me, I'm going to do my best. If you decide to help, you'll be most welcome I assure you. At the moment, I haven't any idea what I'll do nor how to go about doing it. But I'm going to try.

"I'll tell you something else I've learned. I'm a profoundly ignorant man. I no longer buy the idea that if one's heart is pure, then the 'Presence' knows all the answers and will take care of everything. I think that's nonsense for sure.

"I've tried to do that. And I'll admit, once in a while it has worked. That's what has made it all so confusing. Every now and again, and in spite of odds, something completely favorable has occurred apparently brought about by forces outside myself.

"But I'll tell you something else, too. Most of the time it hasn't worked. A great deal of the time, in spite of my 'calls' and in spite of the best I can do, forces outside myself have dumped on me."

Ruth was quick to interrupt. "Maybe you feel that way because your heart really isn't pure."

"I'm going to accept that, Ruth. I'm going to take it a step farther. My heart isn't pure. It has never been pure and I have a sneaky idea that it never will be. Perhaps the 'Presence' is pure and perfect, but I'm not. And at is one thing I'm sure about.

"So be advised. I'm not perfect. I make mistakes. I've made a ton of them. I'll probably come up with additional tonnage. If you can't endure that then you have no business associating with me, I'm not saying that I'm going to do nothing hut make mistakes. Obviously, I'll do my best to eliminate error. But if we work together you have to accept the possibility that I'm going to do a brody every now and then."

Ruth frowned. "Bob, do you think there are Masters? Are there forces outside one's self that are wholly good?"

"I don't know, Ruth. I really don't know. I was so sure at one time. I do think there's something out there. I'm reasonably sure of that. But whether it's good, bad, or maybe just mischievous, I can't say for sure. Perhaps it isn't even 'out there'. It could be a part of each of our inner selves that nobody understands."

"I believe in the Masters."

"Fine." I smiled at her. "I wouldn't tamper with your beliefs."

"I believe in them, too," Eddy said.

"I don't know anything about it," Margie said. "But I like the idea of working for a proper goal."

I laughed. "Freedom is quite proper, Margie."

Amidst the general smiles and nods, Lorna spoke. "Well, I don't know about the rest of you gals, but I want to get some more education. And after that I want to get married."

"Spoken like a true woman," I said.

"Are you implying that all true women should want to get married?" Ruth demanded. "I'm a woman and I most decidedly do not want to be married."

"You see how imperfect I am," I said. "My statement was clumsy. I didn't mean to imply the meaning you extracted."

Edith shifted impatiently. "I want to help you, Bob. Let's cut out all this discussion. What's the first thing we ought to do?"

"My first task," I said, "is to stop fooling around and get a job. "

"No. " Edith squared her shoulders. "The first task is to find another place to live. This apartment is too expensive. And look at Margie. She ought to be in bed. Let's get relocated. Margie has to give notice and quit work."

As so frequently happened, Edith put our feet squarely on the ground. And we stayed together.

In a few days, someone located a furnished house for rent on Arapahoe Street, not a great distance from the Ashbury and still in the 14th District.

Under protest, Margie gave up her post at one of the hospitals and retired to her room shortly after we had made the move.

It didn't take long to find a job. Indeed, one of the benefits accruing to any candidate seeking office is the heightening of his profile. The GOP betrayal wasn't held against me. People accepted double-dealing and betrayal in politics, and my experience convinced many that I had lost because I refused to compromise.

About this time, full-page ads began appearing in the LA Times, sponsored by a group calling itself the Wage Earner's Committee. The ads captured enormous attention.

The spokesman for this Committee was a man named McConnell. He ran the ad once a week. It called for ordinary wage workers who didn't want to join the Union to join, instead, the Wage Earner's Committee. The committee was taking a stand against the "Labor

Boss." It contended that the Unions were the source of difficulty in the United States. The Committee objected to the strike, the Union dues, the assessments, the fines, the picketing, and most especially to the Union's ability to collect membership dues by having the employer deduct them from the worker's paycheck before he saw it.

The ads showed that most strikes actually cost the workers money, despite a raise which, after weeks or months, they might receive. The cost in lost pay was frequently never earned back. Meanwhile, they forced prices up for everyone.

This Committee wasn't interested in attacking the Teamsters, or the Steel Workers, or the Electrical Workers Unions. They attacked Unionism with an all encompassing wrath.

They showed that the "Labor Boss" was wallowing in big money that he extracted—sometimes by force—from the meager pay of workers. Further, the Labor Boss had little respect even for Union members, referring to them as "weed heads," dummies, and dopes. On top of this the Union paid no taxes and was exempt from anti-trust regulation.

The ads were brilliantly conceived and hit the public squarely where it lived...in the pocketbook.

When McConnell was interviewed on radio, on TV, or in the press and queried about the size of his organization, he was adamant. He would give no details. There were "thousands" in the organization and thousands. More were joining every day. The dues were $1.00 per year. Each ad cost over $1,000. It all fit.

Thus, when Mr. McConnell telephoned me at our new place of residence and wanted me to call at the Wage Earner's Headquarters in Glendale, I was happy to oblige. The Committee had a job opening for an Extension Director.

This was the kind of job I had hoped to find. I could be paid and, at the same time, I could use my talents in one phase of the crusade for freedom. The Unions and the "Labor Boss" were engaged in reducing the freedom of their members, the employers and the public alike. And all to line their own pockets in the creation of a monopoly of political and economic power.

The Committee offices were in a small building on Glendale Boulevard. I shook hands with McConnell, two other men and a woman, all of whom were directors of the organization.

If I took the job, what would my duties be?

I would become one of the spokesmen for the group and, in that capacity, I would make speeches at various gatherings in an effort to enlarge membership. Further, the committee wished to offer its services to any particular businessman who was was having difficulty with Union organizational efforts. My job would, in such cases, entail a discovery of the true economic situation of the company. Having found it, I was to communicate it to the workers one way or another.

What would the job pay? The amount was disappointingly small. I would receive $100 every two weeks. I would also have to provide my own car and gasoline.

McConnell expressed great confidence in my ability to speak. He was apparently favorably impressed with the campaign I had conducted and he had the feeling that I hadn't compromised my position. Further, he had somehow taken the trouble to learn of some of my prior experiences with Unions. He was confident that the stance of the Committee was in harmony with my deepest personal convictions.

I asked the size of the membership. McConnell assured me that the actual numbers was a closely guarded secret, as were the names of members. Reprisals against individuals—many of who were also Union members—had to be guarded against.

Was there a chance for more money later? I was assured there was. As membership grew, made possible by my own efforts, there was no reason I couldn't receive more. At the moment, they were spending everything as fast as it came in.

McConnell, himself, was impressive. Tall, lean, with a slight greying at the temples, he looked to be about fifty. He was probably older. But he was a vigorous, intense man. His eyes held, he stood straight, and his sentences were crashing accusations against everything the Unions thought and did.

I took the job. At home, there was immediate rejoicing. Although the money was small, the crusade was on its way again.

I began where I had terminated my campaign. I was in demand as a speaker, and it was no trick at all to be rebooked as a representative of the Wage Earner's Committee.

Within a week or so, came the first application from a businessman who wanted help in opposing the Union.

A Union had invaded the Knickerbocker Plastic Company of Glendale, and an election was going to be held. The laws were such that the owner could not speak to his employees in defense of all the allegations the Union publicly made against him. Most of the charges were simply bald-faced lies and vicious innuendoes.

I asked to see his books. He had had two or three bad years during which he had survived on borrowed money. Now, at last, he was getting into the black and making profits for the first time in four years. The Union's demands, if granted, would put him right back into the red again.

After looking at the books, I asked for an opportunity to meet with the employees to let them know the facts. The businessman didn't want me to reveal what I had learned about his financial condition, but I insisted they were entitled to know.

The bulk of the employees were allowed to quit their posts and come to an area in the plant that, at the moment, was idle. I stood on a chair and laid the story out. With blackboard and chalk, I showed them in black and white just where the company stood.

I explained to the workers, who at the outset were bristling with hostility, that Knickerbocker Plastics was a highly competitive business. One of the reasons their employer had been reluctant to tell them of the true economic condition was that his competition might gain by that knowledge. If others knew of his plight, they might put the pressure on. Further, some of them might quit and migrate to a competitive firm.

I showed them that if they held a strike and won it—although it might appear advantageous—any advantage would be at great cost to them. In the long run, it would be detrimental. Most of them would lose. And in time, there would have to be lost jobs. Vacancies wouldn't be filled. Some would have to be dropped.

Someone called out: "How much is he paying you to say this?"

"Nothing at all," I said, truthfully. "I'm a director of the Wage Earner's Committee and even the Committee doesn't pay me extra for this talk. I get the same salary whether I come here or stay away."

This was true and some must have believed me. The election was held a few days later, and the Union lost.

But the Union has many weapons. A couple of weeks later McConnell said to me, "Bob, the Union has filed charges against Knickerbocker Plastics for interfering with an election. Some Union reps are coming by to talk to you about it."

Later that day two men appeared. One of them not at all to my surprise, was the Chairman of the Republican Central committee, who had promised me financial help in my campaign, and then, without explanation, given the help to Jack Hardy. He was an attorney and had been hired by the Union.

He began by saying that he was acting for the NLRB and anything I might say could be used against me in court.

"What court?" I asked. "Do you mean that kangaroo court of Labor Boss Stooges called the NLRB? If so, it has no jurisdiction over me."

"It could take you to court," he warned.

"So could anyone else," I said. "So, what's new?"

"Come on, Bob," he said. "We're old friends. You can tell me all about it."

"Sure, we're old friends," I said.

We were in a small room abutting the main office of the Committee headquarters and I could hear McConnell's delighted snort from the adjoining room.

The Union man spoke up. "We're not here to debate," he said. "I want a copy of the speech you made at Knickerbocker Plastics."

"There is no copy," I said. "I spoke extemporaneously"

"Do you remember what you said?" he asked.

"Sure, I do."

"Then I want you to write it down and make it available to me."

"Fine," I said. "I'm a professional writer and sneaker. "What do you pay per word?"

"Pay?" he looked dumbfounded.

"Of course, pay! You want everyone paid for his efforts don't you? Or is the Union now going to advocate work without pay?"

"We never pay for these things," the Union man said.

"You do this time," I said. "Or you get nothing. In most cases I get less than this, but in your case, considering everything, my price is 50¢ per word. And the speech is very long. Will you meet my price?"

The Union man cursed and sputtered. The attorney, my "friend" laughed.

"He's got you there," he said. "He's within his rights."

"As a matter of fact," I said, "I am now eager to write it all down. At fifty cents a word, of course. I may pad it a bit, but you'll have it. All of it."

"Can he do that?" the Union man asked.

The attorney turned to me. "How much did Knickerbocker Plastics pay you for the speech?"

"Not one cent."

"Then why not treat us the same way?"

"I was glad to make the speech. For free. I considered it my civic duty to make the speech. But now that it's in demand, it has a commercial value. Pay me, or forget it."

"Let's forget it," the attorney said. "We can do without it."

"But it would help if we had it."

"You want to pay this man's price?"

"Never. " The Union man glowed with hate.

" If the speech existed in writing we could subpoena it. We can't subpoena something that doesn't exist. You'll have to pay or forget it." The attorney didn't appear particularly crestfallen.

"Let's get out of here," the Union man said, heading for the door.

"I can write on other topics, too," I called after them. "Whenever I have a market. Just remember my price."

McConnell was jubilant.

Shortly after this episode I had my first opportunity to appear on television for the Wage Earners.

Somehow a debate had been arranged by one of the television stations. It had managed to obtain the head of the Retail Clerk's Union, a man named DaSilva. He and his assistant would be two members of a panel.

The program department phoned the Wage Earner's Committee as the natural source of an opposing view. Another director and I were assigned to the panel.

The subject was similar to the question I had debated before in South Bay. Instead of focusing on the Steel Workers, this time the question was: "Do Unions have Too Much Power?"

McConnell took this opportunity to coach me. "The Union specializes in carrying the attack," he warned. "They will take the offensive if they can get it. If you can turn that around and initiate the issues, then you'll probably win. Do the same kind of thing you did with the Plastics Union."

This was my first appearance before television cameras. The set consisted of a large divan on which the five of us sat. The Moderator was in the center, the Union men on one side, the Wage Earners on the other.

Several quart bottles of Sparkletts—the product of the sponsor—were on a coffee table in front of the sofa.

The confrontation started with the Moderator spelling out the issue and introducing the participants. I would he fourth in line, the other three would get in their licks first.

I had asked for this arrangement, deliberately. If the others shot first, then I'd have a better chance of getting the range, as I saw it. This had pleased everyone. McConnell had been right. The Union wanted the first shot and planned to wipe us out before we had ever begun. And as I had anticipated, DaSilva and his henchmen were well prepared.

This time I wasn't going to be drawn off by attacking the persons rather than the issues. I had done a bit of homework, too. When my turn came, I said: "Before we proceed further, I think it would be a good idea if these gentlemen of the Retail Clerk's Union would tell the viewing audience what they do with all the money they collect.

"According to the figures we have had compiled, the Unions of this country receive a monthly income of $80,000,000 tax free. Do you Labor Bosses draw all that down in salaries and expense accounts? If not, what do you do with the money?"

"That's a very great deal of money! That's 960 million dollars every year that the Union spends any way it wishes. Nearly a billion dollars. And it pays no taxes, It isn't subject to anti-trust and is rarely even challenged in this area.

"So, before we can judge just how much power the Labor Bosses have, I'd like to know where the money goes."

DaSilva looked as if I'd kicked him in the midsection. He'd never heard of $80 million, much less $960 million. He didn't get that much money. But the figure was in the ballpark, even if not absolutely accurate. It was probably conservative, based on membership numbers, the amount of dues, and the fines and assessments collected overall. I had deliberately avoided an over-statement.

The Union Boss was a skillful opponent. He recovered on the instant, and changed the subject. He went back to an account of all the good the workers experienced with the increased wages gained for them. My compatriot took him on. The talk went back and forth, avoiding the subject of money.

The Moderator brought me back in. "We'd like an opinion from

Mr. LeFevre on that last point," he said, turning to me.

"Before I respond," I said, "I would still like to know what the Union does with $80,000,000 per month every month of the year. Would you be so good as to answer that question, Mr. DaSilva?"

DaSilva sputtered, came up with a mumble, and then returned to his text. The other two joined in.

A pause ensued and I took the floor. "I think the television audience is entitled to have an answer to the point I've raised," I said. "What do you do with all that money?"

Before I could blink, DaSilva's assistant sprang into action. He grabbed one of the quart bottles from the coffee table, raised it over his head, and came for me. The camera, its two red eyes staring, dollied in for a tight shot.

DaSilva motioned and the assistant's face turned the color of paper-mache. He looked at the camera, crouched, and put the bottle back where it had been. Then he sank back in his place.

From that moment, the Wage Earners had it all their own way. We never did get an answer. DaSilva said he didn't know. Don't think we didn't leap into that opening. We shredded their protestations like a series of "eyes only" documents.

The thirty-minute program ended amid a barrage of telephone calls congratulating the Wage Earners.

For days after that episode, as I moved about town, people I had never seen would suddenly light up with recognition. I'd be stopped in the street or in buildings. Everyone was concerned with my well being.

McConnell wasn't. "Don't worry about a thing," he told me. "As a matter of fact the Union may have taken out an insurance policy for your protection. If anything happens to you over the next several months, everyone will believe the Union was responsible."

Chapter LXXV

The Wage Earner's Committee was possible in Los Angeles because of the city's relatively non-Union climate. San Francisco was in Harry Bridges' pocket, which pocket was in the trousers of the ILU (International Longshoreman's Union). Los Angeles, on the other hand, was largely Open Shop.

This advantage, seen from a different viewpoint, was detrimental. The pressure from Unions to get more members and dues was comparatively low key in LA. Had the voice of the Labor Boss been more strident, a far greater number of people would have been driven toward Committee membership.

Committee growth was slow. McConnell lauded me every time I made an appearance or was involved in radio or television interviews. No raise in wage was mentioned. Sometimes even my pittance was late and, on occasion, it was only partial. The business of being a crusader, especially in causes that will predictably take years to bring to fruition, is not lucrative.

The American mentality isn't geared to slow, solid growth and development. Further, the more government intrudes with regulations and controls, the greater the tendency toward the "fast buck."

The primary reason relates to banking practices—geared and controlled as they are by Federal and State statute and law. At an earlier time, dating to my boyhood, credit was hard to find. Banks were slow to put out the cash. But when they did, they usually didn't expect miracles in repayment.

In the first dozen years after the creation of the Federal Reserve System, the ability to borrow was broadened, but requirements to repay were intensified.

When the "I Am" group, under my leadership, had purchased the house on the River Drive in St. Paul, we were expected to make one payment of principle per year, although interest was paid monthly. I would never have been able to arrange a loan at all except that I owned property and had been steadily employed for several years at one firm. The interest on the loan was 5%. I thought it terribly excessive.

Today, thanks to government intrusion and the resulting

hyper-intensity of all money markets, and interest rates fluctuate at triple or quadruple figures almost week by week. Payments are rarely deferred on anything without stiff penalties.

In the 1950's, this tendency was already making itself felt. You didn't start a business, and then grow with the neighborhood, gradually establishing a firm and reliable foundation. Rather, you got in for a large and rapid profit. The higher the interest rates and the more rapidly they fluctuated, the more this became necessary. You had to make it big and fast, or fail.

When the money climate is heated to this extent, those who financially support crusades want quick results. They shy away from any commitment that won't show immediate return in the achievement of goals.

The downswing in the economy—occurring in 1948 and undoubtedly affecting my businesses in San Francisco— brought still more government involvement. Credit might have disappeared, temporarily. But it would have been followed by slow, steady, reliable growth rates.

Instead, businessmen and others championed further government intervention. The Federal Deposit Insurance Corporation came into being and insured bank deposits by tying tax income to the picture. Now the taxpaying public at large was financially backing the deposits of those with savings.

Thus, crusades that entail broad educational efforts are constantly pushing for federal tax dollars in support. Government involvement feeds on itself. The more it occurs, the more it seems necessary.

So it was with the Wage Earner's Committee. If we would draft legislation and try to get it enacted, money could be raised. The quick answer, imposed by law, could always get dollar support.

To the credit of McConnell and others involved, this avenue was shunned. The growth and power of the Unions had enlarged the government's tax base. Indeed, the real danger in the Unions wasn't from the idea of getting a better deal for workers. It arose from the Wagner Act and the distortions occurring under it, wherein the Unions obtained legal backing and support.

I was caught again between my commitment to the "crusade" and the economic necessity of paying bills. Right at this juncture, after only a few months working with McConnell, I was offered a job with a much better salary.

A remarkable man in Los Angeles, named William Stephenson telephoned. He was a brilliant tax expert and made a living by trouble-shooting excessive taxes being paid by private individuals and firms. He had learned of my crusading abilities and wanted to organize something he proposed calling "United Taxpayers of California." Meanwhile, he would analyze the taxes being paid by each of his clients, and then take up the matter on a one-to-one basis with the taxing authorities. Rarely did he miss. Almost without exception, when Stephenson studied the taxes paid by a given client, large or small, he was able to argue for reduction with such knowledge and skill that he would get at least a portion of what he wanted. He was well known and highly regarded even by government people whom he constantly opposed.

I asked for specifics. What would my job entail, if I accepted the post he had in mind?

I would continue making speeches for various clubs and organizations. I would try to find members for United Taxpayers. I would go on radio with a regular weekly program that his organization would sponsor.

The pay offered was more than double what I was getting. It was an opportunity too good to pass up, and radio sounded great. Reluctantly I resigned from the Wage Earner's Committee as its Extension Director and took a post with Stephenson.

I began writing a series of radio programs that were called "The Voice of Freedom." Stephenson brought a quarter hour once a week on KHJ, one of the major radio stations in the LA area. Despite the Union boast that I would never be on the air again if I had the temerity to leave WTCN, I was back on a regular broadcast schedule.

This new task gave me a chance to renew my studies begun at Falcon Lair. I invented a game called "Taxes" and outlined the concept to my new boss. Stephenson was enchanted with its possibilities as a device to help bring members into United Taxpayers. He bankrolled the manufacture of 1000 sets.

The game was conceptualized with a format similar to that of Monopoly. Instead of a single board, each of

the players had his own. By rolling dice, each player worked, obtained money, got raises, or paid taxes. In the process, he "improved" his board (standard of living). He bought land, built a home, furnished it, accumulated funds, enlarged his business, and so on.

The feature of the game was the "tax collector." He had the power to intrude on any player at any time in order to increase taxes, confiscate some of his property for the "public good" and generally to harass the player he selected.

The game engendered a universal dislike against the tax collector. This player was armed with a small box called the "pig." When the tax collector, at his discretion, plunked it down in front of a given player, that player had to satisfy the "pig." Other players redoubled their efforts to improve their lot at the time their fellow taxpayer was under duress.

The winner of the game was the player who reached a certain standard of living ahead of the tax collector. If none could reach it, the tax collector won.

I vividly recall a game in our home on Arapahoe played by the women. Ruth was the tax collector. She was so efficient at collecting taxes that, for a few moments, it appeared that all the players were about to physically attack her. Indeed, I felt it prudent to intervene before a hair-pulling episode took place. Needless to say, Ruth won. But it took a couple of days for the other women. to return to civility with her.

The game awakened each player to a realization of the very situation he was experiencing in real life. And curiously, the party selected as the tax collector immediately took on the typical attitude of any government employee who finds it difficult to understand why people are upset with him. He is only following the rules, doing his "duty," and doing it for the "public good."

The game was, in fact, a splendid study in psychology. It furnished a fast-moving evening of great emotional intensity, and a kind of bitter hilarity, if there is such a thing.

The game brought about something of a misunderstanding between Stephenson and me. I had designed the game, expecting that he would handle the marketing. Stephenson had anticipated that I would know all about marketing the product I had designed. The truth was that neither of us had the foggiest notion of how to get it into the market. Stores wouldn't take it. The big companies weren't interested even in looking at it.

Stephenson suggested some "Taxes" parties be organized. There, we could bring together taxpayers and use the game to introduce them to the realities they were up against.

The problem with the game has already been stated. It tended to engender personal animus toward the tax collector, so that it had a divisive effect over all. If anything, it was too graphic. As a matter of fact, I have learned it may merely have been ahead of its time.

Currently, there are several games on the market similar in format although, in my view, none as gripping and exciting. Nor as dangerous. Anyway, the game turned into a financial loss, and Stephenson had laid out considerable money. My various activities hadn't brought in revenue at a level commensurate with the expenditure.

I could see the handwriting on the wall when my radio show wasn't renewed after the original thirteen weeks. Yet Stephenson liked me and I was very fond of him. He had hoped that I might be able to develop into an expert so that I could understudy his own remarkable performance. This was beyond me. I have never been attracted by mathematics and Stephenson had a calculator for a mind. He enjoyed translating everything into numbers.

I was assured that I could continue working indefinitely for United Taxpayers. My evaluation of my usefulness didn't correspond to his assurance. Stephenson, in his specialty, was a vital unit in opposing the socialist takeover. If my broadcast and other activities were becoming a financial drain, a parting of the ways must occur. I did not wish to be a cause for the weakening of Stephenson's effectiveness.

One day Stephenson, his secretary and I had lunch together. I laid it out bluntly, as I saw it. His activities would be stronger without me. His fundamental honesty was such that, despite the growing respect we had for each other, he had to agree with my analysis. I gave him two week's notice.

Before we left the table, I recall this exchange.

"Bill," I said, "I've been associated with the Wage Earner's Committee, as you know. The organization believed that the most serious threat to this country and American concepts and practices came from the Labor Boss.

"Prior to that I ran for office. In the political circles I was in, Russia and Communism were viewed as the most serious threat. What do you think it is?"

He looked at me closely through his thick lenses, glanced at his secretary, and then looked around the restaurant to see if anyone was listening to our conversation. He shifted uneasily, and then said, "Come with me, and I'll tell you."

When his secretary presumed she had been excluded, he said, "That's an inclusive invitation. In a public place like this, one never knows who might overhear."

On the street, instead of heading for the office, we walked slowly in the opposite direction amid throngs of noonday pedestrians. "This is the safest place to say things you don't want others to hear."

"There are plenty of people around," I observed.

He turned to make sure no one was matching our steps from behind. "Lots of people make for solitude," he said. "True loneliness is in a crowd that isn't listening."

I chuckled. "Shrewd. I've noticed that myself. But why not wait until we get to the office?"

He shrugged. "It may be bugged."

"What do you mean?" Back at this date, the expression was new to me.

"Eavesdropping devices have sometimes been installed I offices such as mine to find out what I'm up to."

"You're kidding."

The secretary spoke up. "No, he isn't. We found a tiny microphone once. During a political campaign, as a matter of fact."

"I can't expect you to understand this entirely, Bob. At least, not at once. The real danger to this country comes from the government itself.

"We've got to have a government."

"Of course. I'm not suggesting otherwise. There are certain things such as public streets, sewer systems, fire and police protection, and so on that can be far more efficiently and economically handled by a public agency than by private companies. At least, that's my view of the moment."

"I'm not having trouble with that idea."

"But there is one agency of government viewed by nearly everyone as sacred that is engaged in wrecking everything."

I felt a chill down my spine. It was my turn to look around to see if we were being tailed.

Stephenson smiled. His face had a far-away look. "It's the public school system, Bob. I don't dare say that openly. But that's it. The school system is a separate, distinct, and unique government all to itself.

It has independent taxing power and authority. It can confiscate property. It can and does control the view-point of future generations. And it's sacred. Chastity, motherhood, and the public schools are equally sacrosanct. Were I to criticize it to my clients, I'd lose my credibility."

I asked a few more questions and Stephenson provided statistical data from memory. In a few brief moments, he had uncovered a danger I had never even guessed at.

Because of my respect for the man, I didn't debate him. But I felt he must be overlooking some pretty important items. I didn't buy it. At the same time, I didn't forget it.

Back at Arapahoe Street, I took Ruth into this confidence. She could be trusted without reservation. My own view clung to the popular notion that it was Russia and the "foreign influence" of "communists and communist sympathizers" in government that was responsible. The "International" Trade Union movement appealed to me as a far more logical bulls-eye for the crusade target.

Ruth grasped the significance of Stephenson's position better than I did. "It might interest you to know," she said, "that Mr. Stephenson isn't alone in that view. Did you know that there's a newspaper publisher in Santa Ana, whose editorials have been attacking the public school system for years?"

"Really?" I said. "How does he get away with it?"

"I don't know," she conceded. "But why don't I pick up some back issues of his newspaper? You could read what he has to say. It could be important

"Do that," I said.

Within a day or so she had collected half a dozen editions. R. C. Hoiles, the publisher of the Santa Ana Register was an outspoken critic of government compulsion in the school system. I read a number of the published editorials and most particularly, I took notice of a column written by the publisher himself.

Two things impressed me. Hoiles was one of the worst writers whose prose I have ever struggled with. However, his logic was irrefutable. He was devastating.

I remember saying to Ruth, "My gosh, Ruthie. I think Hoiles may be right' And Stephenson, too, of course. But I could never say that in any of my speeches. No one would believe me.

I also recall Ruth's reaction. "Where is your dedication to truth? Are you afraid to say it?"

After a pause, I said, "Yes. I guess I am. But all in good time. Perhaps things will change or develop in such a way that I can come out publicly in that area. For right now, I wouldn't dare. Remember, I'm hunting for a job."

At this particular time, Ruth was employed by an organization as much engaged in the "crusade" as I was. It was called "Spiritual Mobilization" and The Reverend Fifield of First Congregational Church was involved in it.

The principle factotum of the organization was a man named James Ingebretson. A third participant was a handsome, young man named William Johnson. The major chore undertaken by this group was the monthly publication of a little magazine called "Faith and Freedom." Johnson was editor.

There were a number of other people, who were making magnificent contributions to this publication. A well-known professor named V. Orval Watts, who held a Ph.D. in economics, worked closely with them, either as a staff member or as a free lance contributor. The work was inspired in part by the outstanding efforts of a man of considerable stature who had been the President of the Los Angeles Chamber of Commerce, named Leonard Read.

I was informed that Read had helped to inspire the creation of "Faith and Freedom. " But he had gone to New York and was himself organizing an eastern group called "The Foundation for Economic Education."

I was urged by Ruth to apply for work with Spiritual Mobilization. I did so, but nothing came of it. The organization wanted people of "prestige." My abortive campaign for Congress, coming as it had after that flurry of Falcon Lair "love cult" publicity, hadn't provided it. Rather, I was looked upon as something of a "street fighter" useful, but not really smart enough to make a serious contribution.

Meanwhile, Read lured V. Orval Watts away from Spiritual Mobilization and also hired Ayn Rand, recently arrived in this country as a Russian refugee. While Watts was still in the Los Angeles area, I invited him to call on us.

A group of my co-workers, plus our "family," listened to Watts as he set forth the principles of economics. It was a revelation to we. Watts stated the realities in a language that anyone could understand. The principles he set forth in lay terms were essentially the principles set forth by the "I Am" in transcendental, metaphysical terms. I was captivated by what he said.

I invited Watts back for two or three more visits before he left for New York. Each time I asked him to discuss a new phase of economics. Nothing I asked caused him the slightest hesitation. I recalled my friend, the Major, during the orientation course I had taken at Lexington, Virginia, while in the service. At last I saw where his information had come from. He, too, must have been an economist of the free market variety.

Watts had been unable to find work at any institution of learning. Free market education was not wanted. The country had been captured by the writings of John Maynard Keynes of England—a young, aspiring economist who was destined to make a name for himself in this country. He had stated, "We're all Keynesians now."

Then, a free market economist named Milton Friedman—together with another well-known economist named Beardsley Rummel—helped to write the check-off system for income tax collection.

Their intention was commendable. The costs to the government of collecting taxes, which many people avoided or evaded, was staggering. By siring a withholding tax law, the government could eliminate all those costs. It was the view of Rummel-Friedman, that taxes could be reduced if the cost of collecting them could be shifted to employers.

The result was increased taxation. Further, the costs of government were not reduced. Instead, a quasi-police agency called the Internal Revenue Service hired increasing numbers of bureaucrats whose job was to examine returns and to bring to "justice" any who avoided or evaded. Whatever it had cost before to collect the funds was now increased to make certain by the use of assumed police authority, that they were collected.

Back in 1950, as Watts explained it, any economist who taught the principles of free market economics virtually assured himself of prolonged unemployment. Major institutions of learning were already obtaining large grants from government. Those same institutions didn't want to "bite the hand" that was feeding them. They viewed as anathema, any professor who would challenge the right and power of the state to intrude in economic affairs.

"You mean, " I said to Watts, "that what you are explaining to us isn't available on the American campus?"

"Perhaps in a few places, Bob. Certainly not many. Universities don't want us. They want to stay in the good graces of Washington, D.C. Even private universities are susceptible to government pressure since private donors hesitate to make contributions to a school which is conservative in its economics departments."

"But education is what we need," I said, thinking of Stephenson's position.

"I agree. However, it is even difficult for writers or news commentators to take a position which opposes the onward march of the state and the state takeover of business and property."

One day, Ruth approached me with a book in her hands. "You ought to read this, Bob." She handed me a copy of Rose Wilder Lane's "Discovery of Freedom."

I accepted the volume and began to read, intending to peruse a chapter from time to time. I couldn't put the book down. As the pages turned, my excitement mounted. Lane knew how to say things in a way that got under your skin.

In discussing the book with the family later, Ruth explained that this particular book had been so significant to Leonard Read, that he was making it the centerpiece of his newly formed organization.

According to information Ruth had picked up at Spiritual Mobilization, Rose Wilder Lane didn't like her own book and wouldn't permit it to be re-published. One of the giants of General Motors, a man named Henry Grady Weaver, had read it and tried to obtain permission from Rose Lane to reproduce the book in quantity. She didn't want the money. Reason? She didn't want to pay that much in the way of taxes. And she wouldn't pay Social Security taxes no matter what.

So, Weaver had asked for permission to re-write the book in his own words. Rose Lane apparently told him she couldn't care less what he did with it. So Weaver had prepared a paraphrase of the volume. It was this paraphrase, called the "Mainspring of Human Progress," which Read was using.

I obtained a copy of "Mainspring." I found it lacked the fire and drive of the original, even though it was well done. Indeed, in one respect it was an improvement. Miss Lane had apparently written "Discovery" in the white heat of anger at what government was doing to this country. She hadn't gone back to check her manuscript for errors that might have crept in. She sent it off to her publisher who immediately bought it and issued a first edition of 1,000 copies.

Weaver had eradicated some of the errors, although not all of them in my judgment. In making it more accurate, he had extinguished much of the flame.

When a mind such as mine has been virtually empty, and then is confronted with complete and compelling arguments, each new fact looms large. I learned that R. C. Hoiles, the publisher of whom I have written, had located one such error, telephoned Rose Lane, and criticized her so severely that he may have been the reason she turned against her own book. Despite errors, the book is probably one of the most influential to emerge in this country during the 20th century.

Having read "Discovery" as well as a number of other works, I began viewing myself as well informed. If Watts was correct about our educational institutions—as well as Stephenson, Hoiles, et al—then surely the time had come to do something about it.

Of course, I needed a job. And I was still looking. I had made applications at all the radio stations. I had also applied at several television stations, which were just beginning their sensational rise into national prominence and influence. Applications had been favorably received in most cases. I believed it was just a matter of time before would be called upon to fill an opening.

Meanwhile, as I marked time, I could begin to communicate the information I had acquired. I organized a series of classroom discussions and proceeded to sign up a few people each of whom paid a few dollars for the opportunity of listening to me talk about the danger to freedom brought on by socialist or communist influence in the country.

I invited Watts, Bill Johnson, and a brilliant young fellow named Herb Cournelle, to one or another of these meetings. They were all affiliated more or less with Spiritual Mobilization, and made impressive additions to my own offerings.

I wrote an article about China and offered it to "Faith and Freedom," which rejected it. I handed it to a political friend who had it introduced into the Congressional Record. It was also published by the Wage Earner's Magazine.

About this time, the Reverend Fifield called me into his office. He wanted to organize a committee that would back me as a candidate for local city government. He wanted to get a good start in the campaign, because of anticipated opposition. Would I take kindly to such a proposition? He was planning ahead for 1952.

I turned down the offer. I had seen enough of politics. And I explained to Fifield that my concerns were for the nation, itself. I really knew nothing about local affairs and didn't want to be involved with any more of the kind of betrayal I had already experienced. Education was needed, not more elections.

Fifield expressed terrible disappointment.

Again and again, I called at the radio and television stations, trying to keep my application near the top of the heap. I was treated courteously but there was nothing for me. Time was passing and bills were mounting.

In the midst of these actions, Lorna was married and went off with her fine husband, Jim Hamilton. Loy joined the choir at First Church. Margie completely recovered her health.

From San Francisco, my oldest boy, Bob junior, enlisted in the Marines. After taking his basic training at Camp Pendleton, he was stationed somewhere east of Barstow in preparation for shipment to the war zone in Korea.

Then, Mama Reuling arrived from Baltimore. She had decided to come west again. Because we were so crowded at our address, she rented a room in an adjacent home and took her meals with us.

These events, piling one on top of another, kept me hopping. But it was the kind of hopping that didn't pay off. It appeared to me that some desperate measures were needed.

I don't know where the idea came from. Suddenly, out of the blue, I knew I had to go to Florida. It made no sense to me, but this was the kind of hunch I'd had before, which had paid off. In Florida, I would get back into radio.

When I announced this decision to Loy and the others, they were understandably surprised. Loy wanted to know -f I had had a job offer. I had to tell her that I had not.

Although I denied it, I'm sure the family was convinced that I was receiving some kind of metaphysical guidance. They smiled knowingly among themselves, the more I disclaimed any such direction. So, I made preparations to leave for a quick run to the Sunshine State.

As I was about to depart, a job offer finally arrived. KFI, one of the two largest and most prestigious radio stations in the Los Angeles basin, had entered the television field. The top men were thoroughly favorable to free enterprise. The offer was to join their new endeavor as a director of TV productions.

I felt that I should have a job as a newsman or at least in some capacity as a performer in front of the cameras. Upon checking, I learned to my dismay that they were afraid to put me there. I was "too" controversial, "too" outspoken.

I explained that I was not a technician and really didn't know how to hold down the job of director. Patiently, they assured me that they would teach me. Although I was to be invisible as far as the public was concerned, it was believed that my presence on staff would help maintain a high level of performance among their staff.

Their cautious attitude miffed me. If they really believed in free enterprise, why didn't they stand up and say so? In a fit of pique, I stated that working with them would be a mistake. I wasn't one to mince words or pull punches. I wanted high visibility. Working behind the scenes wasn't my particular helping of spinach.

Besides, I had this inner conviction that I had to go to Miami, I was still engaged in "feeling" my way. I hadn't yet learned to think.

Chapter LXXVI

As the weeks slipped away following the election, the Socialist tide kept rising. My political adventuring had at least accomplished one thing for me. I had grown politically aware. I read the headlines in a new way. The news stories took on additional dimensions. Radio and TV broadcasts highlighted the same trend.

The people of the United States, without comprehending the issues involved were drifting into the hands of the statists who wanted to control everything. If a person viewed the American dream as somehow related to the American heritage, then the daily events took on alarming overtones. Our past said that in America each person was free to try, to win or lose on the basis of his own skills, ability and perseverance, and then to enjoy the fruits of his labor as he saw fit. The new America was emerging as the product of the legal firm of Crybitch and Whine.

All you had to do was to organize the crybabies, complain in one loud bellow of pain, and then start to whimper that it was up to the government to solve the problem. This was political fodder of the first water.

Someone was sure to come forward to make a career out of the difficulty at public expense through some new agency, bureau, or tax procedure. And the government got bigger, the people got smaller. Their willingness to address their own problems and to solve them—or to at least live with them—was eroding in favor of political paternalistic panaceas.

I had to fight it. I had to do all I could if I loved my country. And I loved my country (the American Revolutionary image) so much that it hurt. I had shifted from one job to another because I had to crusade. Actually, I could have found a job with good pay, had I been willing to put aside my patriotism. My nuclear family wouldn't hear of it. I would have been miserable had I given in to the temptation to seek income alone. No. I was a crusader and my job must bring me a living and allow an expression of my devotion to a cause larger than myself. S

Socialism was winning and tire was slipping away. When Miami emerged in my consciousness as a shining Mecca it was already

September of 1951. With the assistance of the family I managed to amass a grand total of close to $80.00. I cannot recall the exact figure, but it was considerably short of $100.00. I could delay no more. It had to be enough. With it, I could drive to Florida, get a job and drive back.

Gasoline was about 28 cents per gallon, including taxes. A full tank for my aging Chevy cost between $3.00 and $4.00. I could anticipate at least 300 miles per tankful. A round trip, crossing the country both ways would total about 6000 miles, or 20 tanks. That would cost between $60 and $70 and whatever left could go for eating, sleeping and other nonessentials.

There was no margin for error, or failure. And I knew no one to whom I could turn in an emergency. My hunch or "inner-direction," or invisible mentor drove me. Obstacles meant nothing would overcome.

I have driven many thousands of miles on America's highways and for me the best procedure is to get an early start. Loy got up with me, prepared a hearty breakfast, and a bagged lunch I could carry. I drove away from the residence about 4:30 one September morning.

I was easing out of San Bernardino as the first rays of dawn dimmed my headlights. I had to stop for border inspection at the Arizona state line. Much earlier, California had placed an embargo on the importation of fruits and certain plants. Arizona had gotten into the act and now stopped all vehicles heading the other way with its own list of contraband.

The delay was minimal but I took the occasion to fill the tank and settled again behind the wheel. No time to eat. My goal was Miami. Nothing must deter me in my frantic dash.

I became ravenously hungry about noon, but I was still in Arizona. I opened my prepared lunch with one hand and kept driving as I devoured a sandwich. There were two. I saved the other for supper. When the tank needed filling, I found a filling station and took a long drink of water. Then back to the wheel and the feel of the road.

I had calculated that I'd be in Texas by the time darkness came, but I was still miles west of the border somewhere in New Mexico when I had to turn on my lights. I ate what was left of my lunch and kept going.

I drove all that night, only stopping to fill the car and to drain myself. Morning arrived and I was feeling a bit weary. But if I stopped to sleep, the cost of a room at even a cheap wayside motel would cut cruelly into my meager funds. A good meal would be just as refreshing and, so, I pulled into a truck stop. I indulged myself in a gorgeous feast consisting of eggs (in butter) fried potatoes, pancakes, toast, orange juice, and coffee. And plenty of jam with even more catsup to take away the taste of the potatoes which were slightly rancid. I was shocked when the bill totaled more than $2.00.

I was restored to vim and vigor and driving was fun again for awhile. For a very long while, all my driving was in Texas. The state is as big as rumor has it.

Then came Louisiana. I raced across the state, stopping for another meal, always giving priority to the car's needs. The second night descended as I crossed the Mississippi River into the state of that same name. But I didn't bother with sleep. I had to keep going.

Mississippi was traversed, and so was Alabama. Neither seemed large compared to Texas. But my speed lessened as the long straight stretches of highway farther west were replaced by roads more inclined to turn and loop.

The third morning found me in Florida. And Florida is a big state when you take the southern route. In my mind's eye, I was almost at my destination but the entire day was spent in crossing to Jacksonville. Then, I turned south for the final four hundred miles to the great Metropolis that had become my Golconda.

Early evening arrived as I came through North Miami. During my brief food breaks, I had been examining a list of radio stations that operated in the city. I wanted to apply at a station that emphasized news.

As I entered the range of various radio signals I tuned in all Miami stations, one by one. I settled on the "best" stations according to my immediate reaction. There were two: the CBS affiliate; and, the NBC outlet. The latter was owned and operated by the Miami Herald, with the call letters, WQAM. I would apply at both.

But time was passing. Before reaching the central part of Miami, I stopped to service the car one more time. I also used the payphone to call the two stations managers at their respective studios to see if I could set up an appointment for the next day.

I was exhausted. But I pumped a lot of pep into my voice and had a lucky break at WQAM. The station manager had stayed in his office later than usual and my call was accepted.

I explained that I had just driven in from Los Angeles. As a newsman with experience, I was hoping for a berth at QAM. Could I please have an appointment?

The station manager quite properly explained that I should talk to his program chief and production manager, but I overrode the suggestion. I wanted to see him first. Then, I'd talk to anyone he wished.

Luck was with me. Perhaps the manager was impressed by the fact that I knew what I wanted. He agreed to see me at 11:00 the following morning.

I tried to make an appointment at the CBS competitor, but I was too late. Heartened by one firm commitment for the next day, I cruised the downtown area until I found a hotel that looked on a par with my purse.

I had a three-day's growth of beard and was bleary-eyed. But I had my good suit on a hanger, a clean shirt, and—in a little case—reposed my toilet articles.

A room was available for me if I would pay in advance. The fee was $4.00. It was a lot of money but I had to look the part when I confronted the big man on the morrow. I paid up, went to the room, and stripped.

The Miami heat was already getting to me. In actual fact, the temperature of Miami is quite similar to that of LA. But there are two major distinctions. In Los Angeles, the evenings are cool and there is a wide fluctuation of thermal intensity every twenty-four hours. In Miami, the nights remain warm.

Additionally, there is much more humidity in the Miami area, despite the fact that both cities are coastal and the air is moistened.

In any case, I was both hot and harried. I was too tired even for a shower. I stripped the bed of all but the lower sheet, put my body in a reclining position, and flopped my head on the pillow. That was that. I was asleep in an instant.

I was awakened by a pre-arranged call from the desk. I had perspired so much during the night that the place my body had occupied was sopping wet. But I was marvelously refreshed.

I showered, shaved and dressed with care. I indulged myself with my favorite breakfast at a nearby restaurant and drove to the Dupont Building on Flagler Street.

Everything worked in harmony with my hunch. The manager appeared to be favorably impressed. I talked to the production manager who went over details. My salary was agreed upon. I had an audition that was a breeze. Then I was introduced to Gordon Shaw, the news director. He wasn't too sure about me, but he was third in line. The decision had already been made.

When could I start work? I explained I would have to return to LA and bring back my family, including my small son. Would the third week in October be satisfactory? All was agreed upon. Could I manage so much in such a short time? I never doubted it. I was riding a wave. How it would work, I didn't know. But it would work.

By one o'clock I was ready to start my return trip. I was just as eager to get back as I had been to arrive. I stopped at a curio shop along Flagler and purchased a ceramic doe's head and fawn, a memento for Loy. Then I had the last good meal I could afford.

Behind the wheel, I roared along the highway heading north, exulting that my hunch had been correct. This is always the trouble with hunches and other forms of gambling. They sometimes pay off.

My return to the West Coast was a repetition of my mad dash toward Miami. However, one night's sleep every three days isn't enough. I felt drained. The hunt is always mightier than the kill. Going east, the adrenaline was pumping. There was the possibility of failure.

But I hadn't failed. I had hunted the quarry and made the kill. My adrenaline went to bed and pulled the covers up. Failure keeps one keen. Success lulls.

I fought the urge to sleep. I pinched my legs, taking tiny folds of flesh between finger and thumb. I made myself black and blue. I slapped my face. I opened the windows so that the rushing air would keep my eyes open. I played the radio full blast.

I stopped for coffee whenever I found an open cafe. I could afford nothing more. Once, I pulled off the road, got out and marched around the car, kicking the tires. It seemed to make me less drowsy. For perhaps another ten minutes.

I drove in a daze, mechanically. As the sun came up behind me I managed to sign a new lease on alertness, particularly as I indulged in a scant, cheap meal. But the day was long. Somehow I managed.

The second night was pure torture. At last I pulled off the road, determined to sleep in the car with the doors locked. Perversely, once I had parked, I woke up and couldn't manage an audible signal to Morpheus. Sitting there wide-awake made no sense. Off I drove again.

I had made an error. I should have taken time to spend another night in bed before trusting myself on the highway. But as I counted my remaining cash, I knew I had to make no error. If all went well, I could just make it home with no more beds and no more breakfasts.

I played mental games. I counted telephone poles and approaching cars, I tried to remember license plate numbers, and dreamed of my welcome in Loy's arms.

As the third night descended I was still miles from home. I had left Miami shortly after noon. My driving was nothing short of grim. My eyes were glazed, my grip on the wheel intense.

I imagined myself having fallen into the hands of Communists. They were torturing me to get me to divulge national secrets. They would get nothing out of me. I set my jaw. I could endure anything they could dream up. My head kept nodding. I would have momentary blackouts and would jerk myself out of it still roaring along at better than fifty miles an hour. Fortunately, there was little or no traffic. And the farther west, the straighter the roads.

Then it happened. With a spasm I came wide-awake. The car was jolting across desert lands at full tilt somewhere in Arizona. Where was the highway? I didn't dare slacken speed. I knew from experience that a car can bog down in a sandy spot and I had no funds for any such luxury as being towed.

Off to my left I saw a pair of headlights and dimly heard the muted sound of a truck moving eastward, or a paved surface. Route 66 must be over that way.

I increased pressure on the throttle, slid in and out of a dry wash, but managed to veer in the direction I had noted. A few more jolts and my nodding headlights picked up the reflection of Macadam. Fortunately, there was no ditch at roadside. I thundered and spewed gravel, and then managed somehow to find the smooth traction the tires needed. The car swerved onto the highway and, again, I faced the west without slackening speed and with my heart pounding. I didn't fall asleep again.

To reach home from that point was a routine, deadly, boring, sleep luring routine. But on the evening of the final day of driving, I pulled in at Arapahoe Street, red-eyed, shaggy with beard but triumphant.

I had been gone six days and six nights.

The family was eager to have the news. My verbal report must have been a model of direct simplicity. "I got a job. I'm going to bed. Tell you the rest later." They were compelled to wait for details. When I sat down to take off my shoes, I fell asleep. Loy had to help me into bed.

The evening of the following day, we made our plans. Loy, Tommy and I would leave within a week or ten days for Miami. Others of the family who wished to come would stay behind temporarily to give notice to their employers, to terminate our rental agreement, and to wind up details. Then, they could follow whenever they were ready.

All agreed that my trip east had been successful. WQAM was a major radio outlet. I had lined up a good job this time. The pay was good and I'd be a newsman. Perhaps I'd even find a welcome for my commentaries on the news. The future seemed bright.

Ever practical, Edy brought us back to earth. "Where's the money coming from for the trip?"

"I don't know," I admitted. "But it's got to come somehow."

"Don't worry," Ruth said. "It's obviously the right thing to do. We'll get the money."

"How?" Edith asked. "You haven't any money. Bob hasn't any. I loaned my last twenty to help pay for the trip you've just had. I don't have any more. We have expenses here, too, remember."

"I've got to get it, Edy," I insisted.

"I'm not trying to oppose you, Bob. I agree. You certainly should go."

"Maybe I could borrow it."

"Not before you pay back what you owe. I need money, too, you know."

"You'll get it, Edy. You know that."

"Of course I know it. But it's going to take several months of preparation it seems to me. You can't possibly leave in two weeks."

I shook my head. "Something will open. It must. I arranged to have the job start by mid-October."

"Then you were a fool," Edy snapped. "Why don't you telephone and explain? Ask for a delay."

"I was just plain lucky to find an opening. They don't come up often. If I'm not there when I said I would, I'll simply go on a waiting list. I'm on a dozen of those around here and have been for six months."

Edy nodded. "I guess it's your problem, Bob."

Thus far my hunch had paid off. Was I to be stopped now? Edith was right. I could travel many miles on short rations and no sleep. I couldn't ask that of Loy, and certainly not of Tommy. At that moment, if memory serves, I had less than 25 cents remaining in my pocket.

The remainder of that day I did my best to figure a passage through this maze of poverty. I began to agree with Edy. I had been a fool. It was so characteristic of me. When I saw what the best position was I took it, never bothering to figure out how to get there. I had said the right things at WAQM. But it appeared that I had promised to deliver where the means to achieve delivery didn't exist.

Sometime within the next twenty-four hours, the telephone rang. My mother was on the line. After that memorable visit when Loy and I had journeyed to Minnesota, she and her new husband, Doctor Ed Cook, had moved to Southern California.

They had decided against San Francisco and, instead, had purchased a small house in Inglewood where we had visited on occasion. Mother had chosen that location in part because my sister, Lauris, and her family lived in Gardena not too far distant. Lauris and her husband, Frank, had six children and mother had made herself useful to Lauris, as a good grandmother should.

During 1950, in the midst of my campaign for Congress, Ed Cook, Mother's husband, had died. With some of her remaining assets, Mother had purchased a trailer home and parked it in the side yard of Lauris' home. She had been living there, taking her meals with my sister and her family.

But Lauris' children had grown and some of them were in the loud and mischievous stage. Mother wanted and appeared to need far greater peace and tranquility than her current location provided.

Mother's sister, Coral, lived in East Aurora, New York. Coral's second husband had also died, and the two elderly sisters had been in close communication by mail. Mother and Lauris had quarreled.

The spat was over the noise the children made.

Mother's voice on the telephone was pinched. She had been crying. "Robert," she said, "You must help me. I'm in terrible trouble."

"What is it?" I experienced a sense of guilt. I had been so busy trying to solve my problems that I had given little thought to any that she might have.

"I've got to get away from this place," Mother said.

"Why? I thought everything was fine."

"Well, it was. For a while." There was a pause. She was all choked up.

"Mother, what is it? Tell me."

"It's the children. I simply can't stand it anymore. They never give me a moment's peace. They are rude and loud and Lauris can't or won't control them. I've got to go someplace else."

"Golly, Mother. I don't know what I can do. I've just landed a job in Miami and Loy and I are going to be heading backs that way very soon. You know we don't own this house on Arapahoe. We only rent. I couldn't have your trailer here."

"I know that, son. I don't expect that. I've worked things out with Coral. I want to go live with her."

I experienced a small sense of relief. "Well, that doesn't seem like a had idea. If that's what you want, I suggest you go. What do you what me to do?"

"I want you to take me there."

"Take you there! What do you mean?"

"Well, I have a few things I don't want to part with. And I simply can't ship them. You have no idea of how helpless you become when you get to be my age. I want you to drive me back there in your car. I'll be glad to pay you for your services, you know. And you can load up the car with my things. It's not so much; it's just that I want them with me, and I want you with me, too. I couldn't stand a train trip. Is that too much for a mother to ask of her only son?"

"Of course not, but you see, I've got this job opening..." my voice trailed off. Perhaps this was the very avenue through which financial help would come

"I'll make it worth your while, son. I don't have a great deal of money but I'll pay you enough so you can take me back to East Aurora, and then return to California. "

The idea crystallized. "Mother, how long would it take you to get ready?"

"Not long at all, Robert. I'm ready to go right away. Any time. Whenever you can manage."

"This just might work out for both of us," I said. "I have to go to Miami. Would you pay enough so that after I left you in East Aurora, I would be able to drive down to Florida?"

"Certainly. It can't be any further from East Aurora to Miami than it would be from East Aurora back here." She was eager. The tears had gone.

"The trouble is, there won't be room in the car for your things," I said. "I'll be taking Loy and Tommy. Could we afford a small trailer hitched to the car, which would carry your things as well as some of ours? Could your budget stand that?"

"How much would it be?"

"I'll find out, but I'm sure it won't be a great deal. That's why I thought of it. Today you can rent a trailer, and then leave it at your destination. The cost is quite reasonable, I'm sure, but I'll find out exactly."

"Please do it right away," Robert. I simply can't stand it here. I've got to get away. At once!"

"If you'll bankroll the move," I said, "we're in business."

"Oh, Robert, I'm so thankful. You are wonderful to come to the help of your Mother this way."

My guilt returned. "I think it's the other way around. You're helping me. I'm afraid I've neglected you. I thought everything was swell with you at Lauris' and all."

"It's terrible. I can't stand it another minute."

"You'll have to give me time to make a few arrangements. But don't worry. Your wish to go east couldn't have come at a better time."

"Robert?"

"Yes."

"I'll give you $300. It's worth that to me. Can you manage with that?"

"I'm not sure, Mother. You're in no condition to do the slam-bang kind of driving I'm capable of alone. It might be a bit more. Let me do some figuring."

"All right, son. Call me back as soon as you can."

I broke the news to Loy and the others. With careful management the trip to the east could now be paid for. However, when I added up costs of overnight stops and meals, plus the trailer rental, $300 was on the scant side.

Mother was more eager than before. "I have a few thousand, Robert. It's all coming to you anyway, when I go. So you might as well have enough to make this trip."

"I don't want your money, Mother."

"I know you don't. But you're entitled to pay for doing me this service. What if it does cost $400? Or even more. There will still be plenty left for me to use as long as I'm around. Room and board with Coral won't be much at all."

And so the arrangements were made.

Ruth, Margie and Edy decided without much hesitation that they would continue as our nuclear family and follow us east as soon as possible. It might take two or three months to manage. Victoria would return to San Francisco. She subsisted entirely on government funds and could not leave California without losing her subsidy.

My oldest son was serving in Korea. I learned that David, my second son, had also decided to enlist in the Marines. Mama, Loy's mother, obtained a job managing a residence for girls located not far from First Church. Lorna had been married and she and her new husband were doing well.

I called on many of the friends I had made in the 14th District, letting them know that I was leaving for Florida.

At last we were ready to go.

We loaded the trailer with our own things, and got an early start the following morning. In Gardena, we added Mother's possessions to our own and got her into the rear seat with Tommy; Loy and I sat in front.

We hadn't gone far before I realized that Mother was not as well as I had presumed. She experienced a few serious memory lapses, and had difficulty in getting in and out of the car. She didn't complain. Whenever I looked around to see how she was fairing, she had a smile on her face.

The trip took longer than I had anticipated. The car broke down in Nebraska with a generator problem. While having it repaired, Mother experienced a stroke. We rushed her to the local hospital where she spent the night. She was released into our care the next morning. With admonitions to make things as easy for her as we could.

At a motel in Indiana, we got Mother into her room, taking a second room adjacent to hers to hers. She agreed to knock on the wall if she needed anything. When an excessive amount of time passed without a signal, I went into her room to find that she was in the shower and had forgotten how to turn off the water.

Loy and I got her dried off and into bed. She seemed so happy having us taking care of her. But she was becoming increasingly dependent.

In Pennsylvania, the trailer got a flat tire. The weather was cold and wet. Finally, I located a man at a rural garage who could supply us with a used tire that fit. Tommy got a big thrill out of that experience, and he has referred to it often. The strange things children remember! It certainly wasn't thrilling to me.

Then, as we began to approach our up state New York destination, Mother seemed to gain strength and better command of her mind and her limbs. However, she had a tendency to limp and was not in the best of condition when we at last reached Coral's home.

My mother's side of the family are all diminutive and it was a delight to see how bright and sharp Coral was, despite her stature being less than Mother's. Mother could stand under one of my arms but Coral WRS at least two inches closer to the floor. They fell into each other's arms and Mother rallied, filled with joy and confidence. It was like a homecoming.

I took my aunt aside, explaining the problems we had been through respecting Mother's health. She downgraded their importance and, indeed, the two sisters gave evidence of being mutually benefited by one another's company.

We spent a night in East Aurora, and after unloading Mother's possessions were again on our way.

Loy was filled with nostalgia as we neared Baltimore, but due to our extremely precarious finances, I ruled against a stopover to look up relatives. So we continued southward, taking the shortest route.

It seemed as though we had been born in the Chevy when at last we drove through Florida's Hollywood and descended toward North Miami. Then, without warning, the brake fluid drained away, leaving us with little ability to decelerate. It happened to be Sunday. I crept into filling station after filling station trying to obtain repairs.

It was hopeless.

The final few miles we drove at a snail's pace. Finally, we found a motel with a vacancy sign and had a place to spend the night.

There is an old saw to the effect that "the Lord looks after fools and children." The sentiment expressed appears vindicated insofar as I was concerned. I had returned to Miami on the date I had promised, and I had managed it acting both like a fool and a child.

Leaving Loy at the motel, I drove to the station, spent an hour getting re-acquainted, and promised to return for my first newscast later that day. To begin, the program director wanted me to work with Shaw on the six o'clock news until I was entirely familiar with procedures. This meant that I would have the entire day ahead of me until about 3:30 in the afternoon.

Loy had busied herself with apartment and house rental ads and, even though the Chevy was a lethal weapon without its brakes, we managed to limp around town and settle on a place of residence.

Thanks to Mother, I still had enough cash to make a payment of two week's rent in advance. Our new home was on the second floor in a brand new subdivision in North Miami. Neither Loy nor I liked the place. but it was clean and well within our budget.

The apartment we had found was partly furnished. With the few things from our trailer and with Tommy very much in evidence, we had completed our move, and were at home.

Chapter LXXVII

In 1951, Miami was a Paradise. Prio Socarras was the dictator of Cuba and the influx of Cuban refugees had not yet begun. Fulgencio Batista was the important strong man of Cuba, temporarily out of power. Tourists flocked to Miami Beach by the tens of thousands each winter. Loy and I learned rapidly that the people who lived in Miami on a year-round basis were among the kindest and most generous on earth. Most Americans had never heard of Fidel Castro.

As a newsman, I had to absorb as much of the local scene as I could. I digested the history and background of the people, the events, and the flora and the fauna that had made the place what it was.

My job was ideal. I began working with Shaw on the six o'clock news. Presently, I was trusted with the eleven o'clock news on my own. Within a matter of a few weeks, I was an integrated part of the news team, consisting of Shaw, another radioman, and myself.

Most of our broadcasts originated from the newsroom of the Miami Herald where a soundproof studio had been built for that purpose. The policy of the station, which I heartily endorsed, required each radioman to write his own copy. We were not among the "rip and read" boys who serviced the teletype machines of AP and UP and INS (the latter two had not yet merged). They went from telecopy to tell the world, without comprehending what they were talking about.

For our local news we were not only aided by the latest edition of the newspaper but—working in the city room—we also had advance information on some fast breaking stories. It was a fine layout. I've never seen a radio news operation that surpassed it.

Most of my working time was taken up with copy preparation. I could anticipate an hour's effort to prepare a fifteen-minute broadcast. I was never over-worked. I was well paid. And I had plenty of time to do other things as well. The big news show was at six o'clock. There we had a full hour and the entire news team, sometimes augmented by a Herald sports reporter, or some other man from the Herald. This produced total coverage.

Tommy had reached pre-school age and we managed to get him

into a kindergarten school in North Miami. Loy got a part-time job as a hostess in the Burden Department Store tearoom and, between us, we brought in a good income.

Meanwhile, we kept in touch with the second part of the family, still winding up affairs in Los Angeles. This task took more time than I had anticipated. However, it was done supremely well. Late in November, the girls arrived having driven across the country in Edy's car.

I had anticipated their coming and rented an apartment across the hall from ours in the same building. However, after only a few days, it was clear to all of us that this arrangement was not satisfactory.

One of the major problems had to do with distance. Commuting into town took too much time. And we learned that jobs for women with the skills and specialties Ruth, Edith and Margie possessed weren't readily available in Miami.

Ruth was hired almost at once as a secretary. However, Edith found nothing to her liking and—good sport that she was—she took a job as a waitress in a Howard Johnson restaurant. Margie had even more of a problem, although she finally won a splendid position as a therapist and became much in demand.

Meanwhile, Loy found a better post at an auction gallery. Finally, Edith obtained a bookkeeping position, so it all worked out.

Right after Thanksgiving, we went house hunting, seeking a large place such as we had enjoyed in San Francisco, Beverly Hills, and Los Angeles. Good fortune accompanied our efforts and we were able to rent a partially furnished house originally built by the Tiffanys, we were told. It was on a corner of Brickell Avenue, a few blocks south of the canal and only a block distant from the bay.

This property would classify as a small mansion. It had five bedrooms, a sleeping porch and a separate structure in the rear containing two separate apartments and a garage. We managed to rent the apartments to tourists each winter, which rental boosted our income.

The main building had marble floors and a marble stairway to the second floor. The place was built like a fortress, including a reinforced wall that separated the sidewalk from the front yard.

The reason for the wall soon became apparent. The property was situated at a corner where Brickell Avenue made a thirty-degree turn to the left, if you were heading into town. Some two miles south of our location was the causeway that would take motorists across the bay to Key Biscayne. Brickell Avenue was a main thoroughfare at this point.

Many a driver, heading toward Miami late a night, would fail to notice that angle in the avenue until he was at the intersection. Then, with squealing brakes he'd negotiate the turn. Sometimes negotiations would break down. In that case, there would be a smash up against our wall, a lamp pole or one of the inevitable palm trees. Without the wall, those same vehicles might have come up on our porch or even have invaded our living room.

Having time on my hands between broadcasts, I set out to get acquainted. Thanks to my political experience, I knew how to do it. When you want to meet a businessman, a man of the professions, a man of affairs, it's usually the easiest thing in the world. You call on him.

I began by going to the Chamber of Commerce where I immediately met a young employee who was as concerned about the inroads against the business community as I was. He put me in touch with several important people who shared our mutual concern.

There was one drawback to the thinking of the man at the Chamber, which kept me at arms' length. In his opinion, the "Communist Conspiracy" was nothing more than a conspiracy by the "Zionist Jews." As he saw it, Karl Marx was a Jew and just about every evil in the world could be traced to Jews.

Not "all the Jews," mind you. Just the "Zionist" Jews. A book had recently been published entitled "Iron Curtain Over America." He loaned me his copy and it was easy to see how he had arrived at his conclusions. I had run into this same type of thinking during my campaign in Los Angeles. There I had met a man named Gerald L.K. Smith and another named Wesley Swift. Both were dedicated "anti-Semites." Indeed, Swift had taken a brief interest in my campaign and promised to get me "tons of money" if I would come out publicly against the Jews.

Through him I met a very wealthy woman who, Swift informed me, would drop a bundle in my lap if I'd line up on his side. Swift had furnished me with some literature, including copies of a lurid hate sheet called "Spotlight" put out by someone named McGinley.

I had discussed this whole matter with family members and others. I had already arrived at the conclusion that these people who hated Jews, or "Zionist" Jews, were way off base. While it may have been true that the Russian revolution had closed churches in the Soviet Union, I didn't detect the growth of Synagogues there. The Russian revolution had spawned Atheists rather than anti-Christians per se. Further, I had learned there were plenty of Atheists who despised Communism.

Thus, the attempt to get me to believe that the world was divided between Christians and Communists (the latter directed by Zionist Jews) had already earned my distrust and rejection. I told Wesley Swift that I wanted nothing to do with him or with money from sources he could control.

When the young fellow at the Chamber began to recite the same litany, I gave him short shrift. I read his book, and while I couldn't dispute it's alleged "documentation," I told him it "had to be wrong." I simply rejected out of hand any attempt to make it Jews the root of the problem.

I recall a part of the conversation. "Bob," he said, "If you check into it you'll find that Jews dominate the Communist Party in this country and in most others."

"By the same token," I told him, "Jews are also into everything else including the anti-Communist movement. I wonder if you aren't simply envious of the drive and intensity that many Jews seem to have. I'm not surprised to see them in Communist circles. And I'm not surprised to see them in business, the professions and the arts. While a lot of us 'so-called Christians' twiddle our thumbs, they go out and forge to the top in plenty of areas."

"Don't tell me you're a Jew lover," he said. "Don't you know how ugly and disagreeable Jews can be?"

I nodded. "Sure, I've met some ugly and disagreeable Jews," I admitted. "And I've met some ugly and disagreeable Christians. And I'll tell you something more. I think the effort to stir up hatred against a person because he's a Jew or a Christian, is about as ugly as ugly gets. You're off base on this one."

"But what about the facts?"

"Just what *are* the facts?"

"I mean the ones in the book."

"Yeah. The book is devastating. If true. Frankly, I don't believe it."

"But it's all documented!"

"Even if it's true it still doesn't make your case. I admit there are probably some evil Jews. But evil isn't limited to Jews. There are fine people and dreadful people in every category you can name."

I'm happy to report that this gentleman was the only man I met at the Chamber who expressed sentiments of this sort. And it may be instructive that he didn't remain in that position long. A few weeks later, I learned that he had departed Miami.

Despite this unpleasant interlude, the man had done me good service. I met three men who were to become in instrumental in what followed. The three were Bob Overholzer, owner of a credit company, John Anderson, a prominent attorney, and Roy Page, an elderly man of means, retired. The three began to introduce me about town and through them I became acquainted with a great many splendid people.

Presently, I was on good terms with the Babcock. Construction Company. The owner hired me to write and present a fifteen minute commentary using the same format I had employed back in Los Angeles in my "Voice of Freedom" broadcasts. I called the new show: "Past is Prologue."

Since the program was sponsored, I had no difficulty 1n obtaining airtime. The station manager was delighted. I had visibly increased his business. And I was well paid for this effort.

Then, through Overholzer, who seemed to know everyone, I met a man named Larry Brooks who ran a collection agency. I sold him on a second 15-minute commentary to be offered once each week and thus had a second independent sponsor.

With these added financial gains, I cleaned up almost all of the debts left over from my misadventure in San Francisco.

Before I left Miami, I had paid off most of everything I had owed, except some funds still due Ma Gray. It took another four years before I was able to wipe that one off the books.

Ever since my brush with creditors during the Falcon Lair days, I had avoided using a bank. I had learned, to my sorrow, that the government had access to anything they wanted in any bank. Privacy in banking was a privilege reserved for the Swiss. In 1948, among other creditors, was the Federal Government. My Chapter 13 procedure did nothing to write off delinquent taxes. The Feds are always the last to let anyone off the hook.

However, I had also learned that the Feds (at least at the time of which I write) were among the least innovative. They apparently relied upon information they could obtain from banks. Since I had no bank account of any kind, the Feds had apparently lost track of me.

As my earnings improved and I began retiring my debts, everything was handled on a cash basis. I saved my money in cash, put it into an envelope, and attached it to the underside of a dresser drawer with Scotch tape. I told no one at all of this procedure.

What the girls didn't know, no one could get them to tell. I acted like a felon with my own earnings. And I must confess that I felt like a felon because of the secrecy. I did owe the money, even though I was paying it back as fast as possible.

While we lived at the Brickell Street address, someone ratted on me and I was visited by an agent of the FBI, and then by the IRS investigator. The latter and I went around for a few bouts because I refused to tell him where I banked. I am sure he thought some banking official was in cahoots. I was finally able to get the IRS to compromise the sum still owing from my 1948 income tax. They excused interest and penalties and I paid the principle sum.

But I had grown very wary of what the government could and would do to a private citizen who, in fact, was doing the best he knew how. I accepted this attitude as a problem arising from the "Communist influence" with which the Federal Government was saturated.

I consulted with my trio of new friends. With my radio connection I was already engaged in telling the story of free enterprise as best I could. But much more needed to be done. What had to happen, as I saw it then, was a reformation within the government. We had to check the voting records of members of Congress and weed out the ones who tended to follow the Socialist line.

Suppose we started an organization in the Miami area for persons dedicated to free enterprise? Could we not, by such a process, hope to endorse "good" people for government and actively oppose the "bad" people?

The idea was warmly received. I contacted Mr. James Fifield of First Church back in Los Angeles. In LA, he had sponsored of "Freedom-Clubs" that he helped to organize in many cities of the U.S.

I wrote for information, telling him that I believed it possible to start a Freedom Club in Miami. He provided literature and general procedural suggestions. With this material as a guide, a Freedom Club was put together. We began attracting a number of prominent people to our roster. Roy Page had access to some very important individuals. Through him I met Vining Davis, chairman of the board of ALCOA. Through other friends of Roy's, I met such personalities as General Mark Clark and General James Van Fleet. Davis lived in Coral Gables and was already a very old man. The generals came as honored visitors. Van Fleet, because I invited him as a speaker for one of our Club meetings, Mark Clark because of other persons he knew. But I had nothing more than a "hi there" opportunity to become acquainted, particularly in the case of Van Fleet. I had a number of meetings with him, after learning that he favored private enterprise. I did my best to convince him that he should run for President.

There was no question in my mind that Van Fleet favored the idea. But he had already learned that Eisenhower was thinking of running in 1952 and he was reluctant to throw his hat into a ring that might be dominated by a higher piece of brass.

The format of the Freedom Club was established. We would meet once each month for a gala banquet to listen to someone of national prominence who we would bring to Miami for the occasion. Louis Budenz, a re-canted Communist bigwig, came at my invitation for one such meeting.

By far the most interesting speaker we ever attracted to one of these affairs was Tom Gaskins. No one had ever heard of him until I received a letter from him as a result of one of my commentaries.

Gaskins was a Florida "cracker." He wrote me about a run-in he'd had with the Department of Labor. Gaskins explained that he was a "squatter" who lived at the edge of one of Florida's great swamps near Palmdale. There, in a shack he had constructed from packing crates and native materials, he and his wife had raised a family and enjoyed a precarious living by selling cypress knees.

The cypress knee, he explained, was a strange growth that emerged from cypress tree roots, often many feet removed from the trunk of the tree they supported. The knee was not a new tree nor a burl. It was not a disease. It was a peculiarity of cypress trees and he offered himself as the world's greatest authority on them, which, in fact, he was.

Stripped of bark and cured by sunlight, the knee—often of artistic and grotesque shape—took on an amber glossy sheen. The knees were conversation pieces that he sold his "production" to wayfarers who happened to stop at his remote location. Aside from these occasional sales, he and his family survived on what they could grow, find, or hunt down in the swamp.

It seems that a vagrant had wandered by one day and Tom had made a deal with the man. If he would stick around and help Tom with his harvest of knees, he would be fed and given an occasional dollar when available.

The man was delighted and the two had developed a good working relationship. For an unschooled son of the swamp, Tom was astonishingly facile with the English language. He was outraged by the government's welfare program. Tom had to pay taxes whenever he bought something and he never asked anything from the government, except to be let alone. The land he occupied was submarginal and no one wanted it. He was happy and productive. He had no ambition to be a wheeler, a dealer, a mover, or a shaker. He was living proof of the fact that material things do not make for happiness. Tom was a happy man, and his family was proud.

Somehow the Labor Department learned (probably because Tom kept writing letters to the Tampa Tribune attacking welfare) that he had someone working for him. So one day, the Labor Department sent two agents to investigate the wage scale he was offering and to subpoena his employment records.

It was this event about which he had written to me. Intrigued by his account, I put it on the air. I invited Tom to come to our Freedom Club and to tell his story to those who attended the banquet.

We rented the ballroom of one of the leading hotels. Our club had already made news by bringing in some national celebrities and more than 300 people turned out for this affair.

Tom arrived in town, took one look at the size of the banquet hall, and nearly turned tail to run. He had been in Tampa only once and Miami was a much larger city. Tom was overawed. I had great difficulty in persuading him to make the talk as he had agreed.

I convinced him that the audience was on his side; they were real people and not just a bunch of rich phonies; all he had to do was to recite in simple words the run-in he'd had with the Labor Department. Tom was scared to death.

Loy and I sat on the dais along with the President of the club and a number of local luminaries, including a State Senator and some prominent business people. At my immediate left sat the production manager of my principal competition, the CBS outlet. Tom was there, quaking with anxiety and every few minutes requiring my intercession to keep him from bolting for the door.

The banquet was a glowing affair. The lights were bright, the linens clean, the silver and glassware sparkled. The men wore ties and the ladies were resplendent in formal or semi-formal attire. There were several courses and Tom's reaction to what was commonplace to most have already made him the center of all attention at the head table.

Finally, after a few announcements concerning future meetings, I introduced the speaker of the evening.

He arose, trembling visibly. I smiled my encouragement and Tom began. He'd had no speaking experience of any kind. But he was real and he was honest. With both naivete and forthrightness, he told his story. After sketching his background and bringing the audience up to the first visit by the Labor Department, he had us in the palm of his hand. He paused at this juncture, with timing that would have been applauded by Jack Benny, and capped his remarks with: "So I wrote a letter to the Tampa Tribune."

There was an appreciative chuckle. Tom was startled. He got a further grip on himself and told how the two men had re-visited him. Another pause. "So I wrote a letter to the Tampa Tribune."

The dilemma of the investigative agents began to be appreciated. Tom kept no records at all! He couldn't turn over non-existent documents. But he could and did, "Write a letter to the Tampa Tribune."

By this time the audience was with him so totally that they were breathing in cadence. The auditorium was completely hushed except for Tom's voice and those telling pauses, followed by, "So I wrote another letter to the Tampa Tribune."

The final episode took place when the agent returned and agreed to cancel the investigation if only Tom would stop "writing letters to the Tampa Tribune."

It was superb. The CBS rep sitting next to me, a man of some corpulence, rocked in his chair with mirth to such an extent that—but for my restraining arm at the critical instant—he and his chair would have toppled off behind the dais.

The place roared with approval. Tom got a standing ovation and showed by his expression that he couldn't understand it at all. He had provided us with evidence that anyone who was honest and who would communicate the truth had a chance to win by his own towering integrity.

In terror, Tom whispered to me. "Why are they laughing? Are they mad at me?"

"They love you, Tom," I whispered back "You've given us a great speech—a great experience."

Tom shook his head, still baffled.

That meeting stands out in my mind as one of the great moments in a lifetime of experiences including many speeches and banquets.

Gasping for breath, the CBS man shook my hand.

"What an experience," he said. "Gaskins is a 'natural.'"

That he is.

Chapter LXXVIII

The Republican Party of Florida in 1952 was anemic, discouraged, and impotent. I felt no loyalty to the organization as such. However, the protestations and platform gave vocal support to the free enterprise system (more freedom, less government) and I was inevitably drawn in that direction.

Those who wished to enlarge the state and make it more of a participant in private affairs came from the Democratic Party as a rule. However, since my slight acquaintance with economic principles, as spelled out by Watts, Johnson, Cournelle and others from Spiritual Mobilization (including Ruth, who brought many of the ideas home for discussion) I was beginning to detect a remarkable similarity between the two parties. If anything, both the Deems and the GOPS behaved much the same way. The Democrats openly favored more government, and proceeded to enlarge it. The Republicans openly opposed more government, but in their behavior did much the same as the Democrats. Ergo, both parties enlarged the government, one candidly and openly, the other clandestinely and protesting all the way.

Since the Republicans were out of power they were the natural source of opposition. It seemed to me that I could assist in creating an effective two-party system in the south and, thus, enlarge the voice of protest. Such action could bring pressures to bear against the Socialist phalanx squeezing in on the economy.

I now understood what Party politics is about. In actual fact, Party members by themselves can't elect anyone. The Party serves as a catalyst bringing together a point of view deemed desirable. Then it promises to deliver programs that will crystallize the point of view into law. Thus, each Party sets itself up to champion "the desirable" "the good," or "the generous. " Any number of Parties can play the game.

My growing coterie of friends and well wishers could hardly achieve much in the way of political influence by having one Freedom Club meeting per month. We needed another organization that would convene at least once a week. We wanted numbers, high visibility, and a constant flow of words in favor or our position.

The informal committee of three helped to put together a meeting where we discussed the idea. One young attorney in attendance was named Harvey Klein. He suggested that a breakfast meeting was probably best since so many had evening appointments, but nearly everyone was or could be free at breakfast.

I thought that a splendid idea and went to work on it. We put together a rather remarkable format that proved nearly as popular as our larger and more prestigious Freedom Club banquets.

Each of our Breakfast Club meetings featured a political candidate or office holder as the main speaker. The purpose of the club was to put our guest on notice. Our organization was politically outspoken and would favor those who put restraints on government. One of our active members was a socially prominent woman who obtained the use of the Women's Club building for most of our meetings. This setting gave us some of the political clout we wanted.

We constructed a giant high chair, complete with hinged tray that looped over the occupant's head and hung to the rear when not in use. During the Breakfast Club preliminaries, we would put our speaker in this high chair, the seat of which was a good six feet above the floor. With the tray swung over for use, a large plate of scrambled eggs would be placed before him. One of our officers, often Bob Overholzer, who loved the task, would then ask the candidate to repeat an oath of fealty to the principles of free enterprise. The bib would be fastened under his chin, one hand thrust into the scrambled eggs, the other hand raised in solemn oath. Phrase by phrase the speaker was asked to repeat the oath. It was hilarious. The speaker had to be a good sport to put up with it and his willingness to thus be demeaned went a long way toward instilling at least a temporary humility.

In short, we let our guests understand that party affiliation meant little to us. We wanted performance from both Parties and from anyone we might favor. We wanted an end to government growth, a reduction in taxes, and a cancellation of government's roll as Big Daddy Charity.

While I was making a name for myself in this fashion, Loy was hired to sing at Bayfront Park at least once a week for open-air concerts that were conducted there.

By this time, the actions of the Miami Breakfast Club and the Miami Freedom Club had brought us to the attention of the GOP at national headquarters. I began to hope that we could and would effect the election results.

In Chicago, during July, the Republicans dumped Bob Taft, and chose General Eisenhower. I was dismayed by this turn of events. I was sure that Eisenhower had little comprehension of free enterprise and would simply be a "yes" man for various pressure groups. However, I was heartened to learn that Richard Nixon had been selected as Ike's running mate.

I let all my friends know that I was personally acquainted with Nixon and that he was a strong anticommunist and a stout defender of the free enterprise system. My very brief association with the Nixon senatorial campaign hardly qualified me as Nixon's "friend." However, I had become a "name-dropper" because in politics, dropping names picks up votes.

The Democrats had their convention in August and chose Adlai Stevenson with John Sparkman as his vice-presidential hopeful. Again, I felt encouraged. Sparkman had been to Miami, and I had met him. This flimsy contact had convinced me that Sparkman would listen to reason.

Stevenson was an unknown quantity, far too intellectual and erudite for the common man.

I was sure that if Eisenhower would campaign in Miami, his appearance would strengthen our efforts. In process, it would help to put muscles into the two-party effort south of the 'Mason-Dixon' line.

To assist in making this event a reality I began writing letters to Nixon and to Republican Party Headquarters, urging a vote seeking into Dade County. Whether my letters carried any weight I'll never know, but it happened that just such an excursion did take place.

As things worked out, I was on duty at WQAM and couldn't manage to get away for Ike's speech at Bayfront Park. Loy and others of our family were there. Loy was introduced to Ike and shook hands with him. She reported afterward that the man was a "light weight," with a poor handshake. He seemed to agree with everyone who spoke to him regardless of what was said. She was disappointed.

Meanwhile, I phoned Nixon's headquarters on Key Biscayne and arranged for a press conference that he granted later that night after my 11:00 o'clock newscast.

I notified the Herald and media newsmen that they should be

present. A temporary headquarters had been established in some tents pitched on the beach of Key Biscayne. As quickly as I was off the air, I streaked for this rendezvous hoping to show Nixon that the GOP in South Florida could at least get a good and favorable press.

Some ten or twelve reporters were present by the time I arrived, but Nixon was in one of the tents and wouldn't emerge until we were all present.

I informed his liason man that I was anxious to shake hands with him again, reminding that I had served in his senatorial campaign in California.

The liaison man took this information into one of the tents. Presently Nixon emerged and came plodding across the sands. I was standing in front of the other reporters. Presumably they held back hoping to get pictures of Nixon and me shaking hands, possibly embracing, whatever GOP cronies did after a long separation.

Nixon halted some fifteen feet away. He peered at me closely. I was grinning from ear to ear, bursting with eagerness. The light wasn't too good, even though there was a moon and a lovely, clear sky. Nixon and I had never known each other well, but surely he would accept me. Then, after a few brief remarks, we'd be in gear. I had been singing his praises to all and sundry. No one was certain about Ike, but Nixon was "our man."

Instead of a friendly greeting, I felt a wave of hostility. Nixon turned to his aide and whispered something. Then he abruptly turned about face and went back to his tent. There was no press conference.

I was crushed. Worse, I was now jeered by my peers. I had undoubtedly overstated the case. But when is politics void of hyperbole? Nixon could have gained advantage at that moment. Instead, he threw away a proffered hand of friendship, doing it with apparent anger and disgust.

Despite my disappointments in political affairs and the affront to me personally, my reputation in South Florida was apparently undimmed. So, I was not surprised when I was approached by a businessman from Fort Lauderdale. The Fort Lauderdale Daily News, owned and operated by the Gore family, was constructing a television station. Television would be the coming rage. Would I be interested in a move to Fort Lauderdale to become the news director of WFTL-TV?

What would I be worth to them? They offered a wage 25% higher than my present earnings from all sources. Plus an opportunity to earn more when special shows were needed. And I would have it all my own way and establish news broadcast policy.

This was a most tempting opportunity. Still, I had finally put the pieces together in Miami and was beginning to wield some influence. One of the most difficult chores a person performs is to accurately evaluate his own assets. Most of us think more highly of ourselves than the facts warrant. At other times, I was guilty of excessive negativity concerning what I had and what I had done.

In this case, I decided that due to the nearness of Fort Lauderdale I could take the job there, boost my income, and have a larger impact on more people through television than radio. Additionally, I would be able to commute to Miami. So, I reasoned that I could have my cake and eat it too.

The final factor was the personality and character of the man who had been hired to manage WFTL-TV—a gentleman named Nick Quirts. I've often wondered what I might have done had it not been for Nick. Had I stayed in Miami, what might have eventuated? No one can ever know, of course, We cannot re-write history. However, in moving away from Miami, I gave up far more than I had anticipated.

I was wrong about commuting. When I moved out of Miami, the two organizations I had put together languished. They became increasingly less active and less important. In a year or two they were gone.

Of even deeper consequence was the loss of my great friends. I do not mean to imply that the folks of Miami turned against me. They didn't. But friendship is like a garden that needs constant attention. If a friend is worthwhile, he must be cultivated and loved. This requires frequent contact. From a distance of thirty miles, such daily contact didn't occur. I have often keenly felt the loss.

But Nick made the sale. He came to Miami, took me out to dinner, and laid out the proposition. It turned out that Nick was a free enterprise supporter without equivocation. They are rare and he and I were buddies from the beginning. In my discussion with Nick, I obtained affirmative responses to all my questions. As a department head of the new station I would have things my own way.

I had been before the cameras only briefly in Los Angeles, my largest exposure occurring during the debate with the Retail Clerks. How could Nick be sure I was the man for the anchor, the policy, and the whole kettle of fish, when I hadn't even had an audition?

No problem. I was the man he wanted. He had discussed the question with others. He needed me. I could write my own ticket. The offer was too flattering to turn down.

Then, as Loy and I took off house hunting in Fort Lauderdale so we could make the move. Another man appeared on the Miami scene. His name was Jim Fradkin and he worked for Merwin K. Hart in New York City. It seems my reputation had reached Gotham and Hart was interested in obtaining me as a PR man and a radio "expert" in the big City.

Since I had just accepted a new post, I was in a position of great independence. I explained to Fradkin that I thought it better to be a big frog in a small pond than a tadpole in the ocean. I would stay in Florida.

My independence didn't dim Fradkin's ardor for my services. He persisted in asking what it would take to get me to New York. I had heard of Merwin Hart. He was one of the few conservative voices that had consistently supported Constitutional government, human liberty and the free enterprise system. But I didn't want to go so I put it this way:

"Jim, it's very flattering to have you express interest. Naturally. But hiring me isn't going to be easy because I have what I want down here. However, if you persist, bear in mind, you wouldn't just be getting me. I travel with my staff. I have three women who work with me, plus Mrs. LeFevre and our small son. So, you'd have to hire four of us, me and my staff. That's four salaries, not one. And I'd need my own suite of offices and the latitude to make myself effective. That's a pretty big package. Are you sure Merwin would consider it?"

I anticipated Fradkin's objections. He would say that I was unreasonable and I would agree and tell him to forget it. Instead, he licked his lips, explained that he was a fundraiser for Merwin, and that he'd be in touch with me later on. I hadn't made myself less desirable quite the reverse. He was sure, now that he knew my demands, that Merwin would be even more eager to have me than he had been before.

I told him he was dreaming and thanked him for lunch.

Loy and I found a furnished house for rent in Fort Lauderdale and as quickly as it could be arranged, the move was effected. We had Tommy enrolled in the Miami Military Academy, a private school. This was situated at the northern outskirts of Miami and since it was a boarding school, he could stay there getting good schooling while we concentrated on the television industry.

Thus, shortly after accepting the post of news director, all of us left the Brickell property, and took residence in another large domicile more convenient to the television studio. It wasn't as grand as the Tiffany place but it was satisfactory.

Kirsta was amenable to almost everything I suggested. Loy wanted to become familiar with television, and she was immediately given a thirty-minute slot that she called: "Busy Fingers."

Loy has always had a fine sense of color and form in addition to being something of a musical genius. She probably could have been a professional interior decorator. this program got her a good audience and eager participation by various artists and craftsmen who did things with their hands.

I am a person who is fascinated both with people and ideas. I am not a technician. Thus, it wasn't until after we had made our move and were ensconced at WFTL-TV that I learned the significance of being U-HF instead of V-HF. The H stands for high frequency. Most of the television sets sold up to that time were designed to receive VHF programming only. The V stands for very. Very High Frequency.

WFTL-TV was unable to obtain a VHF license and had to settle of U (ultra) HF. So, to my dismay, I learned that instead of competing with other TV stations on a head-to-head basis, our signal was lost to the majority of set owners.

It was Nick's contention that the UHF bands would quickly become as commonplace as VHF. And it was true that the newer sets had extended capacity. Also, converters could be obtained so that sets not so endowed originally, could finally pick up UHF signals.

But Nick was mistaken in his judgment. Although today UHF is commonplace, the entire band above 14 or 15 is still outside normal viewing by vast numbers of TV viewers.

I began with two daily newscasts and one cameraman, called "Lucky." To fill up our broadcast day and to carry out my deepest wishes, I was also given the final slot in the broadcast day, which in our case was 10:00 p.m. This was my time for commentary on the day's news. It would run as long as I cared to stay on the air. When I finished, we signed off until the following day. Usually, I managed an hour.

I found that TV producers made little attempt to operate with precision when it came to time. Starting a program a bit early or a bit late didn't seem to bother anyone.

It bothered me. So I began demanding a discipline from my fellow broadcasters. I am happy to say that this insistence on punctuality brought a number of improvements.

My commentary was my pride and joy. Even if we had few listeners, I gave it all I had. The program was sponsored. Because we were neophytes and hadn't yet developed all of today's techniques, we made many errors. To open the program the camera focused on me while an announcer read the commercial. The commercial ran for 60 seconds. So I had to sit, looking at the camera or staring off into space (or both) for a full minute! Have you any idea how boring that can be?

Try it sometime. Time yourself. Get a stopwatch and stare into a mirror for a full minute. Before half the time has elapsed you will be hoping never to see that face again. A person's admiration of his own face will last only a few seconds. After that...ugh!

I experimented with ways to avoid that deadly interlude by providing movement. Aha, why not do what newsmen do? I would have a typewriter at my desk. As the camera blinked its red eyes I would take a piece of paper, put it into the machine and begin to type.

I tried that. It takes less than three seconds to get the paper in place and begin working the keys. Want to know what is more boring than looking at a staring face for 60 seconds? It's looking at a staring face that is staring at a typewriter making clacking noises for 57 seconds.

What else could I do? I tried to add a dimension by starting to type, pausing, picking up the dictionary and looking up a word, then resuming the finger exercise.

The first thing I learned was that if I took too much time seeking a word I looked like a fool. So I had to grab the tome, turn pages for three seconds, find the place in one second, and then hit the keys again. Staring time has been reduced from 57 seconds to 53 seconds. Worse. The audience always wanted to know what word had given me the problem. It's called "detrimental empathy." You've hooked them, but to no purpose. It's a distraction.

I don't know what gave me the idea but I finally went to a drug store and bought a pipe and some tobacco. As the camera came on, I sat in an easy chair with what I hoped was a thoughtful expression. After a few seconds I reached for my pipe, took up some tobacco and filled the bowl. The camera dollied in for a close-up. Don't try to explain it. Putting tobacco into a pipe is fascinating.

Better yet, it takes time. Lots of time. Then, with the bowl stuffed, I'd reach for a match. The match would flare. I'd hold it over the bowl, puff a few times until rewarded by a cloud of vapor.

Do you know how long that takes? It takes a full minute and it grabs everyone's attention. Perhaps it's the fire, perhaps the smoke, perhaps the reflective expression. Whatever it is, this stage business I devised proved to be just right.

With a cloud of smoke still wreathing my head I'd make my opening remarks. I'd lay down the pipe and never use it again until the next day's broadcast.

Because of this, I developed the habit of using the pipe whenever I needed a bit of time to reach a decision. So, I'd take the pipe to meetings and, if a question were asked for which I had no ready answer, I'd go for the pipe and the stage business.

If a person stalls and won't answer at once, many lost respect for him. But if the staler goes for his pipe, everyone seems to gain respect, presuming that profundity will somehow emerge. They wait eagerly, yet patiently, for the drama to run its course. What a marvelous bit of camouflage it is.

Actually, tobacco is filthy. Pipe tobacco usually burns the lips and tongue. It's a constant nuisance and is probably a substitute for thumb sucking. But who was I to argue with results?

Chapter LXXIX

After working at WFTL-TV for about a month, Nick Kirsta called me into his office. The *Fort Lauderdale Daily News*, the Gore enterprise owning the station, wanted to conduct a drive for new subscriptions. They were willing to sponsor the six o'clock news. But they wanted a format that would really grip attention and get results. Could I devise something?

I assured Nick that I had a format in mind, but it would be costly. We had only one camera crew. It consisted of "Lucky" who was required to take pictures, record the sound, and then bring the film in for development. This was before videotape had been devised and the time involved in shooting, developing, editing and cueing into a newscast presented a major obstacle. I had already complained, suggesting that a minimum requirement would be three camera teams, each of which needed at least two persons, preferably three.

Our handicap can be glimpsed by anyone knowledgeable in the field, when I report that "Lucky" also did the developing and editing of the film he shot. Thus, if we had one film clip per newscast, we thought we had scored. Aside from that single piece of sound on film, the viewers had the thrill of watching the face of the newscaster as he read copy. He winked, made faces, and tried to be worthy of attention.

With the "state of the art" as it then existed, Nick didn't want to put money into equipment that was undergoing development so rapidly it became obsolete every three months or so. So I got a thumbs down on suggestions along that line. Instead, Nick wanted me to devise a format that would be gripping, but minimize the use of film.

I studied newscasts from major television studios and learned that their programs weren't much better than ours although they were spending from five to eight times more per program.

Everyone seemed eager to maximize the use of film. But even when the latest equipment was available, along with ample manpower, the film clips used were already history rather than news by the time they were shown. Newspapers were faster than TV. But the really effective news media was (and in my judgment still is) radio.

Since my new format was going to use film sparingly, the logical way to go was to use the visual effect of a newspaper city room, combining it with the immediacy of radio.

I designed a set that portrayed the city room of a daily newspaper. I brought two teletype machines (functional) onto the set so the audience could actually watch the machines work, see someone service them, tear off the copy and bring it to the desk where it would be read.

I placed myself at the head of that desk as editor-in-chief. Then, I hired reporters from the paper to handle all the positions. One presented international news, a second handled national stories, a third, sports, and a fascinating man who also worked for the *Daily News*, named Orville Revelle, covered the local scene.

We refrained from the kind of set so common today, in which participants become panelists. Instead, two men on either side flanked me at the long table. We faced each other as we would in a newsroom. Orville and the sports caster prepared their own copy in advance. The other two depended on the teletype printers.

Thirty minutes prior to show time, we'd assemble our first batch of copy and have stories fairly well distributed before the cameras came on. I did obtain a full complement of studio cameras (three), so that we could move from reporter to reporter with ease and vary our picture with close-ups, shots of the teleprinters, or whatever seemed vital.

Each reporter had his own microphone but was told to ignore the cameras altogether. Our job was to get out the news. The director would handle everything as the news developed.

Next, I insisted on informality. If a story broke which surprised us, reporters were to make whatever comments they cared to make. Thus, we'd have an on-going dialogue conducted by professional newsmen, who had had years of experience and a background of information no "rip and read" man could be expected to provide.

I hired Ruth as my assistant. She serviced the machines during the program, tore off the stories, and brought them to me. I'd assign them and she'd hand them around. Sometimes, I'd offer the lead myself, and then hand the rest of the yarn to the appropriate reporter.

We obtained immediacy. Today, most television newscasts are virtually choreographed in advance. Indeed, long before news time, anchormen come on touting the stories they are going to present. For example, we have a story of a murder, a fire, a policeman's ball, and an interview with a celebrity. Pictures at six.

When we went on the air, we weren't sure what stories would be used or what would happen as we progressed. This is immediacy. The hype used today virtually destroys it. Our presentation was *news*.

We obtained immediacy in another way. I asked for—and got—*carte blanche* on the use of the telephone. Thus, when a story broke on the wire, I would ask Ruth to get the leading figure in the story on the phone. I could telephone anywhere in the world for the latest information, or to develop an angle not yet appearing in the copy,

Due to FCC rules, we were responsible for what went on the air and there were a number of words that were taboo. Since we had no way of knowing what someone might say on the phone, we piped the phone conversation through a tape recorder, transcribing both my questions and the answers. This obtained with a three-second delay. Thus, on the phone my lips would go "out of sync" and we would advise the audience of the reason. It was a useful device. On occasion we kept curses off the air.

When possible, as when we had advance warning, we'd try to get a picture of the party I was calling and put that on camera, using a divided screen.

Reporters with me were urged to feed questions to me that I might not think of. Spontaneity was the result.

We called the show, "The World Today." It was a winner from the first. Dealers selling TV sets in Fort Lauderdale reported a rush of business from those seeking to buy ultra-high adapters or trading in old sets for the newer models already equipped for UHF.

Frankly, the show was so exciting, that none of us remembered we were on the air once the program opened. It was almost as though we were making up the front page of a daily and agreeing among ourselves what should be covered and how much space should be given.

In the first month of our operation, our program scored six news "beats." These included one each in New York, Los Angeles, Wisconsin (Senator Joe McCarthy), Havana, Cuba (the ousting of Prio and the rise to complete power by Fulgencio Batista) and an unusual angle on the assassination of Prime Minister Mossadegh. A nephew of the victim, who happened to be in Fort Lauderdale, walked into the studio and made it possible to develop background on the killing that no one else had.

Believe me, I was proud of this show. Despite our poor position channel-wise, we sold subscriptions for the *Daily News* until the paper begged us to lay off. They were expanding more rapidly than their plant could handle and they had to take time out to enlarge press capacity.

My reputation as a public speaker continued without abatement. I made myself available in Miami, Fort Lauderdale and all points in between. Thus, when I wasn't on the air or preparing a program, I was rushing somewhere in connection with a talk before this or that organization.

One day the Fort Lauderdale Council for the Girl Scouts of America sent a representative to our studios, asking me to talk at some important meeting. I had an available date and agreed to make a presentation. The negotiator asked what my subject would be. I responded that at that juncture I really didn't know. We were some two months away from the meeting and who knew what would transpire in the meanwhile. She shook hands and departed, assuring me that she would be happy with my choice of subject.

A few days later, she telephoned. "Mr. LeFevre, have you decided what you'll be speaking about before the Girl Scout Council?"

"No, I haven't," I said. "Frankly, I haven't had a moment even to think about it."

"The Council needs to know the topic quickly. We have to get out publicity. You know how it is."

I was under pressure at the moment with airtime for a "special" coming up fast. "Miss" I said. "We agreed when you were here that whatever my topic, you'd be content. I'm sorry, I won't make that decision for probably another month. You may announce that I'll be there. If that is not sufficient and you must have a topic at once, why don't you book someone else?"

"Oh, no. No. That won't do at all. We want you."

"Then we're all set. You have me. Let me think about it and, perhaps, I can figure something out soon. Give me at least a couple of weeks."

"Can't you do it sooner than that? "

I was beginning to feel irritation. "Look, Madam. I am under a great deal of pressure constantly. Indeed, I've got to put this telephone down within two minutes and make a dash for the studio. I'm due on the air."

"Wait a minute, Mr. LeFevre!" Her voice sounded frantic. "It's just that we don't want you to talk about the United Nations. That's all. You can have any topic you want except that. Will that be all right? You can agree not to talk about the UN, can't you?"

This time I was angry. "As you know," I said, realizing that my voice had taken on a cold steel quality, "I haven't decided. But if I decide to talk about the UN, that's what I'll talk about. Nobody censures me. Since you've already decided what you don't want me to talk about, why don't you save yourself and me a lot of time and trouble? Get yourself another speaker." I slammed down the phone and raced to my position on set.

When I came from the studio an hour later, the lady was waiting for me in my office. She was embarrassed and uncomfortable. "Please forgive this intrusion, Mr. LeFevre. I didn't have an appointment but I have to see you. It's urgent. You *must* agree not to talk about the UN."

"Why must I?"

I strode to my desk and turned to face her. I didn't invite her to sit. "Look. I didn't come to you seeking an opportunity to speak before your group. You came to me. You agreed I could choose my own topic. I intend to.

"Now you approach me and plead with me not to talk about the United Nations. I have no reason to know why you've made that request. But the more I think about this talk, the more I am inclined to talk about the United Nations. Yes. In fact, that's it. I've just decided. When I appear before the Girl Scout Council I will speak about the UN."

"Oh, but you can't do that!"

"Yes, I can. You'd be surprised."

"I've made a terrible botch of things, haven't I?"

"Not really. Actually, you've helped me select my topic. If I appear for your meeting, the UN will be my topic. Since you don't want me to talk about it, why don't you simply get someone else? You have plenty of time. I'm sure you can find someone who will talk about something else."

"But we want you."

I smiled. "Then you do have a problem."

"Oh, dear. I'm so sorry. Won't you please reconsider?"

My smile was broader. "Not a chance."

"Don't go away," she said in apparent desperation. "I'll be right back." She literally ran from the office.

Ruth came in. "What scared her?" she sniffed, shrugging after the subsiding whirlwind.

"I did," I admitted. 'She insists that I talk before the Girl Scout Council. But she also insists that I refrain from talking about the UN."

Ruth looked astonished. "She's got her nerve."

"True enough," I said. "And with that she can always get another speaker."

I was in the midst of dictating letters when the Girl Scout Lady returned. I permitted the interruption and saw her at once. She entered, carrying a paperback copy of the Girl Scout Handbook.

"I raced home to get this for you, Mr. LeFevre," she said. I believed it. She was out of breath. "Read the Handbook and you'll see why you mustn't talk about the UN."

I laughed. "I'll let you in on a little secret," I said. "Up to this moment I have never read the Girl Scout Manual. Up to this moment I have seen no reason for reading it. I have no intention of becoming a Girl Scout. Therefore, I have no intention of reading the Manual. Thank you for the offer. But, no."

"But you must!" She was panting. "Please, Mr. LeFevre." She opened the book quickly and turned to a dog-eared page. "Here, read that page, anyway." The manual was thrust into my hands.

"I will not read this..."- My voice trailed away as my eyes inadvertently picked up a phrase: "The Constitution of the United States is very much like the Charter of the United Nations."

I gaped. Then I hastily read a few more sentences. I could hardly believe what I was seeing. Slowly I stood. "You have opened my eyes," I said. "And you are right. This is something I must read. And you may be very sure that this will be my topic before the Girl Scouts. If I had any doubts, they are gone now. It is high time the good ladies of the Council learn what is in this Manual. "

"I've really done it now, haven't I?"

"Yes, you have."

"Well, I'm not through, Mr. LeFevre. There are others who will have something to say. And to your employer."

She tossed her head and marched.

A couple of hours later I received a message from Nick. I was to come to his office the following morning, at a specified time.

When I reported in, Nick was grinning. "I hear you've been something of a bully to the nice ladies of the Girl Scout Council," he began. "Want to tell me about it?"

As briefly as possible I spelled out what had occurred. He listened gravely.

"Is that the way it happened?"

"Yes, Nick. Further, Ruthie was a witness to some of it. Meanwhile, I took the Manual home and read part of it. It says a great many things about the United Nations, but most particularly it makes it clear that the Girl Scouts of America aren't the Girl Scouts of America. They are International Girl Scouts with something of an allegiance to the UN rather than to the Constitution. And they try to make it appear that the Constitution and the Declaration of Independence and the Bill of Rights are all very much like the UN Charter. They aren't like it at all. I'm familiar with the Charter. This Manual, Nick, is unAmerican, in my judgment."

"That's a pretty serious charge."

" I intend making it."

He nodded. "I'm with you right down the line. But you'd be surprised at the pressure they're putting on me. I won't even tell you who has talked to me requesting that you be disciplined or fired."

"Am I going to be fired?"

"Hell, no. I'm with you all the way. You're right."

"Thanks, Nick."

"You *are* right, aren't you?

"Yes."

"What about that speech?"

"If I make it, I'm going to talk about the UN. And I'm going to rip it apart. But, Nick. The way out for them is so easy. They aren't obligated to me in the slightest. All they have to do is get another speaker."

"Why don't you write up this whole episode? Go over it in detail. Make it as complete as you can, including your differences with the

Manual. Make a comparison of the Constitution with the Charter. Whatever. Get it all in.

"Then, we're going to launch a campaign of our own."

"A campaign?"

"Yes. They've threatened a boycott unless you and I do as they say."

"Hey. I didn't think they'd go that far."

"Write it up, Bob. And make at least fifty copies of the whole thing. I want it for ammunition. We'll fight fire with fire."

"Yes, sir. With pleasure."

It took two days to produce 36 pages. Ruth copied the opus. Nick took half and asked me to circulate the other half.

I mailed out my twenty-five copies to various people I knew in Miami and elsewhere. I had learned about a conservative publication called: "Human Events." And I included the newsletter in the mailing. The editor of "Human Events" was a well-known writer named Frank Chodorov.

Within a few days, a letter came from Chodorov returning his copy. It would be considered for publication provided I would cut it down to a size corresponding to their format.

I went to work on the copy and eliminated about ten pages. Ruth went after it, and lopped off another eight. We'd cut it in half. I sent the abbreviated version back to Chodorov. He phoned asking if I objected to further reduction which he could make.

I gave him carte blanche and he proceeded, commenting that it could have been a good article if I had learned how to write. Chodorov was a master at it, and my report, under his deft handling, read well.

The next issue of "Human Events" was comprised of my report. It was entitled: "Even the Girl Scouts." It took the country by storm.

Suddenly my name was in wire service stories as the man who was picking on little girls. Herb Block did a cartoon showing me as a big bully glowering over a cluster of cringing little girls in uniform.

Before the matter ended, the Girl Scout Council recalled that particular edition of the Handbook and reissued it, with the portions I had targeted either deleted or rewritten with an altered meaning.

My attack had actually been aimed at the United Nations and the personal challenge to my freedom of speech. But newsmen like an angle. They twisted it into an attack on little girls. But since I was an anticommunist I had learned to anticipate this type of thing.

In those days, if a person waved the flag he was at once "controversial." If he spouted off in favor of Communist doctrine, he was called an intellectual and his broad comprehension of current events was accepted as beyond question.

And thanks to my experience with the "I Am" I knew better than to expect comprehension from the media. This would hold true, even though I was a member of the Fourth Estate myself. So, the reporters and wire services twisted my article, which was an effort to protect the Girl Scouts from propaganda and brainwashing. The article became opposite of what it was.

Reporters and police alike, acquire a jaundiced view. They are constantly exposed to a certain segment of society that is aggressive and exploitative. Understandably, they believed that there is no other segment and that man qua man is a lost cause.

One further event of note should be chronicled concerning my news career in Fort Lauderdale. Senator Joe McCarthy and his wife came to Key Biscayne for a week's rest.

I had talked to McCarthy on my "World Today" program. Learning that he was in Miami, I made an appointment for an exclusive interview. Taking Lucky and his camera, the two of us went to his retreat.

I had been enthusiastic about McCarthy's roll as a leading "Red" fighter. With his full cooperation, we "set up" and McCarthy readied himself for a televised interview. After the normal introduction, in which I established his identity and asked a few questions about the particular phase of his on-going probe of Red influences in the government, I made a statement like this:

"Senator, you have done an outstanding job of establishing that there is, in fact, a threat of Communism in the government. But, I wonder, sir, if this is enough. Do you plan to stop with this?

"It's been my experience that many Americans don't really know what Communism is. They identify it with Russia or with something that is bad, but they really aren't aware of what it means. What do you think of establishing some kind of educational institution so that we not only learn who the Communist sympathizers are but additionally, learn what Communism is trying to do?"

I thought the question more or less routine. I was completely unprepared for what followed.

McCarthy leaped to his feet and with a clenched fist pounded on a table top with such violence that items, including a picture, took a life of their own and fell to the floor. The picture broke.

"No! No! No!" he roared. "No education! You have to expose! Expose! Expose!"

I gulped. "Do you really mean that?"

"I never meant anything more in my life! Expose! Expose!"

His wife intruded at that point and terminated the interview.

Outside, Lucky said, "Sorry, boss. I didn't get it all. He jumped up and I couldn't swing my camera in time. Did you expect that?"

I shook my head, mystified. "Lucky," I said, "I thought I'd given him an easy one. He could have come out for education. He might have made a friend or two if he had. I hate to say this, but I'm beginning to wonder if he has all his marbles."

"You want my opinion?"

"I think I can handle it."

"He's out to lunch."

Chapter LXXX

I hadn't heard the last of Jim Fradkin. The man from Merwin Hart's office in New York reappeared in Florida. It seems my terms had been agreed upon. There would be paychecks for Ruth, Margie, Edy, and me. Loy, Tommy and I could move to the big city whenever we could manage the details.

Before agreeing, it seemed expedient to fly to New York for a personal reconnaissance. A red carpet welcome had been arranged if I had been uncertain before, the treatment afforded swept away my remaining doubts.

I was taken to a luncheon at the University Club. There, rubbing shoulders with a host of important men, my ego was stroked and I was allowed to preen and posture. I was introduced as the young man who had already accomplished so much in Florida. The National Economic Council (spelled Merwin Hart) was going to bring me to New York so I could go on the air in that city and repeat my successes.

This was heady stuff and I returned to Fort Lauderdale to give notice to Nick Kirsta. Our entire stay in Florida had spanned the latter half of 1951, all of 1952 and '53 and the first half of 1954. In something short of three full years, I had become a personality—if not a celebrity—in southern Florida and had made friends with a host of splendid people. Now, like Caesar, I would march to the north and take the big prize. At least, that was how I looked at it.

Thanks to the organizational work I had done in Florida, I was now known to just about every Conservative group in the country. A man named Arnold R. was putting together a national amalgam of organizations to be known as the "Congress of Freedom," and I had already given it my enthusiastic support. I had met Archibald Roosevelt, from the conservative side of the Teddy Roosevelt family. I also met Vivien Kellums, Mary Cain, Lucille Cardin Crain, Thadeus Ashby, and a number of other men and women who were known and admired for their stand in favor of the Constitution and the concept of free enterprise.

Bill Buckley had graduated from Yale, in search of God and man, and I numbered him among my friends.

Flattery and a fat paycheck can sometimes act like blinders and a bag of oats to a hungry horse.

Merwin was a man of his word. We were granted the necessary time to find a suitable abode. Manhattan was too expensive, considering the size of the establishment we wanted, so we looked in Connecticut. We found a lovely house in Greenwich on King's Street. Danny Wolfson, whose brother was a stock market whiz kid and well-known in financial circles, owned it.

Danny agreed to rent it to us at a good stiff rental, on a month-to-month basis. The place had eight bedrooms and was a warm and graceful structure at the top of an orchard with at least eight acres in apple trees.

Additionally, there was a separate building for a gardener. We wanted it as an office and presently employed it in that function. The rooms were large and so well lighted by the sun that our problem with it related to temperature. It was altogether too warm and there was no air conditioning.

Meanwhile, in keeping with the arrangements made in advance, my three girls and I were furnished offices on the 75th floor of the same building. Within a week, the transfer and transition had occurred and we were on duty with the National Economic Council.

I don't know the source of the misunderstanding that immediately surfaced. I'll take the blame. Indeed, I can hardly slough it off. In all that had been said prior to our move, I had understood that I would be broadcasting for Merwin on some radio station in the city. Now, as it turned out, Merwin had no intention of buying time on one of the stations. Rather, he expected me to get on the air, either because I was a celebrity or because I would very quickly be hired by one of the stations as a staff newsman.

I managed an appearance on TV as a celebrity, flanked by Bill Buckley. The two of us debated a couple of well-known leftists. My appearance was a case of "show and not tell." Buckley was enormously well informed on all manner of trivia. I wanted to debate issues and ideas, not personal habits. Personal traits make excellent fodder for gossip and who gives a hang about ideas? I think I got in one or two good licks but Buckley lapped the plate clean. He handled both his opponents with ease, and my presence was more a matter of decoration than anything else.

I made the rounds looking for airtime. I went from one broadcast studio to the next. It was conspicuous from the start that I was not a celebrity. I wasn't even a personality. I was just one more guy with some jerkwater experience, trying to land a broadcast slot.

My inactivity was dreadful. I went up to Irvingtonon-Hudson, where I met Leonard Read of the Foundation for Economic Education. Through him, I met F.A. (Baldy) Harper, an economist—formerly at Cornell University—and other members of the remarkable staff of key people Read was assembling.

I had learned of this organization back in Los Angeles. Now I asked Baldy if Read was attempting was to organize an actual school where the ideas of free enterprise (as V. O. Watts had spelled them out) could be taught.

Baldy, to my surprise, replied in the negative. Such a school would be impossible, he informed me. How marvelous if it could be done! But it could not. Baldy had researched the area and was convinced, and Read was similarly warned off.

Read was concentrating on offering one and two-hour lectures, either in person or with the help of his staff people. Additionally, he was publishing a revitalized *Freeman* magazine, which had recently been purchased from three people—Henry Hazlitt, Suzanne LaFollette and John Chamberlain—who had themselves picked it up from Albert J. Nock.

Additionally, Read was building his operation around the revised Henry Grady Weaver version of *Discovery of Freedom* now called *Mainspring*. As former head of the L.A. Chamber, Read knew how to raise money and everything he touched glowed with his genius.

But Baldy agreed. What was needed was a school. Unfortunately, it was beyond everyone's reach.

Read saw to it that I was invited to a luncheon sponsored by FEE. On this occasion I met Ludwig von Mises, the Austrian savant. His classic work, *Human Action,* had won plaudits from the remnants of the conservative wing, which had been driven into hiding and near extinction by the charging hordes of the political socialist do-gooders.

It was nearly impossible for me to understand Mises, for he talked with a particularly thick accent in extremely erudite terms. Later, when I had an opportunity to read his book, I found myself enthralled. In his writing, there was no accent and I found his book easy to understand. Many have expressed difficulty with it, but I can assure them that it is limpid and clear compared to Mises' verbal presentation.

Thanks to Nora Laidlaw, back in California, I obtained an introduction to Henry Hazlitt. At this time, he was writing a weekly column on economics for *Business Week Magazine*. To my astonishment, Hazlitt knew of me. He had been enthralled with the work I had done with the Wage Earner's Committee. We enjoyed each other's company and got along very well indeed.

I also met a young fellow who was being touted as a "comer." His name was Murray Rothbard. He, his wife, and a household pet rabbit lived in an apartment in the 80's. Rothbard was already the center of a group of admirers and was making a name for himself as an economic genius. Unfortunately, Rothbard had been stricken with a phobia that prevented him from traveling. It is the fear of open spaces. Many are afflicted with its corollary, the fear of closed spaces. But it is a malady that requires serious treatment and cannot be shrugged off or ignored. Perhaps, because of this phobia, Rothbard turned to the typewriter rather than the train. His output was becoming prodigious. He stands today as perhaps the most prolific of all free market writers of our time. [Murray Rothbard died in January 1995.]

While I was busy getting from group to group and meeting some fine people, Merwin appeared to be content with my efforts. He expressed no disappointment that I had not been grabbed up and put on the air. The disappointment was mine. I was doing very little to warrant the splendid wage I was drawing. And, quite candidly, although my girls pitched in to help to the degree they were called upon, they too had little to do.

One other insect had come to lodge in the National Economic Council honey jar. I began to detect a trait of anti-Semitism in Merwin. He was not overt. And he was such a gentleman on each and every occasion that few could take umbrage. I learned a great many things from Merwin and to this day retain an admiration for him. But a fundamental suspicion bracketing an entire segment of the population appeared to me unreasonable, and a matter of prejudice.

I broached the idea that the National Economic Council found a school, so that free market ideas could be studied in depth. Merwin agreed with Read and Baldy Harper that the job was too large to be undertaken at this juncture. Rather, the N.E.C. was using the political approach, lobbying for tax reduction, and seeking repeal of particularly onerous regulatory commandments.

Merwin came up with a counter-proposal. Since it now seemed that my appearance on the airwaves from New York was going to be delayed, he would underwrite the setting up of a new organization, which I could head. He visualized something called "United States Day" and the creation of a "United States Day Committee," which would seek to have a specific day set aside to honor the U. S. Constitution.

The Fourth of July commemorated the Declaration of Independence. But September 23rd was the anniversary of the ratification of the Constitution, a date which few knew of and no one celebrated.

I confess to a lack of enthusiasm. It seemed to me that the rank and file of America was dismally uninformed of the great sweeping changes taking place in their country. Waving the flag for the Constitution wouldn't inform them of anything. Conservatives were aware, but their response was much the same as Merwin's. If we can win some elections, all will yet be well. The changes were unwelcome. Conservatives wanted to bring back the "good old days."

They objected to Communism and Socialism because the principal thrust of these ideas demanded the growth and dominance of government.

Their procedure entailed the exact malady they opposed. If the Conservatives could gain enough power in government, which would surely result in governmental growth, then they would have the *power* to hold the Socialists at bay.

But if the problem dealt with government size and power, a growth of government and dependence upon it was bound to be counter-productive. I expressed the thought to Merwin. While it was true that I wanted "my side" to win, I wanted to win because I was right and not because I was strong.

If ideas of free enterprise were correct and understood, then they would triumph. If the ideas were incorrect, they should not win anyway. Truth was what was needed, not a measurement of political biceps.

This argument was not altogether original with me. Read, although fearful of establishing a school, was definitely committed to truth. Further, he was committed to the educational approach rather than the political one.

When Merwin responded that winning was the important matter, I pictured the affair at the Biltmore in which Nixon had said much the same thing. My alienation was emphasized by Nixon's scurvy treatment of me on the beach at Key Biscayne, which I also remembered. From that moment forward I lost sympathy with the National Economic Council and its political methodology.

However, I couldn't simply throw down my shovel and walk. Merwin had laid out a great deal of money and I was morally obligated to deliver something.

We gave up the offices in the Empire State Building as the first step in a move to economize. Margie, Ruth, Edith and I set up offices in the out-building at our home in Greenwich. While I didn't approve of the political approach, it did seem worthy of effort. In all my talks—and they continued even in New York City—I stressed the Conservative position. This was that our problems in the United States arose from a failure to adhere to the Constitution and the Bill of Rights. "All we must do," I told many an audience, "is get back to the Constitution, the Bill of Rights, and the Declaration."

It seemed to me that our drift into socialist ideology was occurring largely because of judicial decisions from the Supreme Court, which, since Roosevelt, had taken on a "liberal" tinge. Liberal in this case had little to do with liberty. The word was taken to mean generosity. And the generosity exhibited had to do largely with taxpayers' money.

I stressed the importance of the Constitution. The activities of a "United States Day Committee" could help that emphasis, and in consequence, turn us back into more traditional (earlier) Constitutional interpretations.

With Merwin showing the way, the United States Day Committee was organized and the first effort made to bring about a national observance. The girls labored through long days and far into nights to get out mailings. They contacted the Conservative wings of both major political parties and anyone else who might take a belated interest.

Meanwhile, the Congress of Freedom, which I had joined while still in Miami, was growing apace. I kept in touch with this group by mail and by telephone, winning their support for my current efforts.

There came the time for an annual meeting of the Congress of Freedom. Some of the founders, including Arnold, were aging, less active, or had already died. I offered the leading members of the organization the facilities of our home in Greenwich for this meeting. Some fifteen or sixteen of the most active arrived at the appointed time.

At this meeting, I was chosen as Executive Director for the group. We took as our project a major undertaking.

At the close of World War II, the United Nations had been organized in San Francisco. With one accord, we viewed this organization a waste of time and money, a blot on our national honor, and a sounding board for every Socialist group extant.

The Congress of Freedom proposed that—on the tenth anniversary of the date of the founding of the UN—we would meet in San Francisco, hopefully in the same building used by the United Nations. There, we would spend several days denouncing the UN and showing that we should dismantle this first embryonic attempt at a world government.

If big government was evil, and we deemed it to be, then a world government would be the worst of all. A public statement in opposition would be timely and possibly influential.

I accepted the task of bringing this convention to fruition. I felt I could achieve both it and the United States Day effort at the same time. Naturally, this was done with Merwin's full knowledge, although he admitted doubts that I could ride both horses at once. He wanted me to confine myself to his brainchild.

Merwin was right, of course. My heart wasn't with the U.S. Day group. We did achieve some recognition. We contacted every governor in the country, and managed perhaps a dozen state proclamations in favor of the Constitution on September 23.

We urged every patriotic, right wing organization to rally 'round the flag on this occasion. We got nothing from the federal government.

Meanwhile, the Congress of Freedom began flexing its muscles and I became increasingly embarrassed. I was being paid by N.E.C.; I was doing very little for its brainchild, the U.S. Day Committee, but putting plenty of time in on the Congress of Freedom.

I began casting about for new employment, revisiting all my radio contacts in New York and calling on everyone I could think of.

Finding a job was one thing. But finding one that would make it possible for me to continue to crusade for America was another story entirely.

I notified the Congress of Freedom leaders of my wish to move on. Strangely, it was through this contact that my next job was located.

One evening at home in Greenwich, my telephone rang. The party on the line was Harry Hoiles, publisher of the *Gazette Telegraph* in Colorado Springs, Colorado.

Thaddeus Ashby, one of the leaders of the Congress of Freedom, had been working at the *Gazette* as Harry's editorial page editor. Thad wanted to move on and that post would be open. Thad had given Harry my name, and he was calling me to see if I'd care for the job.

I knew full well that I had no particular skills as an editor. However, I had written a few items, including my book with the "I Am" which I wanted to forget; *The Primer to a New World,* and the item on the Girl Scouts, which, (thanks to Frank Chodorov) had been written well enough to take the Girl Scouts by storm.

I could see myself as a writer. Thanks to my zeal as a crusader, I could also see myself doing anything and everything that needed to be done on behalf of my country. Could I become an editor? Obviously. No problem.

We discussed further elements of the job. The pay was next to nothing. If I accepted, I would lose 75% of my present income and the girls would again be out of work. I told Harry I'd have to think it over and call him back.

We had a family discussion. I got out the atlas to learn where Colorado Springs was located. I had crossed the country several times, but my routes had either been northern or southern and I had never been in Colorado.

As I studied the geography, one thought kept intruding. Thanks to all my contacts and efforts, it seemed to me that the worthiest goal would be to create a school that would concentrate on economic freedom. It would teach the right of a person to own property and to use it as he saw fit, provided that he intruded on no one.

Colorado Springs was nestled at the base of Pike's Peak, one of the grandest of the Rocky Mountains. The scenery was spectacular, the town relatively small. It was, in terms of the total territory of the

U.S., close to the center and, thus, equally inconvenient for practically everyone.

If I managed to organize a school, Colorado was located in such a place that those who came would have to really *want* to be there. Also, by virtue of its location and the population density, if I fell flat on my face, everyone wouldn't have to know.

Like Read and Baldy, I believed that setting up a school would be impossible for anyone. Anyone, that is, except me. I could do it. And there had been universal acceptance of the idea as desirable.

The creation of an educational edifice was Mount Everest for the cause of freedom. Someone had to show that the summit could be achieved. I had demonstrated some ability to scale a few foothills. It was clear to me that I must make the attempt. Colorado Springs was the place to begin.

The girls looked at me as if I'd lost my mind. But, then, I'd lost it before and things had worked out one way or another. Loy was in favor. The spirit of adventure was as strong in her as it was in me.

I called Harry and set up my terms. I would require a month in which to give notice and wind up my affairs. I also advised that I was obligated with the Congress of Freedom and that I would have to give some of my time to that effort, including a full week's absence from the newspaper during the convention when it was held in San Francisco.

Harry accepted these conditions and I notified Merwin that October 1954 would serve as my final month with N.E.C.

Before leaving New York, I made an appointment with Baldy Harper. He was the one man who had expressed the keenest interest in a school. It turned out that Baldy was coming into the city and we arranged to meet at a mutually convenient hotel.

To my amazement, Baldy began our meeting by expressing complete disgust and disappointment with Read. It seems that Baldy had spent a great deal of time researching ideas relating not only to economics, from which discipline he carried his doctorate, but also to politics and government. It was Baldy's firm conviction that a consistent position had to be taken. As he saw it, there was nothing a government could do that free men outside of government couldn't do better, more efficiently and certainly, more morally.

Indeed, many articles that had appeared in the *Freeman* magazine under Reed's management had demonstrated that various expressions of government were unneeded, counter-productive, and even vicious.

However, when Baldy had requested Read to denounce government per se as a moribund, obsolescent device to be phased out of existence, Read had balked.

Baldy was convinced that the only reason for Read's reluctance to take a consistent position was money. If the stand were taken, which Baldy felt was the only consistent and honest stand possible, then funding to the Foundation would be cut off. Rather than lose income, Read was compromising, as Baldy saw it.

I managed at last to steer the conversation to the question of a school. What would Baldy think if a real freedom school were organized and set into motion?

The economist fairly drooled at the prospect. A far away look shone in Baldy's eyes as he envisioned what could be achieved with such an instrument. He expanded on it at some length.

"Mr. Harper," I finally said, "Would you care to teach in such an institution if it could be started?"

It was clear by his reaction that I had described the gates of Nirvana for him. But he shook himself free of the spell. "It's a marvelous dream, Bob," he said. "The problem is, it can't be done. So there's no point in dwelling on it."

"But just for a moment, Baldy. What if a virtual miracle occurred? Suppose that somehow a campus were provided, money made available, and so on. Would you care to teach in such a school?"

His answer was typical. "I don't know that I'd be the best teacher, Bob. I can make up a list of splendid men and women who could probably teach better than I could."

I chuckled at this. Baldy tended to depreciate his own talents. "Obviously, a school would have to acquire a faculty of more than one person," I conceded. "That's not my question. Would you be willing to be one of those persons?"

The far away look returned. He took some time, thinking about what I had asked. Finally, he said, "It could be a turning point for the United States," he said simply. "I would certainly want to help in any and every way I could."

I couldn't tell him that it was in my mind to achieve that very goal. I wasn't sure I could do it. And why build up hopes? Besides, I knew what he would say.

He would go on at length about the impossibility. And what could I say when I had never attempted anything of such magnitude before?

We dropped the topic. And when the meeting ended, I secretly vowed that—if and when I put together the instrument I had in mind—Baldy would become the kingpin in what I planned.

I had no illusions about myself as a teacher. I had never taught and I had no desire to teach. But I could organize. What a school I could bring into existence! I'd put the pieces together and Baldy would manage it.

I would forge excalibar. Baldy would become King Arthur to wield the sword on behalf of liberty in America.

Chapter LXXXI

Our plans were complete when the October page was torn from the calendar. We left New York, Edith driving her Plymouth. I drove the big Buick sedan I had obtained in Florida. Loy and Tommy were in the lead vehicle with me; Ruth and Margie shared Edy's transportation.

The first part of the journey was uneventful. Loy and I had been over approximately the same route more than once and the girls were relatively familiar with it as well.

As we entered Nebraska it occurred to me that, in approaching Colorado Springs, it would be meritorious to come in from the east, rather than the north. I can't recall why this seemed important. Perhaps I had a romantic notion of seeing the looming colossus of Pikes Peak rising slowly above the horizon. Then, as we approached, we would make out the profile of buildings. We would see this remarkable city of the mid-Continental Rockies, nestling at the foot of the Rampart Range, as Gstaad nestles in the Swiss Alps.

Whatever my reasoning, somewhere in Nebraska the road forked and a southern sweep looked like a good bet on a secondary, little-used route. It is incumbent upon every leader to do a certain amount of leading. Since I was at the head of the expedition, I swung left, down this smooth but relatively narrow highway. Edy dutifully followed.

Within a matter of a few minutes, we were out of touch with every trace of civilization except the road itself. In 1954, there were at least two geographical areas in the U.S. that from the highway appear to be uninhabited. One of them was the entire state of Nevada—Reno and Las Vegas, excepted. The other area was eastern and central Colorado. I had crossed the former several times, but Colorado was new territory.

There was no traffic. This may be an exaggeration. Perhaps, in fifty miles, we would pass another vehicle. If there were man-made structures, they were away from the highway and out of sight. Places on the map that appeared to be centers of trade or habitation proved to be one or two ramshackle "public" buildings, with five or six domiciles scattered about. To add to our growing feeling of isolation, the sky clouded over, the sun vanished and we drove in afternoon gloom.

Loy kept peering off to the right in hopes of seeing mountains. Her eyes were rewarded with nothing but endless prairie, stretching in all directions.

"Shouldn't we be able to see the Rockies?" she asked.

"We're too far east," I told her. "There's a junction up ahead somewhere and then we'll turn west again. After that, it won't be long."

We drove on and on.

"Are you sure about that junction?"

"Certainly."

But I was becoming concerned. I thought I had calculated the distance accurately. My eyes began to turn to the falling needle on the gas gauge. And the roads were so narrow at the speed I maintained, I wondered if I might have zipped past a crucial crossroad without seeing, it. If so, we might continue all the way to Texas, without a filling station or a restaurant in sight. Much less a place to spend the night.

In the rearview mirror I could see Edy, grimly following. The girls must be apprehensive, too. I pulled to the side and stopped.

"What's the matter?" Loy asked in alarm.

"Nothing.

I walked back to the Plymouth. "Everything okay?" My voice radiated manufactured cheer.

"Sure," Edy said. Margie and Ruth nodded.

"When do we eat?" Margie asked. "I'm famished."

"It shouldn't be long," I said. "There's a junction or a crossroad of some kind up ahead. We'll turn west again and after that, why, no time at all. "

"Then, let's go," Ruth said.

"There's less traffic than I expected," I said. "And no signs. Keep your eyes peeled. I don't want to miss that turn."

"I'll honk if you miss it," Edy gave assurance.

"How's your tank?" I asked.

"Don't worry. I'll have gas left over when you run out," Edy said.

She was probably right. I got back behind the wheel and on we moved in tandem.

The clouds lowered. I turned on the headlights and Edy's forward beams blinked in the mirror. The fuel indicator gave growing evidence of coming vacancy.

At last I was rewarded. A battered arterial stop sign stood beside the road and a smaller black and white rectangle indicated that Colorado Springs was to the right somewhere.

We executed the turn and I picked up a bit of speed for awhile.

We began running into patches of fog and I had to decelerate. The occasional patches gave way to constant thin vapor. Visibility was fair to poor and we moved more cautiously. The road was straight as a taut wire, but, not being certain of it, I couldn't afford to take chances by acceleration.

"Mother," Tommy said. "I'm awful hungry."

"It won't be long," his mother said. "Where are the mountains?"

"Don't you see them? They're right up ahead."

Loy peered through the windshield. "I don't see anything."

"Neither do I," I said. "But on a clear day I'm sure they'd be visible by now."

"I don't think you know anything about it," she said.

"You're right," I admitted. "I don't. But I have studied the maps. They're there all right. They've got to be."

We drove on and on. The roadbed slowly climbed, the highway turned in a graceful curve and outcroppings of rock were visible through the fog. The fuel gauge registered empty. The motor throbbed on with nothing better than a memory of gasoline vapor to keep it running.

"We're probably in the foothills right now," I said.

We gained a slight summit and then the road curved again and went down hill to more endless, flat prairie. It was interminable. Slowly we poked through the fog, which grew more and more dense as we progressed.

"How long is this going to last?" Loy asked. "And where is Colorado Springs?"

Somewhat testily I snapped, "The answer to both questions is: I don't know."

"Humph!"

Lights flickered out of the void on our left.

"You see," I said in triumph. "Civilization at last."

"Is this Colorado Springs?" Loy asked. "If it is, where is it?"

"We must be in the outskirts," I said. "We'll keep on to the center of town." To myself, I added, "Or until this crate stops altogether."

Then aloud, "There should be enough street lighting so we can find a hotel or motel."

I patted Tommy's leg. "And get something to eat, young man."

"I'm hungry, Father."

"I know. Just hang in there a bit longer. Our journey is nearly ended."

We probed forward like a burglar in a dark hallway with only an occasional window gleaming fitfully through the engulfing mist.

Suddenly, the highway broadened and we turned about forty-five degrees to the right. Now we were rewarded by the glorious evidence of human endeavor. A red neon sign produced a pink aura above the highway and the legend on the beacon read, "Wrangler Motel." In smaller letters, the sign said: "Horses boarded."

"I see why it took us so long," I said. "We were supposed to make our entrance on horseback."

I used the turn signal, needlessly informing Edy of what I had seen, and pulled into a parking spot at the Wrangler Motel. The Plymouth pulled up alongside.

The gas gauge and my stomach gave the same reading. Before I could reach for the key, the engine stopped. Even the carburetor was bone dry.

All six of us got our feet on the ground and relieved our stiff muscles by moving around. Then, with one accord, we entered the motel office.

Our luck was with us. The motel was clean and the owner, a friendly man with a weather-beaten face, made us welcome. There was a dining room at our service as well. It was after eight o'clock when we sat down to eat. It was nine o'clock when we turned in. But there were no protests about going to bed.

The last thing I said to Loy as she prepared herself for the night was this: "Get a good sleep, Hon. Tomorrow the fog will be gone and we should have a breath-taking view to the west."

The next morning the fog had obviously not heeded my message. It was thicker than before.

We had a hearty breakfast and I used the telephone to notify the business manager of the Gazette Telegraph that I had arrived in town. It happened to be Sunday morning and I inquired as to the best locations for renting a good-sized residence.

It was my intention to use the day to locate a house. I could report for work the next morning. The manager's parting shot was that, whether I found a suitable residence or not, I had best report on Monday at the proper time.

I had to send Edy to a filling station a couple of blocks away so I could get enough gas to prime the carburetor and get the engine running again. She had been correct. She still had fuel in her tank.

Finally, restored with food, rest and gasoline, we all climbed into the Buick to explore the city in which to establish a school that would teach and sustain the American virtue of free enterprise.

As we drove around, Loy expressed growing disappointment. Fog was everywhere and the city appeared to be laid out on flat terrain. Views are important to Loy. It appeared that we must be miles from anything worth looking at. The city, itself, was small compared to all our prior experience. I took a certain amount of friendly guff for my failure to provide a mountain. Before long, some of the guff wasn't too friendly.

As the morning wore on, the fog gradually dispersed, and, at last, visibility returned. The effect was breathtaking, and I was vindicated. Immediately to the west of the city, an enormous mountain rose with its summit snow capped. The main street through town is called Pikes Peak Avenue, which ended abruptly at a large hotel called the Antlers. Between and above its twin towers, the great mountain discovered by Zebulon Pike loomed in majesty. To right and left of this monolith, the shoulders of the Rockies stretched north and south, providing a great barrier. Colorado Springs was located exactly as the maps had shown.

Something like enthusiasm came to all. We visited the Garden of the Gods, Helen Hunt Jackson Falls, and, at last, the world famous Broadmoor district.

It was here that we found our first residence in Colorado Springs. Number One Elm Street was just below the Broadmoor Hotel. It was vacant, partly furnished, and available. We managed a relatively inexpensive rental since Colorado Springs experiences its major tourist season in summer. The owner of this imposing domicile anticipated few inquiries until April or May of the following year. We managed our occupancy on a month-to-month basis without a lease.

Finally, we headed back to the Wrangler Motel. The girls could manage the chores of getting services turned on and taking possession of the place after I reported for work the next day.

The Gazette Telegraph was located on Pikes Peak Avenue only half a block away from the Antlers Hotel. On Monday morning I called on the business manager who took me in to meet Harry Hoiles, the publisher.

My new employer proved to be slight of build, with a smooth, clean-face, and eyes that never left mine as we talked. My attempts at pleasantries—expressions of being glad to join the *Gazette*, and so on—were met with stony-faced silence. Nothing I said or did evoked a twinkle in an eye or a twitch of a lip.

Harry appeared to be devoid of humor. Any attempt at levity was treated as a distraction. He was all business.

Over the telephone from New York, I had been led to believe that the writer of the editorials would be a most important person, putting out the official view of the newspaper. Across the desk from Harry Hoiles, I learned that writers were the lowest of the low. At the bottom of the list were people who wrote editorials.

My new boss laid it out. I would write what he wanted me to write. Further, I was to be consistent in everything I wrote. Prior editorial pages were produced, the editorials of Thad Ashby—the man who had recommended me for the job, and immediately left town. I looked over several. Writing such material didn't appear insurmountable.

The paper was a "Freedom" paper. That meant the editorials would be about freedom. Everything I wrote, if Harry were to approve of it, would have to support the concept of humans as free beings.

I found myself becoming increasingly uneasy. I am a person who likes to do things. I like being busy. Harry let me know that, without exception, the people he had employed in the job I was undertaking tended to be lazy. He wouldn't tolerate that. I would write. If I wasn't writing, I would study. Read. Learn. And then write more.

I felt as though I were already under suspicion, not because I might have done something wrong, but because I wanted to write. It became crystal clear that there would be nothing of the "cult of the personality" insofar as my job was concerned. Of particular distress was my discovery that my name wouldn't even appear on the editorial page. I was to be an invisible man, a ghost who would express the views that Harry held.

I felt it only fair to set the record straight on my side of the desk. So I laid things out as I saw them. I loved my country, I was a crusader, fighting for freedom. I was accepting the job because I viewed it as a means to an end. That end was to argue for and awaken a love of liberty, of the ideas and ideals embodied in the Constitution, the Bill of Rights, and the Declaration of Independence. So long as the job helped me do those things, I would work like a demon. If the job didn't permit me to do those things, then I'd leave. I wasn't in love with the newspaper. My mistress was Liberty and it was this celestial being I naught to serve.

Harry asked me what I felt about free enterprise. I thought the question unnecessary in view of what I had already said, but I laid out my feelings there, too. I believed in the right of every human being to own property, to manage it as he saw fit, and to win or lose on the basis of his ability.

Harry nodded at that, and I had the impression that he found my response satisfactory. There was no smile, no warmth.

I also filled Harry in on my background. I mentioned the "I Am," stressing that I had served with the Ballards only briefly, which was true. But I brought up the lawsuit in which I had been named as a co-defendant in a federal mail fraud action. Naturally, I put myself in the best light I could. I had written a few things and mentioned them all. Harry had read my article about the Girl Scouts in *Human Events*. I didn't tell him that Frank Chodorov had largely provided the form of that article. I began to sense that I had a great deal to learn.

Another matter, which I had brought up during our earlier phone conversation, was my commitment to the Congress of Freedom. I had reserved two weeks so that I could serve as Executive Director. During that period I would have to be away. This had been understood and Harry nodded without giving a sign of approval or disapproval.

Harry went on to explain that the kind of people he really wanted to bring in at the *Gazette Telegraph* were those who took an interest in the business affairs of the paper. Freedom Newspapers was an expansion operation. They would, with the passing of time, be buying more newspapers. They now held fourteen of them, all fairly small. *The Register*, in Santa Ana, California, was the primary enterprise.

Suddenly that clicked. Hoiles. Ruth had brought Mr. Hoiles to my attention when we lived in LA at Arapahoe Street. Hoiles was the man who had come out against public schools. I had told her I couldn't see how I could take such a position. It became increasingly clear that I could and, if I stayed at the *Gazette Telegraph*, I *would*.

Something else clicked. I remembered a scene at Cité Universitaire in Paris, where a fellow officer had pointed to a young Captain recently arrived. I had been told that he was the son of a man who owned a newspaper in Santa Ana. The loyalty of the newcomer to the United States had been discussed because the newspaper had been highly critical of the government for putting Japanese Americans behind barbed wire in concentration camps.

I asked Harry if he had served in the Army during World War II, and I was given an affirmative answer. I didn't check further, but leaped to the conclusion that Harry was the young Captain pointed out to me. It was many years before I learned that Harry had never visited Cité Universitaire in Paris.

My new boss was a tough minded, two—fisted fighter for every idea he believed to be correct.

Later that day when I talked to the girls at our new home, I expressed some dismay at the personality of my new boss.

Ruth was immediately on my side. "Do you think you can get along with him?" she asked.

"Frankly," I said, "I don't know. Harry is a tough nut."

"Maybe you ought to quit at once and we'll all go somewhere else."

"We're in no position to do that," I said. "We laid out a lot of money on first and last month's rent, even without a lease. And we've spent quite a bit getting here. Frankly, we're stuck. This one has to work."

There were expressions of disappointment and concern. "Maybe you've made a mistake, Bob," Edy commented.

"It's sure possible," I admitted. "I've made lots of them. But there is something else. I know it. Let me be entirely frank. I'm not sure how good a writer I am. I have written a few good things. This job is going to demand enormous discipline from me. Probably I won't like it.

"But there is something more important. With a daily deadline, I'm going to have to produce. Harry won't keep me on because he likes me. I don't think he likes me. I'm not sure he likes anyone.

"But I can learn from him. And from the daily demands of a deadline. If I'm going to be effective in our fight for freedom and in our hope of doing anything to offset the threat of communism, I need to be a good writer. So, I'll tell you what's going to happen.

"I 'm going to go to work every day like a good little boy. And I'm going to produce. I'm going to work like hell. Harry's going to find out that I'm not lazy, even if other writers are. And I can learn. Harry knows a lot and seems perfectly willing to teach. So? Well, I don't have to like him and he doesn't have to like me. But he's going to like what I do. He's looking for an end result and I'm going to supply it."

"He sounds forbidding," Margie said. "There may be some unpleasantness."

"So what?" I said. "The trouble is, I can see his side of things. If he'd had a lot of people who are lazy and who don't know their jobs he probably has just cause for feeling and acting the way he did.

"I'm going to demonstrate that I'm cut from a different bolt of cloth.

"Is there anything I can do?" Ruth asked.

"You'll be the first to know if there is," I said. "Gals, we're going to have to make this one work."

Our conversation ended there, but my thoughts went on. A small, persistent nudge deep within me kept repeating. I needed Harry. He was exactly what was called for. And, curiously, I found myself liking the man. He was tough. But there was a basic fairness. Harry was the kind of person who stated things honestly and firmly. He wasn't one of your "waltz me around again, Willie" types.

If I could manage to produce what he wanted, he would be solid in his support. I had met the personification of the Rock of Gibraltar. Quietly, I made up my mind. Harry *would* approve of my output. And he would finally approve of me. If there were to be a breach between us, it would have to come from him. I would give him no cause for anything except whole-hearted acceptance of my best.

Chapter LXXXII

During my first week at the *Gazette Telegraph*, I was like a man possessed. I *had* to make good.

I thought about writing. I read. I put paper into the typewriter and removed its innocence by streaking it with inky symbols of my thoughts.

I dreamed about writing. I talked about it. I ate with it and slept with it. Harry wanted short, terse copy, with protein words, lean and target-centered. I wandered across literary moonscape, bleak and almost untrodden.

Harry wanted local comment. I knew nothing whatever about Colorado Springs. Had I been asked to discuss the habits of the African Wildebeest, I would have had an easier time. And on top of this, Harry wanted me to write about liberty. But I was to refrain from contradiction and be above reproach in matters of consistency.

To heighten my anxiety, Harry watched over me with unblinking, clear blue optics. When I erred, he was patience itself. He took me aside and tabulated my mistakes logically, painstakingly, minutely. When I chanced upon a paragraph or idea that worked, my reward was silence, but my output remained in his hands. Everything else was returned. A national forest of paper was at my disposal and I felt as though I were trying to push this supply through a single mail slot, equipped with an automatic rejecter.

Fortunately, in departing, Thad Ashby had left some surplus editorials. They were being used (two a day) while I was trying to get the feel of my job. How I admired Thad's writing ability.

Carefully, I prepared my first editorial. I struggled with it all that first week, getting ready for my first explosion into print which would occur on the first Monday of the second week. Finally, I took it in so Harry could approve. He read it, responded with a nearly imperceptible nod, and asked what else I had ready.

I told him I was still working. I fielded a stony stare and went back to my desk.

I looked over the editorial page for the umpteenth time and decided that I'd like to redesign the whole layout. Instead of having the top half of the two left-hand columns for my copy, I thought the page would look better if the first two columns were used in their entirety. This would require two full-length editorials (about 800 words each), plus a brief one or two liner to break the columns at the fold.

I sold the idea to Harry and, thus, got myself in even deeper. But I was determined. I was going to show him I wasn't lazy! And somehow I managed to produce. If I do say so, that first editorial was pretty good. The short one was much too long, and the long one that followed could have been improved if Chodorov had been around with his blue pencil meat axe. But Harry approved. I must have some redeeming virtues. My writing appeared in print. The world seemed not to notice, but I knew.

I made it a rule to be at my desk early each morning. I worked, I slaved to bring the words together around an idea. I was often still at my desk when others had left for the day.

Again and again I'd take copy in to Harry. In his own time, he'd read it. Then, he'd call me back and talk to me about something in it of which he didn't approve. I'd have to re-write.

The man never forgot anything! He tripped me up on one inconsistency after another. His grasp of the subject was prodigious. If I wrote that the government was out of line in taxing the poor with disregard for their well being, it would probably be approved. But if two or three weeks later I implied that a tax on someone with more money was all right, he would ask me to define "poor." Which person was "poor" and which one wasn't?

When I suggested that I was poor and he wasn't, he asked if I wasn't making a comparison based on a very loose use of terms without proper definition. Compared to any number of people both of us could name, he was poor. I was poor compared to him, but he was poor compared to them. Where does one draw the line?

Gradually I began to see the principle he was sustaining. It had little to do with "rich" or "poor." It had to do with the right of the individual to do his best with what was his. Rich and poor were value words having no precise meaning.

I was slowly attaining some measure of organized thinking when my telephone rang one morning. My Aunt Coral, in East Aurora, New York, was on the line. Mother was dying. She couldn't come to the phone but Mother was calling for me. It was an emergency. Would I please come at once?

Without hesitancy, I agreed and rang off. Then I raced in to tell Harry of the crisis. I needed a few days off to get back to New York. Could I please be excused?

Harry took the occasion to have me sit down and listen to a discourse on the subject of basic honesty and devotion to duty. I could hardly believe it. As he talked, I saw what was wrong. He didn't believe me. He thought I was pulling a fast one to get a few days off!

Oddly, as my feelings boiled in mounting anger, I could see his side of it. He had probably had experience with other people who pulled that kind of stunt. And considering the kind of background I had—my shifting from job to Job, my experience in mail fraud action, and so on—I could understand why he greeted my sudden request for time off with a jaundiced eye.

I said, "Harry, I don't think you believe me. My mother is dying and I will go to her. I don't want to lose my job but if that's what this time off is to cost, so be it. I'm going to go."

He said, "You understand that I won't pay you for time you're away."

Seething, I replied, "I'm not asking to be paid for work I haven't done. And if you care to, I'll give you my aunt's phone number and you can check and verify the facts."

He thought about that. Reluctantly, he gave permission for an unpaid break in my schedule.

Before the day ended I had made arrangements to fly to Buffalo. Also, before the day ended, Aunt Coral called again to say that Mother was gone. I told her I was coming.

My sudden trip to the east was a sad interlude. I had convinced myself that I had learned to be tough-minded and that I could attend the funeral without a tear. But when I saw Mother in her casket, there was no way I could manage my grief. She had been marvelous to me. She had lavished her affection on me. Not only had she brought me into the world, but she had also been my good angel throughout, never believing anything against me, even when I was clearly in the wrong.

There were only a few details that demanded my personal attention, but there were a few. Coral had handled everything beautifully. Mother had left a Will and I was the principal beneficiary.

But what was I to do about my job at the newspaper? My pride had been mortally wounded and I could hardly bear the thought of returning. But another side of me responded. This treatment arising from contempt was what I needed. I had always been willful and headstrong. My mistakes were humiliating. Harry was being fair' Damn! I had to admit it. I wasn't a good writer. I was learning things I should have learned years earlier. Harry was cold, apparently unfriendly, but tan his hide, he was *right*! I was getting priceless experience. In reality, I ought to feel gratitude.

I took my pride by the throat and wrestled it to the floor. Let Harry do his worst! I had often gotten by because of my personality, my ability at repartee, and my smile. But could I produce? Harry didn't give a fig for my charm. He wanted results! By all that was holy, I'd see that he had results. I'd show him!

Meekly, I returned to my poorly paid, enormously demanding toil.

Now I was caught up, both by the discipline of the press and the organization of the Congress of Freedom.

The girls had obtained jobs. Tommy was enrolled in school. Loy stayed at the house and made it a home for all of us.

In the evening, and sometimes late into the night, we toiled for the Congress, making arrangements. We obtained the Veteran's War Memorial Building in San Francisco for our big meeting scheduled for April of 1955. Then, every day we'd go to our respective employments to earn our keep.

I was acting like a field marshal. By telephone and letter I called on various members of the Board of Directors of the Congress to perform this or that chore. Then, one day a call came from Thad Ashby, my predecessor who was now living in or near San Francisco. He was in charge of some detail respecting the April convention.

After the opening pleasantries, were out of the way, Thad said, "What were you planning on doing during the convention, Bob?"

The question made no sense. "What am I going to do? Why, I'm going to be right there In San Francisco. I'm going to be running the show. "What did you think?"

"You can't come back here."

"What?"

"You can't come back here."

"Is this some kind of joke?"

"You know damn well it's no joke."

"Thad, I don't know what you're talking about. Of course, I can come back there. Trains and planes are running." I laughed. "Has there been a big storm at Donner Pass? Don't worry, I can get through somehow."

"I'm talking about what you did when you were here before." Thad's voice dropped to a whisper. "You'll never show your face in this town again."

"I'd like to know why not. I haven't done anything to keep me away."

"Come on, Bob. You can level with me. I know all about it."

My head was spinning. Thoughts of the "I Am" and my real estate experience, as well as all my other activities in San Francisco, flashed before me. And Pearl. What did Thad mean, he knew "all about it?"

I said, "I assure you, my good friend, that I will be there when I say I will. I'm planning on showing up about a week or ten days in advance of the convention so I can help with final arrangements. Stop sounding like a spy in a two-bit novel."

"Don't try to con me," he said. "At the last minute you'll have an excuse so you don't have to show."

"What will happen if I do show?"

"I don't know. Probably you'll be arrested."

"What for?"

"You know."

My anger surfaced. "Thad, I'm busy. I'm in no mood for fun and games. If you have some information, I'd like to know what it is."

"You've seen the report."

"Report. "What report?"

"You know. The one put out by Retail Credit."

"Retail Credit! What in hell has that got to do with me? Sure, I had some financial difficulty at the Jefferson Hotel and I guess my credit can't very good. So what? This whole convention is handled with cash. I've raised nearly enough and admissions will take care of our expenses."

"It's not just your credit. It's the other things you've done."

"Like what?"

"It's all in the report,"

"I haven't seen any report."

"Really?"

"Thad, I have seen no report whatever."

"About the "I Am?" And "Mankind United," and so on. You know."

"I have never seen a report made out by Retail Credit."
"Honest?"
"Honest."
"Well, it's all around out here."
"Do you have a copy?"
"Sure thing."
"How about being a good scout and sending it to me?"
"Can do. Really, you haven't seen it, huh?"
"Right."
"I'll send one right away. You'll see why you can't show up."
"Thad, I was in the "I Am" back in 1939. This is 1955. I did nothing wrong in the "I Am." Perhaps I was foolish being connected with t, but I did nothing wrong. What was that other thing?"
"Mankind United?"
"Yeah." I was puzzled. Dimly I recalled hearing the phrase but I knew nothing about it. "What about Mankind United?"
"You helped put that outfit on the map. It's listed as subversive."
"I know nothing about it whatever."
"You probably figure you covered your tracks, but they've dug it all up."
"Then they've dug up something that doesn't exist. Please send me a copy. Right away."
"Will do. And then, let me know what you decide."
"I've already told you what I'll do. I'll be in San Francisco when I say I will. But I sure want to see that report."

I told no one about this conversation until a few days later when a letter arrived from Thad containing a six-page, single-spaced report put out by Retail Credit Company. I went over the report and was appalled.

The document was an interesting blend of fact and fiction.

What was particularly enlightening was that it had been prepared at the request of Jack Hardy, my erstwhile political opponent from the 14th Congressione1 District in Los Angeles.

Suddenly, I understood why so many of my friends and well wishers began crossing the street so as to avoid talking to me. And, again, I saw the familiar touch of the press, which so often takes the adversary approach in trying to discover truth.

My career had been unearthed. But it had not been set forth in an unbiased manner. Virtually every statement was in the form of an accusation. By now the public is familiar with the process. They've seen it often enough on television even if they don't road.

The party conducting the interview begins by stating the most innocent activities in a hostile manner. For example, "You admit, then, that you went to bed at nine o'clock on the night of January 10th?"

Clearly, there is nothing criminal about going to bed either at nine o'clock or on January 10th. But the tone and manner is such that one is eager to deny. So the interviewee cavils. "Hell, it was probably a few minutes *after* nine."

"It was *later* than nine!" Again, the hostile glare, the look of accusation.

"Well, I didn't check it. Or if I did, I don't remember."

"Aha. Then, in fact, you don't know when you went to bed, is that correct?"

"I wouldn't 8ay that. I went to bed about nine, perhaps a bit later."

"But you didn't check!"

"That's right."

"If you didn't check, then how do you know?"

"Well, I don't really know, I guess."

"Aha. Then why did you say that you went to bed at nine o'clock when, in fact, you don't know when you went to bed because you didn't check?"

By now the interviewee is rattled and feeling an overwhelming sense of defensiveness. And interestingly, anyone reading or listening is beginning to assume that the poor wretch is guilty. Guilty of what? Who knows? Or cares? He's just guilty, that's all. And, thus, the sharp reporter for the press or for a credit company damns with adversary questioning.

So with this Retail Credit report on me.

I had been born. (That establishes that we are talking about a real person.) I left school prematurely to get married. (Aha. Suspicious mount.) I had worked at a radio station in Minneapolis where I had made the employees upset because I talked about my religious views. (And all this time, I thought they were upset because I was anti-labor boss.)

I left that job to become the announcer for the "Great I Am" which was later indicted for mail fraud. I was named in the indictment. (Now we know, don't we? This is a bad man we are talking about.)

I had gone to work for Mankind United, writing its books and various publications, which had been branded by the Attorney General as subversive. (This was news to me. But clearly it is part of the pattern of criminal behavior. What can one expect from so desperate a scoundrel?)

I had written my own book in support of the villains in the mail fraud case.

I had gone into business in San Francisco. The business failed, and I had taken bankruptcy under Chapter 13.

I could see why the Republican Party had repudiated me. Indeed, I could see why Thad Ashby was certain I would shy away at the time of the convention.

I could see something else as well. If Harry Hoiles ever got his hands on this document, every suspicion he had about writers would be confirmed in me. I would be summarily discharged.

Some of my achievements were included in the report. But they were included in such a manner as to make them appear despicable and the result of devious cunning. Had I seen that report about someone I didn't know, I would have made certain that I never met him. And it was out, had been copied who knows how many times, and had been circulated so widely that even Thad Ashby had one.

I trotted into Harry's office and laid the report on his desk. "This is terribly important," I said.

"Thad Ashby sent it to me from San Francisco. Some of it is true. In fact, I've told you about most of what is in there except for the things that aren't true."

I told Harry that it had first been issued in 1950 and that, until this very moment, I'd never even seen it. But no one could possibly know how far it had gone or whose hands it had fallen into.

Later that day, Harry summoned me to his office. His countenance was dark. Since some of it was true, and since it had been put together by a reputable firm, why was I asking him to accept that some was false?

I went over the report with him, sentence by sentence. I showed him that what was true was presented in a negative light. Taken alone and without the innuendo with which the document reeked, it would not have been incriminating. I had done things that were not wise. Was I the only person in the world who had ever been guilty of poor judgment?

The most damning item had to do with Mankind United, which I denied flatly. Harry didn't like that. He was sure Retail Credit wouldn't have put it in unless there was something in my past that had been documented.

When this most unpleasant meeting ended, Harry said, "You will have to get Retail Credit to retract this report."

"They'll never do that, Harry. Much of it is true. Why should they retract it?"

"If they don't, I will have to dispense with your services here."

I could understand that. Nobody would wish to have the man on the payroll described by Retail Credit.

"We're coming up on that meeting in San Francisco for the Congress of Freedom," I said. "Retail Credit is a California corporation. While I'm on the west coast I'll do my best to get at the bottom of this and I'll try to get a retraction."

"If what you are telling me is true," Harry said, "you have grounds for a legal action for libel and slander."

"You want me to file suit?"

He looked at me, and icicles formed. "Get a retraction. If Retail Credit will provide it without a lawsuit, fine. If not, you must sue. And you must prove in court what you have tried to prove to me."

"Otherwise?"

"Otherwise, you are through here."

I took a deep breath. 'All right, Parry. I hate to go into court. All the silly things I did in my early life are going to be dragged out and I'll be made to look like an idiot. But in its most damning area, this report is false. If I can't manage it any other way, I'll sue."

Harry nodded.

"Will you at least give me the interval between now and the termination of the convention in San Francisco? I'll try to get it resolved without a suit."

He thought about that. "You reserved the time for yourself when we made our arrangement on the telephone," he said. "I will keep my part of the bargain."

"Thank you, Harry."

At home we made final arrangements for the Congress. The family was as shaken over the Retail Credit report as was I.

I would leave ahead of everyone else and fly to San Francisco. Edy would drive to the west coast, taking a bit of time to visit relatives in the Walnut Creek area, after which she'd show up in San Francisco to help in any way possible.

Loy would come later driving our car and bringing Ruth and Margie. Tommy would spend the time with a marvelous ranch family we had met and learned to love. Their name was Rapp and they had a spread east of Colorado Springs. They had a small son close to Tommy's age.

Meanwhile, Ruth phoned her mother to see if some of her extensive influence might be brought to bear so that Retail Credit would back away from the document it had authored during my ill-fated political campaign.

Chapter LXXXIII

As we made our plans for my departure to the west coast, Loy came down with the flu. My sweet wife has always been blessed with astonishingly good health. However, when she does succumb, everything falls apart. It appeared that she would be unable to attempt the trip. Ruth and Margie, neither of them confident of their skills as chauffeur, agreed to come to the Congress of Freedom only if someone else would drive them through the Rockies. Loy would be happy to oblige. Provided, of course, that she was up and about. Loy had only just learned to drive, but had complete and justified confidence in her ability.

With decisions to be made and final arrangements still to be accomplished, the time came for me to head for San Francisco. Reluctantly, I turned everything over to my bed-ridden spouse and the others, asking them to solve the problems. I took off for the Golden Gate, emotionally in turmoil. I was counting on having Ruth, Margie, and Edy help with the work of the convention.

Ruth, Margie and Edy had, in fact, put the Congress of Freedom together. Loy had held everything else together. The four ladies were my good angels and I needed all of them to make the Congress work. It looked as though Edith would arrive, but the others would not. It was always made to look as though I did it all. In fact, it was a team effort with the ladies carrying the load.

I took a room in a working man's hotel, not many blocks away from the Jefferson and close to Van Ness Avenue and the War Memorial Building. My first act was to contact Ruth's mother, Ethel, letting her know of the Retail Credit report and furnishing her with a copy. She set out to get to the bottom of it and reported back before the convention ended. Ethel was amazing. She managed, and I have no idea how she did it, to obtain an agreement from Retail Credit not to issue the report any longer. However, she was unable to affect any changes in it. So far as Retail Credit was concerned the information was factual. Ethel apparently convinced someone inside the organization that while the information might have been true, it was unnecessarily harsh; I was a good guy and not a bad guy. Therefore, they would withhold most of the information unless they got into a bind of one sort or another.

In short, Ethel assured me that I would be free to return to San Francisco, go into business, and re-establish credit provided I kept my nose clean. This was a development Ethel wanted. Of course, I had no intention of returning permanently to San Francisco, at least at that time.

This "understanding" had no official status at Retail Credit, but I hoped that Harry Hoiles would relent and a lawsuit avoided.

Meanwhile, conventioneers began to converge on the city and I was immediately up to my ears in work, trying to handle the details that normally would have been managed by my girls. Fortunately, Edith put in an appearance a few days early and was quickly assigned a task—that of keeping all the accounts straight.

Everyone was so cordial and cooperative among the directors of the Congress that I began to hope Thad might have kept the Retail Credit report to himself. Each of the directors had his own tasks to perform and our entire convention shaped up in preparation for the opening.

I kept in touch with Loy by telephone. Finally, she decided, despite her illness, to come west. She drove the Buick, with Ruth and Margie accompanying her. But there was additional disturbing news. The owner of our home had decided to double our rent. So we would either have to pay or move out. The new rate was beyond our means.

I told Loy not to worry about it and forced it out of my own mind. But I knew that when we returned to Colorado we'd be in a new turmoil of activity finding a place to stay. Provided I could keep my job.

At last, Loy dragged herself from the sick bed. Getting behind the wheel, she, Ruth and Margie drove to the west coast arriving in San Francisco before the opening session. Immediately, Ruth and Margie plunged into managerial details and the Congress formed up properly from that moment. Loy's arrival was a great morale booster for me. Before the convention ended, she had been fully restored to health.

The Congress of Freedom was an outstanding success. We had a host of able speakers, including the man who had done so much toward awakening an understanding of economic affairs in my mind, Dr. V. Orval Watts. Also included was Westbrook Pegler, the man I had seen in Cleveland beginning the character assassination of

"Daddy" Ballard. We carried Pegler's column on the editorial page of the *Gazette Telegraph* and that gave me access to him.

Again my concern with the great question of karma surfaced. This was a basic tenet of the "I Am" doctrine.

"Daddy" had certainly been vulnerable in many of the things he had said from the platform in Cleveland. Had his utterances created negative karma? I knew how reporters twisted things to make a good story. I knew that Pegler had taken some of the symbolism of the "I Am" and distorted it by ridicule. In serving as an instrument for Daddy's downfall, had Pegler, himself, created negative karma for Pegler?

"Daddy's" karma had come home to roost. Would Pegler ever face the same kind of character assassination he had himself contrived in the Ballard case. I didn't get an answer to that question during the convention. But Quentin Reynolds brought a legal action against Pegler at a later date because Pegler had accused Reynolds of being "pink," or sympathetic to communism.

As it turned out, Pegler lost that legal skirmish when some of Pegler's own copy was read in court. Pegler quickly identified the writer as a "commie," not recognizing his own handiwork. From that time on, Pegler's star moved from the firmament, and he suffered the same character destruction he had initiated in the Ballard case. Events of this sort make one wonder, and turn many people toward metaphysical and occult enquiry.

What distressed me about the convention was the frequent innuendo that the problems of this country came from an abandonment of the Christian religion. This insertion of a religious issue had nothing to do with the convention, but it became a bone of contention. Although nothing was said, the impression was created that the American malaise was a Jewish conspiracy, that communism was a Jewish conspiracy, and things equal to the same thing are equal to each other.

There were two young men who served as directors of the Congress. I had great faith in both of them. One was a man named Johnny Hart, the other was Willie Carto. My intention was to recommend one of them as my replacement as executive director. They appeared to be equally capable. I wasn't certain who would do the better job.

I found the time, even though I was acting MC for the sessions, to take Willis aside to discuss his ideas. I had not detected it before, but I learned that Willis was firmly entrenched in an anti-Semitic stance. I pleaded with him to abandon such a fruitless and unjustified position. I must give Willis credit. He could have pretended and had he done so he probably would have deceived me. I wanted to back him. But he was honest and forthright. He sincerely believed that the Zionist Jew was the vortex of universal conspiracy and unrest. Reluctantly I gave up on him. Johnny Hart had to be my choice of successor. Johnny was surely under no such illusions.

Moreover, before I could summon Johnny for a private conversation, he asked to see me. We met and to my consternation, Johnny began by denouncing me and declared he would do his best to unseat me as executive director, and have me kicked out of the Congress.

He refused to tell me the reason. He merely said, "You know why." I presume I did. Thad must have seen to it that a copy of that abysmal credit report had come to his hands. "Mankind United" was a "bad" organization and I was apparently its "intellectual source" for strategy and tactics. Had Johnny accused me of participation with the outfit I could have denied it. But it's poor politics to deny something specifically when one has been charged only in vague and general terms. Apparently Johnny was doing his best behind the scenes to have me declared *persona non grata*. I wanted no such mark against me. I had no way of knowing how many other directors knew of the report or were affected by it. If any.

I called my family together and also managed to corral Bill Johnson, formerly with Spiritual Mobilization who was at the Congress. Bill was a very brainy person and I felt I could gain by having his advice.

We met in my hotel room and I spelled out my dilemma. I wanted to be re-elected as executive director. I certainly wanted to retain my post on the Board. However, it was doubtful if my job at the newspaper would permit me to serve more than a few months. I wanted to prevent the achievement of the political move to oust me in disgrace.

Ruth wanted me to resign at once and turn the reins of the Congress over to the Board. Then, we could all walk out and go home. I was reluctant to do this. That was the kind of thing I had done before when I felt that principles in which I believed were being violated. What course of action should I take? No one likes to quit under fire, even though there may be times when such a procedure is wise.

As I had anticipated, Bill Johnson had some ideas. He suggested that winning re-election to the Board and as executive director would be easy if a few simple rules were followed. Then, it was his recommendation, that I resign altogether. The tone of the meeting indicated that it would not be in my own best interest to continue with the Congress in any capacity.

The by-laws of the Congress required that, immediately following the convention, we hold our annual meeting and elect the new Board and the executive director. Following Bill's suggestions, the entire affair was managed as he had outlined it. My re-election, while not unanimous, was achieved by a clear majority.

Following this victory, I tendered my resignation. I had no one in mind as my successor and said I would be happy to work with any party chosen by the new Board. I would surrender all records, funds, and accounts in A-one shape.

The Board also decided to publish a book that would recite all the events of this particular Congress. Thad Ashby was given the job of putting it together. In due course the book was issued as a memorial to the work done by those who participated.

With the Congress out of the way, and my chore in respect to it an accomplished fact, our family and I drove back to Colorado in our two cars. I reported to Harry Hoiles that I had managed to win the agreement of Retail Credit not to circulate the faulty report any longer. Since I had attained only an "off the record" agreement, Hoiles was not satisfied. A lawsuit must be filed or I must look for other work.

Clearly, I had to find an attorney and Harry would offer no help of any kind. It was all up to me.

In the course of my brief sojourn In Colorado Springs had met a wealthy man, living in the Brookmoor District, named Bob Donner. Donner was an avid anti-communist and I sought him for advice on the matter. I showed him the report and spelled out the damaging, untrue elements. Donner we instantly on my side.

Donner was a supporter of the *Gazette Telegraph* and was aware of the direction of my editorials. He immediately concluded that the Credit Report had been put out by "commies" in an effort to "get" me. Further, he had an attorney friend in San Francisco named Aaron Sergeant, another staunch anti-communist. Sergeant would be glad to be my attorney, he was sure.

Since the Retail Credit report had been issued during my political campaign and since in that campaign I had made no secret of my antagonism to communism and my support of the free market, Donner could have been correct.

But he was shooting in the dark and I had no way to prove or disprove his conclusion.

I told him of my financial dilemma. Sergeant would require a retainer fee. I didn't have that kind of money. Did Donner know of anyone who would lend me the money? Donner was a shrewd man with a dollar, but finally decided that the only way to go would require his own participation. He advanced the necessary sum and I was able to win Sergeant as my attorney.

I had to fly to San Francisco for a quick trip for a face-to-face meeting with the man who was to represent me. There the necessary papers were signed and the lawsuit filed. I learned that in matters of slander and libel one sues along two avenues.

Part of the total sued for is called "compensatory damages." These are the real losses allegedly suffered by the plaintiff. The other avenue is called "punitive damages." Here, the plaintiff calls upon the government to punish the offender far in excess of the actual damages. The amount to be paid by the defendant is, of course, determined by the court. But it is customary in most of the cases where punitive damage is awarded, to grant the money to the plaintiff, thereby establishing an interesting motivational syndrome.

In libel and slander matters even though the government is deemed to be acting for the people, as a whole, the reward goes to the individual plaintiff. This motivates attorneys and their clients to sue for very large sums.

This is particularly true when the client enters into a percentage arrangement with his attorney, in which he agrees to Fay court costs and a minimal fee. Moreover, he and the attorney split the winnings along a pre-arranged percentage line. Such was the deal I made with Sergeant.

The legal action was filed in Federal Court on the grounds that I was living in Colorado. Had I continued to reside in California, where the defendant had its principle offices, a state court would have heard the case.

I returned to my waiting desk at the Gazette Telegraph with a lawsuit on file and a newspaper story published in San Francisco, as evidence of my action. Sergeant had estimated that it would take at least two years to get on the trial calendar.

Since Harry was a man of honor in all things, I now realized that I had virtually a guarantee of a job, for at least the length of time necessary to bring the legal matter to termination. I would have to see to it that I gave no grounds to upset this arrangement.

I had other problems confronting me. We had to move or begin paying a huge rent.

Colorado Springs is something of a watering place for the horsy set, People who love to ride, or who admire horses for any reason, like to come to the Springs when the weather is good. During summer months, the population of the city swelled by thousands and nearly all the large homes on the market are rented out at high rentals to those who can afford every luxury. That, indeed, was what was happening in respect to Number One Elm Street.

I followed the rental ads in the GT with devotion and the results were discouraging. Large places at reasonable rents in summer simply weren't available. We thought of obtaining adjacent apartments in conventional apartment buildings—a procedure none of us wanted, but even that proved too costly for consideration.

One Sunday an ad appeared concerning a large property in Cascade, a suburb of the Springs located part way up Pike Peak via Ute Pass.

With the entire family aboard, we drove up the gorgeous canyon west of the city learning that Cascade at this time was little more than a wide place in the road. By asking directions we finally located the property, which turned out to be a huge log cabin, made of native tree trunks and having a distinctive beauty all its own.

The owner, Alice Leck, a widow, showed off her estate. We fell in love with it at once. Unfortunately, it wasn't as commodious as it appeared from the outside. However, Alice had built two other cabins on her land, one of which she planned to occupy herself when she rented the big house. The second cabin could be made available to us along with the log structure.

The best part was the rental fee. It was very close to what we had been paying at Elm Street. We took the deal. Margie and Edy would sleep in the adjacent cabin. Ruth, Tommy, Loy, and I could be in the main building where we would take all our meals,

The living room was sensational. It had a high, beamed ceiling, rising to a peak with a gigantic fireplace at one end of the room. The immediate item of interest in the furnishings was a full sized pool table.

Loy's first comment when we saw it was, "Well, that will have to go."

Alice Leck smiled somewhat enigmatically and said, "All right. But why don't you leave it for awhile? Then, if you want it out, I'll have it moved."

Clever woman. It was impossible to ignore a really fine pool table. After we moved in, we began puttering around with it and before long we were addicted. Even Tommy, just tall enough to see over the rail, learned how to line up a cue.

Our first summer in Colorado Springs was spent in Cascade, in a building that reminded me alternately of Heidi and Lincoln. And when the ensuing winter came upon us at the same address, we found we had one marvelous advantage by being situated on the mountain.

We could park our cars facing away from the house, aimed downhill. If we had difficulty in starting an engine, we had only to release the brake. Somewhere between our house and Colorado Springs, a distance of more than ten miles, the engine would start.

At the newspaper, in addition to writing editorials, I became the editor of the editorial page. The number of editorials I had to alter or rewrite diminished.

The biggest news in Colorado Springs had to do with its being chosen as the site for the Air Force Academy.

When I had served in the military, there was an Air Corps, which was part of the Army. Now the Air Force was created as a separate and distinct branch of the service. A spot about twelve miles north of the city had been chosen for the campus, for its new military school.

The second major item to take my attention had to do with our competition. Colorado Springs was one of the relatively few small cities that had a competing newspaper. Our opposition was called the "Free Press." It was owned and operated by the International Typographical Union (ITU) which also maintained the Old Printers

Home in the city.

I learned from Harry that the origin of the paper had occurred during a strike against the Gazette.

In earlier years, the Broadmoor interests and the Penrose family had owned the paper for which I worked. They had sold it to Freedom Newspapers long before I appeared on the scene.

Shortly after the paper had changed hands, the ITU had brought a strike action against the Gazette and put out a picket line. The Union had been opposed so successfully by Hoiles management that even with a picket line, the Gazette gained in circulation and advertising.

Despairing of winning anything or of interrupting Gazette Telegraph publication, the Union had at last decided to whip the GT at its own game. It had organized its own newspaper, employing it as a substitute for pickets. Indeed, in its first issue the Union had made this observation on its own front page, serving notice that the Free Press was the device by means of which the strike was to be continued.

The strike had never been settled. It was so far out of date that newcomers to the city had no knowledge whatever of what had gone before. We did our best with editorials and with news stories to keep the public informed that our competition wasn't a true newspaper and that it hadn't been organized for that purpose. It was a self-admitted "strike weapon."

According to the calculations Harry had made from data obtained from within the Union, the Free Press was a colossal loser. It was in the red by at least three million dollars. It lost money every day of the week and double the amount on Sundays. To pay for its losses, the Union was assessing the rank and file of its own Union and had leached millions from them in fines, assessments, and various other "emergency" exactions.

Even in the face of this competition, Harry would often take stands that he knew in advance would be unpopular. He was concerned primarily that his position was right in respect to the concept of freedom. Then, he would go ahead.

Thus, to my amazement and delight, we published reams of material showing what a gigantic boondoggle the Academy construction was. Beginning with a request for a mere 10,000 acres (certainly a fair amount of land), the Academy ended with more than

60,000 acres.

The city fathers, the merchants, and most of the important people wanted the Academy with all the dollars the Federal government could channel into the region as a result. We took the side of the American taxpayers who were being compelled to pay for the expensive, extravagant construction.

What was particularly rewarding to me was our outspoken position in respect to unions and to the government school system. These were topics that, in other communities, were viewed as sacrosanct.

Harry believed that only the truth was sacred. we endeavored to keep our opinions out of our news stories. Often, indeed, reporters were upset by the editorial material we published daily on the page reserved for that purpose. But on that page, which was mine to edit, we recited the story of what was happening to this country under the onward march of government as it grabbed up first one thing, and then another.

During this first year at the *Gazette Telegraph*, I found myself enthralled with what I was doing. I wasn't certain as to how many read what I wrote and offered. But I had the satisfaction of believing that I was reaching those whom cared to read. It was an exciting and stimulating period.

Chapter LXXXIV

My desk in the newsroom of the *Gazette Telegraph* was just large enough to hold my typewriter and prop up one elbow. The desk and I became inseparable companions. My concern for my country and my determination to actually become a writer provided the mucilage that glued me to the job.

Thanks to my earlier experience with the "I Am," I had already developed some mental discipline in coping with abstractions. There was one profound difference between the stance required then and the one I now had to learn.

The Ballards, reportedly taking their cue from the Masters, spelled out every thought and tied those thoughts to the appropriate actions. One didn't have to think; one was supposed to obey. It was my task to write on the subject of Human Liberty. But I was not to tell anyone what to do. Each had to seek the facts and make his own decisions.

Liberty or freedom had to be the base on which I rested all my arguments. In that case, I had to know what liberty and freedom were all about. This meant that I had to think it through for myself.

The newsroom of a daily newspaper is filled with sound. At first I resented the hubbub, because it was all-pervasive. I had to shut it out. Later I became grateful for the tumult that annoyed me. It literally compelled me to exercise my mind at a level of concentration I might have had difficulty in achieving without it.

I learned that it was actually *fun* to think. Conceptual thinking is, to my way of looking at it, the most fun of all.

Imagine a globe, exactly like a large soap bubble. Imagine yourself inside that bubble assigned the task of learning the particulars of how the bubble is made and figuring out its utility, if any.

Every concept is like a bubble. It is a subjective room existing in the space-time continuum of your mind, and nowhere else. Things in the real world of time and space exist. If you doubt their existence, you can kick them and they will kick back. But in the interior bubble of your own concepts you have to do your own kicking back.

When you learn about things, you are learning the true nature of what exists. Or, at least, you are trying to learn it. You are no more than one step away from the thing itself.

In conceptualizing, you are taking a second step. Not only must you be aware of what exists, you must discover *human meaning* to what exists as it relates to you and to others.

Human meaning doesn't exist unless you put it there. That is what conceptualizing is all about.

Does this mean that a concept is false? Not at all. But it does mean that your premises must be accurate both in your primary and secondary suppositions, or your conclusions will carry no weight. When one learns to conceptualize correctly, one's conclusions are valid, even though the conclusions never become things that exist as three dimensional objects in the world we live in.

In the spirit of adventure, let me take the subject of freedom and liberty (concepts) and enter into a giant bubble with me and see where we are led.

Here I will be both the kicker and the kickbacker. And we have shut out the real world, here in this bubble of intellectualizing.

What is freedom?

Human freedom in America is in jeopardy. Exactly what is it that is in jeopardy?

People in other countries look at America, calling it a "land of freedom." Those of us here apparently feel we are losing our freedom. But in other countries, it is felt that migration to America would attain the freedom already lost. Who is correct?

What does freedom consist of?

Several factors go to make up a package we call freedom. Clearly, the first factor would have to be: Freedom to think. The next factor would have to be: Freedom to choose. Then, there would have to be the factor: freedom to act. There may be other factors, but these would certainly be primary.

Are we in America losing our freedom to think? It would appear so. Our eyes and ears are inundated minute by minute with importuning, pleadings, political protestation, and reams of data.

Time to kick back. The reason we are being inundated with all these data and importuning isn't because we no longer think, but because we still do. Those seeking command over our sensory perceptions want us to think, but they want us to reach the conclusions *they* believe to be beneficial to them.

Then, it is not our freedom to think that is in jeopardy. Rather, the losses we may be experiencing relate only to the limit placed on what we think about. Clearly, none of us ever think about something we know nothing about. Because of the explosion of information occurring in the 20th Century, Americans have more to think about than any other people under the sun.

If we understand our own natures, then freedom to think is not in jeopardy although freedom to obtain accurate information could be.

Indeed, were a man given a choice between thinking what he is told to think or dying, he might choose to die. Even an executioner cannot change the thinking of his victim. Most of us would probably choose to utter a lie, seeking to convince the executor that we had changed our thought. By telling a lie, we would preserve our lives.

In fact, we would continue to think as we pleased. We just wouldn't let anyone know. For example, Gallileo, before the tribunal, recanted his findings to convince his captors that he had changed his thinking. But under his breath he muttered "Nonetheless, they (the planets) still move."

The ability to think one's own thoughts cannot be destroyed merely by argument, pleading, or the introduction of data. Drugs (physical items), electrodes planted in the brain (physical items), or other devices that could induce brain injury or interfere with brain functioning might alter thinking or to prevent it entirely. But thoughts or threats do not alter thinking. One's thoughts are not in danger unless some physical means is brought to bear.

If a person does change his thinking, it is that person who effects the change. Thus, while certain persons or institutions are engaged in altering thought by physical means of one sort or another, the people do not face jeopardy from this category.

What of freedom to choose? Choosing is a *mental* activity. Any ordinary person can choose what he will.

He merely concludes that he prefers A to B. That is where choice occurs, in the mind.

The ability of Americans to choose is in no greater jeopardy than is their freedom to think without choosing. Unless physical means are provided, one is at liberty to think what thoughts he will, and to choose what he pleases.

Then, is freedom in jeopardy?

What of freedom to act? Ah. Here is the threatened area. We may think what we please, but are we free to act as we please? We may choose what we will. But are we free to act upon our choices?

A man in prison can think what he pleases and can, in fact, choose to be out of his cage. But he cannot act out his thoughts and choices. He 1e physically restrained. And because he is physically restrained we say he is not free. He has been physically made prisoner. He cannot exercise his freedom.

Conceivably the man in prison deserves to be there. But what of those of us out of prison? Are we free to act? Do those of us who have injured no one deserve to have our freedom to act taken from us?

This is the point of friction. Freedom to act is in jeopardy in America. It is in jeopardy all around the world. It can only be in jeopardy because physical means have been devised and are being taken to impair or eliminate the individual's freedom to act.

What about the freedom of Americans to act as contrasted to the freedom of non-Americans to act? Many non-Americans have come to this country because they have been told this is the land of the free. Large numbers of them have learned after their arrival that they are under duress in many new and strange ways, each of which restricts their freedom to act.

A conceptualized conclusion now begs to be stated. Freedom to act in America is in jeopardy.

How much freedom to act should exist?

If each of us were able to act out his thoughts and choices, the result might be chaos and destruction. I know of no reasonable person who would care for such an eventuality. Is freedom then equivalent to chaos and destruction?

It is clear that persons exist who use their ability to think and act as they please, who inflict injuries on others. Perhaps the freedom we have lost in this country represents no loss, but a gain.

Before considering this possibility, we must now firm up that part of our bubble that has taken shape and form. Imagine, if you will, a huge sheet of plastic, cut like the skin of an orange segment. We now glue this to the inside surface of our bubble. This segment of pigmentation now becomes a permanent part of our concept. It says Americans are not free to act as they please.

It appears that we now require two words because there are two meanings to freedom that we must consider the constructive and the destructive.

We could say: freedom, sub-one; and freedom, sub-two. Then, we could ascribe different meanings to the two sub-sections. Rather than that, we already have two word es Freedom and liberty. I will use them.

We might have said that freedom conveys one meaning and license another. License could be used as a term to denote a negative application of freedom.

I will arbitrarily employ the terms "liberty" and "freedom," ascribing to each specific meaning. Thus, I am stipulating certain definitions, not to demand acceptance but to further communication. Ideas are like nectar served in a goblet. The purity and integrity of the nectar is our objective. Different goblets must be used or we will adulterate our concepts and have punch instead of elixir. The goblet is the word used to convey the nectar of thought.

Let me stipulate that the term "liberty" be used to denote man's natural ability to think and act as he pleases. In this sense, all men are born in liberty. This is why I use the word. I do not wish to say that all men are born in a state of license. While parents may often view their unruly offspring as qualified candidates for the term license, it seems reasonable to note that in thousands of choices and actions performed by children license (negative freedom) does not appear.

Consider our bubble again, and let us conceptualize once more.

If it were possible for a person to exist totally alone with neither parents, friends, acquaintances, associates or children to make their presence known, then the word "liberty" might be the only one required.

Such an isolated individual could never have his liberty challenged by another person—there being no other person available. Nor would such an isolate impinge on the choice or actions of others. Circumstances in this case would simply mean that the individual could think and act as he pleased. The only question that could be asked concerning his choices and actions would relate to their implicit wisdom.

By using liberty in this sense, I am now free to employ the term "freedom" within the practical context of real life. I wish to use the term "freedom" to denote the social and economic condition of man wherein he lives with or near other human beings. However, we must bear in mind that each of these persons has the natural ability to inflict injury on anyone else. Freedom would be that state in which persons are capable of inflicting injury one upon another, but for one reason or another, don't. Such a society, properly organized, could be a free society.

This would mean that one's natural liberty to act is mobilized positively. Such would be a state or condition of freedom. The ability to act negatively would still exist. But it would not be employed. Freedom would exist then, only when individual liberty remains unimpaired.

Time to kick back. What if we have a man born in state of liberty who happens to fall and break a leg. Hasn't he lost his liberty? Not really. He has lost his mobility. His choices and actions may be curtailed as a result of his accident but no human being inflicted him with the broken leg. He fell out of a tree and landed awkwardly. The tree did not injure him. It did not single him out for specific and unique action. The only conspiracy against him arose from his own ineptitude.

But what if another man reduces an opponent to helplessness, and then breaks his leg? Now the first man's liberty has been taken from him by a second man. We have a state of non-freedom, because one man acted deliberately to reduce or destroy another's natural liberty.

An individual who finds his liberty curtailed by an act of nature, or by an act of any natural species other than man, has not lost his liberty as a result of human action. He lost his mobility (more or less) as a result of natural law of one sort or another.

This is not the area of our jeopardy. We are in danger from others of our own kind, just as they are in danger from us. We may also be in danger from the elements, from wild animals, from disease and countless other perils. Nature does not conspire against us.

It is up to us to understand nature and the nature of wild animals, disease, broken bones...and the like.

If we are injured, it is our own fault.

In short, if it were impossible for one human being to inflict a physical injury on another human being, no matter what or how he tried, then the term liberty would suffice. No human being could impair another's liberty.

But because a man is capable of injuring others of his kind, we must show two results each of which could descend from liberty. Men can associate with each other and refrain from inflicting injury. Men can also inflict injury upon their associates. When men refrain from inflicting injury upon others, we have a state or condition of freedom. When men do not refrain from inflicting injury, we create a state of non-freedom (in whole or in part).

Now take a look at the segment of pigmentation we glued to the interior of our bubble.

It is exactly correct. Liberty isn't in jeopardy. As a natural condition it is bound to exist. It is freedom that is in jeopardy, which is what we said,

Let us provide two more segment-shaped pieces that we now put in place on either side of our first segment. They will read: Man's natural liberty to think and to choose is not endangered. The other segment will read: Man's freedom to act is in peril.

We have postulated human beings living in a societal condition and we have postulated a single individual living in isolation. We may now move away from the latter. While isolation might occur once in a great while, it takes at least two to propagate. And it takes many to produce the goods and services we must have if we are to stay alive. Therefore, we will move away from the segment dealing with liberty. It is freedom that is in jeopardy and a most particular kind of freedom. The freedom to act.

Some method must be found to restrain human beings so that their ability to do as they please does not conflict with the ability of others to do as they please. Without such a method, and given the full range of choices for the natural expression of one's liberty, freedom might well become impossible.

Ability to act is bestowed upon each person, individually. Additionally, each of us has the ability to limit or remove the ability to act from others by means of force. How do we control the human ability to act in such a way that man's natural liberty will not be impaired within a social context?

Two methods immediately loom. We can organize an instrument of force and coercion and use it to compel everyone to act as we think he should. Or we can ask that each individual restrain himself in regard to others.

There do not appear to be any other choices. Either each person controls himself, or some instrument or agency will be used to forestall or prevent a negative employment of liberty.

But now we have a new problem. Each of us would approve of a condition in which each of us would be able to exercise his own liberty, while the liberty of others who *might* improperly act is restrained.

Apparently, human beings, in respect to freedom, have a certain ambivalence. We want freedom for ourselves and restraints for others. To deal with this ambivalence we have traditionally bargained with a group of strong men and surrendered some of our freedom to them, thus placing them above ourselves. Called by various names, these strong men formulate government.

The merit of the government is presumed to reside in its elevated position above everyone. The government, it has been argued, will restrain those who might injure innocent people and will leave everyone else alone.

A new problem immediately emerges. The men whom we now call government begin by being human. They are as prone to injure others as the rest of us. But they have an advantage when it comes to inflicting injury. If "government" injures someone we view the act as "right" or "just." If a person not in government performs the same act, we would call that person "wrong" or "unjust."

All "modern" societies suffer from this difficulty under any and every government devised. Thus, all modern societies suffer from a philosophic contradiction. Right and wrong, just and unjust no longer serve to identify the character of a given action. They serve, rather, to identify the person performing the action.

Still another problem appears. For its very existence, men in government take sums of money *they* believe to be adequate from those who earn the money. Thus, everyone is injured to a degree, to prevent anyone from being injured in any degree.

Further, with the passing of time, what is "adequate" at the hands of those governing becomes larger and larger. Government persons still have liberty and can think and act as they please. The rest of the population is *under* them and must obey or suffer loss, indignities, or death. Thus, government removes our freedom under the pretext that it is only through government that freedom can be obtained.

The human record in setting up and dealing with governments

has a melancholy consistency. All governments reduce freedom and some destroy it altogether.

Time to kick back. What other procedure is available? Given human nature and man's capabilities in respect to each other, there will surely be some who will misbehave.

This is true. But curiously, the same phenomenon exists with government fully functional. Indeed, it appears that unless a total dictatorship is provided, the criminal element will tend to enlarge in direct ratio, to the growth of government. Moreover, if a dictatorship is provided, then freedom is banished at once. And the single justification for government's existence is to provide a climate so that we can be free.

Obviously, there are only two avenues. We can do our best to educate and train individuals to refrain from aberrant conduct. Or we can refuse to run the many risks involved and create a state. With state control, there is less risk that a given individual outside of government will run rampant over others but along with this is the virtual guarantee that men in government will.

We have a Gordian knot. But our task is to learn. We are not yet ready to make a recommendation. We are ready to provide two more segments to our bubble. Our first new segment will read: All governments without exception reduce freedom for all individuals living under them. Some governments eliminate freedom entirely.

The second segment will read: If we seek a free society without some agency of forceful restraint, then we are at the mercy of the aberrant individual who, if he thinks and chooses in certain ways, can predictably reduce or eliminate the freedom of some persons in society.

Our final segment will read as follows: There is no risk-free method presently known which can provide a state of freedom. We must produce additional concepts to learn which route offers the fewer risks.

By making use of this conceptualizing procedure and making certain that I accepted nothing at all until the conclusion became inescapable, I worked painfully toward a view consistent with reality. Not as I wanted things to be, but as they were, in fact.

When this is done, I developed a set of building blocks from which ever higher and lovelier structures arose. This is the process I followed in writing editorials for the *GT* and for Harry.

Gradually, step by step, I developed a philosophy from which I have not had to deviate. The conflicts and inconsistencies were worked out at the beginning.

It isn't always a happy philosophy. I often wish things were other than they appear to be. But reality is whole and wholly consistent, A philosophy based on reality must echo its holistic quality and be equally in harmony with that which is.

Chapter LXXXV

Writing is slow work for people like me. A person cannot write faster than he can reason. True, he can get words into line on paper. But in my case, writing means re-writing, again and again.

If A is true, and B is true, then C has to be true. If C turns out to be true, then it becomes a building block, a new A. One searches next for a new B. And so on. I know of no way to make this sound exciting or even interesting. But this is what I did, finding it exhilarating. My editorial output increased and improved.

Before 1955 ended, word came from the attorney handling Mother's estate. The Will had passed probate and I would find myself on the beneficiary end of a $4,000.00 inheritance.

My bills were virtually out of the way. What I had borrowed from Bob Donner in the pending legal action was outstanding, but under control. Mother had provided me with a nest egg to help with my future. Was it possible, at last, to pay all debts and have a clean slate?

I broached the matter with the girls. Perhaps the time had come to establish the school. The idea, though dormant, had never been far from my thoughts.

What would be required? Only one way of proceeding had ever been successful for me. If I could find a large building with a reasonable amount of land in conjunction and if the parcel could be purchased for as little as $4,000 down, then we could all move into that new building, just as in San Francisco and Los Angeles. Our individual earnings would be spent on our own livelihood anyway. So, if we became proprietors, we could keep our jobs, pay rent to the property we were buying, share our meals and—in the process—have the use of a facility that would serve as a school.

The girls were favorable. Indeed, Edy suggested we begin at once in our cabin in Cascade. But the Leck property was too small. Because of our location in the center of the USA and of the pioneer nature of our educational endeavor, we'd have to offer residence facilities. We would have to seek students from across the broad United States. Ours could never be a neighborhood day school.

We planned to teach free enterprise. Who wanted to learn about that? We'd have to offer potential students something sugarcoated. He'd instill the principles of economics surreptitous1y, while they weren't looking.

It would be desirable to offer our schooling during summer months when people were more likely to travel. What we needed was something in the nature of a Dude Ranch. We'd try to offer a two-week vacation in a mountain setting, with schooling thrown in as a bonus. We could charge the students for board and room. We'd have to take in enough by serving meals and offering living accommodations to pay for everything. If we could find a property that would accommodate this kind of multiple purpose, and if we could get our hands on it for only $4,000, we'd be on our way.

"Wouldn't it be great," Loy suggested, "if we had log cabins like this one, on a large piece of land. Then, we could build other cabins and we'd have a rustic setting people would enjoy." She was right. It would be out of the ordinary. People would come to experience life in the mountains, and we could teach them in spite of themselves.

We had become enchanted with the building we occupied. Such a building had atmosphere. He believed that atmosphere would be an inducement, not only to attract enrollees but also to engender a scholarly stance. Didn't Lincoln begin his educational efforts in a log building?

Before attempting step number one, I approached Harry Hoiles. I had become proficient enough in writing editorials so that I could handle the chore in half a day.

I began by reminding Harry that my purpose was to teach the truth regarding free enterprise. I was a crusader for liberty, not a newspaperman. I was at the paper and delighted with the opportunity. But I had a proposition. I would continuo doing my work as before. There would be no change, either in volume or quality, except, hopefully, I would continue to do a better job.

Meanwhile, I wanted to be excused in the afternoon. If I had half my time to myself I proposed to start a school and devote myself to teaching. To make it worthwhile, I proposed taking a cut in pay. Thus, he could lower his editorial costs but his editorial page would remain the same.

He listened to everything I had to say, showing neither pleasure nor displeasure. Inscrutably, he finally nodded. "I'll think about it.

I'll get back to you."

With other people, such a statement would have been a brush-off. But not with Harry. If he had disapproved he would have said so. Further, when he said he would think about it, he would do Just that. And when he said he would get back to me, that is what he meant.

I communicated his reaction to the girls and they felt I had been turned down. Big events were shaping up at the Gazette Telegraph. Despite our competition, the Gazette was expanding so nicely that we had outgrown our pressroom. The building we were in didn't have enough land to add an enlarged facility.

Harry was preoccupied with building plans. A new location had been found and construction begun. It was believable that a derailment of my proposal had occurred.

The family talked about it and I conceded that if Harry did say "no," then I'd have to stay on the job as before. Even with that anticipated S4,000, we would be in no condition to do anything without at least half of my present income to work with.

There would be a delay, perhaps a long one. We'd move as soon as we could. Meanwhile, I urged the girls to believe that when Harry said he'd got back to me that is exactly what would occur.

A week passed, and Harry called me into his office.

This time he smiled and asked me to sit. This was unusual. I at once feared the worst (a pink slip) but hoped for the best (approval). I tried to look nonchalant.

"To build a school," Harry began, "will take a lot of money. You don't have any. I won't give you any. What makes you think you can get the money?"

What a question! Right on target. I gulped. "I don't know that I can, Harry." I took a deep breath. "I've put together a mailing list. I began it in Florida and we have about 3,000 names of come of the best conservatives in the country. I've corresponded and talked to quite a few of them. I'll let them know what I'm doing and try to get their support."

"What makes you think they'll give it?"

"I don't know that they will. Some of than probably will. I'm sure all of them won't."

I gripped the arms of the chair. "Here's the way I look at it. If I don't ask, I'll never find out." I paused. "I'd hate to think, later on in life, that if only I'd asked, I would have had support."

Those candid blue eyes continued their unblinking stare.

"I will have $4,000," I said, and told him of my mother's Will. "If I don't try, Harry, I'll always believe that there was something I might have done and that I didn't do. And I don't want that on my conscience. The country is coming apart. Free enterprise is almost unheard of in our schools and colleges. You know that.

"I think I can do something about it. Maybe. I'd rather try and fail than not try. At least that way, I'll know I did the best I could. I'll have to be content with that."

Harry nodded. "All right. Let's just suppose you get the money. Frankly, I doubt it. But let's suppose. You have the money. What makes you think you can get anyone to come out here to Colorado Springs, to sit in your class to learn about free enterprise?"

Again, a zinger. "I don't know that I can get anyone, Harry. But I have the same problem. What if I could, and then didn't try? I'd always believe that I could have done it, but that I was unwilling to give it a chance."

Another nod. "Very well. Let us suppose you have the money and students are willing to come. What makes you think you could teach them?"

My heart felt like the bull's eye on an archery range, with Robin Hood doing the shooting. "You've got me, Chief. I don't know that either. I'm not a teacher. But I know something about free market economics. I think I can communicate it verbally as well as I do it in writing, and probably better. If I can manage some of it, I'm sure I can find others who will work with me in that area. There are plenty of free market exponents right now who can't find work. Of course, I can't afford anyone at the outset so I'd plan on doing the teaching at first. And I don't know that I can do it at all.

"But you know my answer. It's the same as before. Maybe I *can*! But if I don't try, I'll always believe I could have, but didn't get the chance."

This time Harry smiled. "Do you have a place in mind?"

"No, I don't," I admitted. "But I wasn't even going to look if you disapproved. I'm not asking you to guarantee my efforts. I'm only asking you to let me have the time so I can try. And you'll be saving money!" That last was my trump card.

He sat at his desk, nodding, apparently to himself. Finally, he said,

"Very well. You can have the time."

"Oh, thank you very much." I sprang to my feet.

"But there is one part of your proposition I won't approve."

My heart sank, "What's that, sir?"

"Your pay. You'll receive the same pay as before. You'll be doing the same amount of work."

"Really?" This was totally unexpected.

"Of course, it I find that it distracts and prevents you from doing your job, it will have to stop."

"I won't let that happen."

"All right, then." He turned to a stack of papers, and I was dismissed.

At home the girls were impressed. "Harry's a strange man," Loy said. He seems so cold, so detached."

I know," I agreed. "It's disconcerting. But I'll tell you something. Harry is absolutely okay. He's tough. He has to be. But he never leaves you in the dark. You can believe him. If he tells you anything, that's the way it is. And it isn't that way for right now. It's that way from here on. He doesn't shift his position. He's as solid as a rock."

"Is that good?" Ruth asked.

"It's different," I conceded. "But I'd rather deal with a man who rarely smiles but who means what he says, than try to do business with someone who smiles to your face and cuts you down when your back is turned. Harry's aces with me. And think. I get the same pay! Now that's something!"

Our search for the type of property we wanted took us out of Colorado Springs—south, west, east, and north. There was plenty of unimproved land available. But my plan demanded living quarters for six people at the outset. And everywhere we looked, the warning cry was constant. Check on the water table. Don't take land, however attractive, until you are certain water can be found or provided in some way.

He found some beautiful places priced well beyond our wildest hopes. We discovered some suitable housing, without adequate land. And then, one day, a real estate agent called me. He had learned that I was looking for a property and he had something he thought might provide the particular combination of features we sought.

A Denver family owned half a section of land (320 acres) in the

Rampart Range, north of Palmer Lake and south of Larkspur. It was clear of encumbrances and contained several cabins in questionable condition. The land was situated at a point where Plum Creek crossed it from the high mountains on its way to the Platte River. The family in Denver had turned this one-half square mile into a game refuge and called their holding "Glenrose Park."

The next Sunday we drove to the location specified and as we left the Perry Park Road, turning in across an ancient cattle guard, it was as though we had at last come home.

The site was magnificent. At the gate and along the creek bottom, the land was approximately 7,000 feet above sea level. Most of it was wooded with secondary growths of Douglas Fir and Ponderosa pine. Included were clumps of aspen, scrub oak, and willow. Something better than 250 acres of the terrain was steep and virtually impenetrable because of the density of forest growth. Within a quarter mile, the land rose to 8,000 feet above sea level.

Plum Creek, little more than a rivulet in summer, gurgled and splashed across the flat meadowland. Wild roses and banks of flowers grew profusely. Nearly half a mile removed from the entrance were the cabins, snuggled into the slopes, each on its own relatively level ground.

Never had I seen the eyes of the girls light up with pleasure as they now did.

We parked and strolled—no, that is too citified. We parked and climbed up and down some of the many trails in evidence. We located an old logging road part way up the first rise and wandered along the unused, overgrown path between the trees.

Margie looked at me and said, "This time, you've struck twelve." She was right. On a scale of one to ten this property went off the chart.

But what about the cabins? No claim had been made concerning their livability. We had been furnished with a key by the realtor. An ordinary skeleton key would have served as well. All the cabins were painted in rural railroad yellow. They weren't attractive but they were there.

We entered the largest. It had a solid stone and concrete foundation and was two stories in height. The first floor was a concrete slab and contained a bedroom, storage room, bathroom, and a screened-in porch. The bathroom had a shower but no tub.

A stairway, as steep and narrow as a fireman's ladder, led up to the second story entirely above ground. It contained two rooms, one of which had a fine stone fireplace. Additionally, there was a screened-in back porch. The largest room, that with the fireplace, was about 18 feet by 12 feet.

There was no furnace. The smaller room on the second floor was the kitchen, endowed with a wood burning stove. This building, with some modifications, would be livable.

We entered the second most prepossessing structure. It, too, had a solid foundation of rock and concrete. There was a large front porch, one fair-sized room and two smaller ones, with a john and wash basin in the basement. No place to bathe. No furnace and no fireplace. And no place to cook, either.

Further, the floor canted dangerously in a northeasterly direction and the doors stuck, indicating willingness on the part of the building to seek a better location.

A look at the other buildings, six in all, and my heart sank. They could hardly be dignified as buildings. No foundations, no insulation, no interior finishing of any kind. The exterior siding provided the interior decor. Each had an electric light dangling at the end of a ceiling cord. No plumbing. No heating. They were little more than canvas tents without the canvas.

We gathered in the meadow. I shook my head. "This is the finest land for our purposes I've ever seen. Or imagined. It's great. But did you see those cabins?"

The girls were apparently as glum as I.

"That two-story cabin is okay," I said after a moment. "I think Loy, Tommy and I could survive in it. No heat, except the cookstove and the fireplace. Frankly, I wouldn't ask anyone to live in any of the other places without extensive remodeling and renovation."

"What about that second one," Ruth asked. "It's pretty rough. But if we could get a bathtub put in and fix it up a bit, I think the three of us could live there."

There was no enthusiasm in response.

"What about heat?" I asked. "Colorado winters aren't accompanied by heat waves."

"It can be fixed up," Ruth insisted.

"The two-story place has to be fixed up, too," Loy chimed in. "It's a wreck."

"Bear in mind," I said, "we have only $4,000 to work with. With it we've got to buy the place and do all the fixing. That won't give us a lot of money."

"No, it won't," Ruth was intent on pushing. "But we can work fast. I don't mind working and working hard when we have something worthwhile to work with and to work for."

"Let's look around some more. The big question has to do with water. At least both of the cabins with foundations have running water. That's a start."

Our explorations continued. It turned out that each pair of cabins, other than the two with foundations, had an outdoor privy nearby. No running water for any of them. Clearly, they were a lost cause.

As we explored the water system, the whole project appeared to be a lost cause. The property had no well. The water used was pumped directly out of the creek and pushed some three hundred feet up hill to a giant 5000 gallon galvanized metal tank. The pipes were above ground. Then, additional surface pipes carried the water by gravity into the two cabins.

With the coming of winter, the first freeze would eliminate water service altogether.

We were not concerned with the purity of the water. This was a stream fed by mountain springs and the water was as fine as one could discover. Our very first requirement would have to be a well, probably near the creek where we could be virtually certain of an underground supply. Then we'd have to install a complete pressure system with pipes a good four feet below the surface to protect from frost. Either that, or forget taking up residence. Without residence, there was no immediate hope of generating enough income to keep the place going.

Again, we returned to the meadow and sat in the car. At last, I broke the silence.

"Well. we've all had a good look. The real estate agent thinks we could buy it for as little as $4,000 down. The full price is S32,000, which works out to $100 per acre. fortunately, here in Colorado, mortgages don't work the way they do in California. Our first payment of principle, interest, insurance, and taxes will occur one year later. We'll have twelve months to get the thing working.

"I had hoped we could do something with those six extra cabins.

I had in mind turning them into housing for students with at least one for a classroom. They are purely impossible. We'll have to tear them down, save the lumber and, somehow, build a real building that can be used. We're going to have to do the work. We can't afford to hire help."

"How much is the interest on the unpaid balance?" Edy asked.

"Five percent."

"That's pretty steep."

"I know it. Butt we don't have any leverage for bargaining. We either take it on the seller's terms, or we forget it."

"How big will the payments be?" Edy probed.

I did some figuring, "We'll have an annual payment to start of around $1,800 per year. That includes everything."

"I'm for it," Ruth said at once, "with only one proviso. Bob. you have to promise me that the first priority is going to be a bathtub. I will not live in the woods for a whole winter with other people, none of us bathing."

"Hey, wait a sec. First priority is going to be the water system itself. And don't forget, there's a shower in the large cabin. We could all bathe there. If and when we have our water system."

"No," Ruth stated it flatly. "Promise that bathtub, Bob. I don't like showers. I'm for it, provided we have a tub."

"What about the rest of you?"

"I love the place," Loy said. "It won't be too bad."

"I saw a trout," Tommy volunteered. "I almost caught it."

"It is a beautiful location, Bob." That was Margie.

"What about living quarters?" I asked her.

"Quite dreadful," Margie admitted. She shrugged. "I've seen worse."

"It's going to cost a lot of money," Edy cautioned. I don't see where it's coming from."

"It'll be close all around. But maybe we could do it."

"You know my position," Ruth said. "Promise me."

"I know. The tub. Okay, the tub's a promise."

We all looked at each other. Nothing more had to be said.

I took a deep breath. "I'll make an offer."

"If you do," Edy said, "you're going in way over your head."

"I know it. And you know it won't be the first time. But I'm going to do it. Maybe we can make it work."

Chapter LXXXVI

The deal was made. Loy and I bought the property in our name using Mother's inheritance. I wanted to create a corporation so that I would not be the owner of the property. At that moment the time lag involved might have prevented the purchase.

Remembering the United States Day Committee and the lessons I had learned from Merwin Hart, I tried to draw together a group of trustees, solicited from the ranks of Conservatives whom I knew. I failed. The idea of establishing a school was too large an undertaking for anyone. As a matter of fact, the attack against me in San Francisco had created a credibility gap. People were polite. And who could blame them if they were suspicious of me. It was now too late for second thoughts. We had title to 320 acres of land. Further, until we had a water system that worked, we couldn't move onto the property. And we had no money to pay workers.

In Colorado Springs, a small businessman named Bill Froh owned the "Enterprise Tent and Awning Company." He had had a run-in with the local authorities that tried to intrude into his business with some absurd ukase. He had fought them to a standstill. I had never met him. But I had written an editorial in his support.

I walked into his store one afternoon and introduced myself. I spelled out my dream. I also spelled out my lack of money. Despite the fact that Bill was a complete stranger, I asked if he would co-sign a note at the bank in the sum of $2,000. That was about as brassy an act as I had ever performed.

Bill hardly hesitated. For a brief moment he stared at me. Then he grinned, offered his hand and said, "Sure."

Bill's credit was good and, with his signature, we drew the necessary funds and hired a couple of men from Palmer Lake to put in a well and the necessary ditches for piping.

Here I was most fortunate. One of the men was named Norris Romack. There was hardly a chore I could mention that he couldn't perform. He said he was a plumber, an electrician, and a carpenter. And he wasn't kidding. Best of all, he wasn't afraid of working hard. Nor did the sight of a spade discourage him.

Our entire plumbing system was put in so skillfully that we never had a problem with it. The job even included a cesspool. The cost was under $1,000.

Thinking of the coming winter, I purchased a second-hand Jeep. I wanted the four-wheel drive. I knew that snows could be deep in the mountains, and we could hardly afford a tractor with which to clear the stuff away. If we couldn't push the snow to one side, then we had to be able to get through it. I counted on the four-wheel drive for that.

Someone advertised a bathtub for sale, second hand. I bought it, got it aboard the Jeep, and headed for Glenrose Park. The Jeep promptly broke down.

With the tub still in it, the Jeep was towed to a garage where mechanics located the trouble. The gear that converts from two-wheel to four-wheel operation had cracked. So we had the axle replaced, and the job took three days.

At last, I was able to fulfill my promise to Ruth. But there was much more to be done in that cabin. Indeed, before we moved in, substantial remodeling had to occur.

There were three rooms in the cabin, plus a cement hole for a basement. We tore out one of the partitions, built two others and came up with four rooms, one of which was the bathroom. Norris moved the fixtures from the basement, installed the tub, and the cabin was livable.

A boiler was put into the little basement so hot water would be available. This same facility was installed in the larger building that Loy, Tommy and I were to use. Up to that time, cold water was all that was available. Now we had two sets of pipes in both buildings, and we began to appreciate what our pioneering ancestors must have experienced.

We gave the interior of the girls' cabin a paint job. Ruth's favorite color was purple and she covered the floor of her room, the largest, with a purple pigment about the color of a ripe plum. The rest of us thought it quite dreadful, but it was Ruth's room. It also became our first office.

In the larger cabin, other things had to be accomplished. The lower floor had walls that were nothing but poured concrete. Norris taught us what "furring" was. To save money, the girls and I did the interior cosmetic work. We put in a knotty pine finish thus making the grey concrete disappear. I drew the task of putting paper on the ceiling. To my joy and amazement, it stayed there after I finished.

Meanwhile, I gave full service at the newspaper, but I worked every afternoon on the property. Margie landed a job at a hospital in Denver and had to commute much further than the rest of us. But she was game. She bought a car so she could hold down the job.

Nor did I forget our purpose. We were going to have a school. Barry cooperated and we managed a bit of publicity in the Gazette about the project we had undertaken. I called for volunteers to come out to Glenrose Park to help us take down the cabins that were to be converted into a school building. For a series of weekends, numerous people who worked at the Gazette, plus a few others, came out to our lovely land and tore a couple of the cabins apart.

In process, I learned something else. The lumber in these cabins was so old and weather-beaten as to be virtually unusable. We saved as much as we could, but boards kept breaking and splitting. We continued anyway.

If the wood was useless as building material it would still burn, and we had a cook stove and a pot bellied stove to be fed all winter.

While these exercises were in process, we prepared a flyer that I proposed to mail to those who might make contributions. But before we could do that, simple honesty demanded that we form a corporation. I could hardly solicit funds to improve a property that was in my own name.

We obtained the services of an attorney who advised us that we must have a board of directors. The girls were willing, of course. But if this was to be more than a family affair I had to bring in some people from outside.

I have already mentioned a ranch family with a spread east of town. Tommy had stayed with them during the Congress of Freedom. I approached the rancher, Bob Rapp, a good conservative. Bob was willing and I asked him to serve as a director. I also asked Bill Froh, who also agreed. The lawyer proceeded to draw up a non-profit corporation called, "The Freedom School."

Bob, Bill and the family met at the property for this auspicious occasion. I produced the papers showing our incorporation. At the same time, I deeded the property over to the corporation. In return, I took back a non-interest bearing note, which the corporation could redeem at any time it had the financial capacity to do so.

A celebration seemed in order. We should have planned a picnic, but—preoccupied with legal formalities—I had forgotten all about so trivial an item as food. The nearest store that might be open on a Sunday was 26 miles away.

We searched our cars and the ladies searched their purses for some forgotten tidbit we might share to express our mutual trust and goodwill. Carol Rapp found a bouillon cube in her purse. Margie discovered a tea bag.

Loy was called upon to perform her magic. She made a pot of very thin bouillon and boiled water for some weak tea. The bouillon cube had a beef base so I refrained, but I did share a cup of tea. Somehow, it was a feast. Our project was launched!

With Ruth's help I carried on an extensive correspondence. Ruth was a secretary second to none. The pamphlet describing our efforts was put in the mail and a trickle of small contributions started. Edith kept total control of all monies and managed with a fist so tight it seemed to be bound shut with friction tape. Most of our contributions were $5 or $10 bills. It takes quite a few donations of that size to pay for the mailing of a pamphlet, let alone to build a fund for the work to be done.

However, we had things in order and moved to the property. That was a joy in itself. The weather was fine, but winter would soon be upon us.

I was so eager to begin work on the school that I could think of little else. Being on the scene was a help, but that alone wouldn't do the job. We'd have to start construction as quickly as possible. First of all, a general classroom had to be provided, and then sleeping accommodations for our enrollees had to be built. To begin construction, money was the first requirement. Our attention quite naturally turned to our fund drive and efforts we had already started in that direction.

The location of the school was in such a remote spot in Douglas County that no mail delivery was available. We rented a post office box in Colorado Springs and either Ruth or I picked up the mail daily. One day I opened an envelope from a man who signed himself Reno Sales. I presumed this to be a pseudonym. When I found a check in the envelope for $1,000, I came up out of my chair. I showed the cheek to Ruth. "We will succeed," I said. "I'm sure of it now."

I learned that Reno Sales was a geologist who had worked with the Anaconda Copper people in Montana. He had retired as a man of some means and somehow our efforts appealed to him. He gave us a real boost.

Reno Sales was his real name. In Montana, his reputation was firmly established. His industry and integrity are still remembered by all who knew him. His was the very first sizeable contribution we received.

I expected more of the same magnitude but many, many months were to pass before anything of that size showed up again. Financially, we were in the doldrums, and moved at a snail's pace.

Winter came and, with it, some heavy snows. I was familiar, of course, with the Minnesota winters and believed that since Colorado was further south there would be less to contend with. How wrong I was. We were in the mountains at 7,000 feet, Further, we were on the northern side of what is called the "Palmer Lake Divide."

Ferocious storms followed one another over the mountains. Our cars were parked at the base of the slope in the meadow, and we had no garage for them. We now had four vehicles. Edy and Margie each had their own and I still had the Buick. The Jeep was assigned to Loy so she could do the shopping and get around. It constantly broke down and Loy hated it.

Morning after morning, Edy, Margie and I would descend early to our parked and sometimes nearly buried vehicles, to get them started. Ruth would drive into town either with me or with Edith. Sometimes we would have as much as a foot of snow at the school, and then discover that no snow whatever had fallen in Colorado Springs. The Palmer Lake ridge diverted the major thrust. The Springs had mild winters. Twenty-six miles to the north, we faced heavy weather much of the time.

One Sunday morning, Loy found me hammering some boards together. "What are you up to?" she asked.

"I'm making a snow plow," I explained.

Loy's expression was dubious. "What do you know about making a snow plow?"

"Nothing." I kept working.

"That doesn't look like a plow to me."

"It's a new invention." I had constructed a simple upright panel of boards and nailed a small platform behind it. "Here's how it works," ~I explained. "I'll hitch this plow to the Jeep. The Jeep can get through the snow pulling a load. I'll ask you and the gals to stand on this platform to give the whole thing weight. Naturally, it ought to be made of steel but we don't have any.

"The panel will move the snow. I'll put it at a slant, so the snow will be brushed off to one side. I really ought to make two of these and nail them together in a V. But I can't find enough good lumber and besides I'm not really good as a carpenter. But it's solid and it ought to work."

"You won't get me on that thing."

"Don't be like that. It's really half of a plow. The weight you can provide eliminates the necessity for the other half."

"Well, I like that!"

I grinned at her. "Not what you think. You aren't heavy. But it should hold four people. That ought to do it. Four is heavy."

"What will you be doing while we're standing on this thing?"

"Someone has to drive the Jeep," I said.

Loy snorted. "Forget it."

"We'll do it right after breakfast, Hon. It's a bright sunny day and we've had some fresh snow. We'll plow out to the gate and that means the cars won't get stuck. It'll be fun."

After a fine meal, all of us, including Tommy, descended to the meadow where I had everything in readiness. I explained the theory. All the women had to do was stand on the platform and firmly grasp the top of the panel. I promised to drive in low gear. It looked like a lark.

Ours was an enclosed Jeep, so Ruth and Tommy sat on the tailgate to warn of any possible contingency. There was only enough room for three on the device anyway, since I had overlooked the increased size of women wearing parkas and heavy coats.

I put the Jeep into gear and tried to move. The engine stalled. Finally, after several tries, the Jeep with its living ballast in tow, moved slowly down the road. The snow forced the half plow to one side and little was accomplished.

I stopped to survey the results. "I guess I was wrong about having the tow ropes of different lengths," I said. "I'll make them even so we can move straight ahead. The snow is light. We should have no problem."

Adjustments made, I got into the driver's seat again. I had been going too slowly, that was obvious. This time I started without difficulty and we moved at about ten miles per hour.

There was a chorus of screams and shouts from the rear. I stopped at once.

An indifferent nature, in some much earlier age, had deposited an unyielding rock in the road. The bottom of the "plow" snagged on the rock and, in less than a second, the panel had fallen forward, slapping the ground with such intensity that my "ballast" had their wind knocked out.

Fortunately, none were injured, but that ended the experiment.

One of the interesting features of winter in Colorado relates to frequent thaws. We'd get snow, sometimes very deep snow. Then, for a few days, the sun would shine and the snow would melt and run off. Standard fare in Colorado was what we used to call an "open winter" in Minnesota.

A few weeks later, we had a run of mild weather and most of the snow vanished. I decided that in the available interval, we ought to install some kind of an intercom system. To have a proper installation would have cost a couple of hundred dollars, and we didn't have it to spare. We had a telephone in the larger building, but if messages had to be delivered, someone had to bundle up and sometimes wade through snow to the lower building. Then, the party wanted on the phone, or for other reasons, had to bundle up and wade back up hill.

I saw an ad promoting a "do-it-yourself" intercom. The dealer of the hardware store carrying the item offered no guarantees. He said that if it was installed properly it "ought to" work.

We understood, virtually as an article of faith, that anything we could do ourselves would save money in the long run. So, I now offered myself as an electrical engineer to run wires between the two occupied buildings, and then make the simple telephonic connections at either end of the battery-operated gadgetry.

I suppose I had begun to think of myself as entirely competent in all building trades, except snowplow construction. After all, the barn was still standing. And the ceiling paper in our bedroom continued to cling, in defiance of gravity, without a bubble or gap. I had participated in both procedures. I had even helped with the knotty-pine furring. I shouldn't have trouble with anything that "ought to" work.

We were blessed with another mild weekend without snow. I took the ladder we had used in making the barn and climbed high in a

Douglas fir just outside the screened-in porch of our house.

There, I tacked up several strands of lightweight wire. When completed, the lines would rise from our porch a distance of perhaps sixteen feet nearly straight up. Then they would descend almost vertically to the window of Margie's bedroom some thirty-five to forty feet further down the slope. The reason for these sharp angles was to lift the wire above the heads of anyone walking about on the hillside.

All went well until I and turned to make my descent. The tree I was in had been trimmed of low branches and I had done my work standing on the top rung of the twelve-foot ladder. In turning, my foot caught and pushed the ladder to one side, where it balanced precariously for a moment, and then toppled down the hill.

Naturally, I grabbed the trunk of the tree in a loving embrace with arms and legs. However, my muscles were not adequate to the weight they were suddenly called upon to support. I came down the tree like a fireman dropping to the main floor at the sound of a four-alarm fire.

There were small twigs and branch stumps all the way to the ground. They gouged and jabbed me in an extremely private and personal area. For a moment I thought I had become the beneficiary of an unintended vasectomy.

Margie had been watching my antics from her bedroom window. She was convulsed with mirth and concern at the same moment. She was worried about my back. It took a while for me to breathe normally and to assume an erect position but there were not lasting ill-effects.

I proceeded with the balance of the installation that never did work satisfactorily. Instead of being able to talk back and forth as I had hoped, we were finally able to use a buzzer system. Believe it or not, I did manage a pair of buzzers. Clearly, I was becoming expert.

One more experience is worth noting. I had drawn up the plans for our first building. I decided that the efficient way to go was to attach the first new building to the house. By locating it in this position, it would extend to a point immediately above the girls' building. Then, we could put in some kind of a stairway between the two buildings.

The new building would have a basement and a floor above

ground, just as the house had. The upper floor could be the classroom, with one end used as a library. The underground room would be for recreation and study. I wanted our guests to have the benefit of a pool table as soon as one could be afforded.

This building site would require excavation of the hillside. It would also require the removal of a number of trees. That would take time and money. But anything we could do before hiring professionals would save money.

With a spell of good weather on a weekend, all of us were outside, enjoying nature. I had planned for this exercise. I had a saw, axe, and rope.

I gathered the women and Tommy below the tree I had chosen as my first target. It was the largest. I explained the project. We would cut down that tree and get it out of the way.

I had read Ernest Thompson Seton with boyhood devotion and admired the manner in which a good woodsman could "throw" a tree anywhere he wished. I knew it would be impossible to convince the family that I was a good woodsman, since I had never cut down a tree. But I had devised a method of procedure that, I trusted, would overcome my inexperience with consummate ease.

I pointed upward, explaining the problem. A telephone line ran from a pole to the house. It hung perhaps ten feet from the tree. If the trunk toppled in that direction, the telephone line would be snapped like a dry twig. On the downhill side of the tree, electric lines ran between the house and the girls' building. If the tree went that way, zap, and no electricity.

The solution was conspicuous. The tree must be felled in such a way that it dropped between the lines.

Now a final problem. It was a very tall tree. If it swung to the north as it came down, the top of it would crash into the lower house, even if it missed the phone lines. Conceivably, it could cave in the roof. There was only one channel in which the tree could be safely brought to earth. The tree must fall east by south between the two sets of lines and away from the lower building.

Hastily, I admitted my lack of knowledge and experience before I could be reminded of it. But I had the solution ready.

"This is why we're all here," I cried. "Even you, Tommy. You have a vital part to play. I'm not much good as a tree climber. I'm sure I don't have to embellish that statement."

I received silent, grinning agreement. "This is where you come in to make the tree cutting possible," I said to my small son, age nine, "I want you to shinny up the tree with this rope and tie it tight as high as you can go.

"Once the rope is in place," I continued, "I'll chop down the tree. When I have it nearly cut through and ready to fall, I want all of you gals to pull on the rope. We'll stretch the rope in the direction we want the tree to take. I'll stay at the base of the tree and push. That way, my ignorance can be overcome and the tree will naturally follow the direction of pull."

"That will take a lot of muscle," Edy said. ~I don't think we're strong enough."

"Not at all," I insisted. "The tree will not be pulled down, it's going to fall of its own weight once I have it cut. It's only the matter of direction. The rope will guide it, not force it."

"I'd rather be excused," Margie said. "It sounds a little complicated."

"It's easy as falling off a log," I said. "Come on, Margie. All we need is one, good hard tug. You see the tree is stupid. I'm afraid it won't fall the way I've told it to. You will be the tree's brains and bring it down in the correct piece."

"I don't think I was hired to chop trees," Loy said. "I think you're crazy."

"Crazy or not, please help. Everything we can get done beforehand will save time and money. You know that."

Finally, I won grudging agreement and Tommy went up the tree. Filled with the importance of his role, Tommy did an excellent job. He tied a good, firm knot and came safely down again. The next step in the process was mine.

First, I took the buck saw and, with Edy helping on the other end, we cut through much of the trunk. I tested it several times as we worked but there was no give. The tree was still firmly upright.

Now I took the axe and, trying to remember my Seton, I moved to a new location on the trunk and began to cut a wedged-shaped gash. The chips flew and the amount of wood still in support looked mighty slim.

I rested briefly and then pushed on the trunk. This time the tree moved slightly and didn't appear to move back. If a wind came, it would probably fall.

"Get on the rope, people!" I shouted. "I think it will start down if you pull and I push at the same time."

With some under-the-breath mutterings, the women lined up along the rope in the correct compass bearing.

"Now!" I gave a good push and the girls gave a half-hearted twitch. The tree slowly began to topple.

"Pull! Pull!" I shouted.

To my dismay, instead of pulling, the girls dropped the rope and scrambled for their lives. It hadn't occurred to me. I had asked them to pull the tree down on top of themselves'

My two cuts on the tree had done the trick. Instead of coming down as I had planned, the tree now pivoted on the remaining upright fibers and with a great swishing crash descended to the roof of the girls' cabin, knocking down the electric lines. Fortunately, the lines didn't break.

Later, we got Norris back and he put the lines up again and repaired the roof. I decided that cutting trees had to be put in the same category as making snowplows. Neither was my line of work.

Chapter LXXXVII

The *Gazette Telegraph* moved into a magnificent new building east of the center of town and on a rise overlooking the business district. I was delighted to find that plans included a private office for the editorial editor. It was situated in the newsroom and next to Harry's office.

Shortly after the move was made, Harry's secretary decided to resign. I thought of Ruth as a possible replacement. Ruth had been working as a secretary ever since our arrival in Colorado, but she hadn't found a post where her full range of skills was required. Her jobs had been humdrum and unrewarding.

I suggested that she approach Harry for the job, suddenly available. She did I so, and obtained the position with no difficulty. It wasn't long before Ruth demonstrated her superior ability as an editor. When I had finished with the page, she would go over it and almost always find a way to improve it, or correct some typos I had missed.

From this date on, Ruth and I worked together at the Gazette. It was a period of learning and development for me that has had no parallel in my life.

I would write my editorials. Ruth would ask questions and debate with me on every issue. I'd whip that bit of writing into the best shape I could. Then I'd take it to Harry. Nothing I wrote ever got into the paper without Harry's personal okay. I was the "official" voice of the publisher and Harry took nothing for granted.

Consistency was the watchword. The newspaper was in favor of human liberty for every individual. That meant that at no time could I take a position that might conceivably diminish the right of each individual to his own freedom. The right of each individual to manage his own life and his own affairs, regardless of anything and everything else, became my constant theme.

All of us are in the habit of rationalizing any position we take. Indeed, we are so skillful at rationalization that we are capable of supporting the most convoluted and contradictory positions. I eagerly supported pro-freedom ideas but until I began this intensive writing chore, I hadn't been tested and tested again as I now was.

Harry and I butted heads, argued, sought to demonstrate our positions, and gave each other a thorough course in logic and logical expression.

At the outset, we followed the advice of Harry's father, R.C., who favored shock therapy. I wrote with gloves off and pulled no punches. Since we favored the right of each individual above the alleged right of any organization, I presumed that the people of Colorado Springs would support the newspaper's editorial policy. We were "for" each of them. We did not favor any kind of meddling in the peaceful and productive pursuits of anyone. That meant that we disapproved strongly of government intrusion and intervention.

I was rocked back on my heels to learn that very few people liked our policies. The paper did well because it was a good newspaper, but it succeeded often in spite of what I wrote. Perhaps it was successful because only a few read my editorials.

Later, R.C. changed his position in respect to shock tactics and favored a "selling" approach. I adjusted my writing accordingly and we did our best to state the case firmly, but in a gentler, more persuasive manner. A handful of businessmen and a few others were enthusiastic about our policy. By far the greater number despised it and took occasion to show their distrust and animus for me, the "official voice" of the *Gazette Telegraph.*

Slowly, oh, so slowly, we were building a fund so we could begin construction. Then, one day, a letter came from a friend of mine who lived in Kansas City. He wanted to make a contribution but apparently had no cash to spare. However, he said he would like to give us a horse. Surely, with all our land, we could use one. All we had to do was pick up the animal.

How does one pick up a horse in Kansas City? I thought of going back and riding the horse the distance. Ridiculous! I knew nothing about riding. Considering the distance, it would take days. It was a good thing I was so little informed or I suppose I might have tried it. I was in a frame of mind to tackle anything if it would help the overall effort.

A much more practical procedure was suggested. Why not rent a horse trailer, drive to Kansas City, and return? If I left on Saturday afternoon, I could get pick up the horse, turn around and get back to Colorado Springs sometime on Sunday. Then I'd be able to report in for work on Monday as usual.

I finally convinced Edith that a horse would be a real plus so far as the students we hoped to attract were concerned. I wanted the atmosphere of a Dude Ranch. That takes horses. Some might come because we had a horse. Somehow we'd manage to get them into a classroom, too.

Loy asked if she could come with me. Then it turned out that, while the girls were entirely willing to look after the property in our absence, they were incredibly busy and wouldn't have the time to look after Tommy. So, Loy decided that Tommy would be no trouble. We'd take him as well.

With the logistics planned by mail, we made the arrangements and one Saturday, right after work, Loy, Tommy and I set out.

The weather of the plains appeared to be manufactured in the Rocky Mountains. Even as we left the Ramparts, heading east, a storm began brewing behind us.

This was to be one of those mad-cap shuttles I had engineered before in my somewhat checkered career. Our drive east was essentially without incident. We had rigged a bed for Tommy in the rear seat of the Buick; he was never a whining or importuning child. There was never a problem with him. Loy and I would both stay awake. On the return journey, Loy could help by keeping me awake. Loy is a superb traveling companion. In the event I became exhausted, she was competent as a driver.

We kept the radio on and learned that the storm, which was just beginning as we departed Colorado, was revving up into a major event. But we were ahead of it, racing to our port-of-call, so we could acquire one free horse.

It was about nine o'clock when we found the home of our donor. It turned out that he was "horse poor." He had about thirty animals, which were kept on a large tract of unimproved land right inside the city. He wanted to thin out his herd and was as glad to see us as we were to arrive.

We were urged to spend the night, but I explained my problem. It would have been wonderful if we could have stayed, but we declined the invitation. So, about ten o'clock we drove to the corral and my good friend, expert with horses, rounded up the mare he had in mind for us.

It proved to be a large somewhat raw-boned pinto named "Daisy Mae." I had thought all pintos were "pintsized." I learned that pinto meant a horse with brown and white markings, an animal often called an Indian pony.

To my unskilled eye, Daisy Mae was anything but prepossessing, but the donor explained that she was one fine animal. And he was right. But now the best part. Daisy Mae was "with foal." So we were actually getting two horses out of one effort. Daisy Mae was due anytime and we hoped to get back to Colorado before the blessed event occurred!

Somehow, we lured Daisy Mae into the trailer, bribing her with a generous supply of oats. Once all was secure, we bade our host a hasty farewell and were again on the road.

But now we drove into the wind and faced the blackness of storm clouds that blotted out stars and the moon. Within thirty minutes after clearing the city limits, the storm broke.

Loy was listening to the radio. "Bob," she said, "there's a tornado up ahead. They've just reported it. I think we're heading toward it. What if Daisy Mae delivers her foal while we're in the midst of a storm?"

"We'd have a problem," I agreed.

"Don't mares lie down when the baby comes?" Loy asked.

"They do in the movies," I said. "But I don't think Daisy Mae has seen many pictures. If the foal comes, she's going to have to drop it standing up. She couldn't possibly lie down in that trailer."

"That won't be good for her."

"It won't be good for any of us if we meet that tornado, either."

The rain came down in torrents and the windshield wipers had to lift off sheets of rain. The trailer began to sway behind us. I stopped the car and got out into the cascading fall. I had placed a canvas over the top of the trailer and I thought it might have worked loose. Everything was shipshape, but Daisy Mae was frightened and had apparently been throwing her weight from side to side. The wind was ferocious and the canvas was flapping like a gattling gun. I managed to tighten it.

Animals are intelligent creatures. I have often found that I could explain things to animals. I spoke to Daisy Mae above the roar of the storm.

"I don't know anything about horses," I shouted. "But you've got to stop milling about. You could wreck us all. If you'll be a good girl and hold everything, we'll get back to Colorado. And there you'll have a pasture all to yourself that's bigger than anything you've ever seen. I can promise you that. But you've got to cooperate!"

Daisy Mae rolled her eyeballs at me and gave no sign that she comprehended. It was the best I could do and I hastily got back into my seat soaked to the skin.

"How is she?" Loy asked.

"Everything seems fine. She's just not used to riding through a storm. I think she'd like to get out of the trailer for a bit but we can't do that. Our only procedure is to keep going as fast as we can."

"What's that roar?" Loy asked. The sound of the storm was perceptibly stronger.

"Probably the tornado," I said. I ground the gears and off we went again.

"I think the tornado is right above us," Loy observed.

"Could be." I said. "Tornadoes are tricky things. They are big funnel clouds that mostly stay upstairs. They are accompanied by high winds and we're sure getting a high wind now."

"What if it doesn't stay upstairs?"

"If it comes down on top of us," I said, "we'll all be mincemeat. Otherwise, we'll be okay."

Pell-mell we continued our drive.

In another thirty minutes the storm began to wane. Presently, the wind abated and we drove on in pelting rain, but nothing worse. I stopped again and Daisy Mae had gentled and was eating oats. She was sure big.

Gradually the dawn came up behind us but, by then, we were in Colorado and making good time.

The next day was crisp, clear and the air was clean, a lovely contribution to our well being. At long last, we bumped across our cattle guard, used the access road and finally parked in the meadow.

The girls came down the hill to share in the
arrival of our new acquisition. Amateurs that we were, we contrived Daisy Mae's departure from the stall. And we still had only the one horse.

"The mare's pregnant," I told the girls. "We came home under a tornado and I was afraid we were going to get a foal in the middle of the trip. But everything is okay now."

Our donor had provided us with a badly worn saddle and bridle, as well as a rope halter. As we tethered Daisy Mae and carried the other items to a safe place, I realized that the horse's arrival meant something more. He'd have to build a barn. In the summer the horse could forage. But with foot-deep snow over everything, the horse would have to be protected. Besides, there'd be two horses.

The used lumber we were saving would have to go to build a barn. And we'd have to do that right away.

Tommy suffered no ill effects from the trip and, after naps, Loy and I felt fine again. Meanwhile, Edy had prepared a feast for us. Eating it, we made new plans.

The next day, after work at the Gazette Telegraph, I consulted with Norris. Did he have any ideas about building a barn? I told him that the girls and I could build it, but we'd need help from him with electricity and also with the roof.

Norris had ideas. He urged a gambrel roof as the strongest and best for our purposes. Then we selected a spot in the meadow for the structure and paced off the space I figured we'd need. The structure would be about 60 by 20 feet with a second floor storage area for fodder.

"It should go in on a cinder block footing," Norris insisted. The boards will rot out if they rest on the bare ground."

I figured a cinder block footing just one block in height and ordered exactly that many. Then, during the afternoons, we all worked on building the barn. Norris supervised and charged us a minimum for his services. He was great.

We didn't bother with cement to hold the blocks together. That cost too much. We just dug a shallow trench and laid the blocks end to end around the entire periphery. They weren't even trued up. But they were there.

While barn building was in progress, one of my nephews, Jollun Kassebaum, showed up. We put him to work, tearing down cabins and nailing boards at the barn. Also, some of the Rapp family put in appearances and gave us a meaningful assist.

The fourth of July was coming and, since that is the anniversary of our Declaration of Independence, I extended an invitation to all the people who were friends or who had helped us. We would have a picnic and shoot off some fireworks at "the school."

Something in the vicinity of forty people showed up for our celebration. But Daisy Mae gave us our biggest thrill. Sometime during the night of July 3, she delivered her foal. It proved to be another pinto mare, who was promptly named Liberty-Belle—"Libby" for short. We took the birth of this four-footed addition to our "family" as a happy omen of fruitfulness.

Among those in attendance were the entire Rapp family (Carol Rapp and three children) and Mr. and Mrs. Bill Froh. Also, as something of a celebrity, came Rufus Porter. He was a well-known "hard-rock" poet, who had been a prospector during his early years up in Cripple Creek and Teluride. He was accompanied by his wife and regaled us with marvelous stories.

Rufus had a gift for us, too. He brought with him a big old hound dog, named Doctor Kline. By now we had a German Shepherd named "Princess." The two animals got along well.

We discovered, after the picnic was over, why Mr.. Porter had been glad to give up the hound. The dog had a problem with his digestion, during which he apparently accumulated great quantities of gas. This invisible essence escaped him at frequent intervals, leaving no one in doubt as to his whereabouts. He was a fine animal but in perpetual bad odor.

Princess was well behaved and could live inside or outside as the seasons warranted. But Doc Kline was something else. I tried to acclimatize him to staying with the horses. After the barn was built, even the horses turned up their noses at his arrival.

Rufus had suggested that Doc Kline would serve as our first PED. (Pretty Hound Dog.) We decided that the correct letters after Doc's name would be PHEW. One day he wandered away. We never saw him again.

Chapter LXXXVIII

By August of 1956, we had lived at the school for nine months. We had conducted two fund drives, built a barn, and obtained a mare and a filly. Financially, we were about where we had been before we started.

Edith had managed our money so skillfully that we would be able to meet our annual payment of principle and interest, pay off our loan at the bank, and keep going.

But where was the school? In our very fires fund drive we had announced that we were going to build. We were no closer to building than when we made the first announcement.

We had a family meeting. "It's time for a new fund drive," I said. "The last one is tapering off. But people won't give money to the school if nothing is happening. We have to report progress."

"We haven't made any," Edy said. "You can't report what hasn't happened."

I nodded. "What I'm suggesting is, we've got to make something happen."

"What are you planning?" Loy asked. Her face was eager.

"I'm going to borrow some more money." Loy's eagerness vanished. Ruth shook her head. Margie tried to appear detached, but she looked as if she had bitten into a slice of lemon rind. Edy came out fighting.

"I'm against it," she said. "We've worked our tails off. We've done coolie's work. We've put in long hours. Why don't we just have another fund drive? If we move more slowly we won't have a debt hanging over us."

"That's what I'm getting at," I said. "Our second fund drive brought in contributions from fewer people than our first. If we have another in which we repeat what we've already said, we'll see a further decline. And if we don't do something pretty quickly so we can report progress, we'll lose credibility and a lot of friends."

"Bob's right about that," Ruth said. "But I don't like to think about more debt. Edy's right on that point."

"It seems," I said, "that we're all of one mind. We don't want new debt. And we must report progress in our next fund drive."

"I thought you were for borrowing more money!" Ruth snapped.

"I don't want to, Ruth. But will someone tell me how to proceed without it?"

Some glances were exchanged, and several glum faces looked my way.

"If Bill Froh has any sense he won't sign another note," Edy said. "He's lucky to be getting off the hook. Besides, I'll bet you're not thinking of borrowing a mere $2,000."

"You're right on both counts," I admitted. "I wouldn't ask Bill again. And we'll need more than $2,000. I've been getting estimates on the cost of our first construction. The cheapest materials we can come up with and have anything substantial will be logs. We can copy Alice Leck's cabin and build the same kind of building.

"Alice gave me the name of her builder. He is an old mountain man named Charlie Heits. I've talked to him. He tells me he can let us have all the logs we want at 5¢ a running foot. That's $1.00 for a 20 foot log. Further, if we give him the job of building it and pay him $1.00 an hour, he'll deliver the logs to us here with no added cost. He's one of the few men around who knows how to build with whole logs.

"We've got to build a minimum of three buildings to start, as I see it. The first will abut the house. It'll have two stories, the upper one containing the classroom, the lower floor for recreation.

"In addition, we'll put in two residence cabins one story high, each able to accommodate four people. We need one for men, the other for women. As I figure it, that's the bare minimum."

"How much will all that cost?" Edy asked.

"Well, there's more than just the logs, as you know. We'll have to put in a cinder block foundation for each unit and that will cost. Then there's roofing and wiring and plumbing in the residence cabins. I figure we can build all three for $7,000."

"$7,000!" Edy gasped. "Where'll you got that much money?"

"I have no idea," I admitted.

"Wait a sec, Edy," Ruth said. "That's not expensive at all. Are you sure you can do it for only S7,000?"

"I've done a lot of figuring," I said. "Of course, I'm going by Charlie's estimates, plus the estimates we have from Norris on the other work. $7,000 seems about right."

"I'll bet it'll run more than that," Edy said.

"Golly, I don't really know. I'm guessing. But that ought to be in the ballpark. I'll tell you one thing for sure. We can't keep going back to the same people saying, 'Look what we're going to do!' We're going to get some snappish letters saying, "Tell us what you have done!"

Ruth nodded. "You're right on that point. I'm already beginning to feel like a con artist. After all, we've accepted quite a few dollars from people who don't have any more than we do. They contributed because they believed in us. We've got to deliver or we'd better get ready to return their money."

"We don't have any money," Edy grumbled.

"Exactly. So unless someone has a better idea, I'm going to see if I can borrow about $7,000 somewhere."

Edy shook her head. "It's your show, Bob. But you really do stick your neck out."

"I don't like it any more than you do," I admitted. "But I don't see any other way to proceed except to give up."

"We surely can't do that," Margie said. "It's a gamble. But so is everything else."

"I'll bet we can do it," Loy said. "Everything we've done so far is impossible anyway."

"You just don't understand money," Edy growled. It's hard to get."

"And who says I'm going to be successful?" I asked. "I'm not at all sure I can borrow that much. I just want to try. Okay?"

Edy shrugged. "It's your funeral. You have to sign for the money. I'm glad I don't."

The next day I asked for and got an appointment with Harry Hoiles. I spelled out our situation. I stressed the fact that we were up to date on all fronts and had paid all bills when they were due. Further, we would meet our annual payment and were already completing the payoff of the money Bill Froh had helped us get.

"So," I said, getting to the punch line. "I'm asking you to co-sign a note for me, Harry."

"I can give you my answer on that right now. No." Harry didn't mince words.

"Do you find me untrustworthy?" I asked.

"No. I don't. But my dad advised me never to co-sign a note for anyone. I never have, and I don't propose to begin now."

"You won't consider it?"

"That's right. It's out of the question."

My heart sank. "You're probably right," I admitted.

"Further, I can't say that you didn't warn me. You said it would cost a lot of money and it sure does."

"There's something else, as well."

"What's that?"

"You have a law suit pending. Until the air is cleared on that, your job is on the line."

I nodded. "I know." I took a deep breath. "Okay, Harry. If you won't co-sign a note for me at the bank, will you lend me the money yourself? I could give you a second trust deed on the property."

He looked at me as if I'd lost my senses. "If I won't co-sign what makes you think I might lend the money?"

"Harry, I don't think you will. But the difference between no and yes is just one word. And I have to ask. What if, later on, you told me that if I'd asked, you'd have said yes."

"What will you do if I say no?"

"I guess I'll just go around town asking other people. Maybe Bob Rapp will."

"The Rapps are deeply in debt already. I doubt if Bob's signature could get you that much."

"I won't know that, either, until I ask. And there are some others. I keep meeting new people all the time. Bob Donner might. I'm sure he's good for it."

"Don't you still owe him money on the legal action?"

"Yes, I do. But I'm not in arrears. And I'll handle that fine…unless I lose my job. "

"What if you lose the law suit?"

"I'm not going to lose it. I've told you the truth about that report. The court will have to concur. It's the truth!"

Harry looked steadily at me. "Let me think about it."

"Think about what?"

"Think about lending you the money. I'll get back to you.

I walked out of Harry's office in confusion. What a guy. He wouldn't consider co-signing. But he was willing to think about making a personal loan from his own funds!

A few days later that is exactly what he agreed to. He didn't want any interest. As for a trust deed, he didn't want that either, unless I failed to meet a scheduled payment. Then, as a matter of honor, I would belatedly supply him with security. If Harry hadn't already won my loyalty and affection he would have won it then. At that moment, Harry grew to Titan-size in my mind.

Prior to this moment, whenever anyone would criticize the Gazette Telegraph or Harry Hoiles, I would listen with a show of polite restraint, and then seek to rebut on the grounds of principle. No longer. Now when a critic raised his voice against Harry, I cut him down without pausing for breath. Harry's integrity made him a great man in my eyes. I let others know it.

With a splendid sum in the bank account of the corporation, we went to work at once. Charlie Heits was hired to bring out the logs. Norris was hired to pour a concrete slab at the base of the excavation, as soon as we had the first building site cleared. Then cinder blocks were purchased so that one full story could be erected. The logs would be cut and placed on the blocks.

At the same time the footings for the first building went in, I asked Norris and his crew to provide a second slab in the meadow large enough to give us the base for a six-car garage. We had done so well with the barn I reasoned the girls and I could erect the garage.

We still had plenty of old lumber remaining, as we hadn't yet raised all of the original cabins slated for demolition.

Knowing the severity of some of our winter storms, I wanted to get the cars under cover. It was September and winter comes early in the Rockies.

While all this was taking place, I arranged for propane gas service. Instead of trying to heat our residences with a pot-bellied stove and a fireplace, we put in space heaters. We retired the old wood range from the kitchen and put in a gas range.

Presently, a shiny silver tank with 1000-gallon capacity nestled snuggly against the base of the hill at the end of the meadow. Pipes ran upward to provide gas in both buildings. I hadn't included these costs in my $7,000 estimate. But, somehow, we'd have to manage. That first winter had been too rough to repeat.

Now on afternoons and weekends, the girls and I gathered at the site of the new garage. With lumber torn from its prior position as siding, we sawed and hammered and spliced, putting up a shelter for the vehicles.

Norris helped us with measurements. When we had the building finished, he hung the six big overhead doors I had purchased. The roof slanted from front to rear with an 18-inch declivity. I figured that would be sufficient for drainage.

When the garage was finished, we painted it a deep green. The barn had been painted a healthy red. So with voluntary labor for the moat part, we had erected shelter for cars and horses. And the shelters for the family had been greatly improved, with better heat and other amenities. Now we could concentrate on the first school building.

Loy has often told me that I have a "weird" sense of humor. I'm sure she's right. Of course, I insist that it's part of "my charm." What does get me into trouble, on occasion, is my effort to be funny without changing facial expression. Perhaps I was overly impressed by Buster Keaton in my youth. So I sometimes say things which, to me, are facetious. However, the person hearing my remarks could conclude that I was being completely serious, since my face might not give away the secret. As a matter of fact, that's why I often find humor where others don't. It is because they don't. To me, this is mischievous. Loy says she has found it malevolent.

An event occurred at the school that perhaps should have cured me once and for all of ever trying to be funny.

The days were already getting short. I drove into the meadow from town, having spent some of the afternoon running errands. Long shadows from the west were darkening the land.

Parked near the garage, at this moment partly completed, was a huge truck-trailer carrying my order for cinder blocks for the main building. The engine was still running but the driver was leaning against the flatbed, looking confused.

"Hey, Mister," he greeted me. "Know anything about these blocks? I was told to bring this load to The Freedom School. Is this The Freedom School?"

"You've come to the right place," I assured him. "That's my order."

"Will you sign for it?"

"Sure. Where you going to unload?"

"Right here."

I nodded. The actual building site was ninety feet up a steep slope. One look at the size of the conveyance and I realized that whoever had assigned this vehicle to the job had had no idea of getting the blocks to that site. The failure was my own. I could have explained that a smaller truck would have been desirable.

It was possible to drive up the hill in any conventional vehicle. We had ourselves put in the road by clearing small trees and shrubs. In fact, we had constructed a loop, both ends of which came to the meadow. At the left end, where our garage would stand, a narrow, graduated slope snaked through the trees and along the edge of a drop-off for about two hundred feet. At that point it turned left and climbed more steeply, coming up alongside our house, then turning right and ending on a piece of level ground approximately at an elevation equal to our eave-line.

The other entrance to the loop was at the far right end of the meadow. There, a very steep ascent went upwards for about sixty feet, turned right and went up another sixty feet at an acute angle, then turned left again and came out on the same bit of level ground.

Anyone could drive up from the left side. The ascent was fairly gradual until the very last. But the momentum required for ordinary driving would probably get a vehicle up the last few yards. It wasn't easy, but it could be done. However, if one tried to go up the other way, skill and daring were essential.

One had to get about fifty yards away from the start of the slope, then aim, and accelerate to the degree possible. One roared up those first sixty feet, veered, zoomed up the second sixty, swung left at the precise moment, and then immediately braked. That would do it.

If a person attempted to be cautious, the ascent was impossible. The reason had to do with the nature of the soil.

The Rampart Range is a ridge of very tired, very old mountains. It was originally a granite outcropping. But in eons of time, the granite has decomposed and it is now no more than shale and dust, mutually distrustful. Nothing binds it in position except the laws of gravity.

Momentum and momentum alone will permit you to scale the heights. If one drives with reasonable care or allows for any reason, he must back down. There is virtually zero traction. The wheels spin and dig deep ruse. The only vehicle that can move up that slope slowly has consistently proved to be a Caterpillar tractor. Or possibly a very heavy road grader or farm tractor equipped with chains. I'm sure a tank could make it, although I have never seen that tried.

All of this was well known to me. But I was disappointed in the size of the rig, so I said, "The building site happens to be up there." I pointed.

"You think I'm going to drive this load up that hill?"

"Frankly, I don't. I just thought I'd mention where we need the blocks. If you unload them here, we'll have to get others to carry them up."

The driver cocked an eye at the dark and forbidding trees and the opening on his left where the road began. "There ain't nothing on earth that could get me to try it," he said.

"I understand." I actually did. And I was in agreement. But then, that little imp who always wants me to try for a joke prodded my funny bone. "Of course," I said, "a really good driver could do it."

This was calculated to make a good driver sputter. It's called a needle. But I kept my face straight, rolled up the window and drove over to the barn. I had purchased a couple of salt blocks for the horses and wanted to store them.

That task completed, I looked over at the garage. The van had disappeared. I listened. The truck engine was laboring and through the trees on the slope I dimly saw something move. Good Lord! The man who had said nothing on earth could get him to try was tooling up that forbidden incline!

I leaped into the Buick, aimed it at the right hand end of the loop and literally flew up the hill braking on the level strip. Nothing in sight! So I compounded the felony. I drove past the house and turned down, hoping to meet the tractor-trailer before it executed the turn and was irretrievably committed. I was too late. The big job, moving slowly and inexorably, had turned and started up the last lap. Our two vehicles were nose to nose when we both stopped.

I put the Buick into reverse, trying to back up the hill. This strip, alongside our house, was as steep as the grade I had just soared up. I dug a pair of ruts and went nowhere.

I got out and then marched over to the driver where he still sat in his cab.

"I didn't think you'd try it," I said.

"You said you wanted this stuff up here," he said.

We stared at each other. "It's all my fault," I admitted. "Can you back down?"

The driver used his mirror and managed something of a view from a window. "Not a chance," he said. "At this angle I can't control the trailer."

"I see. Well, set your brakes and let's try to figure this out. Come out of the cab and we'll look it over together. Maybe you can back down, slowly."

"I can't set the brakes."

"Why not?"

"My emergency brake's broken. The foot brakes are hydraulic. I have to keep my foot on the pedal with the engine running. If the engine stops, the rig rolls."

"Ye gods," I said.

"Yup," he said. We were obviously in agreement.

By now the whole family was on hand. The problem didn't have to be explained.

"Why don't you get the Buick out of the way, Bob?" Edy asked.

"No traction. I can't back up."

"Then cramp your wheels and come forward."

"The road isn't wide enough to pass."

"You can shove the Buick out of the way in that spot between the trees."

"I'll never get it out of there."

"Maybe the Jeep could pull you out later on," Ruth suggested.

"That blankety-blank Jeep couldn't pull a leaf off a tree," Loy said. "I hate that thing."

"That's not really the problem," I said. "Obviously, I can't stay here. But I'm only about six feet away from the truck. If I move forward, even with my wheels cramped, I can't turn in so short a space. I can't back up at all! I'll just make it worse."

"Well, you've got to do something," Ruth said.

"Come on," Edy said. "We'll all help. "Cramp your wheels and we'll help shove the front of the Buick out of the way. And we'll help push it up hill enough to get it turned. Get that driver out here to lend a hand."

"He can't," I explained. "He has to sit there with his foot on the brake with the engine running."

"Come on, let's try."

Ever so carefully, I let the Buick slip forward slightly with wheels cramped and with lateral pressure. The girls actually caused the Buick to skid in the right direction, thanks to the uncertainty of the footing.

Rocking the Buick backward in its ruts, and then letting gravity pull it slightly forward, the girls literally turned the sedan until its nose was clear of the truck. Then I put it in forward gear and moved out of the road into the underbrush horizontal to the slope. The driveway was no longer blocked.

I climbed out of the Buick in triumph. "Okay," I shouted. "The road's clear."

The driver nodded, shifted into low, and the rear wheels spun. He tried a little rocking and got deeper ruts for his pains. The wheels were halfway to their hubs in shale. He shook his head. "No good."

"Ruth," I said. "Get on the phone and call the Triple A. Tell them the problem and get them over here. They can bring the tow truck up the other way, and they've got a cable and winch. They can haul the truck forward enough to get it moving again."

"Right." Ruth started away and I called after her.

"Call Norris, too. Tell him to get a couple of men out here right away. We're going to need some muscles before we're through with this one."

Edith grinned at me. "You sure do like to get into difficulties, don't you LeFevre?"

"I sure do."

"What made him try it?"

"It was my fault. My sense of humor. I kind of needled him. He'd already said that he wouldn't attempt to drive up and I thought he meant it. I kind of pushed him into it."

Loy shook her head. "Dumb. Dumb. Boy, is that dumb.

"I was just trying to be funny."

"You're about as funny as a four-alarm fire," Loy flared and stomped off.

Grimly, the driver sat in his cab, the engine running, and his foot on the brake. In another forty-five minutes, Norris and a couple of his friends came in from Palmer Lake. They took in the situation at a glance and weren't even ruffled. In the mountains, one can always expect the unexpected.

In another quarter hour, the tow truck appeared. I explained to the driver how to get up the hill and he walked over the course first, as a championship golfer surveys the rough. By now, it was night and we had lights on wherever we had bulbs.

The tow truck made the slope with no difficulty. Fortunately, there was a large tree right at the top of the ascent and the tow cable was pulled around the tree through its protective pulley.

At last the cable was in position on the forward end of the cab. Working together, the tow truck winched the cable and the gears of the truck cooperated. Up the slope came our load of blocks, like a giant whale being pulled from the deep.

Nearly at the top, the tree was abandoned and a new set up arranged. Now the tow truck could move down the steep slope on one side, as the truck came up the last few feet on the other. Presently, the payload stood on level ground and the crisis ended.

Norris and his men helped the driver unload.

We ate a late supper. I got more than my share of kidding. Unfortunately, my sense of humor remained. Or, perhaps it is fortunate.

Anyway, it still gets me into difficulties on occasion.

Chapter LXXXIX

Since our purpose was the establishment and operation of a school that would teach and sustain the principles of a free market, we could not rely on government for assistance. We wanted no government favors, no federal funds, and no help of any kind.

At the same time, we wanted to avoid as much governmental interference as possible. One of the primary reasons for locating in the middle of Colorado had been the distinctly rural environment. The more sparse the population, the fewer the government restraints.

Douglas County, which contained the site we occupied, had a population of about 5,000 people and 20,000 cattle. The county seat was Castle Rock, named for a large butte northeast of the tiny city, which might have been used by early Utes as a lookout, or as a place for tribal dances or other ceremonies.

Our corporation had been organized as non-profit and we hoped to pay no taxes. The attorney advised that, to obtain tax-exemption, we would have to demonstrate for more than a year that the corporation was non-profit and that none of its directors were profiting personally.

We anticipated no problem in establishing this fact since our directors were paying for most of what we were doing. The corporation was profiting from our efforts, rather than the reverse. At the moment, however, we were not entirely certain we wished to go that route. Since we wanted no government help of any kind, would seeking tax exemption not be in violation of our?

At this juncture, we didn't have to decide that issue since we weren't eligible yet to file for exemption. But there was one point I insisted upon. I did not wish to operate in contravention of any government legislation. I wished to avoid all possible government restrictions and exactions. I was not ready for open defiance.

My decision was based on strategic, rather than moral considerations. I anticipated that government people would not applaud the teaching I was planning to provide.

I suppose I felt a bit like a man about to rob a bank, who takes great care not to violate the traffic laws while driving to the scene of the crime. If one is to be caught for an offense, it would be better to be condemned for what one really does than to go down to ignominious defeat on some trivial technicality. Better to be hanged for sinking the Titanic than for scratching its paint.

We were about to erect a building. Wasn't it essential for us to have a building permit?

I had already been through the mill on that score in San Francisco, and I wanted no repeat. So, one bright afternoon I drove from the Gazette to Castle Rock and entered the building housing what little government exists in Douglas County. The building contained perhaps as many as 20 rooms and was about the size of the guesthouse I had on Nob Hill in San Francisco.

With no difficulty, I found the appropriate office and presented myself to an elderly man, whose weather beaten face gave evidence that he still earned the bulk of his living out-of-doors.

We shook hands. "I am president of a non-profit corporation," I said, "which plans to build and operate a school on the property in Douglas County known as Glenrose Park. We recently purchased it from a Denver family and are now ready to construct. I want to take out a building permit."

He surveyed me steadily for a moment. "Let's see if we can locate the property on the platt book," he said. Together we poured over several detailed maps contained in a large tome. Finally, we had it pinpointed, a tiny rectangle on the map, shaded slightly different from every adjacent property.

"Is that the place?" he asked.

I nodded. "That's it, all right. I can tell by the course of Plum Creek that crosses the land. Also, by the location of Perry Park Road. That has to be it."

He nodded. "That's a ranch," he said.

"Actually," I said, "it's been a summer camp. It hasn't been used as a ranch. But we are converting it to educational use."

"Our records show that it's a ranch."

"Why is it shaded that way?"

"That's the zoning. It's a ranch. But it's zoned so you can do what you want with the place without rezoning."

"Well, that's a break," I acknowledged. "So it's legal for me to build a school. That's what we're planning. May I have a permit, please?"

"Your place is a ranch, Mr. LeFevre."

I started to protest and paused. "All right. Let's say it's a ranch. Now, I'm about to convert the ranch to a school. And I'll need a permit for the building we are going to put up."

"You don't need a permit."

"I don't?"

"No. You've got a ranch out there."

"Do you mind spelling that out?"

"Like I say. You have a ranch. You don't need a permit. You can build anything you want. Put in a barn. A silo. Another house. Don't matter at all. On a ranch you don't need a permit."

"What if I put in a school building?"

"You can call it a school if you like. It'll go on our records as a ranch building."

"Look. I'm not doubting your word. But are you sure the County Commissioners will go along with that?"

A deep rumble was intended as a laugh. "A ranch don't need a permit for building. That's all there is to it."

I thought about that. "One time, back in San Francisco, I had a man in the city and county building office tell me I could construct an addition to a building I owned without a permit. I got into a lot of hot water. I sure don't want to repeat that experience."

"This ain't San Francisco."

"Gotcha. Tell you what. I'd really like to get this decision in writing from the Commissioners. I don't want to cause you a lot of trouble. But, if I did have to take out a permit what would it cost?"

"Well, how big is the building going to be?"

"It'll be a simple rectangle about 20 by 60, two stories, fireplaces at one end up and down, and the other end will butt onto a two-story building already in existence."

"Twenty-by-sixty, eh?"

"Right."

"Two stories?"

"Right. Bottom story of cinder block, top story, whole logs. That's the package."

The man scratched some figures on a pad. "I figure $11.00 would cover it. Only there's no need."

I pulled out the checkbook. "Let me write you a check for $11.00. Please submit this and my application to the County Commissioners. If I don't need the permit they can return the check with a letter. If I do, then send the permit."

The clerk shrugged. "Like I say, you don't need a permit. But you got a right to play it safe if you want to."

"Thanks," I said. "I hope you know I'm not doubting you. It's just that I want it in writing one way or the other. I've got directors to please, too."

"Fair enough."

Back at the school, Edy congratulated me. "Now you're showing some sense, LeFevre."

"Thanks, Edy." I didn't get many of those.

The cinder blocks were soon in place and the time had come for logs. Norris and his helpers had laid the planks for the subfloor and the basement was roofed over. Now Charlie Heits took over.

Charlie was an old mountain man in every sense of the word. He was already in his late 70's, grizzled and tough as scrub oak. Logs were no problem to him. He drove an old flatbed truck that listed badly to starboard. Without a helper, he'd bring out twenty to thirty logs at a trip and flip them off the truck like a Paul Bunyan playing with toothpick.

The logs looked old to me. They were without bark, gray, and weatherworn, and I wondered if we were being short-changed.

Charlie explained. "Logs is the best buildin' stuff they is," he said, looking so piercingly into my eyes that I could almost feel pressure on the rear of my cranium. "That is, if'n ya know how t' use 'em.

"Them early pioneers dint understand um. They'd go out 'n chop down a bunch a trees 'n stack um up fer a year er so to season um. Thas not th' way.

"What ya want is fire-killed stuff. These here come outa the National Forest. There wuz a big burn about 70 yar ago. I know th' place and the forsters let me cut um. Fact," he smiled, "they want me t' take um. So, they don't cost me nuthin'. An the forsters thenk me." A stream of red tobacco juice hit the dirt.

"It's like this here. A tree what's been fire killed stands fer years after the burn. That's what ya want. The fire takes off the branches, most of th' bark an' kills the tree. Any sap left in th' trunk runs down an' goes, cause th' tree's still upright.

"When ya cut a green tree an' lay it on it's side, the sap goes to the bottom all along th' log. Ya put that log in a buildin', n' ya turn it so's it'll fit. When the log gits warm agin, the sap goes t' th' bottom agin. The log twists. Th' chinkin's thrown out.

"Them old-timers used t' cuss them logs. They wuz allays havin' t' re-chink.

"Thar ain't no sap in these here logs. They done all their twistin' awreddy. Put one o' these in a buildin' an it stays put."

I nodded in comprehension. I was learning something.

"So long as th' trunk keeps standin' it don't rot. 'stead, it turns hard. I got you good stuff."

"I believe it, Charlie. Thanks for explaining."

"Another thing." He pointed to the butt ends of some of his recent additions to the huge pile. "I sawed them down. It's quick. But it ain't no way t' treat a decent tree. Trees got no respect for saws.

"An when I build, I mainly use th' axe. See the grain in th' log? The saw cuts across an leaves th' grain open. Rain and moisture seeps in. No good. When ya use an axe, the log ends is sealed. I chop both ends to make an edge. Then I put th' edges in, first one slants t' the right, next t' the left, and so on. That way, each log sheds rain and it don't drip on th' one underneath."

There was more to building with logs than I had dreamed.

"Ta keep the logs apart," Charlie went on, "I use little block. o' one-inch pine nailed in place. Then, t' hold um together, I drill a hole in the upper log and counter-sink a nail."

"A nail?" I couldn't imagine a single nail holding much of anything in position.

"Yup. A hundred an' twenty-five penny nail. Here's one." Charlie produced a fourteen-inch spike from a keg. "At th' corners the logs is notched so they kinda shakes hands up an' down. When I git through, you couldn't budge one o' my walls with a bulldozer."

I was ready to believe it. "What about chinking?" I asked.

"Here's how I do it. I cut a stretch o' galvanized metal mesh eighth of a inch thick, 'bout ten inches wide 'n tack it to the underside a' each log goin' in place. When the log's in position, I bend down one side o' the mesh and tack it to the lower log. Then I stuff spun glass insulation into the space. That's the best. Wool's good, but spun glass insulation's one good thing that's new, so I use it. Most of the new-fangled stuff ain't worth a damn.

"When I got the space all stuffed I tack down the mesh on the far side. None of that'll ever get thrown out. Finally, I spread concrete on th' mesh on both sides an' you got yer chinking. Best they is."

"It sounds okay," I admitted.

Charlie nodded. "Keep an eye on us, boy. You'll see."

So the work began. It was unbelievably slow. Charlie brought out two helpers and the three of them toiled during daylight hours and sometimes long after dark.

I learned that each log went into position a minimum of three times.

It was first selected and put in place. There it was marked, removed, and trimmed. The edges were hewn at both ends and the notches cut. Care was taken so that whatever curve was in the log was most advantageously placed.

Then the log was put back to make certain everything was correct. Sometimes further trimming was done.

Finally, it was taken down again and the strip of metal mesh nailed along what would be its bottom side. Meanwhile, another workman placed the one-inch blocks on top of the log already in place above which the new one would go.

The log was hoisted into position the final time and now the holes were drilled and the spikes driven deeply into the log below. The chinking would be accomplished when all the logs were in place.

While this careful, customized procedure was underway, a letter came from the County Commissioners of Douglas County. They had discussed our building proposal and had made a ruling. The 320 acres we had was a ranch. That was final. We could build whatever we wished. From their point of view, we had been, were, and would continue to be a ranch. My check, uncashed, was returned. At least we were not in legal difficulties on that score.

"It's time for another fund drive," I said one evening at dinner. "We can show some real progress."

There were general expressions of satisfaction.

"Do you have some ideas?" Ruth asked.

"Yes, I do. Remember, this building is only the first. We have two others to put in for housing. But we're in motion and I think we can make it. So, it's time we spelled out what we're going to offer and begin trying to attract some students. Otherwise, come this next spring, we're going to have a facility and no one to make use of it."

"When do you think we ought to open?"

"Well, obviously, we're trying to put together a combination package. We're offering a course of instruction along with a vacation at what amounts to a Dude Ranch.

"We're not an accredited school. There would be no reason for anyone to come unless they see this place as attractive and exciting. I think they'll come because of our setting and not because we have anything of import to teach.

"This means that we'll have to operate during the summer months, when people normally take their vacations. So, we ought to open around the beginning of June and stop about September.

"I want to set up a series of two-week seminars. This first year, let's try for a total of six two-week sessions.

"Here's the angle. I think quite a few people would be willing to put up tuition to help pay the tab for a student. So, I'd like to conduct a fund drive along that line. Meanwhile, let's conduct a contest among the people who might like to come.

"I'll rig up a little test and ask everyone interested to take it. We'll award scholarships to those who score the highest."

"How many can we award?"

"That depends on how much money we raise. We'll get all the money we can and then deal off the top. If we have enough we'll give five scholarship. If we have more, we'll give six, ten, twenty...however much money we can raise for that purpose. Bear in mind we'll also accept applications from those who wish to pay their own way."

"What if we don't have enough money to pay for even one?" Edy asked.

"Don't think that way, Edy. We can surely do better than that."

"I'm not opposing," Edy assured. "It seemed a reasonably good way to get started."

We decided, finally, that the full price for board and room and tuition for a two-week stay would be $150.00.

"What do you really want to happen, Bob?" Ruth asked.

"I'm hoping we can find a hundred students. If we put them into six groups we can limit each session to about sixteen or seventeen people. That should be about right.

"Let's think beyond this immediate moment," Ruth said. "Let's suppose everything works out. Suppose we get a hundred. Then what?"

"Well," I said, "what I'm really trying is to prove to Baldy and

Read and all the others that the job can be done. I'm not a teacher. None of us has ever tried to do anything like this before. But if we can do it, others can, too.

"What I'm planning is to put this operation on its feet. Then, I want to turn the whole thing over to some real professors. I'm thinking of Baldy. I want him to run it. But at the moment he doesn't think it can be done.

"I think there's enough support in favor of a free enterprise system to finance a school which will concentrate in that area. Lord knows plenty of people out there are griping about their taxes and claiming that their businesses are being interfered with.

"It seems to me they'll support this effort. As far as I'm concerned, this is an experiment. But I certainly don't plan to do it all my life. I just want to start it."

"Okay," Ruth said. "How long will it take to prove?"

"I have no idea," I said. "But let's call it a ten-year trial run. Let's try for 100 students a year for ten years. That way we might reach a thousand. Perhaps I can do a good enough job to convince one out of ten that free enterprise can exist without any government support or interference.

"How many really consistent people are there in the country right now, favoring the position I will recommend? I'll tell you what I think. I doubt if I could find more than 20 if I looked hard. Most people who say they favor free enterprise are like the people we met on that speaking tour. They want free enterprise at tax time. But they want government assistance the rest of the year.

"I'm going to offer a consistent position. The one I take in the editorials at the G-T."

There was a feeling of general agreement. It went deeper. The whole family was beginning to feel excitement. We were working very hard. But our progress was visible for all to see.

As quickly as we could prepare the material and get it into the mail, we started two drives at once, the first to raise money, the second to attract students.

By now, winter had come in earnest. By February of 1957, our days were short and the snow stacked up deeply, then melted away to make possible more delightful days.

Heits had just finished roofing the second story. A sixty-foot ridgepole, weighing half a ton, went from the fireplace clear to the end wall. Log rafters carried two-inch tongue-in-groove planing that provided the arched ceiling as well as support for the green asphalt shingles nailed on from above.

The windows went in, but the cement finish to the chinking could wait for warmer weather. With our classroom in this condition, I had an application from my very first student.

A young man named Bob Richardson, living in Denver, wanted to study with me. He didn't want a scholarship. He was willing to pay his own way. But he was not willing to wait for June. He wanted instruction about freedom. He wanted it now.

By mail, we worked out the details. He drove forty-five miles each way or two nights each week. The two of us, bundled to the ears, went into the unfinished classroom. We couldn't have so much as a blaze in the fireplace—the flue wasn't ready.

Bob and I sat opposite each other on planks resting on kegs with a sawhorse table between us. There, on a one-to-one basis, we discussed, debated, talked, and listened. I set forth the proposition that man is, by nature, a free being, that slavery is a man-made institution that ensues when someone presumes to take power over a second human being. I argued further that slavery is contrary to the nature of the slave, however beneficent it may seem to the slave master.

I demonstrated that slavery is rationalized, under the name of government and politics, because of the belief that if we didn't enslave others, the others would enslave us. Thus, we practice slavery on some in order that others should be free.

Force and violence can only sustain such a dichotomy. And, while it may be human nature to impose on others, it is contrary to human nature to endure imposition indefinitely.

This was the beginning of the Freedom School. For two hours or more per evening, with the thermometer registering below freezing and sometimes below zero, we sat in the drafty, unfinished cabin to consider the philosophic and economic verities. It may not have been an ideal environment. In another way, it was, perhaps, the best arrangement that could be made.

The teacher was able to put full attention on his pupil, aside from keeping warm. The student, likewise, was able to concentrate. The result was the formation of a life-long friendship that continues to this day.

Bob tells me that those sessions helped provide direction and purpose for his lifetime. He developed into a rare, gentle, sensitive person. I take no credit. These were qualities he had in abundance at the time I met him. All I could possibly have done was to solidify and confirm his own merit in his own eyes.

Chapter XC

So passed the winter in which our first school building came into being. It was clear to me that the nation's economic condition was worsening rapidly. Love of country drove me to do all possible within the shortest time conceivable. Pressure was on me and I kept it on everyone else.

Yet the work proceeded with lagging disregard of the national crisis which seemed to be sweeping upon us. Those few who advanced sums to our cause obviously agreed with me as to the state of the economy, as well as the direction being taken.

We knew that certain principles of human action had been violated repeatedly by the government. We were convinced that a day of reckoning was just around the corner. None of us could yet detect the time frame within which these inexorable forces would produce their inevitable result.

Personally, I worked at the newspaper, had my special sessions with Bob Richardson, kept up my correspondence with about seventy-five different people each week, planned fund drives, and fretted at every delay.

The snows of 1956-57 were unusually deep. Driving to and from work was hazardous. Margie had the worst of it for she commuted to Denver (about 45 miles each way) while Edy, Ruth and I commuted to Colorado Springs about 26 miles each way). Ruth usually rode with me as she had no car of her own, and in any case, she worked where I did. She also managed to convince Harry that her work hours should correspond to mine rather than his. How she managed that, she never bothered to tell me.

Like me, Ruth was something of a workaholic and managed to accomplish all that was required of her.

Loy enrolled Tommy at a country school in Larkspur; drove him to school, picked him up after school, did the shopping for all of us, cooked our meals, and made life bearable.

With four women and one man living together, although we occupied separate buildings, tensions sometimes arose. Actually, it was astonishing that we had no more temper flares than we did. I thought reflectively about that phenomenon. Every one of the women was a vital part of what I was trying to do. Had any one of them walked out, the entire project would have gone into a nose-dive. Women are natural competitors. They tend to be more concerned with establishing warm and rewarding relationships than with accomplishing separate and independent goals.

As I thought about our family situation, I came at last to a conclusion. Building relationships is more conducive to creating tension than devotion to a goal. When a given individual is concerned with how he is accepted and appreciated by another, there's a certain amount of bare-knuckle fighting. The gloves come off. Each person keeps himself in the forefront of his own mind. The question most frequently asked is: "How am I doing?" (In the eyes of another.)

But when a goal is the reason for his association with others— and perhaps most especially when that goal is so large that it is virtually impossible of accomplishment—the question most frequently asked is: "What am I doing?" The ego achieves its satisfactions from the activities it successfully completes. Without the goal, the ego seeks to bask in the warmth of another's approval.

The "how" question tends to engender introspection, while the "what" question stimulates action.

I could now see the "I Am" activity in better perspective. Through it, I could see the struggles that have occurred in all manner of human organizations, religious, business, fraternal.

What made our own family unique came out of the "I Am" training. Four of us had been under "I Am" discipline for years. The consequence was an ability to put a goal ahead of our personal feelings. How we might feel about another person in a given situation, could be shunted aside in favor of achievement.

Margie, without that discipline, nonetheless had magnificent control of herself. British instruction is far more rigorous than what is provided in this country. She had attained a kind of self-mastery and detachment.

I had managed to put together a personal library of about 2,000 volumes. I asked Margie to become the school librarian, to catalogue the books, and to serve as a reference point with students when we finally had them.

Margie protested that she knew nothing about library work whatever. Then, she set herself to the task, read up on the subject, provided herself with every bit of necessary information—and with only an occasional giggle at the absurdity of it—performed as though she held an advanced degree in the discipline.

Loy was the single exception when it came to background. But Loy is unique. I have never met anyone with a disposition half so sunny. She had no training in anything but music. In music, she was professorial as well as professional. She knew her stuff and could do it all.

I began by asking her to cook for us. She learned and did it well. Now, in preparation for the opening of the school, I asked her to become our Director of Facilities. She would have complete charge, not only of the kitchen and dining room, but also of all the physical amenities.

She was staggered and alarmed at first. But she was a good sport and took it in stride. She wanted to know if she could have help. I assured her that in time we'd have help for her. But at the outset, she'd have to do it all. The rest of us could pitch in when we had the time.

But I reminded her that we didn't have much time to spare. Raising funds and holding down jobs away from home didn't leave many hours in the day. I got a look from her that said as clearly as words, "What do you take me for?" In fact, I did hire a helper for her. The amount of work was too much for one person.

But I knew Loy's capacity, and I was right. What I had done without fully comprehending the ramifications of it, was to assist each woman in accepting the goal toward which we labored, in placing it above the personal relationship element.

Loy sometimes complained that the only time we saw each other was when she made an appointment. If she resented the presence of other women, she managed to sublimate the feeling with work with music and with her never-failing smile. And thus we persevered.

One late afternoon, driving in from Colorado Springs, Ruth and I went into a ditch during a blinding snowstorm. When a local rancher finally pulled us out, we found Perry Park Road impassable. Edy had had the foresight to take a room in a hotel and hadn't attempted the drive. Ruth and I were compelled to return to the city where we spent the night. I explained the circumstances to Loy over the telephone and met with zero recriminations.

On one never-to-be-forgotten Saturday, Margie and Edy managed to get home early enough to avoid the worst of a growing storm. By the time Ruth and I showed up at the cattle guard, a blizzard was raging. Hard driven snow, packed down tight, halted the Buick's passage.

I trudged across the twenty feet of drift to our property line, where land conformation and clumps of scrub oak combined to keep out the snow. Then, I walked in to the school, a good half-mile back from the county road, leaving Ruth in the car.

I obtained shovels and the help of Loy, Margie and Edy. Back with the Buick, Ruth and I shoveled from the east; the others shoveled from the west. It took us the better part of two hours to clear a passage. The effort had been backbreaking. But the Buick finally spun and swerved to shelter.

Many people have told me of the joys of living in the country. I was ready to write a treatise on the joy of living in the city, where the snow is plowed and there are hotels, gas stations, electricity, and other people.

The thaws began, and the snow backed away from the territory it had claimed. We had positioned the garage at the edge of the meadow where the sun came out only about two hours each day during winter. The snow on the roof softened and melted, but then froze. A new storm would come, burying the layers of ice under fresh fall.

One Sunday morning, Loy heard a groaning crash of timber. She raced to the point of origin to find that the roof of the garage had caved in under the weight of ice. The 18-inch slope of the garage roof had been insufficient for drainage. By the time the rest of us showed, the extent of our disaster was apparent. One car had been flattened, and two others had been diminished in size.

Putting things to right cost both time and money. We were, again, running short of both.

While all this was taking place, applications for enrollment were coming in a few at a time. We managed to raise enough money to provide eight scholarships. In process, we signed up eighteen others, each person enrolled in a specific two-week period during the coming summer. Yet, our classroom building was still under construction.

I refused to believe the evidence. Something would happen so that we'd finish the building and erect the two residence cabins. Edy wasn't talking about; she merely looked at me with a pained expression.

By mid-May, I knew the truth and couldn't deny it any longer. We might complete the one building in time for our first class. But we had no accommodations. We hadn't even cleared the building sights for the two small cabins. And we were out of funds. As predicted, the building costs, plus the other contingencies, had taken all we had.

In short, we could teach a course of instruction. We would be able to feed the students. But we had nowhere to house them. The time had come to notify those who had enrolled that we'd have to wait for another whole year.

With aching heart, I called the family together. I spelled out what everyone already knew. Everyone except Ruth.

"We've been talking about it," Ruth said. "There's no way we're going to postpone the opening."

"You know I don't want to," I said. "But I don't see any way out. We simply can't bring people out here without giving them places to sleep."

"We still have two of those original cabins standing," Ruth reminded me.

"I wouldn't ask a dog to sleep in one of those," I said. "And these are people who are paying for accommodations. What they're looking for is a vacation. Better to cancel than to house them there. No plumbing; one electric light bulb, and a "primitive" john through the brambles and without lights. Forget it."

"No," Ruth said. "We won't cancel. The lower floor of the classroom building can be converted into a men's dorm, We even have a bathroom in the hall. Just get some cots and we can put the men there."

I hadn't thought of that. "What about the recreation we're planning?"

"Forget it. They'll have enough to do."

"But we do have some women coming, too," I reminded. "We can't put the men and women into the same room, even if we do have handy bathroom facilities."

"Let's take a closer look, Bob. Enrollment varies in each two-week period from four to five people. Most are men. A couple of classes have one woman, and there's two with two each."

"So what do we do then?"

"Well, I'll be willing to give up my room to a guest. I'll sleep in one of those cabins. The weather is moderating, and it won't be bad at all. I'll just camp out there during those classes, that's all."

"I'll give up my room for those two-women sessions," Edy said.

"I won't give mine up," Margie said.

"No need, Margie," Ruth said. "We won't need it. Edy and I can do it."

"Well, I can too," Margie said. "But I don't want to. What if you get some additional enrollments?

A light had suddenly come on at the end of the tunnel.

"Would you gals really do that?"

"Sure."

"No problem."

"My own mother's coming for one of the sessions," Ruth said. "I don't mind giving up my room to her. That's what gave me the idea."

"I think I'm as crazy as everyone else," Edy said. "But if Ruth can do it, so can I."

I stared at these wonderful women. A lump rose in my throat. "I'm in no position to do anything except marvel. But if you gals will do that, I don't see how we'll fail. You are superb!"

So we didn't cancel. In the two weeks before our first students arrived, I frantically dashed about purchasing some second-hand furnishings, some at auction. I obtained extra cots for the unfinished cabins, little more than shacks.

Prior to these final days, I had arranged for some instructors to assist in the teaching department. Employment for those who believed in a free economy was almost non-existent in the country. In consequence, I was able to obtain the services of some brilliant people for very little money. I offered plane fare both ways, room and board while they were with us, and $100 for their services over a weekend or for as long as they cared to stay.

That first year, I won the assistance of Leonard Read, Frank Chodorov, Percy Greaves, "Baldy" Harper, Jim Doenges, and E. W. Bill Dykes. It was a stellar lineup. Indeed, it was the use of their names in our earlier publicity that made it possible for us to attract anyone, I'm sure. And I promised each enrollee that at least one of that celebrated six would be on hand during their particular session.

Read, as the president of the Foundation for Economic Education, was well known in the business community and had already established a substantial following. Percy Greaves was an economist, and a student of Ludwig von Mises, the great founder of the Austrian School of Economics. Baldy was a good friend, an economist, and the man for whom all of this work was being done (still without his knowledge).

Jim Doenges was a surgeon and a brilliant man, who knew how to talk about free enterprise. Bill Dykes, from Canton, Ohio, was a recommendation of Baldy's. Bill was soft-spoken, capable on his feet, and unwilling to compromise freedom.

My plan was to turn as much teaching as possible over to these people and to fill in when necessary.

It wasn't until Saturday, just before our opening on the following day, that the impact of what I was going to do hit home. I had been busy with all the housekeeping details. Jim Doenges was going to be our first lecturer. But he could only be present for two days. And that meant that I must teach full time during ten of the next twelve days.

Nearly in panic, I went to my room to outline ten days' worth of instruction, six hours each day! I wasn't allowed the luxury of time to work over that outline. Too many decisions still had to be made concerning the material wants and needs of our guests.

In haste, I jotted down major points I wanted to get across in class. I filled two pages with notes. That was all I had time to do.

The first June session had four people enrolled. Somehow it all came together. My work at the paper had me up to date on current events. Apparently I knew more about what I was going to teach than I had realized. At least, I was never at a loss for words. The two pages of notes took me sixty hours to cover.

The sessions ran from Sunday night of the first week to Friday night of the second, including Saturday and Sunday. On that intervening weekend, Jim Doenges appeared and performed an excellent job, as I had anticipated.

The final Friday was graduation night. and each of the attendees received a "Certificate of Completion."

The students departed Saturday morning. We literally "tore the place apart," cleaning and getting things ready again. Then, on Sunday evening the second batch arrived, this group consisting of five people.

We kept all our commitments and paid all our bills. The sessions were much appreciated, if I could accept the comments of the students.

Rose Lane came as an honored guest. When I asked her to talk to the students for a few hours, she went into panic. She wasn't a trained speaker, she protested. She was a writer, not a talker.

But I had already promised the students. Somehow, I had to persuade her. "Tell you what," I finally suggested. "Don't talk to them, just visit with them."

"What'll I tell them?"

"You've traveled all over the world," I said. "Tell them about some of your experiences."

"I wouldn't know how or where to begin."

"You've got to, Rose. They're looking forward to it. They've had all they need from me. I'll help out if you get into trouble, but you'll do just fine."

"I feel like an utter fool," she said.

"Come on, Rose. Give it your best. It'll be great, I know."

The dear lady truly had a case of stage fright, but I convinced her to start. I introduced her. She panicked and refused to come to the front of the classroom. Resolutely, she took a chair in the rear of the room, her lips firmly closed.

I knew from my reading of her book that she had traveled through Europe and had been in parts of Asia. I made some inane suggestion respecting her experiences behind what Winston Churchill had called the "Iron Curtain."

Finally, she said, "Would you like to hear how I forced the Russian government to re-evaluate the ruble?"

Everyone pivoted in his chair and she began to talk. As she warmed to her subject, it was as though a spell came over the class. Not a sound was heard except her voice.

One by one, the students left their places and took new positions closer to her, some sitting on the floor at her feet. She never stood up. She just kept talking.

I had intervening duties to perform and tiptoed out. I returned about an hour later. It was as though a tableau had been created. No one had stirred. Rose was now deeply involved in her own experiences and she knew how to tell a story. Everyone was enthralled.

She had finished her first recitation and was already talking about another experience. She kept those students hour after hour with no one having any sense of time passing.

She did it again and again, whenever she was called upon. She always maintained that she didn't know how to teach. She was one of the greatest teachers I have ever seen or heard.

In one of the classes, a young married couple, named Gene and Mary Hauske, had enrolled. When their session ended, they made me a proposition.

Gene was employed at the Boeing Company in Seattle. He now wished to make the Freedom School his life work. He was an engineer and a draftsman and said he was handy with all kinds of tools.

I told him we had no money with which to pay him. He said that was no problem for him. He could easily get a paying job in the Springs. He wanted to devote all his spare time to helping us at the school. Marty appeared to be equally eager.

I hadn't anticipated anything like this. I was deeply impressed and overjoyed. The Hauskes had driven from Seattle in a small van. Gene said he would have to return to Seattle to give notice and to clear up some loose ends. Then he and Marty would drive back before the summer was out.

The Hauskes were people of their word. After an absence of about five or six weeks, they showed up again, with an infant daughter named Jennie. Gene began making himself useful around the property. He was a perfectionist and his devotion to the cause of liberty was as deep as that of anyone I have ever met. He was a person without duplicity, and I found I could count on him completely. He and Marty were wonderful.

All in all, we had a successful first year except for one thing. The anniversary of our payment on the property would come due near the end of September. We hadn't been able to put aside all the funds necessary. Indeed, we had only a few hundred available and the payment was close to $1,800.

One day as the school year was closing, Gene and I sat together on the small porch just outside the door to the classroom. I had already told him of our extreme financial problem. Now I revealed that, although we had done what we had set out to do, our little experiment was drawing to a close. I expressed concern that he had given up a lucrative position to be with us. It seemed certain that his stay with us would be very brief, indeed.

We sat there, like two doomed men, exchanging our feelings of impending loss. I told him of all the avenues I had tried and explained that funds might come in later. But the payment on the property had to be made on time. I could see no avenue of possible assistance. I had tried them all and struck out. There just hadn't been enough students. And the funds from our combined incomes, fund drives, and everything else were insufficient.

Rose, who had stayed on to the end of the final session, happened to come out of the classroom at that moment. That she had enjoyed her stay was obvious. She was bubbling over with good spirits. She took a look at us and her expression changed.

"What's wrong?" she demanded. "You look as if you're waiting to be hanged."

Gene didn't say anything. Tears glistened in his eyes. My own throat was husky. "That's an apt expression, Rose. In a sense, that's what's going to happen."

"What do you mean?"

I didn't want to burden her. "It hasn't anything to do with the classes, Rose. Everything there has been fine."

"I should say," she affirmed. "So why are you so glum?"

I hesitated. There was nothing she could do. Why get her involved? Her look was imperious and I caved in.

"It seems kind of a shame to shut the place down, after this much effort," I said.

"Shut it down!" She stamped her foot. "You are not going to shut it down!"

"I don't want to," I said. "I hate to do it. But I can't figure a way out." I spelled out the difficulty.

"Is that all?" she asked.

"It's enough," I said. "We've met or are able to meet all other obligations. But we're about $1200 dollars short. So, within the next month, I've got to abandon the place and turn it back to the prior owners, or face the Sheriff."

"Twelve hundred dollars!" she sniffed. "That's nothing."

"It's a whale of a lot when you don't have it."

"Well, we'll see about that. I'm not going to let you close this school. It's the greatest thing to come along in the last twenty years. It must continue."

"We have the same sentiment, Rose. But how?"

"You two numbskulls!" she scolded. "Acting as if you've lost your last friend. Well, you haven't." Again, she stamped her foot. "You stay right here. Don't you dare go away."

She went back into the classroom.

Gene's face radiated hope. "What's she going to do, Bob?"

"I have no idea. She's not a wealthy woman. She won't even write anything anymore. She hates Social Security and refuses to pay it. So I think she's living on her meager savings. That's about it. I wouldn't dream of asking her for money. She hasn't got it."

In a minute Rose returned, a check waving from her hand. The ink wasn't yet dry. "Here's your $1,200. That's nothing! Don't you dare talk to me about closing up this place."

"Rose," I protested. "You can't afford..."

She cut me off. "You don't know anything about my affairs. If I couldn't afford it why would I do it? Here. Take the check!"

With mixed emotions, I stood. "Gosh, Rose. Do you really want to do this? I mean....well, thanks. Thanks awfully."

"You two idiots stop looking like that and get back to work. School's not over yet!"

She was right. Rose Wilder Lane came through at a crucial moment and the school was temporarily saved by her generosity.

Chapter XCI

After my first six seminars at the Freedom School my attitude contained a curious mixture of anxiety and elation. I was able to teach. I had done a good job. My family was most joyfully surprised and very respectful of my performance. You may be sure I reveled in their approval.

But this wasn't the way I had planned to go. I wasn't a teacher. In school, I had looked down on the profession. I had taken literally the old saw: "Those who can, do, those who can't, teach." I was actually engaged in proving to Baldy and a few other people that the task could be accomplished.

In addition, at the newspaper I had at last developed a style. I could write a decent editorial. And my beliefs, expressed with consistency and supervised by Harry, were beginning to stir up a bit of controversy in town. A little controversy fuels readership and the paper was growing beautifully. I don't mean to imply that my editorials were responsible for the newspaper's favorable position. Colorado Springs was growing and a certain level of prosperity would come, predictably to any well-managed business. I had the satisfaction of knowing that the controversies to which I may have been a contributing factor weren't serious enough to splash red ink on the Gazette's ledgers.

As my second full year at the newspaper drew to a close, Harry let me know that he was more than satisfied. He did it in a very practical manner. I got a substantial raise. I hadn't asked for lt. It was handed to me, and this despite the fact that I was working only half-days.

Feedback containing praise is a very heavy commodity. It is so easy to believe good reports, so easy to quarrel with those who don't and won't admire.

Thus, while I was patting myself on the back for good performance, apprehension gnawed away. Thanks to Rose Lane, we had pulled through the year financially. Just barely pulled through. What about next year?

The girls, who had helped with such devotion, even living in those disreputable hovels so our guests could have the best, weren't in a mood to repeat that performance. Next year we'd have to have more accommodations. Construction was mandatory.

Nor could we limit our expansion to the cabins I had planned. Administrative procedures, keeping records and working together as a team required space in which to work. And then, there was that recreation program we had hoped to offer.

The successful completion of that first year had provided us with an asset that I didn't yet entirely understand. Our efforts had come to the attention of a number of people who were prominent in their respective communities because of their stand for free enterprise and the early, traditional, American values.

Evidence of this came in the form of a telephone call from Chet Anderson, Executive Director of the Employers' Association of Milwaukee, Wisconsin. Chet wondered if I could come to Milwaukee to meet with a number of businessmen so I could relate to them what we had done. He implied that it was conceivable that some of them might be willing to contribute substantially to our on-going efforts.

I prepared a number of editorials in advance to cover my absence. Taking the train, I embarked for Milwaukee. Air travel was quicker, but it was more costly. Additionally, if I traveled at night on the train, I could take a sleeper and arrive at my destination fresh and ready for business. If I flew, I'd have to spend an extra night in town. Absence from the paper was a privilege I didn't wish to abuse.

Chet had arranged a luncheon meeting that was held in one of the more prestigious clubs in town. Luncheon guests numbered a score or more. I was somewhat awed by the caliber of the men present. Bill Grede was there. He had been president of the National Association of Manufacturers and was a powerful figure with many connections. The elderly president of the big Allen-Bradley Company was in attendance. So were presidents and managers of a dozen other major firms.

"What should I talk about?" I asked Chet. "As you know, I favor free enterprise in a total way. I don't believe that government should have anything to do with the economy in the slightest degree. Therefore, I don't favor taxes at all. I'm kind of hard-nosed about that. Is that what they want to hear?"

"I don't think so," Chet advised. "Why don't you just tell them what you've done?" They've pretty well accepted the theories of free enterprise. They're interested in achievement."

"Well, we haven't achieved all that much. We had only 27 students all year. I was hoping for a hundred."

"Well, why don't you tell them what you've done, and then tell them what you hope to do if you can get support?"

I'm sure my eyes sparkled. In anticipation of just such an opportunity, Gene Hauske and I had put together the plans for a residence cabin plus another two-story building. The additional building would contain accommodations for eight or nine persons on its second floor, while providing office and storage space on the ground floor.

Gene, being a draftsman, had put these plans on paper as line drawings. So I had something to show if opportunity offered. If we could finance both buildings, we'd have accommodations for about sixteen students at one time. And the girls wouldn't have to give up their rooms.

Following the splendid noon repast, in which I had to reveal that I was a vegetarian, Chet introduced me. I am always far more interested in discussing ideas, but I accepted Chet's suggestion and simply gave a recitation of what we had done.

When I finished what amounted to an annual report, I was greeted with stony silence. These men had stared at me without changing expressions. Now, Bill Grede stood. He was a tall, lean man, endowed with a friendly voice and the look of a Sabatini's Scaramouche.

"For the first time in years," he began, "I feel ashamed. The rest of us here are in favor of free enterprise because we are businessmen and we know how vital it is to us. But who are these people out there in Colorado? I never heard of any of them.

"We have an editor of a small newspaper, a secretary, a bookkeeper, and a physical therapist acting like a librarian." He paused, looked at me and smiled. "And your good wife, too, Bob, who must have been working like a defender of Troy under siege." He turned again to the gathering.

"These people, without a penny to their names, went out, got jobs and contributed their own earnings to make free enterprise a reality to and all comers.

"When has any of us ever done anything to equal that? Our interest in free enterprise is self-serving. The interest of these people is above that. Wouldn't you agree, Bob?"

I hadn't anticipated being brought into the discussion. I stuttered and stammered. Finally, I said, "Not altogether. It's our country, too. And, of course, we would have paid out the money anyway. We have to support ourselves, you know."

"I don't know about the rest of you," Bill went on, "but I'll tell you what I'm going to do."

He abruptly sat, reached into a pocket, and produced a checkbook. "I'm writing a check for $1,000 right now. Will that help, young man?"

"Will it help? Oh, boy. Of course it will!" I hadn't expected such an immediate response.

Mr. Bradley was not to be outdone. "I'll give you one for five thousand," he said, and a checkbook snapped into his hand. Others began fumbling for their respective wallets. When the meeting broke up, I had $11,000 with more promised.

I remembered what Merwin Hart had told me. "If you want people to give you money, you have to ask for it." In this case, I hadn't even gotten around to ask.

I was profuse in my thanks and Chet was jubilant that the meeting had gone so well.

When I reported to Harry who had been at the meeting and the sum of money I had collected, he was both astonished and gratified. When Christmastime came, in addition to the raise he had already provided, he gave me a bonus. I immediately endorsed the check back to him to finish paying off the $7,000 loan he had advanced.

Charley Heits was contacted once more, and additional logs were cut and brought to the school. Norris showed up with his younger brother "Link." He was another mountain man—quiet, with a far-away look in his blue eyes, and an unwavering devotion to truth. Norris said that Link was a more proficient man and would like to become active with us. Gene was on hand to help in any and every way possible.

It didn't take long to learn that Link was invaluable. Gene had already shown his enormous capabilities but Link was a man of nature and we were combating nature. At the same time, we were working with it. Link seemed to know everything. He wanted steady work and I took him on as our "wrangler." We had two horses, and it was a good title.

In a sense, that was unfair to Gene. He had arrived before Link and, if money was available, it would have seemed logical to give him the first job. I talked to him about it. He appeared unconcerned.

The pittance I could provide for Link wouldn't have made him happy, he told me. He had already lined up a job in town that would pay far better. He was content to donate his spare time and was as pleased as I to have Link's ability and experience on hand.

But now Edy interposed. Instead of trying to construct two buildings at once, why not erect them one at a time? If we didn't slow down a bit, we'd obligate ourselves and be in over our heads again. And who would hail us out next time? Besides, I hadn't even gotten around to display the lovely plans Gene had prepared. I'd picked up a very sizeable gift without promising anything.

Edy was right. We concentrated on the residence cabin, knowing that we could still use the room under the classroom for a men's dormitory while having a completely separate place for the women. And the girls could continue in their rooms.

For office space, we had largely taken over Ruth's room. It contained her desk, filing cabinets, and whatever business machines we had. Indeed, except for her bed, one would have presumed it to be nothing but an office.

We prepared for a new fund drive. I had managed to awaken the interest of a number of prominent people; I created what was called a National Board of Fellows. There were persons of some prominence, who were willing to let me use their names as points of reference. In fact, they had no responsibility in connection with our efforts. They were encouraged to offer advice, and so far as I can recall, none of them ever did.

We now prepared an annual report coupled with a prospectus and conducted an extensive mailing. The final page of our brochure looked like this:

Board of Directors
Ruth Dazey
William J. Froh
Lois Lefevre
Robert Lefevre
Marjorie Llewellin
Robert B. Rapp
Edith Shank

National Board of Fellows

Mr. John W. Beck
Hemet, California
Mr. Harry H. Hoiles
Colorado Springs, Colorado
Mr. Aldrich Blare
Laguna Beach, California
Mr. Richard Lloyd Jones
Tulsa, Oklahoma
G. Blazey, M.D.
Washington, Indiana
Mr. John Bross Lloyd
Greenwich, Connecticut
Mrs. Mary D. Cain
Summit, Mississippi
Mr. Milton M. Lory
Sioux City, Iowa
Miss Taylor Caldwell
Eggertsville, New York
Mr. Thurman L. Mccormick
Kansas City, Missouri
Mr. Zack R. Cecil
Latrobe, Pennsylvania
Mr. Charles A. Macauley
Detroit, Michigan
Mr. Frank Chodorov
Berkeley Heights, New Jersey
Mr. Roger Milliken
New York, New York
Mr. Ralph Courtney
Spring Valley, New York
Mr. R. E. Nellis
Kraemer, Pennsylvania
Mr. Ralph E. Davis
Los Angeles, California
Mr. Ed Obele
Colorado Springs, Colorado
James L. Doenges, M.D.
Anderson, Indiana

Mr. George Peck
Largo, Florida
Mr. Robert B. Dresser
Providence, Rhode Island
Mr. R. Roy Pursell
Plymouth, Michigan
Mr. Harry T. Everingham
Chicago, Illinois
Dr. E. Merrill Root
Richmond, Indiana
Brig. Gen. Bonner Fellers (Ret.)
Washington D.C.
Adm. Wm. H. Standley (Ret.)
Coronado, California
Mr. W. L. Foster
Tulsa, Oklahoma
Mr. Willis E. Stone
Los Angeles, California
Mr. J. H. Gipson, Sr.
Caldwell, Idaho
Dr. V. Orval Watts
Altadena, California
Miss Corinne Griffith
Beverly Hills, California
Mr. E. L. Wiegand
Pittsburgh, Pennsylvania
Mr. Earl Harding
New York, New York
Mr. Glenn O. Young
Sapulpa, Oklahoma

Some of the people thus lending their names had worked with me in the Congress of Freedom. Possibly because of our efforts in founding the school, the new directors of the Congress had decided to hold their convention in Colorado Springs at the Antler's Hotel.

Mary Cain was now the principal executive of the organization and asked me to attend the convention. I made a brief presentation, explaining what we had done and were engaged in doing in the Rampart Range not far away.

This convention was held in October. When I concluded my speech, in good fellowship and with early memories of them as co-workers, I invited all to drive north out of Colorado Springs so they could visit the school, a mere 26 miles away.

Perhaps as many as thirty thought it would be a great idea, provided the invitation was valid on the final day of the convention. After they had adjourned, they would be glad to come.

This seemed like a marvelous way to spread the good news of the Freedom School. I invited them out for a cafeteria-style supper on their final Saturday.

Loy and everyone else plunged in getting everything ready for this major influx of people. It was the largest single group we had attempted to feed up. And since we included the Hauskes and all the girls—now referred to as "the staff"—we anticipated something better than forty persons, really more than our small classroom could accommodate, and certainly more than our kitchen was designed to handle.

I knew that weather in mountain country can be fickle, but I was certain there would be no problem. Saturday had been balmy in the Springs, although the forecasters were predicting a winter storm in Denver.

Colorado Springs stands at an elevation of slightly more than 6000 feet above sea level and the school campus was at 7000 feet at its lowest point. That thousand-foot rise could make a difference. Also, the school was north of the Palmer Lake Divide, which meant that we often had storms at the school that failed to materialize in the Springs.

Ruth and I, now in our new Rambler station wagon, headed a caravan of more than two dozen vehicles. By the time we turned into the school property and crossed the cattle guard, huge flakes of snow were drifting down.

But daylight was still with us and it appeared to be no more than a flurry. However, I urged these great friends of mine to make all reasonable haste. Many of them were quite elderly. The women wore flowing chiffon with broad brimmed hats and the men were in their Sunday best. Most sported summer weight clothing, some even wearing Palm Beach or white attire.

They toiled on foot up the steep slope. Unaccustomed to the altitude, most of them were completely out of breath by the time they arrived at our main building. However, all came up safely and we spent a most enjoyable time. We managed to feed them all, and then gathered in the crowded classroom for a brief explanation about the school.

By this time, night had fallen and I knew from occasional glances out the windows that we had no time to lose.

I'm sorry to cut this assembly short," I said. "But Colorado snow storms can be tricky. You've got to return to the Springs or run the risk of being snowed in. Ordinarily, I'd take keen delight in keeping you here. But our building program isn't yet completed, and we don't have accommodations.

"So, unless you want to sit up all night, forgive my rudeness, but let's get out of here!"

When we opened the door for departure, there were gasps of dismay. The snow, although light, was already a foot deep and was coming down with complete abandon.

Rarely did the wind reach us at our buildings. The contour of the hills protected us. But I knew that just at our property line drifts could be forming and all the winds of the north could be marshaled to block those final few yards to the county road.

The retreat from the school, with its blazing log fire, out into a bleak and frozen white landscape, was something of a shock to our visitors.

The footing was uncertain and I feared for the safety of the elderly. The staff donned parkas and other winter gear and we all assisted in a somewhat disorderly evacuation. There were a couple of falls, fortunately none serious enough to inflict injuries. It was a perilous experience, but we finally had everyone safely tucked into the vehicle that had brought him.

I went from car to car, explaining. "Turn on your lights. I'll lead the procession and break trail," I explained. "To the degree possible, stay in the tracks made by the preceding car."

By now, the road was invisible. From long practice, I knew where to drive but, without me, they'd never get away. Slowly, like a Conga line, each segment glowing with lights, we snaked our way across the meadow, through the various clumps of scrub oak and came at last to the cattle guard. It was as I had feared. A howling gale was piling up drifts just beyond our line fence.

It was going to be a rough passage.

I stopped and went back along the line of cars.

"I'm going to have to work my way through the drifts," I explained to each driver. "So I may have to go ahead, back up, go ahead, back up and so on, several times. Don't crowd me. Give me the room to maneuver until I get to the county road. That is usually clear as the wind sweeps it.

"However, this is the main point. Once I'm on the road, I'm going to speed up. If not, I'll never get through some of the drifts that are sure to be up ahead. You must do the same. Drivers who don't understand Colorado snowstorms usually reduce speed. If you do, once we're on the road, you'll stall in a drift. I'll open the way but you must try to gauge your own speed by mine."

There were expressions of apprehension but a quick grasp of the problem.

By using low and reverse alternately, I forced my way through the stubborn bottleneck.

At last on the county road, I turned the car and signaled by blinking my lights. I saw the first car start up, then I put my foot on the throttle and raced toward Colorado Springs.

For drivers who were unaccustomed to a now storms, they did a remarkably good job. Some of the drifts I slapped at forty miles an hour. I plunged through only because of the momentum I had built up.

Under conditions such as these, it's nearly impossible to follow in the traces made by the lead car. However, the further south we went, the lighter the snow and the more shallow the drifts.

By the time we reached Monument and the pavement leading to the Springs, we were on the south side of the Palmer Lake Divide. From there it was easy. By the time the caravan arrived in the city only an occasional flake was falling, although the temperature had dropped abruptly.

Driving back to the school, I put into focus the terrible risks entailed in the adventure I had just had. It's one thing to run risks with yourself and what is yours. It's something else to ask others to become involved with you.

There were so many ways in which a tragedy might have struck. Someone might have fallen and broken a bone on our steep slopes. A car could have spun out of control and ended in a ditch. Or, a car could have stalled and been in a rear end collision with a pursing vehicle. Indeed, one or more persons could have been killed.

Again, there had been a distinct possibility that we might not have gotten through those cloying drifts. What would we have done with forty-five people and only fifteen single beds? There wouldn't have been enough food or anything else.

I resolved to reduce risks the students would run when they came the following year. And I'd be sure to explain the risks, and then let them assume the responsibilities for their own behavior after the warning. Frontier-style living isn't idyllic. Nature in the raw is formidable.

Chapter XCII

After my visit to Milwaukee, we were no longer in the financial crisis we had been in. There was never enough money to do all we wished to do, of course. But Edith Shank, who had become our Treasurer and served as Comptroller, was a watchdog it would have been impossible to surpass. She kept us all in bounds.

With a National Board of Fellows lending their names to our efforts, our fund drives were more lucrative. But a problem plagued me in this regard, although I made small mention of it. Most of the persons on our list were Conservatives. My work at the Newspaper, and my efforts to develop and present a consistent philosophy in respect to freedom, had made me realize some parts of the Conservative position were not consistent.

All these people now helping to boost my efforts knew me as a Conservative. I also had a pretty good idea that if any of them listened carefully to what I was saying, they might have cringed and pulled back.

Of course, I was totally opposed to Socialism and Communism, as were they. But upon analysis, many of the policies of the Conservatives actually aided and abetted Socialist and Communist ideas. So long as those ideas were organized and augmented by Americans, Conservatives would support them. The Conservative front was lined up against Russia and its satellites, and the similarity between the two positions was astonishing if anyone cared to study it.

The Conservative confused his country and the principles upon which it was founded with the existing American government. While he was often critical of some of the policies—most notably if they came from Democrats—his loyalty was to government, and not to the ideals of liberty.

On the other hand, the Liberals were so convinced of the Russians (or anyone trying to further democratic processes) that they excused the most atrocious and vicious conduct, as long as it was done by what appeared to be majority vote, "the masses," or "the people."

Conservatives often complained that Russia (communism) was dangerous because it sought to engender war against the non-communist bloc of nations. Some of them were militant about being willing to fight Russia to prevent a war. As Conservatives frequently stated it, America must be prepared to fight so as to prevent war.

Contradictions from the left, or the so-called "liberal" camp, were just as obvious and equally grotesque. The leftists posed as being favorable to conflict until it appeared that Conservatives might block some leftist ambition. In their view, war against a "dictator" and for "democracy" was peaceful. The leftists appeared to be entirely militant against "dictators," those who "colonialized," and any nation that didn't let people vote on everything. The moment the rightists appeared to support a "dictator"—or for that matter, any regime acting in favor of the right of an individual to what he owned—then, the leftists cried foul and favored "peace" by advancing toward war.

Those persons, who like myself, favored peace were branded as being either "Rightists" or "Leftists" depending on the stance of the party with the searing iron. If I favored the right of persons to private property, the leftists branded me as a tool of big business and declared that I was making war against the poor. Conversely, if I refused to support war in favor of some political adventure on the Right, the Conservatives called me a dupe of the Commies and a Peacenik.

I had already encountered this ambivalence during the days of the Falcon Lair "Pilgrimage."

There were a few, of course, who saw through this artificial alignment and recognized that nothing is so destructive of freedom as war. To them, it mattered not at all who was fighting. It was important to underscore that legalized killing, even for a political objective, is still murder. And it is obvious that production and trade—the ebb and flow of supply and demand in commerce and business—demands peace as a necessary concomitant.

The respective battle cries became: "Kill a Commie for Christ," on the one hand and "Kill a capitalist pig for freedom," on the other. Yet, if you examined either Christianity or freedom, both doctrines sternly oppose murder for any purpose.

Inconsistencies marred the American political scene on both major fronts. The libertarian position depolarized these areas of discrepancy. To whatever degree a libertarian became interested in the political scene, he brought a new point of view. He put those who favored authoritarianism in one camp, and those who favored liberty in the other.

The libertarian called for a political climate free of government interference for any reason. The libertarian favored an end to taxation and, with it, an end to all alleged tax "benefits."

The Left called for a political climate in which "the people" would hold all power and would vote on what they wanted. This meant that they favored massive gifts, emoluments and grants from the political state. They sought to make the human race subservient and docile under total political control of a benevolent kind.

The Right called for a political climate in which the state would assist every capitalist, and provide favorable tariffs or other protectionist barriers. But mostly, the Right called for military might. The state created Special Privilege that was a necessary concomitant to the idea of private property.

Both sides wanted taxation for the good of all. They merely debated over how the loot was to be expended. The libertarian favored an end to looting. He hoped to see men free of either benefits or injuries inflicted by any kind of sanctioned central agency.

I had obtained the nominal support of Conservatives because of my stand in favor of private property and my opposition to Communism or Socialism. I had no support from the Left, nor had I sought it. So I justified the use of Conservative names on the grounds that we were in agreement on most issues. Meanwhile, I would make a special attempt to get good conservatives enrolled in future classes so as to assist them in discovering their inconsistencies. If possible, I would help them to upgrade their respective positions.

These ideas began appearing in my editorial copy in the newspaper. They made me an increasingly controversial figure. At the moment, however, I was fully engrossed in getting the residential cabin called Thunderbird into existence.

Charlie Heits decided not to do any of the construction work. He would supply the logs at an increased price, and stop at that point. Link took over as foreman, with Gene Hauske providing invaluable assistance.

Thanks to contacts I had made by mail and in Milwaukee, I was now called upon to visit with various business leaders in widely separated parts of the country. I generally traveled by rail, made speeches, asked for financial assistance, and added many names of well wishers to our mailing list.

In the midst of this entire endeavor word, came from Aaron Sargeant. The date had been set for the legal contest of LeFevre versus Retail Credit. It would take place in San Francisco in a federal court. Since Harry had insisted on this trial, I had no difficulty in arranging time off.

In preparing the case, Sargeant decided to use Ruth as a major witness in support of my position. She had been involved with the "I Am" nearly to the extent I had been. Pearl might have been a better witness. But after interviewing her, Sargeant decided that she might become hostile due to her marriage to Jerry and my first wife's present marriage to her ex-husband. Moreover, Pearl was still using the transcendental language of the "I Am" and might have been difficult for jurors to understand. At least, that was Sergeant's view.

He had correctly anticipated that Retail Credit would seek to attack me on the grounds that I had done some pretty bad things while acting on the Ballard staff. Therefore, they would argue that their report was accurate and justified.

In the interim, since my departure from Ballard employment, Mrs. Ballard had stood trial and been convicted of using the mails to defraud. However, she had won a reversal in an appellate court on the grounds that there had been no women in the jury. Indeed, Ballard vs. The People of the U.S. is a landmark decision in its appellate phase. It was the first time (I have been informed) that the lack of women on a jury in a case where a woman was on trial was viewed as depriving the defendant of certain civil rights.

Sargeant planned to let Retail Credit do its best to make a monkey out of me in the "I Am" affair—my connection to which could certainly not be denied. After that, he proposed to reverse the procedure and show that Retail Credit had manufactured the "Mankind United" portion and that this was both false and deliberate—hence, the damage and libel.

Loy, Ruth and I went to San Francisco and took up residence in an inexpensive hotel within walking distance of the Federal Building where the hearing would take place. Sargeant had obtained a jury trial. Juries tended to be more generous to defendants. They would be more willing to spend Retail Credit's money than a judge, even one who might be disposed to favor our position.

Sargeant had managed to locate Pat Crouse, the former secretary to "Daddy" Ballard. He had been called as a witness on my behalf because he would be able to testify as to what my duties were. He would testify that I was not involved in policy decisions and had done nothing substantive to do with the alleged fraudulent use of the mails.

So many things had happened to me since 1941 (when I resigned) that I only dimly remembered a great many events. It was now the winter of 1957-58.

I won't go into details. Anyone interested can, of course, obtain a transcript of the proceedings. I had the natural assurance that I had done nothing wrong whatever, either in the employ of the Ballards or afterward.

To my dismay, a man I thought of as a good friend—Howard Hammitt, Jr., who had been one of our special group living on Vallejo and Jones Street—had been subpoenaed to testify against me. But Ruth was there and so was her mother, and they were on my side.

If one thing stands out in the transcript it must surely be my embarrassment. I had gone into the "I Am" as a devoted student. I believed. Indeed, parts of what the Ballards taught are true and have stood the test of time. Along with those parts is a welter of imagery, terminology and hocus-pocus that would make a stronger person than I blush. Further, I had actually had a series of deep experiences, called by many scholars religious experiences because there is apparently no other term. Those events are inexplicable, and I am still unable to explain them. I can only aver that they did take place.

The court, quite properly, was not interested in my beliefs. It was concerned with what I had done. In the hostile recriminations, accusations, and innuendo, I squirmed and shifted. Certainly I was an idiot to have been so devoted and whole-hearted that I had never questioned the motives of the Ballards. I had judged them by myself, and I had been naive.

First, I was accused of getting into the Ballard movement so that I could make huge dollar profits. This was easily disproved.

Next, I had written that wretched book, "'I Am,' America's Destiny" for that very purpose. I couldn't deny the intention, but it had flopped and only a few hundred books had ever been sold. Retail

Credit could not establish anything more.

How was I able to get the money together to own the real estate and other leaseholds I had managed to amass? My former employer, Fred Weiss came in as a witness and testified as to my ability as a real estate and business opportunity salesman.

At this juncture, Retail Credit announced that it had obtained access to my tax forms, revealing that I had not paid very much in the way of taxes. Hadn't I then, in fact, been cheating the government and withholding taxes rightfully due?

The judge interposed and threw that line of approach out. He said his court was not going to be used as a fishing excursion to assist the IRS.

Proceeding from that point, the lawyers for my opponent sought to show that after leaving the employ of the Ballards, I had used their teaching as a racket to line my own purse. Howard Hammitt, Jr. testified concerning how much money he had contributed.

Howard was basically an honest man. Thanks to Ethel and Ruth, both of whom came to my defense, I could show that: (1) all the sums contributed went to provide room and board for Mr. Hammitt and at some very fine addresses; (2) the sums were always handled by others, much of the time by Ethel; and, (3) rather than taking money out for myself, I was a major contributor in support of the group effort.

The principal issue that Retail Credit sought to establish was that the mimeographed sheet I had received from Thad Ashby was not issued by them. There was no mark of origin on it. They contended that all valid reports went out on Retail Credit paper under their masthead.

True, we had obtained an identical copy from their own files. But Retail Credit suggested to the court that it was possible some employee might have slipped an unauthorized report into my file. Therefore, the firm itself would not be privy to its preparation and, hence, wholly innocent of what it contained.

If the judge would only rule in favor of that motion, then the case could be thrown out of court as it would appear that the present legal action was filed against an innocent party.

The first day's hearing ended on that note. Sargeant's concern was understandable. The judge said he'd rule on the motion later, and the trial was set to resume the following day.

The second day I was on the stand again, this time with Sargeant engaged in the questioning.

He went over the same ground, giving me opportunity to place myself in a better light. I hope I was able to do so, but my embarrassment at having to reveal my inner hopes and beliefs was profound.

Finally, he got to the point. When had I joined "Mankind United?" I had never joined that organization.

Surely, I must remember. The report said I had written some of the major works. Naturally, I denied it.

Sargeant now turned to the opposing attorney and asked if Retail Credit could please provide their copies of all these documents I had authored, as I had been either unable or unwilling to provide them to him.

The defense attorney stood. It was his turn to be embarrassed. He admitted that Retail Credit had hired teams of investigators. They had combed the country and dug into my background as thoroughly as possible. They couldn't find any evidence whatever that I had ever been Connected with "Mankind United."

I heard a collective sigh escape the jury, and several of the men and women there smiled for the first time.

Sargeant made the most of it and provided a splendid tongue lashing in his summation. Retail Credit's lawyer tried to reestablish the importance of the "I Am" and my own villainy in connection with it, but this time it didn't go down.

The judge ruled on the motion to dismiss on grounds that the paper on which the suit was based was authored by a firm or individual other than Retail Credit. Not so, his honor said. The paper in the record as "Exhibit A" was valid and the work of Retail Credit.

Further, the judge had decided that no question existed as to the injurious nature of the report. I had been injured and substantially so.

Sargeant shot me a look of triumph.

However, the judge proceeded, he would order the jury to bring in a directed verdict of "not guilty" insofar as the Credit firm was concerned. His reason, he said, was the statute of limitations. The paper had been issued in 1950, during my political campaign. I should have brought legal action by 1952. Since the suit had been filed in 1955, it was meaningless and the trial ended.

Outside the courtroom Sargeant was hot for an appeal. He was certain we could win in a higher court.

I turned it down cold. My purpose was to win vindication so I could keep my job. The *San Francisco Examiner* carried a brief report on the court's action and I clipped it to take home and show it to Harry.

I really couldn't blame Retail Credit or others from looking at the "I Am" in the light they had. Men of the world systematically denied the existence of any spiritual factors in our day-to-day lives. I had no illusions that another court would do anything else.

Nor could they be blamed for so doing. Experience had long ago convinced most reasonable people that those who claimed to be acting on grounds of spiritual inspiration were phony, with a private axe to grind. Such was almost always true.

When someone like the Ballards contended that they were under direct guidance from "on high," it was both prudent and reasonable to disbelieve.

So what could anyone think of a gullible man like me, who bought the package, but who actually did have some religious experiences in connection with it? Especially when it could be demonstrate that he wasn't as sharp or as careful in taking care of his own best interests as he should have been?

In vain, Sargeant thumped the drum for the money we might pick up. There could be thousands for each of us! Didn't I need the money? Think of all the good I could do at my new school with a big piece of cash coming to hand?

He couldn't tempt me.

Back in Colorado Springs, I trotted into Harry's office with the clipping in hand. Harry was satisfied, and the *Gazette Telegraph* dutifully carried a small story announcing the outcome of the trial.

Best of all, my job was now secure. I could continue to work in developing the school, seeking enrollments for the next year and making myself more useful as a writer for Harry Hoiles.

Chapter XCIII

My experience in Federal Court was, in my own judgment, a colossal waste of time and money. The court determined that I had, in fact, been injured by Retail Credit. But I had already survived the injury and needed no public hearing, especially one in which my sensitivity to the "unseen" and my naivete were paraded for all to witness. I am not vindictively inclined. I have sometimes felt myself wronged and, at the time, experienced anger and frustration. But that mood passes. It doesn't take me long to recognize that while I may echo with frustration and resentment, there was probably some reason arising from my own behavior that triggered a hostile word or deed.

Probably the worst aspect of that trial was its distraction. It cut across my activities at the school and at the newspaper. It was a humbling experience. When it had ended I decided to listen more closely to Edy, who—with her native caution and financial good sense—had warned me repeatedly against trying to do too much too fast.

One thing was gained and one thing only. Harry Hoiles now knew that I had told him the truth about my affairs. His trust in me grew, and I was satisfied with that. I concentrated on paying my debt to Bob Donner and sought to get back to Freedom School and editorial affairs.

We launched our drive for students for the 1958 school year. We held a director's meeting to engender suggestions about things we had left undone and enthusiasm for what we had done and were doing.

One idea that emerged from the meeting related to the actual substance of my instruction. I was presenting a thoroughly consistent (to the degree I understood it) approach to liberty. Our Board of Fellows, many of who were prominent and some of who were famous, had lent the use of their names as an act of trust. But how many of them actually agreed with what I was teaching?

A great many of them were Conservatives, and the libertarian approach goes beyond Conservatism to oppose all authoritarianism. The Conservative position has often been willing to accept authoritarian actions for what are viewed as "right" reasons. Clearly, few of them would ever come to listen to what I was saying. They viewed themselves (as don't we all), as being totally informed. But was it honest to use their names to promote a doctrine that, in some aspects, might have caused their hackles to rise?

Following the 1958 school year, we decided that we would build a new Board of Fellows. It would be called a "Graduate Board of Fellows" and would consist of persons who had taken our Comprehensive Course and could, in sincerity, give moral support to our efforts. As soon as we had a respectable number of persons so disposed, we would abandon our existing Board, thanking them for their help. From then on, we would use only those conversant with our position.

Another idea was offered, too. Our students had evinced considerable interest in Daisy Mae. Link, our ombudsman in every crisis, had brought a couple of his own horses out to our ample pastures—a service to him and a service to us, in return. Some students had taken advantage of his steeds as well as Daisy Mae. They had gone riding under his watchful eye. Even one student, who was tossed off Daisy Mae's back at full gallop, proclaimed that the experience was worthwhile.

Why not get a few more horses? The terrain was ideal. Wild animals crisscrossed our land, making some marvelous trails. And there were spectacular views in almost every direction.

I exercised my new determination to seek Edy's guidance before I plunged into new expenses. I asked her to assist in preparing a budget for the new year and to allot a sum for the purchase of mounts to be used for student riding.

I confess to a sense of dismay when I found that she had complied with my request. She had budgeted the vast sum of $250 with which I was instructed to expand our one horse, plus the filly, Liberty Belle, into a "string" of horses, complete with tack.

I didn't know how many horses there were in a "string." But I was not about to expose my ignorance to Edy, whom I was sure didn't know any more about it than I did. I could have asked Link, but I realized that on $250 I wasn't going to be able to acquire much in the way of living horse flesh anyway. I took an afternoon off and went about Colorado Springs seeking to buy a few "cheap" horses.

While visiting various stables, I learned what I had not known before. "Tack" meant the saddles and bridles (and other leather goods) and blankets that are indispensable trappings for any western mount. I'm a city dweller. I'd had some vague notion that "tack" had to do with horseshoes which would be "tacked on."

I was becoming better known in Colorado Springs and, with one voice, I was advised to attend an auction that was only a few weeks distant. There, I was told, I could get the best bargains and some really good steeds. However, I was further advised that if I proposed attending the auction as a buyer, I should identify myself in advance to the committee in charge of the auction. Potential buyers, I found, sat in an exclusive section of the audience. The auction was a major event in this outpost of horse fanciers.

I realized that attending the auction might not only give me an opportunity to get horses, but it might also allow me to meet wealthy and important people who use Colorado Springs as a place to stable their strings year around. The horsy set has used the city for years and, to the best of my knowledge, still does. It's one of the finest locations on earth in which to enjoy the various recreations and arts of equestrian mastery.

People who have money invariably interest me. At this time, they were more than a passing interest; they were crucial to my hopes and plans. If I were going to succeed with the school, financial support from persons of means must be obtained.

Further, I have a respect for persons with money. They have, by virtue of their positions, displayed at least one and possibly two forms of economic virtue. They have either earned the money by honest effort— surely grounds for respect. In addition, regardless of how they had acquired their funds, they had managed to hang onto them. That engendered in me a respect that borders on awe.

I have known many people who have made it big at one time or another (at least according to their own protestations.) Most of them are as poor as Job's turkey because they spent it as fast, or faster, than they got it.

The government is out to take every loose dollar, particularly from persons who have an ability to acquire more than one at a time. Moreover, the government is compulsive about ripping out dollars that are fastened down. Accordingly, I mentally tip my hat to the successful. I have never been able to understand those who are so quick to criticize persons of means when in every other breath they reveal envy and lust for what some other person has.

I can sympathize with the hermit who condemns dollars and won't take any for himself. But the ambivalence of the person who damns the successful while bemoaning his own poverty fails to impress me.

I make no bones about it. I love the rich; the successful; those who have more than I do...which is a very large number, indeed.

In any case, I followed the advice I received and contacted the appropriate person in charge of assigning seats to buyers. Presently, through the mail, I obtained a pass, identifying me as a potential "dealer" in equine pulchritude.

Now, in anticipation of this major acquisition and the laying out of $250 in cash, I sought to prepare myself. Would I pass muster among men and women who really knew and understood horses? Obviously not.

My knowledge of horses was non-existent, unless you can consider an exposure to Gary Cooper and western cinema as an educational experience. I must do what I could to at least *look* like a person who knew his way all around a horse.

With this in mind, I visited a local haberdashery that specialized in western attire and came out looking a bit like an incongruous Hoot Gibson. I had the "gentleman cowboy's" attire, complete with striped trousers and a jacket with braid on the back and side pockets.

I had a western shirt, a couple of bolo ties, riding boots—which did provide a certain elevation while pinching my toes—and even a lovely gray Stetson girded by a Lilliputian lariat. I paid nearly as much for this get-up as I had in the budget for horses.

The fateful day arrived and I presented myself at the site of the auction. I showed my pass, was given a double take by the usher, who then seated me with a show of respect anyway. I found myself only three or four rows from the platform, where, I was told, the auctioneer would display his wares.

The auction was conducted just outside of town. The importance of the event was evinced by the amount of land dedicated to the effort. I was in a kind of amphitheater completely open at both sides, but equipped with a large stage in front, a wall in back and a tin roof that arched over the entire area. The roof was supported by mast-like four-by-fours at appropriate intervals.

Non-buyers were relegated to bleacher-like seats that were ranked up the natural slope. There must have been room for about five hundred spectators and the seats were beginning to fill by the time I was seated.

I looked around at my fellow bidders, hoping to detect signs of wealth. Instead, I saw people, mostly males, who appeared to be Link's counterpart. They wore Levi jeans and western shirts; most of them were sans hats and sans bolos. I had scored at only one point. They all wore boots! However, I noticed to my surprise that, with the exception of my own shining unscuffed bunion-makers, there wasn't a square inch of polished leather to be seen. Who were these people? Where were those with the bankrolls?

If I was astonished at the appearance of my peers, the effect was mutual. More than one pair of eyes stared at me as though I had just arrived from outer-space. And... was it my imagination? It seemed to me that, after giving me an up and down and an all-the-way-around, they inched away as though I was a trifle unclean. I sat in royal splendor, quite alone.

Clearly, these are just wranglers and hired men, I rationalized. The owners will show up at the last minute, perhaps with the sound of trumpets. But the last minute came. We still had about twenty-nine sunburned, horneyhanded horse people sitting in the buyers' section, plus one immaculate, corduroyed Stetsoned individual. I did my best to look indifferent and to fade from view at the same time. It didn't work. I was as out of place as a New York cut at a vegetarian picnic.

The stage was about four feet above ground level so all could have a good view. Behind the stage, numerous stalls held the animals that were to go under the auctioneer's hammer. In the center of the stage was a sawdust ring such as once adorned Ringling Brothers' big top extravaganzas. Over at stage left was a slender lectern equipped with microphone and, now, with the auctioneer announcing the program.

It was a true gala. Some dignitaries were introduced. They made brief statements about horses and auctions in general and specifically about the auction about to occur. A western quintet set themselves onstage and plunked and thumped an accompaniment to a vocalist. The nasal overtones ricocheted off the tin roof, taking on some of the tonal patina of this metallic sunshade.

The preliminaries finished, the auctioneer spread his papers on the stand, and cleared his throat. The time had come to spend money.

Meanwhile, I had been doing a bit of mental arithmetic. I still didn't know how many horses comprised a string. But I did understand $250. And I knew about "tack." So, I reasoned I would try to set my top price at $50.00, hopefully picking up at least three companions for Daisy Mae and Libby. That would cost $150 and still leave me with $100 with which to purchase saddles and bridles.

Everyone knows about auctions. One doesn't open his bidding with his final dollar. One tries to come in with a low bid and stop when the ceiling is reached. So, I reasoned, I would open my bidding at $10.00 and work up to $50.00. Beyond that I would not go.

But the auctioneer was already telling us about his first offering. I don't remember the name used. I certainly made no notes. But it was of this genre: We have "Dancing Splendor" out of "Gandy Dancing" by "Royal Splendor." (There was great importance put on genetic information) "And he comes from the "Scuffed Shoe" Ranch which has produced such fine mounts as "Arabian Cry Baby" and "Arthritis Brings St. Vitas."

At this point, a cowboy, dressed like the average bidder, came from stage right with a horse at the end of a halter. The horse trotted proudly, leaped into the ring and obediently went round and round doing the kind of things horses know how to do. The cowboy directed its every move.

I could see nothing wrong with this horse. It had the correct number of legs with a head in front and a tail behind. It appeared to have a modicum of good sense and wasn't hard to look at. Surely it was worth $50.00. I made up my mind. As soon as the auctioneer finished his praise of the animal and called for an opening bid, I inhaled a supply of air so I could trumpet my $10.00 offer.

Someone to my right beat me to it. His cry was, *"Four!"*

Four dollars? That was an odd bid. Was this a golf match? And I thought I was being frugal. While I was trying to regroup someone else yelled, *"Five!"* I didn't let out a sound. From various seats in the buyers' pit came, "six, seven, eight," and so on up to "seventeen." Fortunately, I said nothing.

And then the auctioneer gave me an education. "Sold to Mister _____ for seventeen hundred dollars."

The sorry appearing horse people, who looked like they repaired fences, were the men with the chips. It is only the newly rich who try to look as if they have money. And this, of course, includes all the not-at-all rich, who want to create an impression.

Real horsemen didn't waste their time with $50.00 bids. They bid in hundreds. I didn't know that. It was not all I didn't know. What would I do now? Offer half a bid sometime? Perhaps I could buy a partial interest in a horse.

For more than an hour I sat, as one animal after another made an appearance, performed in the ring, and was hammered away. Prices ranged from above $2,000 per horse down to less than $1,000. I think the cheapest was about $700. I wore a pained expression as if to say: "When are you going to produce the good stuff?"

Then an intermission was called. A stirring on the benches in the buyers' section followed. Most of the people who had been tossing thousand dollar bills around tramped out. I could hear the vans, trucks, and horse trailers moving around behind the stage where mounts were claimed by their new owners and accounts settled.

At last the auctioneer returned and gave a haughty glance in my direction. Only eight of us were left. My attire was in such contrast to the others that it must have appeared as if I owned them and was only waiting for the galley master.

From this moment on, most of the hype vanished. The auctioneer's voice was brisk, and he gave a few "no nonsense" comments. Then, without build-up or a recitation of parentage, the next animal made an appearance.

The cowboy ushering it in didn't trot and neither did the horse. Both ambled. But it was clear to see that each was operating under his own power. The cowboy stepped into the ring first and with some reluctance the horse followed.

Even my untrained eye could detect the differences between this horse and the animals that had preceded. They had been *horses*! This one was only a horse. It's odd what a bit of reverence can do for a five-letter word.

Wisely, the cowboy didn't attempt to get his charge to circle the ring. Instead, he led it back and forth, thus establishing that the creature had two sides, a front and a rear. But it had the requisite number of legs and it was actually a rather well formed animal. It only lacked ambition.

I looked at my fellow bidders to see which one was going to get the ball rolling and found that seven pairs of eyes awaited my utterance. My get-up was going to pay off at last, I waited for them and they, acting in concert, waited for me. I shrugged and, taking care to emphasize the second word, I said, "Ten *dollars*."

My bid was accepted. Apparently something in that dollar range had been anticipated. One of my neighbors raised me by ten. I went to thirty. I heard another go to forty. I said, "Fifty *dollars*," with finality.

The bidding stopped at once. In vain, the auctioneer pleaded that the animal was worth more. But he didn't waste a lot of time about it. He didn't really expect more, he just wanted to prove to the seller that he had tried. The gavel smacked and I had purchased a horse for the precise amount I had planned. Perhaps this would turn out to be a good place to buy a horse after all.

For the next twenty minutes one horse followed another into the ring, with clock-like regularity. I began the bidding in every case with, "Ten *dollars*." Then, I'd follow with the third bid of thirty and the fifth bid of fifty. At that point I'd lean back to show I had lost interest. The others understood. If they wanted horses they had to go above fifty. So they did. Seven or eight horses, each of which would have been mine for fifty went to others at a slightly higher price.

The auctioneer took a deep breath and gave a little spiel. This next animal was a palomino. He had some nice things to say about it. Its lineage was apparently unknown but he said it was a fine little horse, ideal for a teenager or someone even younger.

I wasn't the least bit interested in that, so I immediately leaned back. We planned the Freedom School for adult-sized riders and I wasn't going to buy a midget.

But when the cowboy came out with this creature, it knew its way around. It had ambition, trotted around the ring and gave evidence of a spirit not at all dead. Indeed, the color was light beige and, although it still had a bit of its winter coat clinging, anyone could see that it was a cute, attractive animal with intelligence. With care it could be a winner...in the dwarf class.

I gave visible evidence of lost interest. My fellow bidders, apparently taking their cue from me, all did the same. We all stared with lack-luster eyes and studied indifference.

The auctioneer didn't approve of this turn of events. He cajoled, he pleaded—tears came into his voice. It was really a marvelous horse. It was worth more than many others that had brought good prices. And it had to be sold. Surely, someone would see the wisdom of investing in it.

I am a real softy when it comes to tears. The apparent anguish of the salesman touched my heart. I could see his point. He had to get an opening hid. And for some reason everyone was following my lead. If I said nothing, then it was quite likely the entire buying section would remain mute. I have never been one to shirk an obvious responsibility.

Giving what I believed was a convincing performance of a lack of desire, I said, "Ten *dollars*," and at once lolled in my place.

Another, with something of a quaver in his voice, said, "Fifteen."

That didn't seem quite cricket. I had set the pace by maintaining bidding in $10.00 increments. Some cheapskate had cut it in half. I didn't want the horse, but to clear up that deficiency, I said, "Twenty-five."

A bid followed so closely on my heels, that it surprised me. "Thirty."

Forgetting myself, I said, "Thirty-five."

The bidding stopped at that point. Despite all the auctioneer could do, we all remained stolid and unmoving. I grinned at my neighbors, indicating a willingness to applaud if someone else would get into the act. I didn't want that animal!

But I got him, along with a glare from the man with the gavel.

That little palomino, whom we christened Poco Pal, was without a doubt the worst horse we ever had. In appearance, he was as sweet and gentle as a kitten. One should never be convinced by appearances alone! That horse was vicious. Really mean! And because he was so small and his legs so short, his gate was as choppy as a jackrabbit's. Further, if a person of average height boarded him, his knees came up even with the pommel or else his foot dragged so low that he could break an ankle if the horse stepped over a stone.

I don't mean to imply that Poco was a bucking horse. He didn't buck. He was far too clever for that. Besides, you could nearly straddle him with your feet still on the ground.

No, Poco would stand stock still while an inexperienced tenderfoot climbed into the saddle. He would continue to look meek and submissive while the stirrups were adjusted, his beautiful eyelashes concealing the wicked gleam deep in his optics.

When he was sure his rider was exactly where his personal contours were bestowed to best advantage, without warning Poco would swing his head and bite his rider's shin. He would have calculated range and distance to the precise millimeter and never missed. Further, he could score either left or right and no one could know in advance which side Poco would view as the more tasty.

After riding him, walking—even in cowboy boots—was a pleasure. He also had a mouth as hard as cast iron. On the trail, he'd veer off just to pass between a couple of trees, where he'd try to break your leg. And when the trail was narrow, with a cliff on one side and a drop of eighty feet or so on the other, Poco had a knack of leaning against the cliff on the up-hill side. Then, he moved along despite a person's most vigorous sawing on the reins.

With Loy on his back on one occasion, he took it into his head to lie down and roll over her. Fortunately, he had misjudged her and she leaped clear in time.

But how was I to know all these things beforehand?

In any case, I now owned two horses. With one more, I'd have reached the limit of my budget. The sale proceeded and the earlier routine of bidding resumed.

Every time an animal was sold, the auctioneer would flip over the page and start afresh. His system of keeping tabs on everything apparently provided him with one sheet of paper per horse.

Now as he turned to a new sheet, he frowned and peered closely. Then he turned, left the platform, and went back in the general direction of the stalls. In a moment he returned and took a second look at the paper in front of him. At last, he turned to his audience.

"I'm sorry to have to report," he said, "an error has been made. I have an animal for sale from Such and Such Ranch, which is one I thought we had already sold. It happens to be "Grey Ghost" out of "Anaconda Grey" by "Ghost White."

"This one is a horse!" I knew what he meant, the reverence had returned.

The auctioneer looked sternly at me. "I don't want any ten dollar bids on this animal. He's in his prime and worthy of anyone's stables."

At that instant out came the cowboy, trailing a proud and prancing gelding, almost appaloosa in coloring. The horse clearly knew what was expected of him. The two got into the ring at the same time. The cowboy leaped up on the bare back. They performed beautifully. Grey Ghost could do and would do anything and everything he was told. He understood rein, knee, and voice commands. And that air of nobility that marks a really good animal came with him like an enveloping aura.

"I wanted to hold him over," the auctioneer went on, "but my instructions are to sell." Again, his glance targeted on me. "Do I hear $500?"

I may be a patsy for tears, but I can handle verbal assertiveness. Besides, I had just bought that undersized palomino that I hadn't really wanted. I was not to be intimidated.

"What you hear," I said, "is ten *dollars*."

Someone else immediately said, "Twenty," but a second voice chimed in at once with "thirty." That wasn't the way we had played the game. I always got the third bid and someone had taken it away.

Without thinking I shouted, "*forty*," and then, in panic, realized what I had done. I had blocked myself. If I bid fifty, I'd be raising my own bid.

I didn't have to worry about it. Someone else shouted fifty. I saw that everyone was looking at me again. Fifty had been my top all day. But I had saved $15 on Poco. I could raise the ante and stay within the budget.

In a firm voice, I said: "I will then bid *sixty dollars*."

Silence descended.

The auctioneer pleaded. He shouted. He moaned. And he was as effective as an auctioneer could be.

The other buyers waited, apparently in respect for my next move. I wasn't going to make the next move; it was my bid that was being challenged. Truthfully, I was so excited that I very nearly did raise my own bid, but managed to regain some degree of sanity in time.

After five minutes of importuning the auctioneer caved in. At last, with a sound of bitterness, the gavel swung and I was the owner of the Grey Ghost.

My heart we. pounding. I had a pretty good idea that I had scored a coup. I also had a pretty good idea that I was in fast company and that I could readily be conned by someone smarter.

I got up from my trench and walked to the platform. "I'm through," I said, looking up at the auctioneer. "I only wanted three horses."

Then, disregarding the more dignified procedure of walking

around to the rear, I scrambled up on the stage and took Grey Ghost's halter from the hand of the astonished cowboy. I feared that if I turned my back, then Grey Ghost would vanish. Or perhaps, they'd bring out a ringer and I might be too ignorant to detect the difference until too late. I wasn't going to let this one out of my sight.

Personally, I led my *horse* from the ring and headed toward the exit. At that moment, a voice rang out from the upper reaches of the bleacher seats. "Stop the auction! Stop the auction!"

One of the former bidders who had enjoyed a location in the buyer's circle earlier had returned. He came running down the slope to the stage. "That's the horse," he bellowed. "That one on the platform. I want to bid on that animal. "

He pulled up below the stage out of breath. I confronted him, the halter firmly in my grasp. "Sorry, cowboy," I said. "I just bought him."

"No! Damn! I thought I had that one. I bought another that looks like him. His Stetson came off and was hurled to the ground. "That's one hell of a horse, Mister," he said. "Mind telling me what you paid for him?"

"Not at all," I said. "I bid sixty dollars."

"Sixty dollars!" I thought the man would experience cardiac arrest. "You paid sixty dollars for him?"

"Right."

The cowboy's face took on a crafty light. "Look, Mister, I'll be glad to buy him from you. What would you like? A hundred? Two hundred? Three? Four? You name it."

A very strange feeling swept over me. I felt a knotting in my stomach. This man, looking up at me from below the stage had become my enemy. He was trying to take my horse. He was not going to get my horse.

"This horse is not for sale at any price," I said.

Did I say that? That is what I said. It was pretty stupid. We were so short of funds at the school that an improvement in our financial picture could be crucial.

Of course, I don't know how far the cowboy would have gone. Or could have gone. Based on prices paid earlier I could have probably gotten a thousand, perhaps more. And with it, I could have purchased several more horses, and lots of other things we needed.

But at that moment, the Grey Ghost filled my life. I had to have that horse. Everything else paled into relative insignificance.

I've often thought of that experience. It taught me a very important fact that many people have difficulty accepting. There is no real or objective value to anything. We value things depending on a great many variables. And our view of what something is worth can be altered moment by moment.

I often think of this when I run into people who, with a great show of certainty, tell me that this or that item is worth so much. An item is worth what you can get for it at the time you sell it. Or, the reverse. Values don't stay put. They move around.

What was the Grey Ghost really worth? I have no idea to this day. He was a fine, intelligent animal. He gave us splendid service. When I got him out to the school, Link and the horse had a conversation and reached an understanding. Link would stay on as wrangler, but the Grey Ghost would keep the other horses in line.

From this beginning we gradually expanded our string until, by acquisition and foaling we had a string of more than twenty good riding animals. The students always enjoyed seeing the animals even when they didn't ride. They were a real plus factor for our endeavor.

Edy's thrift was vindicated.

Chapter XCIV

Ralph Williams walked into my office at the *Gazette Telegraph* one morning. He was in his late seventies, and he wore a felt hat and a large grey overcoat. He held himself as erect as a trooper on parade. The April day was moderately warm but he remained wrapped and topped as though the world had cooled.

He introduced himself, telling me that he read my editorials and liked them. This was not altogether unheard of, so I waited for discovery of the reason for his visit.

"I have decided," he said, "that I can trust you."

"That's nice to hear," I admitted. I couldn't quite see where his approval of my writings had produced his visit.

"I would like to arrange an appointment with you," Williams continued. "I have a serious proposition to make. The appointment must be for a meeting at my home. There, if you and I come to an agreement, I believe you will find that what I have to offer will be of great value to you.

"I am busy," I confessed. "But what you've just said is enticing. It's the stuff of which storybooks are made. I don't know you and you don't know me. You've read some of my output and I know nothing whatever about you." I surveyed him with close attention. He appeared to be sincere. His blue eyes burned in their sockets. His cheekbones were hollow, but he was clean and radiated personal pride. His overcoat was worn, but everything about him was as trim and neat as his circumstances permitted.

We set an hour later in the week when I would call and he furnished his address. His house was located a few blocks from Ent Air Force Base in an older residential District.

When he left my office I looked him up in the telephone book. A Ralph Williams lived at the address he had given me. I checked a couple of earlier books. A Ralph Williams had lived at that address for some time.

In the newspaper business one grows skeptical. The world is full of strange aspirations. Reassured by this easily obtained confirmation of identity, I decided to keep the appointment we had made.

Later that week I drove to the address and parked at the curb.

Williams' house was a white bungalow placed on a relatively narrow lot with line fences running on both sides from front to rear. The front lawn was in poor shape, weed choked, and in need of mowing.

There was no doorbell. I knocked.

After a brief interval, Ralph Williams opened the door. He was dressed in a black suit with white shirt and bow tie. He was as stiff and formal as though hosting a four o'clock tea.

He looked at me without smiling, pulled a watch from a vest pocket, nodded as though to himself and said, "You're on time. That's good. Come in."

I had made it a point to be on time, and passed through the door into his house.

But wait. He closed the door behind me and we were still outside. That is, we were under a roof but the structure in which he lived was a house within a house. It stood, complete at our right, with another front door to enter. It was a cottage, less than half the size of the bungalow that contained it.

That portion of the building into which I had come from the street was unfinished. The floor consisted of one-inch planks put and nailed on the bias. At my left was a wall with the suds uncovered, masking goodness knows what on the far side. I was in a corridor that ran alongside the original dwelling all the way from front to rear.

The back door was visible, or rather, both back doors. One could exit into the back yard at the end of the corridor. Or one could walk to the rear of the corridor and enter the cottage from there.

I had never in my life seen anything like this and it was obvious that my host was a trifle embarrassed by even my quick scrutiny and my look of astonishment. He ushered me into the cottage saying, "I never got around to finishing it."

I nodded. This whole thing was taking on a very mysterious air.

I found myself in a tiny parlor, furnished in the style of the 1900's. The place was lined with shelves, make-shift and clumsy. And the shelves were packed with books. There was an old-fashioned library table with a Tiffany stained glass table lamp. Across from it stood a horsehair straight-backed chair, an old mohair arm chair and a floor lamp with silk shade, strings of beads dangling from the edges. A cheap upright piano and a rickety piano seat completed the furnishings.

In a place of honor beside the door was a magnificent bronze statue about four feet tall. The blinds at the windows were drawn and, even with both lamps burning, the place was gloomy. But my eyes were sharp and I bent over the statue.

It was a celebrated masterpiece by Auguste Moreau entitled, "Psyche and Eros." Incredibly lovely.

Williams said, "It is the original. There are no copies." I looked again. The statue belonged in a museum. It was priceless.

"Sorry you can't see the best one," Williams said. "I gave it to the Elks' Club. It used to stand over there." He indicated an empty pedestal by the window. "Please have a chair."

I sat on the straight-back and he lowered himself—somewhat painfully I thought—into the mohair. "I don't have many callers," he said, "so I don't use this room often. Later on you'll have an opportunity to examine the books. Most of them are first editions and a few are numbered editions signed by the author."

There was an expensive carpet on the floor, and battered green shade at the windows. Some of the things in the room were antiques and I could detect that a number of the books were leather-bound. There were no paperbacks. The Williams' possessions ranged from priceless to junk.

"This room is amazing, Mr. Williams," I finally said. "No one could imagine what's in here."

"Let's hope it stays that way," he said. "I'm deathly afraid of intruders. And I do not like strangers."

"I'm a stranger," I said, smiling.

"I hope you won't remain one," he replied.

"Tell me about yourself," I said. "You appear to be..." I almost said, "a character," but decided against the expression. "You appear to be unique."

"Each of us is unique."

"Please call me Bob," I suggested.

"Very well. And my name is Ralph."

He stood offering his hand, so I stood and took it. Ralph was apparently more comfortable when a certain level of formality was maintained.

"I was married at one time," Ralph said. "Miserable woman. Fortunately, we were divorced."

I nodded. What does one say to that?

"Then I fell in love again."

I thought I was to be treated to a recitation but, instead, silence descended and Ralph was lost in reverie.

"Did you decide to enlarge the house for your wife or for the later object of your affections? I asked, bringing him back to the present.

"For my love, of course," he said. "She jilted me."

"La Donna Mobile," I said, "The woman is fickle

"Precisely," Ralph agreed. "But then there was another."

"Ah?"

"But she disappointed me, too."

"No."

"I have had miserable luck. But it may not be luck at all. If a woman is truly comprehended, she will be seen to be fickle by nature. All women are the same."

"Possibly not all, Ralph."

"Oh, yes. All. I exclude none. At first they lure a man, pretending to an interest in him when, in fact, they see him and all he possesses in the light of their own desires."

At last the way was clear for a discussion. Perhaps in this respect a woman is most like a man," I suggested.

"Doesn't a man look at a woman in the light of his own self-satisfaction?"

"It's not the same at all. A man is expected to go out, work himself to the bone, slave day after day, and bring it all home to her. She sits there, playing coy, plotting on how to get more, wheedling and coaxing him for one thing and then another.

"You cannot tell me about women. I have known six. I have saved all our correspondence and I'll show it to you sometime. I have it all filed and cross-referenced. They're all alike. They say divergent things but at heart they are identical."

"You have had bad luck," I said.

"I began to enlarge this house to please the woman I loved. After my wife left, of course. When the second one ran off with the garbage man...can you imagine that? A garbage man? Anyway, I kept remodeling to please the first, and then the next. You see, I had the notion that a man needs a woman.

"After the third, I gave up. I decided that the woman would have to love me for what I am and not for the way I remodel my house.

As you see, I never had reason to finish the task."

"Yes, I see. But that brings me to the place where we made this appointment. Did you ask me here to get my ideas on the subject?"

For the first time, Ralph smiled. "No. Set your mind at rest on that score. I have only one ambition left."

"And what, may I ask, is that?"

"I want to die."

I sat bolt upright. "Die?"

He nodded. "I am looking forward to death."

I squirmed in my chair. "Well, you've come to the wrong person if you want me to help fulfill that ambition."

"I know that. I've read what you have written. It is a shame, of course. If we were truly civilized we would have death parlors. There, a person wanting to die could go, arrange for a spectacular party, invite his friends, or hire a room full of girls with whom to make love. He could have the music of his choice, entertainment—whatever he wanted. And then, at the appropriate time, he could be quietly and scientifically put to sleep.

"Instead, we have such prejudice against death that it has been made illegal. So, in the end, we all break the law.

"I've thought. of course, of committing suicide. But what would happen to all those treasures in that case? The government would get them. And government has no sense of the appropriate, or of the fitness of things.

"I know something about government, Bob. I've worked for the government most of my life. In a minor capacity, true, but that is where I have earned my livelihood."

"Do you have any children?" I asked.

Ralph nodded. "Yes. I have a son by my first wife. He's a no-good. Like she was. He has no sensitivity, no appreciation."

"I am forced to abide by your value judgments," I said. "I'm sure I've never met them."

Ralph paid no attention. "I thought of asking you to kill me. I have a revolver. And you could easily do it. But there's always a chance that you'd be tried for murder, even if we had an agreement in writing."

"I would say it is more nearly a certainty, Ralph."

"So, I am condemned by the government to grow old. I can no longer work. My body is growing stiff. I take no delight in eating.

The thought of making love provides no satisfaction. So, I will gradually wither and lose my sight, my hearing, and my ability to move about. I am condemned to be a miserable cripple, an object of pity, and a public and private nuisance."

Ralph stared at my face, seeking to read my thoughts. "That is why I am turning to you. I am going to ask you to look after me in this twilight of my years. Hopefully, the time will be brief.

"There won't be much to do. I want you to shop for my groceries, once a week, I have the money. It won't cost you anything but a little time. Perhaps I can get you to mow the lawn. The kids in the neighborhood hate me and won't do a decent job.

"Perhaps from time to time you'll sit with me for a visit. Or maybe we can go out for a drive. That's about it. In exchange, I will make you the sole beneficiary of my Will. You will inherit this house and lot, both being clear of debt. You will receive all these objects of art. And, in addition, I have a secret place where I keep my savings. They are not in a bank. When you have proved yourself as my friend, I will show you where I keep it hidden."

Who hasn't read of eccentric millionaires who have lived in impoverished circumstances, but, upon their death, were found to have lots of cash hidden upon their premises. Was Ralph one of these odd balls? It was possible.

"Ralph," I said. "I see in you a man who has grown bitter. I find myself interested in what you say. Your proposition is intriguing, but I am not certain that we will ever be friends. For us to be real friends would require you to take an interest in me and my ambitions to the same degree you ask me to take an interest in you. I'm not at all sure that you would care to try.

"Friendship, if it comes, will come unbidden. So if this arrangement depends on friendship, I think we've gone far enough. However, let me say this. What you are asking is within my ability to fulfill. You've created a sense of mystery. I have no idea how much money you have or what any of this is worth. But let me reveal myself, at least to a degree.

"I am trying to build and run a school. Your house and all that is in it should be worth several thousands of dollars, at least. If you will make out your Will to the Freedom School, I'll be happy to be your errand boy and to do the things you ask. I don't want your property and I don't want your money. Not for myself. But I could certainly use the assets for the school. Your books could go into the school library. Any money as well."

"No." Ralph shook his head. "I don't deal with institutions. I tried it with the Elks' club. But they have changes in management and in policy. I'm sorry now that I gave them my statue. I will leave what I have to you personally, or you may forget the offer."

"You feel that strongly on the point?"

"Yes. What you do with my assets after you get them is your business. But I will leave them to you, personally. Otherwise, I may just set a match to the whole place and go out in a blaze of glory."

I thought about it for a moment. "Very well, Ralph. I'm your boy. I'll run your errands. I do a certain amount of traveling and, if I'm out of town for any reason, I'll either do your shopping before I go or have someone on my staff, probably my secretary, do your shopping for you."

"That won't do. You must attend to it personally. I will never let another woman into my home."

"Life isn't like that, Ralph. I'll agree to look after you as best I can within my schedule. But my own work comes first. I refuse to take you on as my prime interest and concern. I'll fit you in and do a good job. And I'll cover all the bases. But if you are telling me that no matter what, you come first, you will have to find someone else."

I stood. Williams was too exacting, too formal, and too rigid. I'd do it for the school, but not at the expense of my primary endeavors. I started for the door and Ralph's voice stopped me. He, too, had stood. There was a pathetic expression on his face.

"Please, Bob, don't go. I really need you. I...I." He clamped his jaw shut at odds with himself for showing indecision. "I think you are fair and honest. If you have to go out of town, I'll...I'll accept that. I'll leave it, me, all my treasures, in your hands. It will be your decision, not mine any longer."

I didn't want that, either. "Ralph, I'm not going to become your keeper, leading you around on a leash. You're going to keep on making decisions and asking me to do what you wish. And I'll carry them out. I may not do them exactly when you want them done, nor in the way you think they should be done. But I'll give it my best shot. That's all I can promise."

He was reaching for me, as though the dimly lit room had gone black. "That's fine. That will be splendid. I can't expect anything better than that. And, really, there won't be that much to do. I'll try not to be a nuisance. God, that's the one thing I don't want to be!"

"Very well. As I said before, I'm your boy."

Again we shook hands. Each handshake seemed to shut the door on what had been said up to that point. It was Ralph's symbol of showing agreement and acceptance.

"I've arranged for everything. I have my grave bought and paid for. And my coffin. Some day I'll take you out to see where my body will rest. I have a view lot in the cemetery. It's quite lovely."

"I'm sure." I didn't want to pursue the subject anymore. The preoccupation with death was a trifle macabre.

"Won't you sit down again? Please." He was eager.

"Thanks, Ralph. But I do have to go. Give me your telephone number and call me if you want anything. Meanwhile, I'll check with you from time to time."

In the beginning of this association, and while Ralph was still endowed with some vigor, we got in touch with each other once a week. He phoned me on Saturday morning at the Gazette. If I hadn't heard from him, I'd initiate the call. He'd give me a list of items he wanted at the grocery. I'd leave my office on the way out to the school, stop at the store, and make his few purchases.

His diet was austere. Mostly, there were a few cans of vegetables, milk, bread, crackers, and bacon. Once in while a pound of coffee.

He finally entrusted me with a key. After that, I'd let myself in, walk down that unfinished corridor to the back door of the cottage, and enter—calling out that I was on hand.

In the rear of the parlor was a kitchen and a tiny room where Ralph slept and spent most of his time. A bathroom with ancient fixtures completed his accommodation.

After putting away the groceries, I'd go in to spend half an hour or so as a visitor. Ralph was not an exceptional conversationalist. At first, I looked forward to the visits because I anticipated that he would have much to tell me. But he rarely extended himself.

On several occasions, I'd try to interest him in what I was doing only to find him inattentive, disinterested or antagonistic.

He had a file on each of his six loves and I wheedled him to tell me about them all. He answered by saying that the whole subject had been reduced to writing. I could look over the record after he was gone.

I took him out for drives on occasion and, true to his promise, he directed me to the cemetery so that I could examine the lot where he would be laid to rest. He seemed to have a great attachment for the place and was proud of the view from the lot that he had purchased.

I tried and failed to get any information from him as to his beliefs of what happened, if indeed anything happened, after death. Whatever his opinions, he kept them to himself.

When Ralph thought I was becoming disinterested in him, he would dangle his treasures in front of me, telling me that soon he would let me know where he hid all the money he had saved.

One day, he showed me his Will. He'd had it drawn up about the time of my first visit and he had been true to his word. His son and first wife were specifically excluded. I was his sole heir.

As a rule, my own schedule was made up weeks in advance so that if I were to be out of town for any reason, I could let him know. Then, I'd shop for him during the week and buy enough to tide him over until I returned. It was the best answer to the problem of my absence.

On two occasions, we drove out to the school so Ralph could see what I was doing. Each of those visits wore him out. And, while at the school, he simply sat somewhere, saying little to anyone and waiting until I was free to return him to home.

One day, he appeared to be both exceptionally talkative, and eager to tell me something. After trying to recreate the air of mystery, he told me where he had hidden his savings. Then he asked me to bring them to him.

He had been clever in finding a secret hiding place. One of the floorboards in the unfinished corridor outside the cottage wasn't nailed down. But, because the end was concealed under the plate supporting the wall studs, it remained tight. Without Ralph's guidance, it would surely have been overlooked.

In the space between the floor joists, I found a black metal box and took it to him where he sat on the side of his bed in his little room. Using a key that hung from a dirty string around his neck, he unlocked the box and handed it to me.

"I want you to count it, Bob."

The box contained three stacks of bills, each secured by a rubber band, and a copy of the Will. I counted the bills.

"I want you to promise me two things, Bob."

"What two things?"

"First, I want you never to tell anyone how much there is."

"No problem," I said. "I won't tell."

"Finally, I want you to promise me that you won't report this to the IRS. I know you plan to give everything to the school. But this money is for you. All of it. I don't want the IRS to get their filthy hands on any part of it. It's taken me many years to save that much. I won't rest easy in my grave if you betray me."

I thought for a moment. "Ralph, give me your word on just one point. Tell me that you obtained this money by honest means. Your word is good. If any of it has been stolen, I won't promise."

"Don't you know me better than that?"

"I think I do. But why don't you tell me?"

He smiled suddenly. "Good. I earned every cent of it, or it has been part of my pension. It is honest money."

"You have my promise," I said with great solemnity.

After the first two years, Ralph grew visibly weaker. His diet became little more than crackers and milk. In vain, I tried to interest him in food. He wouldn't go out for a good meal and he wouldn't tolerate having someone come in to cook.

I was worried about him and offered to take him to the hospital or to some home where he could receive adequate care. It was the only time I ever saw him truly angry. He railed at me for suggesting it. He ordered me never to make such a suggestion again. Didn't I understand that he was dying and that he wanted to die in peace? He didn't want a bunch of strangers pawing over him.

By this time, my first thought every day was of Ralph. I'd telephone him each morning at nine o'clock to be sure he was okay. His hearing began to fail as he had predicted and, on more than one occasion, after getting no answer from him, I dashed from the newspaper out to his place, in fear that the final curtain had been lowered.

Then, I began to suspect that he was feigning deafness to get me out there. Not that he wanted me to do anything. He just wanted another human being near him.

Finally, his physical movements became erratic. He'd forget to hang up the telephone after a conversation. Or when he tried to dial me, he'd become so confused he'd get nothing but a series of wrong numbers. Then he'd accuse the newspaper of canceling his telephone service.

One Wednesday morning, when I tried to call him, I was rewarded with the busy signal. I knew, or thought I knew, what had happened. He had tried to call me and had forgotten to hang up the phone. I had already raced to his house on numerous occasions because of this and, so, I wasn't too worried.

Besides, it happened that I was hobbling around with two canes, my back having given out. So I waited at the paper, getting my work finished before leaving.

When I finally entered the little room, I found Ralph flat on the floor. He had fallen. In trying to get up, he had pulled a great many items in the room over on the floor with him. He lay in a sea of broken glass, loose papers, and the telephone.

Because of my back, I was physically unable to give him a hand. Had I attempted to lift any weight, I'd have ended on the floor with him.

But there was one happy note. Ralph was fully conscious and he was smiling! "Hello, Bob," he said. "I knew you'd come!"

"My God, Ralph! What happened?"

"I don't know what's the matter," he said. "I haven't any strength. But I know what it means." He was jubilant. "I'm dying."

I managed to retrieve the phone. After a few moments, the dial tone replaced the busy signal and I got through to St. Francis Hospital.

In about twenty minutes, an ambulance arrived and two attendants came in with a stretcher. "I'm sending you to the hospital, Ralph, "I told him. "I can't help you anymore. You've got to be in the hands of the professionals."

"It's all right, Bob. It's all right. I don't mind anymore."

He was carried out and I locked up. His room was in shambles.

Instead of returning to the school, I stayed in town and later called at St. Francis.

One of the Sisters explained they had never had anyone come in quite as dirty or as emaciated as Ralph. But they had hopes they could reverse his condition.

I got to visit with him briefly. His complexion was several shades lighter than I had remembered it. I expected a figure of pathos, but Ralph's eyes sparkled.

I was apologetic. I knew he hadn't wanted to leave his home and I had finally disobeyed his wishes.

He held out his bony hand at the end of a skeletal forearm. "Thank you, my good friend." He wasn't feverish. His hand was warm and soft, despite the absence of flesh.

"Don't worry about a thing, Ralph. The Sisters say you have a good chance."

He smiled in triumph. "They know nothing about it, Bob. I am the one who knows. I will be dead soon." He closed his eyes and all his strength ebbed away. He was asleep and the Sister ushered me out.

I called on him the next day, but he was asleep. And in the middle of the night I received a telephone call from the hospital. Ralph had gone, at last, on the great journey he had longed to take.

He was buried where he had wanted to be. I found that I missed him, although he had often tried my patience.

His assets were sold and turned over to the school. The books, the piano, and a few antiques were moved there as well. That strange, old man had enriched my life in more ways than one. I remember him with great fondness.

Chapter XCV

During the winter of 1957-58, Link and Gene built "Thunderbird Lodge." This was our first residence cabin, designed to accommodate four persons. Old Charlie Heits brought the logs and supervised construction but did no more of the actual building.

We extended the school year, opening on June 1 and closing on September 18. That gave us eight two-week sessions. One of our sessions was ear-marked "history" and another "economics." The remaining six were what we called "basic," the "comprehensive," and finally became known as "Fundamentals of Liberty."

Additionally, we expanded our list of guest lecturers to include: Leonard Read, E. W. Dykes, R. C. Hoiles (the father of my employer at the paper), Louis G. Milione, Jr., Frank Chodorov, Percy Greaves, Jr., William Paton, James M. Rogers, James L. Doenges, Rose Lane, and "Baldy" Harper.

By having such well-known instructors we were able to attract a larger contingent of enrollees, and the year finished with fifty people successfully completing one or more of the courses offered.

Two unforeseen results emerged from this year's efforts. Neither result was welcome, and the cause in each case could be laid at my door. I was not a teacher.

I had taken no training that might have prepared me. I'd had a wonderful opportunity, through my work as editorial writer at the *Gazette*, to think through my subject. But thinking it through and expressing it are two different tasks.

My position had been developed on the basis of consistency. But when I insisted on consistency from my students, I sometimes ran into opposition. Consistency is an important element in logic. Logic is often lacking in the thinking and emotionalizing of many people. We tend to believe what we *want* to believe, not what coincides with reality.

Opposition from students in this area can be dealt with successfully only by an instructor who knows what he is doing. My only tool was dogged persistence and that meant some toe-to-toe verbal slug-fests.

I found I could usually win the argument. But sometimes, when I did, I lost the student. My lack of experience and my attitude sometimes alienated rather than liberated.

We signed up fifty-three people for our various sessions but only fifty finished their respective courses. Three left of their own volition. Of course, we gave them their money back, not even deducting for meals consumed. Full refunds were available to all at any time during the two weeks.

(The total cost was only $150 for the two weeks, which included all books, room and board, plus instruction and recreation. This was clearly a bargain. Bear in mind that a dollar would buy considerably more in 1959 than it now does.)

My staff was so sympathetic to me that none was helpful. When I asked various students who accepted the use of logic, I was informed that the problem was always with the student.

This affirmation caused me to dig in and become even more insistent and dogmatic.

The second unwanted result posed an even larger problem. A few of my guest instructors hadn't yet completed their homework, either. Common courtesy forbade that I interfere. But I could detect the looks of confusion on tee faces of some students, when, after a week of getting the basic uses of the mind under control, some celebrated personality would veer from the path.

This was not true with most of the instructors, some of whom had a far deeper grasp of the realities than I. Indeed, I made it a point to seat myself in each class whenever a visiting savant was present so I could learn from him, too. And I can't begin to express my gratitude for the enormous number of insights many of them provided.

Nonetheless, following the departure of a guest instructor who had compromised his position, I would start over with the group he had been teaching, taking the time to re-establish the principles agreed upon at the outset.

I well understood that my own reputation was nonexistent. Very few would come to hear what I had to say. So the headliners, who brought customers, had to be watched closely so they didn't undo the thrust and purpose of the instruction.

A third problem we still had to surmount was not unexpected. We had approximately doubled our enrollment from the prior year. Yet, we had added only four beds.

Thanks to our fund drives, we were moving along much better

with our finances. Additionally, having undertaken only a small building program during the prior winter, we weren't spending that much money.

I decided we could achieve a better balance if we reduced the number of instructors, notably those who contributed a mixed bag, while enlarging our facilities to accommodate more paying participants.

So, even as classes were going on, plans were completed for another building. Construction began. Instead of limiting this effort to a second residence cabin, as we had originally intended, I sought to take care of our growing requirement for an adequate dining room, as well.

With Reno Sales' permission to use his name, we planned and built what we called "Reno Sales Lodge," This building was placed across the access road and up the slope from our first construction. It was approximately the size of our first building, having two floors. The lower story, we built of cinder blocks and the upper was actually a one-story log cabin placed upon that foundation.

Our plan was to use the main room of the lower floor for a new classroom. A second room on that floor would be used for office space and storage. The top floor was divided into four separate rooms, each of which would house two persons. Thus, Thunderbird Lodge and Reno Sales Lodge, in combination, would provide student housing for twelve and we could use the existing classroom as our dining room.

Across the country, the reputation of the Freedom School was growing. We had begun attracting attention. Loy contributed significantly by concentrating on the food end of our operation. The existing dining room was added to the kitchen space and a cafeteria counter built. We hired an assistant for her and she began baking bread, cakes, and pies. She turned out some marvelous meals.

Our format for each session was now fairly well established,

Loy and I would both arise at about 4:30 AM. She would fix breakfast for the staff after which I would drive off with Ruth to the newspaper. Edy would drive into Colorado Springs a short time later, and Margie would head for Denver.

About eleven, Ruth and I would leave the paper end return to school in time for lunch with all the students.

Meanwhile, the student day was as follows: mornings were unscheduled. Breakfast was served at a fixed time, but no one was required to be on hand. The students spent their mornings sleeping, reading, writing papers (one was due each evening), discussing, riding horseback, hiking, jogging, or otherwise participating in a few low intensity activities such as horseshoes, archery, badminton and so on.

Lunch was served at noon and everyone was expected to be in the dining room unless an emergency interfered. At one in the afternoon classes began and continued until five. There was one scheduled break about three, but otherwise, it was a continuous four hours.

Supper (or dinner) was served at 6:00 p.m. and all returned to class at seven. The evening session ran until 9:00 p.m.

This classroom schedule applied from Sunday evening at 7:00 p.m. through Friday afternoon of the second week, following. On the final Friday evening, we would have a graduation ceremony, awarding a certificate of merit to those who successfully completed their studies. Thus, we had classes for 12 consecutive days (including Saturday and Sunday} plus a Sunday evening session from the beginning. That is 72 hours in class for lectures, discussions, debates, reading papers or reports, and otherwise using the mind.

Such concentrated classroom work was a challenge to nearly everyone. What surprised me was that the students liked it better than the guest instructors did. Almost without exception, the instructors complained that it was impossible for them to present that much material in that short a time. Of course, I permitted them to adjust that portion of the schedule over which they presided, so as to harmonize with their own material and inclinations. This meant that the instructors in charge of a two-week offering, such as a course in history or economics, usually kept the students in class a mere four hours per day, instead of six. And those in charge of a weekend often cut back to no more than two hours per day.

It became obvious to me after a time that students have a far larger capacity for absorbing information and getting it organized in their minds than many of the instructors had in presenting the material. There are always exceptions, of course. But, in general, better than half the time spent in grade and high school is wasted. In college, the individuality of a given institution has to be considered, for here the range in performance is broader. Some colleges and universities waste a great deal of time but others operate with considerable efficiency.

Because of the stringent demands I made on enrollees, while in class, countervailing efforts were made outside of class to provide an air of informality and relaxation. I specified informality of dress, with comfort the keynote.

To assist, Loy varied the menu and produced an attractive array of viands, no two meals alike. Additionally, on Sunday morning, instead of eating in the dining room, or at the table. just outside on the flagstone terrace, we provided a picnic ground at a spot near the creek.

There, Gene constructed a barbecue, and our Sunday morning meal was something to be remembered. We served flapjacks made over an open fire, accompanied by all the trimmings of a hunt breakfast.

For further variation, Loy dreamed up an evening's entertainment for all. Thus, on the second Thursday, after nine o'clock dismissal, all were invited to the dining room, or the classroom (later the lounge) where she sang a number of songs ranging from classics to pop, accompanied by recordings.

Even after we acquired the piano from the Ralph W1lliams estate, we didn't use it for those Thursday night gatherings. None of the staff, including Loy, played. And on those rare occasions when a student was a skilled pianist, there was no adequate time for rehearsal, either for the pianist or for Loy.

I think I am safe in saying that although some of the students may have resented my disciplinarian attitude, they warmed to Loy's happy contributions and her golden voice.

When the school year terminated in September of 1959, it seemed to me that I was at last ready to make the move that had spurred me into this project from the beginning.

I knew that I was not adequate as a teacher, but what I had really wanted to do was to demonstrate that a school, teaching free market economics and the concepts of human liberty, could be established. Baldy, whose influence over me had been profound, was the man envisioned as the educator who should be in charge of all Freedom School intellectual effort.

Chet Anderson, the man who had opened the door for me in Milwaukee, advised that my organizational structure was faulty. What

I needed, he said, was a Board of Trustees. The people we had as Directors were unknown outside of Colorado Springs. What the Freedom School required was a Board composed of persons who were known nationally.

In discussing the problem with Chet, I confided that I really wanted to turn the school over to Baldy. His belief was that Baldy would insist on the formation of a group of Trustees, made up of substantial citizens who were known and respected and whose names would open doors.

I explained about my development of a Board of Graduate Fellows. But this was not adequate as Chet saw it. Most of my graduates, although they might be totally convinced as to the merit of free enterprise and the importance of human liberty, suffered from the same anonymity that accompanied the Directors. Few had ever heard of thee. The school needed backing from persons with prestige and a bit of clout.

Very well, I asked him, whom did he have in mind?

Chet's view was that the very finest person I could possibly get would be none other than Bill Grede, the man who had really gone out of his way to get me moving during that never-to-be-forgotten luncheon at the Athletic Club. Once I had Bill, Bill would help to attract others of like caliber.

This conversation occurred during a visit to Milwaukee wherein Chet's organization had sponsored a three-day seminar which I had put on for him. The opportunity presented itself and I met with Bill Grede and asked him to help as Chet had recommended.

To my joy, Bill Grede accepted. Thanks to him, I immediately obtained another man from Milwaukee as well. His name was Robert W. Baird, Jr., who had a top executive post with the Marine Bank in that city. Spurred on by these developments, I was able to attract four other men of stature to the Board of Trustees. They were: Dr. James L. Doenges, M.D., of Anderson, Indiana, who had won a great reputation both as a surgeon and as an exponent of liberty, plus Ned Kimball, of Waterville, Washington, a well-known attorney, and R.W. Holmes, of Bellevue, Washington, who served with the Boeing Company in Seattle.

This was a significant development. I called for a meeting of the Trustees at the school and they all arrived.

The weather was still delightful, autumn lingered in the Rockies, and the scenery was at its best. There were two more decisions to be made. First, I sought Trustee approval to turn the academic area of the school over to Baldy. Everyone knew him or knew of him and the choice was applauded. Here was a man with consistency of belief, the ability to teach, and the credentials necessary. Baldy had taught economics at Cornell University for a number of years before taking a post with Leonard Read at the Foundation for Economic Education.

I was authorized to telephone Baldy and ask him to appear at the school. We'd pay his way, of course, as well as providing a small emolument for the time involved. He agreed to come at once. He still had no inkling of what was in store.

Meanwhile, another question loomed. Should Freedom School file for tax exemption? In my various efforts to raise money, most of the support I had won had been marginal. That is to say I might garner somewhere between $100 or $500 from a corporation president, who would nearly always advise that if the Freedom School ever obtained tax exemption, a much larger contribution could be justified. In some cases, actual promises of such contributions were made. They were usually followed with a wistful look and the comment: "Of course, if the government knows you are supporting free enterprise, you'll never get exemption."

On this question we all looked to Bill Grede for the ultimate wisdom and Bill admitted that exemption would be difficult. Also, that exemption would not bring about an automatic increase in contributions. In some ways, exemption could provide a negative impact. The operations of the school would come under a certain amount of government scrutiny. We would be banned from any kind of activity relating to political action. There would be forms to fill out regularly. There is a big difference between non-profit and tax-exempt status.

While we waited for Baldy's arrival, this subject was discussed—pro and con. Finally, Bill made his recommendation. Let's try for the exemption. This recommendation was immediately approved.

I met Baldy at the Colorado Springs Airport and drove him to the school. There we were all prepared. During the drive, I sidestepped his questions. It had to be a surprise. I'd planned it that way for years.

At last, I made the presentation. Going back in time, I reminded

Baldy of our meeting in New York City. There, he had exhibited great interest in a school that could be organized for the purpose of teaching free enterprise. He was no longer with FEE and was essentially unemployed at this moment.

I went on to explain that I had accepted his negative predictions as a challenge. From the beginning (as our correspondence would remind him), I had never thought of myself as a teacher. I had experience in organizing and believed that I could organize a school and get it on the map.

It had taken a great deal of time, money and effort, but it had been done. I had hoped to achieve our entire primary building plan within a year, and it had taken two. But our position, financially, was satisfactory. We had small debt that was being managed. We had limited facilities, which could be expanded as needed.

But we now had brought into being a working educational unit that was being used for the purpose intended. With that much in the way of introduction, I now offered Baldy the top position in the school. He had the credentials and he knew what was needed.

I would stay on, if that was his wish, to help manage the physical plant, to raise funds and to promote attendance. I wanted to continue to be helpful. If he wanted. But he was to be the ultimate decision-maker. If he accepted, the school would be his.

With Baldy in the saddle, we'd really be able to make a difference in the future of America. The Trustees were of one mind and so were the Directors. Baldy was the key to everything.

The look on Baldy's face was not the one I had anticipated. I expected, at the very least, some smiles. Perhaps a word or two of congratulation. I knew I had touched him deeply and right at the point where he lived.

But Baldy's look was cold, almost grim. I am sensitive to the moods of others and I must report that he appeared to me to be experiencing a form of panic. My offering was both unexpected and unwanted! I refused to believe that I was picking up that type of signal. I rationalized that Baldy's surprise was what I was seeing, not his sense of shock.

I had planned on his remaining at the school and a place had been prepared for him. He refused to spend the night, although he had been with us as an instructor for two full weeks earlier that year. He said he'd feel better in a hotel downtown.

So with my heart quailing at what I was picking up with my mental radar, I returned him to the Antler's in Colorado Springs. He promised to think over the proposition and to telephone his decision.

The next day, he telephoned, but not to me. He said he would provide us all with a letter in which he would show his reasons for the rejection.

It is incredible, as I look back on it, that I had never considered the possibility that Baldy would refuse. Of course, he would accept! I had assured the Trustees that this was his deepest wish. He had told me as much.

Now, I was stuck. I would have to continue teaching whether I thought myself capable or not. Further, I would have to raise all the money, make all the final decisions, and continue to operate—at least during summer months— from 4:30 a.m. to after nine each night.

In the winter, I would have to travel about the country, putting on smaller seminars, giving lectures, and doing my best to attract support. The whole operation was now my little red wagon.

Jim Doenges was the only Trustee who shared his letter from Baldy with me. Baldy didn't write to me at all, although we had carried on a warm and personal correspondence for years.

Doenges was so shocked at what Baldy said that he extracted a promise from me never to show the letter to anyone. I agreed in advance, and then Jim forwarded the letter. It was lengthy.

Baldy's basic objections were much the same ones he had before I put the school together. This wasn't the time. Colorado wasn't the right location. For an effective operation, the school would have to be in California, as he saw it. And we couldn't get the money.

But more. Baldy cast grave doubts upon me, personally. What was I doing there in Colorado with all those unmarried women out in the woods that way? What about my earlier connection with the "I Am?" How could he agree to work with a person like that? He appreciated the confidence of the Trustees. Perhaps sometime he'd be able to launch an educational institution. But certainly not with me.

Baldy had been one of my idols. Now, he broke my heart. Since Ruth opened all my mail in preparation, she, too, was privy to the letter's contents. She cried real tears and I came close to joining her. The inferences and allegations were deep wounds for her to carry, too. I kept the material from the others, but I could not hide my own sense of an inflicted wrong.

And yet, as time passed and I reviewed the matter, I could understand Baldy. There had never been a hint of scandal connected with Baldy's reputation. My own background was, at least in the minds of some, too lurid to be conducive of trust. I could, at fact, see Baldy's position. What assurance would Baldy have that I might not be involved in another charge of "using the mails to defraud?"

What really hurt was that Baldy never, in all the years that followed, spoke to me on the subject. And, as I learned, the letter obtained rather wide though selective circulation. And that hurt a lot.

Chapter XCVI

I didn't have time to waste feeling bad over Baldy's decision. I had already started the furrow and I must take it to the end of the acre.

There were a number of projects requiring immediate attention. He had to put final touches on Reno Sales Lodge, publish an Annual, issue a Prospectus for 1960, and tour the country far funds. Then, as quickly as possible, I had to build another residence cabin. We also needed to apply for tax exemption and do what was possible to build prestige for Freedom School.

I held a meeting with the Directors. Since I, was going to be responsible for the academic work at the school for the foreseeable future, I must have help in another function. Fund raising took a great deal of time.

I did fairly well at it, but detested the job. Would the Directors approve if I concentrated in other areas of management plus the teaching, while obtaining assistance in bringing in the dollars?

By now the Directors would probably have approved anything I suggested. Few, even among my angels, had anticipated that we would have gotten as far as we had. So, the immediate thought was that we would try to add to our staff by employing someone to enlarge and enhance the fiduciary flow.

With Baldy's rejection I also had a twinge of conscience. I had repeatedly promised all four women that the time would come when they would be paid for their work at the school. Meanwhile, one of the mainstays was the outside income earned by four of us and the non-salaried Herculean labors of Loy on campus.

In fact, without the years of work they all had put in for which there had been no recompense, the school would not exist. So, I suggested to Edith that she begin keeping tabs in the following manner. Each of us would go on salary, figuratively. None of us would be paid, but a bookkeeping entry would acknowledge that the school owed us wages. Then, if and when, we got everything moving as we hoped, we could all obtain our back pay.

And, I suggested that these wages be made retroactive to the opening of our first school year in 1957.

"Let's take Dr. Harper's rejection as a challenge," I told the Board. "It's probably my own fault. I should have let him know what I was planning without springing it on him as a complete surprise."

I was doubtless encouraged by the willingness of my co-workers to follow my lead.

But there was another enormously important factor. My work at the Gazette Telegraph was winning approval from Harry. Taciturn and aloof, as he often was, Harry was an honest and appreciative publisher. Now that Ruth was on hand, working both with him and with me, she helped substantially in making things go.

Ruth was Harry's secretary, as well as secretary for the school and for me personally. This lady had the capacity. Her many talents had developed under pressure. She had become an executive secretary of highest caliber. She was a blue ribbon achiever. Harry was delighted with her efforts and approving of mine.

Day after day, I wrote my editorials, and then took them in to Harry where we butted heads, argued, debated, repaired, improved, or (on occasion) vetoed. Ruth and I both received wage increases and mine was substantial.

The policy of the paper was carried forward to the best of our ability. The view held was this: the newspaper belongs to the public, subscribers, and advertisers. They pay for it and it should reflect what is useful and newsworthy. But the editorial page belongs to Harry. His opinions (and, consequently, mine) were not to color the news stories. Total independence between the editorial content and the news and advertising content was maintained.

To my surprise, I learned that many and probably most of the personnel in the newsroom didn't agree with our editorial policy. I felt this to be a tragic condition. Harry agreed that it was unfortunate, but insisted on complete autonomy for the newsroom anyway.

I have often noted precisely the same schism in many of the nation's news media, both printed and electronic. The opinions of the owners are usually conservative, supporting the right of property owners to manage what they own.

But pouring from the schools is a flood of avid young journalists and fame seekers who have been weaned on Socialist pap by professors with one foot off the scale. They know that sympathy for the underdog is conducive of applause and reputation-building, no matter how the underdog got under.

If a person wishes to be popular with the masses, one must shed tears for those who suffer, take from those who have to give to those who haven't, and do one's best to bad-mouth the successful while excusing the failures.

The public doesn't want to think; it wants to *feel*. Truth is dangerous. It is often unpopular and remains today a scarce commodity.

So, what research would label a "conservative" press has been anti-capitalist in its function, precisely because the owners are scrupulous in avoiding "undue influence." At least, at the *Gazette Telegraph*, we had one page every day where we could stand against the tide and try to influence.

The *Gazette Telegraph* at this time was one of fourteen newspapers owned by the Hoiles family. R.C. Hoiles, the patriarch, had founded the chain by first working in a print shop at about $3.00 per week. He had no help from family or friends. He had literally pulled himself up by his own bootstraps, truly a self-made man.

By a thrift that would have made Ben Franklin proud, he had amassed a few hundred dollars. With this, he purchased an interest in the print shop where he worked. Then, through adroit trades and very careful handling of funds, he had swapped interest for full control, and full control for ownership. He traded the print shop for ownership of a small newspaper That paper led to ownership of a second small paper...and so on. This process had gone on during his entire life.

R.C. was now in his 80's and ran the organization from the *Register* in Santa Ana, California.

R.C. wrote a daily column called "Better Jobs" in which he offered his own view and also quoted numerous authors. He was an omnivorous reader and took the position that the Declaration of Independence and the Decalogue provided all the laws men needed in civilized living.

He was a controversial figure—totally fearless when it came to expressing an opinion. He had been ticketed one time for mishandling his car. In court, he refused to take off his hat or to stand when the judge entered. His observation was that he'd take off his hat and stand up if God appeared t otherwise, no. He didn't believe that any man should show reverence to another simply because of some governmental employment involving a black robe.

The spice of R.C.'s life was argument. People adored him and feared him at the same time. His reasoning was as sharp as a dueling saber and as assertive as a loaded forty-five.

One day, Harry and I got to talking about the "Better Jobs" column. I made the off-hand remark that it was poorly written. Harry was shocked that I would say such a thing. No one criticized R.C.

I repeated my assertion. I wasn't criticizing the content or the ideas in the columns. I was critical of the style, the syntax, and the choice of words. I said, as I remember it: "The only reason this column appears in print is that R.C. owns the newspaper. I'm not suggesting that we abandon it. I'm simply saying that it is a terrible column because of the way it's written."

Harry called his father on the telephone and, inadvertently, I overheard a portion of Harry's end of the conversation. He was letting his dad know that he wasn't any great shucks as a writer. Shortly after this, we dropped the column and R.C. stopped producing it. Our editorial page was easier to read.

But that wasn't an unmixed blessing. The value of a gadfly that stings you with ideas constantly isn't appreciated until he stops buzzing. And then you know you've lost far more than bad grammar.

As for my own writing, it was improving. But I had another talent that apparently impressed Harry favorably. I could talk. And I could think on my foot. I was a "runner-up" to R.C. when it came to being argumentative, although never as innovative or inspirational. No one could top R.C. in that department. Harry wasn't blessed with his dad's loquacity. That was probably why he appreciated my stage presence.

There was something else in my favor, too. I was attracting men of stature to the Freedom School banner. Harry knew from experience the enormous amount of effort that has to go into a successful business undertaking. Thus, when men like Bill Grede and others came on my Board, my puny efforts earned his respect.

The consequence was that one day, and without my urging, Harry cashed in some stock that he owned and presented it to the Freedom School as a generous gift.

The Hoiles, as a rule, contributed very little to any non-profit effort. The simple philosophy was that if a good or service is desirable and the public wants it, then those who benefit should pay for it. If something is offered that doesn't win support, then the offering should be withdrawn and the business permitted to fall.

This is, of course, the free market rule. I had pleaded with Harry that when one is attempting to sell ideas, the rule has to be modified at least part of the time. The people who could benefit from what Freedom School had to offer were: 1) unaware of the benefit; and, 2) often too young to pay for it.

Harry had finally agreed that the market place for ideas had virtually been ruined by government invasion through the tax-supported school system. The public had the opinion that education was "free," while it actually cost billions. The idea of paying for education was almost alien. Harry's gift was an enormous vote of confidence for what I was doing. All at the school were impressed.

During my various travels about the country, I had found myself in a passenger coach with another publisher, Jim Gipson, of Caxton Press, located in Caldwell, Idaho. Jim was a conservative and so opposed to government intervention that many viewed him as radical.

Now that I was going to be responsible for the entire academic effort at Freedom School, I thought I ought to write a book to help remove the taste of the earlier disaster. The various books I had been using in class were good. But each of them, somewhere between the covers, offered ideas that were dependent upon government support.

Since I was striving for consistency, it seemed to me that I should provide a book that rang with the same music throughout. With such a book, I could stop ignoring or explaining the inconsistencies invariably found in the volumes with which I was familiar.

I contacted Jim Gipson in Caldwell, asking if he would be interested in publishing such a book from me. He responded in the affirmative.

Because I had so little time, I wrote a series of editorials that step-by-step explained the doctrine of liberty. I had to write editorials anyway. These were published in the newspaper, gathered, and sent off to Caxton Press.

Jim drew up a contract, my first with a book publisher, and issued the volume. To help make it saleable, I sent the manuscript to Rose Wilder Lane, who—with great courtesy and enthusiasm—wrote a forward nearly as long as the book and a lot more fun to read.

The title was *The Nature of Man and His Government*. The first edition appeared at the end of 1959, and it has remained in print ever since. The royalties have never been heavy enough to cause me to become stoop shouldered carrying the annual check to the bank. But, after more than twenty years, it still sells several hundred copies every twelve months. There have been at least seven editions. By now, about 20,000 have been sold.

Thanks to the interest taken in our efforts by Bill Grede, we were able to enroll some outstanding people for our 1959 sessions. Bill was well known, and rightly so. As a matter of fact, I now recalled that I had interviewed Bill when he had served as President of the National Association of Manufacturers. He had visited Miami, and I had put him on the air.

He had only a vague recollection of the event when I reminded him of it, but it did serve to bring us closer together. In a sense, Bill became my model. In my entire lifetime, I have met perhaps six men of such outstanding character and achievement that they have inspired me. Bill is one of these and stands near the top of the t list.

Among others who came to study with us during the 1959 school year were Chet Anderson, the man who had introduced me to Bill Grede, and a fine couple, Dick and Margaret Schwerman from Milwaukee.

Dick owned a trucking company. After his experience at Freedom School, he decided he wanted to be a publisher. Dealing with ideas, he now believed would be a more worthwhile endeavor than hauling goods.

He approached me with the idea that I write a second book so that he could launch his publishing career in that way. I was under contract to Caxton to submit my next manuscript to them, giving them first refusal. Dick was relatively certain that if wrote down the arguments I used in class, then no ordinary publishing house would touch it.

Somehow I found the time to write another book. This one did not consist of a series of columns, first written for the newspaper. I wrote the volume from my earlier position as a conservative, showing my polarization toward liberty and my inescapable movement in the direction of a consistent libertarian stance.

Dick's feeling about other publishing houses proved to be correct. Caxton turned it down. Dick accepted it and launched his new career.

Meanwhile, Gene Hauske's departure from Boeing had stirred interest among his former co-workers. Several splendid people from the same company, came to the school, including Rollie (R.W.) Holmes, who had become one of our trustees. Through Rollie's good offices, I met one of Boeing's vice presidents, a man named Jay Morrison. Morrison wrote the foreword to the Dick Schwerman book named, *This Bread is Mine.*

Dick was overly optimistic and without experience. I advised a small edition to see how it would sell. In great enthusiasm, he produced 20,000 hard cover copies as a first edition. Neither of us had funds to promote it and it was a financial disaster. We had to remainder the books after the first 4,000 and I was able to pick up most of them. It took me twenty years to get rid of them, but the effort was successful. Today, it is sold out.

I'm happy to say it has become a collector's item and used copies have sold for something in the vicinity of $25.00. Dick's publishing efforts evolved, and he is still going strong in a difficult business.

Meanwhile, with Trustee approval, an attorney named Burgess filed for Freedom School exemption. The plea was denied. Burgess appealed, and after several anxious months the appeal succeeded and we were granted exemption in 1960.

Next, Burgess applied to the State of Colorado as well as to Douglas County for tax exemption of all our property on the grounds that we were a school. Having already obtained IRS approval, the State and the County concurred and we came out into the sunshine of normalcy.

One of the provisions in the IRS Code at that time was that certain workers could be exempted from Social Security taxes. Those who worked for a school were in that category, provided they themselves wished exemption. One by one, as we were able to put people on our payroll. Each employee of Freedom School voluntarily chose to forego the alleged benefits of SS protection.

We had managed to place ourselves outside of government benefits. in every department save three. Our electricity came from the REA, a government corporation. The only other electricity that might have been available would have been from Colorado Springs. We'd have been required to run the lines some 26 miles at our own expense. But this would have achieved nothing anyway, since the city government of Colorado Springs had already gobbled up all the local utilities.

Additionally, we used the mails. At that time, I could see no way around this one. We obtained our students by using the mails. We maintained contact with the rest of the world by this method. And as postal services declined and costs rose, the government was breathing fire and smoke against anyone who suggested that private firms could handle the mail, do a better job and do it for less.

Years before the government had made it a felony for anyone in the country to carry first class mailing piece, privately and for profit. A case had occurred in the state that pretty well kept us from any efforts along that line. The Colorado Fuel and Iron Company of Pueblo, having principal offices in Denver and other major cities, had established a courier service for in-company correspondence. Colorado F&I was taken to court and found guilty of failing to use the mails. It was forced to pay a substantial fine and to abandon the couriers.

The third area wherein we were still dependent upon government had to do with the use of roads. Of course, we were, at least in theory, helping to pay for the roads. Every time we bought gasoline for our growing fleet of vehicles, we paid taxes. And taxes paid by gasoline consumers were supposed to move into a highway fund, and I presume they did.

The only idea I could hatch in this area was to offer to buy one mile of county road—the one we used to reach the school. I don't think the County took the offer seriously, but I made it. It was turned down.

To reduce our taxes in this area, we put in an underground tank and a secondhand gasoline pump. By this method, we avoided retail gasoline taxes. We began to furnish gasoline for all staff care as well as for the tractor that we finally obtained.

Aside from electricity, postal service, and highways, the Freedom School was totally independent of government. All workers at the school were given to understand that we had no garbage service, no water service, no utility service (except electricity), and no fire protection. Certainly we wouldn't call the Sheriff even if we had occasion to do so. We would have to handle all our own problems.

The winter of 1958-59 brought tremendous snows. With spring, as the sun began burning into the snow banks, our tiny creek became a swollen river.

The half section immediately behind the school's property was owned by people named Counter. Our deed specified that they had a right-of-way over our land for access purposes. This easement actually began at the county road and first crossed a neighbor's property. Then, it turned southward and curved around one of the school's mountains, and crossed the creek on a log bridge. Thus, it finally reached the rear of our property at line fence where a high wire gate was kept padlocked.

As the spring runoff reached its height, the log bridge came bounding into view on the floodwaters. The creek had been so high it had washed out the footing of the bridge. The span of tree trunks had been converted into a raft that finally snagged on a bank leaving the icy waters to swirl around it.

As we were preparing for our first June session, my son, Tom, reported to me. He now had the title of Junior Wrangler. He was helping both Link and Gene in their various chores.

"Dad," he said. "The Counters are doing some things to our land."

"What are they doing?" I asked.

"Well, they've brought some big equipment in on their road."

"Like what?"

"Like a bulldozer. And a big crane."

"And where is this equipment?" The contours of the land hid it from my view. In fact, it would have required a small hike for me to get into a location where I could see any part of the Counter's access road.

Tommy pointed. "Up there by the property line."

Fathers are prone to be preoccupied when in the presence of their own children. I was no exception. "Why do you think the Counters have done that, Tom?"

He shrugged. "I guess they have to fix something."

I laughed. "Good. You're right. Remember that big log raft that came down the creek a few weeks ago? That's their bridge. They're going to have to replace it. That's what the equipment is for."

He nodded. "Only that's not what they're doing."

My interest was still marginal. "Of course, that's what they're doing."

"Dad, you ought to take a look. They're not putting the bridge back. They're making a new road. And the new one is on our land."

I frowned. "Are you certain?"

"Don't believe me if you don't want to. But I was just down there. They're putting in a whole new road."

I was annoyed. "All right, Tom. I'm very busy, but if you say so I'll take the time to look for myself."

Happily, Tom skipped ahead of me. Presently, we reached a point of land where I could see the equipment at work. Tom's report was accurate.

A bulldozer was slicing into *our* land and the crane was yanking out *our* full-grown trees. The Counters had elected to carve up property over which they had no easement whatever. I had had no notice of their intention—not so much as a friendly "by your leave."

Adrenaline pumped into my blood system and I was fighting mad on the instant. My brain stopped its normal function. Away flew my philosophy. *Our* land was being violated. The Counters were committing a trespass in the most brazen manner possible!

Although we had occupied our particular location for more than four years, I had never mot any of them. They only used the property during the heat of the summer, so that most of the time they weren't on hand. They were people who lived in Denver. They were so sensitive of any trespasses themselves that I had had stories of guns being fired when hunters or my own son had dared to cross their property line.

But this was monstrous. The Counters weren't crossing our borders; they were tearing up our land. My mind was empty of solution except one. Call the Sheriff. Steps must be taken at once to stop what could only be called errant vandalism.

I raced to the office where Ruth was busy at her typewriter. She saw the look on my face and came up out of her chair. "What is it, Bob? What's wrong?"

"The Counters!" I growled. "Boy, have they got nerve! They are back there with heavy equipment. I wouldn't have known a thing about it except that Tommy came and told me. They're putting a new road on *our* land!"

"Why...why..." Ruth sputtered. "They can't do that."

"They're doing it," I said. "Right now. Get me Sheriff Higgins on the telephone!"

The blood drained from Ruth's face. "You can't call the Sheriff," she said in a small voice.

"What else can I do?" I snarled. "They've got to be stopped. Do you want me to just stand by while they wreck our property?"

"Well no, of course not."

"Get the Sheriff on the line!"

In slow motion, Ruth reached for the telephone. Tears shone in her eyes. "You just can't do this, Bob!"

"You Just watch and see what I can do."

"But it's wrong. Remember all that you've been teaching. You'll be involving innocent taxpayers with your personal problems. Their taxes will go up because of you. Oh, Bob. Don't do this, please."

But she had dialed and I took the instrument.

Margie must have felt the electricity. She made an entrance and Ruth whispered something to her. Margie stood as still as Lot's wife, staring at me with round eyes.

The haze in my brain began to dissipate. There must be something else I could do. Two of my stalwarts were now witnessing the clay feet of their leader.

Higgins' voice came on the line. "Hello. This is Sheriff Higgins."

"Hi, Sheriff," I said. But I had come to my senses.

"I thought perhaps you could help me. Do you happen to have the phone number for the Counters? You know, the folks who have the property in back of ours?"

"Yes, I think so. Just a minute."

The office was as still as an empty church. Then Higgins again. "Yeah. Here it is." He gave it to me. "Anything else?"

"Not this time, Sheriff. Thanks a lot. You know, I've never even talked to any of them. I've never met them. I thought this might be a good time to get acquainted."

"Okay, Bob. If there's anything else, let me know."

"Sure." Higgins had a good idea what was happening.

I hung up.

The sigh that went up from the two ladies was like steam escaping under pressure.

"I could have gotten the number from information," I said lamely. "But I was already ringing his office. I'm sorry. You're right, Ruth. There has to be another way."

I dialed the Counter's number. In a moment, a male voice came on the line.

"Is this Mr. Counter?" I asked.

"Yes. I'm Counter."

"This is your neighbor, Bob LeFevre. The Freedom School, you know."

"Yes?"

"I telephoned to find out if I've done something that has injured you in some way."

"Injured me?" The voice contained a note of puzzlement. "Why, no. Not that I can think of. No. Certainly not. You haven't injured me that I know of."

"Hmmm," I said. "Then that can't be the reason. I thought maybe you were trying to get even."

"What are you talking about?"

"Well, right this moment you have heavy equipment putting in a road on Freedom School property. You've taken out trees, some of them quite large. I've just been down to see it. If you're not trying to get even, why are you injuring me?"

There was an echoing silence on the line. Then a low voice said, "Oh, my God. My God. Of course. That's what you'd think. You're new here. You had no way of knowing. I should have called you. I should have let you know."

"Let me know what?"

"I'm in the wrong," Counter said. "Of course. And don't you worry about a thing. I'll go down and stop that operation at once. I'll put back all the dirt we've moved. I'll replant trees. I'll put in new ones if the ones we've taken are damaged. Let me straighten it out."

A strange line of reasoning now glowed like a bright avenue in my mind. One of these days, my hopes were that we might acquire the Counter property in addition to our own. One of the first things I would do, if I owned that property, would be to put in the very road Counter was putting in. The place he had chosen made a lot of sense. The bridge had never been any good and the spring freshets had demonstrated It.

It was my sense of pride that had been injured. With Counter admitting to error, I suddenly felt very warm and friendly. At his own expense, he was improving what might one day be ours.

Counter's offer was magnanimous. I could stand at the same level.

"Now that you've stated what you have," I said, "I see no reason for that. Why don't you just keep on? You've picked a good place, actually. I think it vas the sudden surprise of seeing the work going on that kind of got to me."

"Let me explain, Mr. LeFevre," Counter said. "Your deed has the location of the easement appalled out on it. I'm not really putting in a new road. I'm putting the road on the land where we have the easement. It used to be there. But some years back, before you came, we decided to put in that bridge and we let the road go. There was a slide and all traces of the road were covered.

"But the bridge was a mistake. This isn't the first time it's washed out. So I decided to put the road back where it belongs and I forgot that you didn't know. I should have talked to you before we started."

"Then everything's fine," I said. "No problem. At least we've broken the ice and gotten acquainted a little bit."

After a few more bits of idle conversation, I hung up. I was smiling. The girls were smiling. Edith had come in and she was smiling. The room was wreathed in smiles.

Chapter XCVII

The lines of development and growth for Freedom School were now established. 1959 had brought an increase in enrollment above that of the previous year. 1960 turned out to be an improvement over 1959. My job was to bring in more and more students on the one hand. On the other, I had to continually enlarge our facilities so we could handle the increasing number.

Time was short. The country was in dire peril, thanks to grievous policies that were destroying the American economy. I sought to do all as rapidly as possible.

My list of guest instructors, guest lecturers, and assistants who joined in this effort began to read like the *Who's Who* in support of American free enterprise.

It may be useful to provide a list of these persons so I will include it here with this preamble as a waiver. I am not seeking to imply that any of them held conclusions identical to my own. There were some whose views were close to mine, and some whose views were distinctly opposed in areas.

I think it is safe to say that all of them favored free and private enterprise. They were appalled at the size and the power of the government of the United States. All of them opposed the growth of taxes. Some opposed taxes outright; some favored a limited and regulated taxation.

Beginning very early, our efforts were attacked in the press from many quarters. We had anticipated that. At this time in America, those who believed in a free or a relatively free market were hounded out of their jobs, driven into obscurity, and held up to ridicule and acorn,

I think I am being honest when I say that at this particular time the Freedom School was the *only* location in this country, where students could enroll in study groups held on a regularly scheduled basis, in which the principles of free market economics would be taught.

Despite my earlier experience with the press in connection with the Beverly Hills Falcon Lair, and also in conjunction with my efforts with the "I Am," I still believed that the press, while it might distort, would essentially tell the truth. My work at the *Gazette* re-enforced that belief.

So, I wasn't prepared for one line of attack that was immediately launched against us. The report said that I was an intellectual tyrant and that all my lecturers and guest instructors had to agree with me or be ousted.

I do not know where the attack originated. But it was hurled against us by so remote a publication as that put out by the Harvard Business School and by as potent a daily as the *New York Times*. And, yet, when I thought about it, I could understand it, even though it was false.

I had certainly been "hard-nosed" when it came to my own students. I suppose one of them made the accusation to his hometown paper somewhere, and the idea quickly spread. In all probability, it was one of those who failed to finish the course with me and stalked out in an angry mood. I had lost three such in 1958. Seven more followed them out the doors in 1959.

I did not demand conformity from any of my instructors. Instead, I made it a point that they were free to express any opinion they felt to be true. I did insist that they be willing to defend their positions. I was so confident of my position and its consistency with liberty that I fully expected my own powers of persuasion to move them toward where I stood.

In this, I was totally mistaken. Each of my teachers, lecturers, and instructors was as convinced of the rightness of his own conclusions as I. I don't think I moved any of them whatever. But the reports continued that I was engaged in a "brainwashing" procedure by means of which I was converting professors as well as students into unthinking, anti-intellectual robots.

With that observation in the record, let me provide the names. They are not listed chronologically, but alphabetically. Some came to help year after year. Some came a few times—some only once. I chose them on their ability to provide solid contributions in the field of human liberty in an interesting and convincing manner. There are 56 men and women in the list.

    Ruth Alexander, Caanan, New York
    Robert W. Baird, Jr., Milwaukee, Wisc.
    George Boardman, Chloride, Ariz.

Frank Chodorov, Berkley Heights, New Jersey
William J. Colson, Seattle, Wash.
Oscar W. Cooley, Ada, Ohio
Robert L. Cunningham, San Francisco, CA
James Doenges, Anderson, Indiana
E. W. (Bill) Dykes, Canton, Ohio
Arthur A. Ekirch, Jr., Washington, D.C.
Gerald P. Foster, Denver, Colo.
Milton Friedman, Chicago, Ill,
George Frostenson, Stockholm, Sweden
Percy Greaves, Jr., New York, N.Y.
William J. Grede, Milwaukee, Wisc.
F. A. "Baldy" Harper, Menlo Park, CA
Harry M. Hoiles, Colorado Springs, Colo.
R. C. Hoiles, Santa Ana, CA
Roland W. Holmes, Seattle, Wash.
William A. Hutt, Cape Town, South Africa
Arthur Kemp, Claremont, CA
Ellis Lamborn, Logan, Utah
Rose Wilder Lane, Danbury, Conn.
Seymour Leon, Chicago, Ill.
Bruno Leoni, Turin, Italy
J. Dohn Lewis, Salt Lake City, Utah
George Loweke, Detroit, Mich.
Elgie C. Marcks, Milwaukee, Wisc.
James J. Martin, Deep Springs, CA
Ruth Maynard, Painesville, Ohio
Neil McLeod, Appleton, Wisc.
Louis G. Milione, Jr., Philadelphia, Penn.
Jay Morrison, Seattle, Wash.
Toshio Murata, Yokohama, Japan
G. Warren Nutter, Charlottesville, VA
William A. Paton, Ann Arbor, Mich.
Sylvester Petro, New York, N.Y.
Myron R. Pike, Colorado Springs, Colo.
Leonard Read, Irvington-on-Hudson, New York
Bryson Reinherdt, Portland, Oregon
George Resch, Appleton, Wisc.
James M. Rogers, Rockford, Ill.

Merrill Root, Wasbash, Ind.
Salvatore Saladino, Flushing, New York
Hans F. Sennholz, Grove City, Penn.
Butler D. Shaffer, Lincoln, Neb.
Elwood P. Smith, Chicago, Ill.
Robert J. Smith, New York, N.Y.
R. B. Snowden, Little Rock, Ark.
Louis M. Spadaro, New York, N.Y.
Charles Stenicka, III, Lincoln, Neb.
John E. Tato, Omaha, Neb.
Gordon Tullock, Charlottesville, VA
V. Orval Watts, Altadena, CA
Roger Williams, Austin, Texas
Ludwig von Mises, New York, N.Y.

Another rumor circulated—in this case by a disgruntled student, easily identified—relating to the school's financing. The story was given to the press in Milwaukee that I was making a fortune out of the school and had set it up as my personal little dollar making racket.

The fact was that I was earning my living at the *Gazette* and paying nearly three times as much as any of the others for the privilege of doing what I wished to do. But the story made its way through channels, including the Associated Press.

Up to the time that story was released, I had been raising a fairly sizeable piece of change from the people in the Milwaukee area. With the backing of Chet Anderson and Bill Grede, who knew how erroneous that rumor was, I continued to get assistance. But the bloom was off. From that time on, whenever I attempted to bring new supporters into the fold, I would have to defend against the allegations that the Freedom School was a moneymaking racket designed to feather my own nest.

It was clear to me that the problem arose from my own deficiencies as a teacher. I wasn't going to back down on my conclusions. But there must be a better way of telling my story and arguing my case so as not to end in an adversarial position.

I am happy to say that regardless of my lack of teaching technique, I was successful as a communicator. The evidence indicates that I provided a reasonably acceptable philosophy adopted, in whole or in part, by more than 70% of those who studied with me. But no one was forced to accept any part of what I told them.

I set myself to learn the methods and the modes employed by my co-workers in instruction. Some of them were absolutely first class. By observation and by questions asked, I absorbed a great deal from Rose Wilder Lane—perhaps the finest storyteller I have ever known. But it would be hard to give her that acclaim without adding that Bill Grede was on another pedestal in the same department. He was a raconteur unsurpassed in my experience. The two of them could hold a crowd for hours at a time in the pin-dropping silence of concentration.

When it came to expounding the doctrine of free market economics, I know of none who surpassed Milton Friedman. He has gone on to win a Nobel Prize in his discipline. But far better than the book that got his the prize was his classroom manner. He was gentle, smooth, totally informed, and absolutely convincing.

We differed on a major point, but I had to disqualify myself when it came to debating It. I wasn't in the same league. He favored a money supply managed by the government and I favored a money supply based on a commodity, such as gold or silver. I had learned to distrust politicians at all levels. But I also learned not to debate Milton. He was a mathematician who could overwhelm me with data. I had great admiration for him, despite our single area of disagreement. And I gained tremendously from his lectures that I attended at every opportunity.

Within the guidelines he had established for himself, I know of none better than Leonard Read. He had a limited number of lectures, but his presentation in each case was masterful and flawless. He had raised the process of communication to a fine art. We, too, differed on one major point and possibly in several minor areas. But all I could do with him was to lead the applause. The man brought an air of polish and elegance to our rustic surroundings. He helped make my enrollees proud of being where they were.

I can truly say that I learned much from these men and women and the others, too. And thanks to these associations—sometimes fleeting, sometimes repeating—I gradually improved my own efforts.

During the first four years of the school, the instructor who probably did the most for my development was Frank Chodorov. Frank had begun his intellectual pilgrimage by becoming a follower of Henry George. As a Georgist, Frank bad gained a well-deserved reputation as a scholar, writer, and thinker. His book, *Income Tax, Root of All Evil,* is still today a masterful examination of the destructive results inevitably following such massive forays against the helpless taxpayers.

Another book of his, *One is a Crowd,* was, in my judgment, a classic. He was one of the few people in the country who could get published even though he was hostile to the popular wisdom that Franklin Delano Roosevelt had been a new Moses whose policies led the people into a promised land of Social Security and dependence on the State.

Chodorov had been editor of the publication, *Analysis,* one of the founding editors of *Human Events,* temporarily the editor of *The Freeman* (later issued by Read), and very active in all conservative and anti-state causes.

Frank was a large, gentle man, with a face so Jewish it could have been taken for the map of Israel. I told that to Frank once, and he agreed in great good humor. He was deeply sincere, serious, and profound. Yet he had a keen sense of humor that surfaced on appropriate occasions.

I had first met him during the Girl Scout episode in Florida and renewed our friendship when we moved to New York. At the time, the anti-Communist wing of the Conservatives tended to think of communism as anything having to do with Russia. Indeed, many of the Republicans with whom I had been active were somewhat paranoid on the subject. For example, Richard Nixon. Frank saw the matter with a clearer eye.

"Communism is a belief, not a nation," he would say to his students. "Most of the Russian people, just like most of Americans, have no knowledge concerning it.

"It is a doctrine, expounded by Karl Marx and many others, who urged the abandonment of private capitalism. It seeks to transfer the control of all productive property—that is, all tools of production and distribution—into the hands of the State."

At this time, some who called themselves Conservatives were actually anti-Jewish. They tended to lump Russia and all Jewry into the same evil stew. Frank was the first man I had met who had truly researched the area. He brought out the fact that the Russian government was persecuting Jews. This was inconceivable to the anti-Semite claque and Frank was attacked for this position. He was also quite correct, as subsequent events have confirmed.

Frank proclaimed that the Russian government was Communist and that the Russian people, on masse, were not. Then, he went on to show that the American government was ambivalent in the area, sometimes backing Communism, sometimes opposing it. On one occasion in class, he pointed out that American politicians were rarely doctrinaire in whatever they did. "They are just political opportunists," he said, "flip-flopping in the direction of popularity and votes. They are totally innocent of any economic or moral principles."

On one occasion, in a session at the school, Frank was confronted with some "die-hard" Conservatives who were more than usually argumentative. He finally turned off their debate by saying, "The trouble with you Conservatives is that you are trying to clean up the whore house, but leave the business intact."

At another time, an interesting debate having nothing to do with what Frank was trying to talk about, erupted between two women enrolled. One of them was a Christian Scientist and the other was a Baptist. They sat across the aisle from each other. They were sniping and sneering at each other's theological position, which was far from the main thrust of economic learning.

Frank, with great patience, sat at his desk, trying to fill his pipe and remain a gentleman. He smoked a charred and well-worn briar. I noted that he often used his pipe the same way I used mine. Filling a pipe always took time and, somehow, this procedure was treated as a sacred rite and few would interrupt the process.

On this occasion, the two ladies paid no attention whatever. Their backs were up and they were verbally clawing at each other. A cascade of loose tobacco fell down and clung to Frank's shirt as he attempted, time after time, to bring fire to the briar and to the subject. He was simply shouted down and ignored.

Finally, the adversaries stopped for breath simultaneously. Frank's sonorous tones filled the room. "The trouble with you Christians," Frank said, "is that you act too much like Jews."

The dissension halted on the instant.

What Frank brought to the school was political realism. He could and did teach economics or history. Most of our instructors in whatever discipline, looked at government and at politicians generally with a jaundiced eye. However, when it came to analysis, nearly all of them proclaimed the manner in which politicians ought to act—not the way they acted in fact.

Frank did better. Not only did he show the manner in which politicians acted, he also demonstrated that—given the kind of government we have—their behavior is predictable. They *must* seek popularity in order to be elected. Winning and keeping power is the primary objective of any party man. This means that any successful politician must pander to what the masses want. And it is predictable that the masses will want money, food, rent, medical treatment, and anything else they can get that is promised to them as a "gift" from the State.

The fact that the government has nothing of its own to give is quickly forgotten in the hoopla of elections. Then, politicians vie with each other in offering "free" benefits in exchange for votes. Indeed, the system we have, as Frank pointed out, is simply public bribery (votes in exchange for largesse) on a scale so vast that few take notice of it."

Frank developed a speech that he gave on at least two occasions as part of a graduation exercise, in which he showed that even if a free enterprise supporter was elected to Congress, he could do very little to change things. In order to get his particular, bill supported by other congressman, he must offer to support bills they are sponsoring. It's called: "log rolling."

Even assuming a persistent and courageous believer in free enterprise, by the time he will have won enough support to enact his own measure, he will have given support to scores of other measures. They would probably nullify the effectiveness of his own.

Isabel Patterson explained the process in her book, "God of the Machine." She showed that modern American politics has introduced a self-serving mechanism equipped with cogwheel and ratchet. It will only turn freely in one direction—that favorable to State growth. Every time one seeks to turn the wheel in the opposite direction, the ratchet slips into place between the cogs and the wheel will not turn.

Because of Frank's marvelous background, ease of manner in the classroom, and his unwillingness to compromise, I invited him to come to our 1961 sessions—not for one or two classes, but for the entire season.

The year started out well. Frank's classes were superb. I began to think that I might, with confidence, turn the entire teaching chore over to him in lieu of Baldy. Then, tragedy struck.

The occasion was a graduation night. The month was July and we were using our new classroom in the recently constructed Reno Sales Lodge. After a few general remarks, I introduced Frank, who stepped to the podium.

His speech started well. He had given the same talk before, but I sat in the front row as eager to hear him as any of the enrollees. Suddenly, he faltered. He stood at the podium, swaying slightly, apparently at a loss for words.

His face turned a pasty white. He continued to talk, groping for words and saying nothing that made sense. He spoke of his mother and of "pretty little girls." Then, he began to ramble, giving out words without a context.

His knuckles showed white where his fingers gripped the lectern. His eyes went out of focus, and I thought he was about to fall. I sprang to his side and gave what support I could to his huge frame. "You're tired, Frank," I whispered. "Please take a seat. Everything will be fine."

Frank wouldn't let go of the lectern. I had to pry his fingers loose. Finally, I managed to lead him back to his chair.

I turned to take charge of the meeting. One of the ladies was crying. Frank came out of his chair and moved to take up his post as a speaker. I intercepted and got him to sit down again.

I suppose I should have immediately adjourned the gathering. I did not. And I'm glad I didn't. Frank wanted his message to get out. I know what it was and, relying on my memory, having heard the same talk twice before, I gave it myself.

No one looked at me during the talk and it is probable that no one heard a thing I said. They all focused on Frank. But, at least, I made Frank's point. I had the feeling that should I hesitate, Frank would have come reeling to the podium to correct me, yet he was nearly comatose.

What we were doing was that important, both to Frank and to me. Indeed, as I wrote in a eulogy which was published later by the periodical, *Fragments*, "the most difficult thing Frank ever did was to stop."

By the time the talk ended, many of the women were crying and the graduation affair was anything but joyous. Marjorie came forward to help and so did some of the men. Gently, we took Frank to his room.

I managed to reach Frank's sister by telephone. She made the necessary arrangements to drive from New York to pick up her brother. Frank had had a massive stroke. Never again was his voice to rise in lecture or debate. He was bedridden for the balance of his life.

A few years later, I happened to be in New York on one of my constant fund raising efforts. I called on Frank who was now being cared for by his family.

I put on an optimistic front and talked to him about all the "progress" we were making. His eyes were bright and he understood what I was saying. In response, although talking was very difficult, he asked a few questions to the point and penetrating about the support I was getting. I had to confess that it was not as great as we could both have hoped, but nonetheless, things were happening that were favorable. We could still turn things around somehow.

Frank shook his head and then turned his face from me, saying no more. I left in tears. America had lost a great fighter for freedom. He died a year or so later.

Chapter XCVIII

I was now very difficult to live with. My devotion to what I deemed to be America dominated all my thinking and acting. America to me was a concept, an ideal. It was a geographic location wherein every member of the populace, regardless of creed, color, ability, national origin, religious preference, or condition in life, could be free to make his own way.

In the ideal America I pictured, there would be no government agency of any kind intruding upon or taxing anyone. There was no guarantee that a person would win. But there would be a guarantee that he could try. There was nothing wrong with helping another, there was a great deal wrong with being forced to help others when, in fact, one might need all his time and ability to forestall his own failure.

Loy complained that I had little time to spend with her. She was right. I didn't. She would quip that if we were to see each other at all, she had to make an appointment. This was nearly true. I had ringed myself with an almost impossible number of chores so that I dashed from one to another at breakneck speed. But I had also tied Loy into a routine that took her time and energy as well. We grinned at each other and swept past like ships on divergent courses.

Fortunately, when it came to Tom, there were other people around who could supply some of what I should have been supplying. Gene Hauske had his own children and tended to be as one-pointed in his concentration as I was. Nonetheless, when one is working with hands and back, children can observe and learn a great deal. Tom was fascinated with Gene and his perfectionist attitude. And Link, who really understood small boys, liked Tom. He became a kind of off-duty tutor, giving my son companionship and invaluable lessons.

I can't begin to be grateful enough, both to Gene and Link for helping to raise Tom, and to Sydney, the splendid man who married my first wife. He provided the kind of paternal model any son could be proud of. I learned the bitter truth: it is quite easy to become a father. It is very difficult to be one. I was not a good father. It 1s my loss. All three boys turned into fine human beings without much help from me. With the kind of fanatical dedication I had developed, it seemed to me that I was doing the right thing, given what I knew within the parameters of my ability to act.

The Directors of the school pleaded with me to hire assistants so that all the chores didn't rest on my shoulders. I was eager to do so. But I was also well aware that each new employee meant a larger payroll—a payroll I would have to bring in.

Link was already on salary and I put Gene there, although he worked as a volunteer for two or three years before that happened. Then, I was able to add Margie to the list. The Directors felt she should be the first, partly because she traveled farther than any of the rest of us for her outside work and in the winter that was truly hazardous. Also, we felt that thanks to her bout with tuberculosis, she was not as robust as the rest of us.

Then Loy went on salary, and so did her principal assistant and other helpers needed to do the housekeeping and cooking chores.

Once Margie had full time to devote to us, I put my own collection of books together with the 2,000 volumes we had garnered from the Ralph Williams library. We began to have a respectable collection of some pretty fine tomes. Margie studied the Dewey decimal system, read the necessary works on library techniques, and acquired the requisite skills. She always bad-mouthed her own ability in this area. However, on occasion, professional librarians and scholars in library method would come by and remark that I had been most fortunate in finding so able a Librarian. She cross-referenced each volume as to author, title, and subject matter; it was superbly done.

By 1961, I knew that the facilities we had were still inadequate. We needed a larger classroom. We needed an administrative section. And we needed more housing for students. Much more. We also needed a real place for a library, where our 5,000 volumes could be housed and students could study.

So, I dashed from city-to-city and back to Colorado Springs, writing my editorials and raising funds. Through the mails, we sent out appeals for help. Everything worked although never did it work well enough to do more than keep us one step ahead of foreclosure.

Bill Grede's name was an "open sesame" at many corporation doors. Thanks to his generous support, I garnered a number of checks in four figures with an occasional check with five figures in it. Harry came in every year with a few thousand, and then, to my great joy, even R.C. Hoiles decided to make a contribution and came across with $60,000 as a gift. That was pivotal sum. It really helped.

I received an application for work from a young man in Salt Lake City named J. Dohn Lewis. The application annoyed me. He made it on a thirty-minute tape cassette. He was demonstrating his ability to be modern. He sought to show that he was a "free man," not bound by conventionality. I responded that the Directors had already determined we would hire no one who had not taken our basic course. We wanted people on staff who knew what we were doing and were in harmony with It.

Dohn and his wife, Penny, came to the school and took the course. He was bright all the way up to glitter and Penny was petite with talent oozing out her fingers. I hired Dohn as an administrative assistant. He demonstrated marvelous ability in preparing fund drive material. He was truly artistic and our mailings became impressive. Also, they cost more. Hopefully—it is impossible to know—dollar input increases came in part because of this improvement.

Chet Anderson recommended another man to help raise funds. He was Jim Swartout who took the course, was truly impressed, and went out to help raise money.

One of the difficulties everyone experienced was explaining the course. It contained so much. There wasn't anything particularly new in it; it simply put things together in a way that made sense. It centered on free or private enterprise. But the material offered was garnered from a score of disciplines brought together as a result of my own studies and experiences. The effect on students was either overwhelmingly positive or overwhelmingly negative. Students loved it or hated it. Few ignored it.

Jim Swartout was our first fundraiser. In reviewing what he would say to the executives on whom he called, he argued that he could make a better case than I could since he could boast about my work. I could not. If boasting would help, why not?

To conserve funds, Jim suggested that the school furnish a car. He'd be traveling a good deal, and both rail and plane travel cost far more than highway usage.

This seemed reasonable, so we invested in another vehicle, and away Jim went. In six months work, raised $1,000. His expenses, plus the car, ate away some $8,000. Additionally, he was having marital problems and I had to conclude that his work was partially ineffective from that cause. Reluctantly, I let him go.

A second young man appeared with his wife, and the two took the course. His name was Grant Corby and he was convinced that he knew how to sell what we offered. He was tremendously excited about what we were doing. Away went Corby. In two years of effort, he failed to win us a single contribution.

In the end, raising money came back to rest on my shoulders.

I was becoming difficult to talk to. When I was asked to establish some particular policy or to make a decision, I'd come up with an answer instantly. Even Ruth complained. "You haven't heard the whole story, Bob. How can you decide so quickly?" she asked.

"Then do your staff work," I snapped. "Give me the whole story. I can only decide on the basis of what information I have."

"Well, I went you to weigh each piece of information. That's why I give you one piece of the problem at a time."

"I'll be frank, Ruth," I said. "I sometimes have the view you've already made the decision and you simply want me to agree. If you've made the decision, it's probably a good one and you don't have to ask me."

"But it has to come from you."

"Nonsense. I don't know anything about running a school. You're here a lot more than I. Your decisions are as good as mine and sometimes better. You know I have confidence in you. With reason."

"But you're the President. Everything depends on you."

"Hey. There's a thought. How would you like to be President? We can vote you in at the next Director's meeting."

She started to cry. "You know perfectly well I can't be President. No one would give any money to a school run by a woman."

"Why not? You're good."

"Bob, stop being absurd."

She was crying, in earnest. "I don't see why you can't take the time to listen to all the information. You...you're making fun of me."

"I'm doing no such thing, Ruth, you're really tremendous. But, okay." I took a firm grip. "I'll slow down. Tell me the whole story. From the beginning."

And so it went. More and more I said to people working on staff, "You know the problem. I expect you to solve it."

I had given full reign to my four ladies. I had never tried to train them for the job. I was undergoing on-the-job training myself. We were making it work. Just barely. To the public we presented a facade of ease, friendship, and everything first cabin.

I realized just how dangerous that could be when J. Dohn asked me for a raise. Somehow he had gotten the idea that we had plenty of money and that I was simply being miserly by not sharing more of the goodies with him. He was worth it, however, so I did give him a raise and took Penny on as a secretarial assistant. The raise wasn't much, but I'm sure it helped.

To make things easier for him, I moved his little family onto campus, thus taking away the large and best room we had for guests. But I could do nothing less. And Dohn not only had his wife, but also a small son.

Meanwhile, in Colorado Springs, I was Harry's "man." Harry called on me from time to time to make talks. I had become so positive in my various assertions that my manner was something akin to "take it or leave it." No one wants to be handled like a hot rivet, and I found myself the target for some pretty heavy animus.

The editorial policy of the Gazette Telegraph was controversial long before I came on the scene. The paper had lambasted the school system, showing what incredibly bad results it was obtaining. I became the visible symbol of the Gazette policy. I gathered to my own bosom the spears and arrows of outraged bureaucrats, pedants and businessmen who were trying to win favors through zoning boards, political log rolling and palm greasing.

One man in particular took a dislike to me. His name was Shel Singer. He owned and operated a radio station. He would come in to the paper on occasion to complain about one or another of my editorials. Harry always defended me, but because I was on the firing line, Harry was able to avoid some of the direct assault. Besides, Harry was a man of means and—particularly in a small community—that fact alone garners respect. People were careful about what they did to Harry. They had little compunction about laying it on the line so far as I was concerned.

On one occasion, Shel happened to come into my office. He took one look at me and turned white. He began to shake as though he had the palsy. When I looked up from my desk, and said, "What may I do for you?" he retreated as though he had been accosted by "Old Nick," himself.

I presumed the men was ill and followed him into Harry's office that he sought as a refuge. When I appeared on the threshold, he railed at me, shook his fist and stormed out.

Harry told me that Shel was certain I was anti-Semitic and had it in for me.

Beginning that week on Singer's radio station, a public service campaign was launched against me, personally, and against the Freedom School. We had begun referring to the school as the Rampart School because we were situated in the Rampart Range of the Rocky Mountains.

Singer's continuity men and announcers had a barrel of fun. On the air they lampooned the school as "Rampage College." They sold T-shirts emblazoned with a single wing, claiming this to be the only "one wing" school in America. Some of their spot announcements were really funny. I laughed in spite of myself. They were effective.

It happened that this campaign against the school was so droll and so popular that Singer won a national award for the smear job he did. Yet, I had done nothing to warrant this kind of attack. It isn't easy to live in a community when the airwaves are crackling with jibes and sneers at you and all that you stand for. People talked about me behind my back and I'd catch them at it. I was a prime object for ridicule.

I can attribute some of it to my manner. And I'm sorry to say that my manners didn't improve as a result.

The Directors at the school argued that the best procedure was to ignore the whole thing. Anything we did would just bring more attention to the anti-school campaign. After all, there were other broadcasters.

I reported to Harry that in Fort Lauderdale I had done a tremendous job in getting more subscribers for the Daily News by virtue of promotion on television. I was convinced that if I could get in front of the cameras again, then I could reverse the impact of this venomous campaign.

Impressed with my arguments, Harry sponsored a thirty-minute television show entitled "Editor-on-the-Spot." I would take the center frame and use the first few minutes explaining some little known facet of the free market. Then, for the final fifteen minutes I would respond to viewers who could phone in questions or bait me any way they saw fit.

When the word got out that I was to be on the air, a sense of excitement was created. There was no doubt, from the very first broadcast, that we had an audience. We were in prime time one evening per week.

The questions I got indicated hostility on the part of questioners. I answered all challenges as best I could, but the result was overwhelmingly negative. The show was buttressed with commercials about how great it would be to subscribe to the Gazette. During our thirteen week run, the newspaper *lost* 4,000 subscribers! This was not the friendly crowd I had known in Florida.

On one particular show, I was explaining our editorial position respecting Unions. Someone telephoned asking me about the "I Am." I thought the question related to the International Association of Mechanics and I said that I knew nothing about it personally. The answer was honest. It wasn't until after I had answered that I realized the party asking the question wanted to know about my earlier background with the "I Am."

I had never alluded to that earlier experience and for the first time I realized that one never really and truly buries his past.

Harry advised that we couldn't keep up a program that was having such an enormously negative impact and I heartily agreed. After I got off the air we rebuilt our circulation. I was grateful that Harry didn't fire me on the spot.

In an effort to make friends locally, I joined the Kiwanis Club. To do so required sponsors and I was pleased to learn that there were a few businessmen in town who appreciated what I was trying to do. So, I joined with their blessing and attended each meeting possible, when I was in town.

One day, a fellow Kiwanian phoned and invited me to appear on his radio program at an early morning hour. He had a talk show and he wanted to interview me about the school. This was a man who wasn't working for Shel Singer and I presumed that he wanted to offer a view in opposition to the hatchet job still bending one frequency in town out of shape.

At the studios at that early hour, my Kiwanian buddy, flanked by an assistant, began the interview. They asked questions. But, instead of letting me answer, they answered themselves and moved onto the next issue.

I wasn't being given a chance.

After about five minutes of this tirade, I spoke up, literally quelling their flow of words. "I think we have our roles reversed," I said. "I was under the impression that you were here to interview me. But you have all the answers. So, I tell you what. Why don't we start over and I'll ask the questions? Then you can provide whatever answer you wish."

I'll never forget the look of consternation on my buddy's face. He sputtered and hedged, and then he and his co-worker agreed that they weren't being entirely fair about it. I summed it up. "In other words, you didn't get me up here to find out what my ideas were. You got me here to sandbag me."

This time, the audience was on my side. The telephone began to ring and the listeners demanded that I have a shot at the microphone. By now, the time allotted had almost elapsed and so a date was made for me to return the following week when my co-hosts would be good little boys. They would ask questions and respond to my answers rather than to their own.

The next time I appeared the show was quite different. I was asked questions and given a chance to respond. Some who telephoned agreed that I had a point here and there. But one woman who phoned made an impression. "Mr. LeFevre," she said, "You scare me to death."

"Do I know you in any personal way?" I asked.

"No. I've never met you."

"Have I ever done anything which injured you in some way that I might have known about?"

"No. No. Not at all."

"Then what are' you afraid of? I am in favor of your rights to own property and to do as you please with it, provided you don't impose on your neighbor. Is that scary?"

"Yes, it is," she said. "What kind of a world would that be?"

"It would be a world of freedom, with each person responsible for his or her own well being."

"It sounds wonderful," she said, "but I'm terrified. What if people believed you?"

What indeed?

Once in a while, I would eat lunch in town during the winter months when I was not conducting classes. One day, I overheard the President of the Chamber of Commerce explain to a businessman that my editorials were about as welcome as "a skunk at a picnic." When he was challenged on the grounds that I made a fairly good speech, his answer was, "It'll be a long, cold day in January before we invite that man to anything the Chamber sponsors."

The very next January the Chamber had a meeting planned and, at the last minute, their scheduled speaker couldn't appear. In desperation, I was called on. The temperature had plunged into sub-zero readings that night and stood at seventeen below when the shivering businessmen assembled in a hotel with a furnace unable to cope with the penetrating cold.

I think I won a few businessmen to my banner by beginning my talk: "I knew I was going to be called upon as your speaker today. This was predicted by your president some months ago when he said it would be a long, cold day in January before I would be invited to speak."

The President of the Chamber didn't always despise me. Sometimes they'd elect a man to the office who didn't want to make government a partner to everything. Such a man would usually be quite friendly. I can recall inviting one such man in particular to come to the school as a guest lecturer, where he did an excellent job.

I was invited one time to go for an airplane ride in a newly designed airplane. The Colorado Springs Airport wanted tax money to expand and our paper favored the taxpayer. If a larger airport was going to do so much for business, why not have the businessmen, who would profit by it, pay for it, rather than tax those who might never use it?

The test flight resulted from a petition that had been filed by an airline. It contended that this new airplane could make use of the runways already in existence. So, I was not averse to the flight and hopeful that the plane would prove worthy.

The airship in question was an abbreviated version of the old DC-3, which had been the workhorse of the allied forces in World War II. A number of people were invited for the test flight. I was carefully seated next to a man I had never met.

As the plane taxied out, my companion offered his hand. He introduced himself as the President of ITU. I refused to shake hands. Instead, I said, "We'll shake hands as soon as you've resigned your present job. As it is, you are my sworn enemy."

My participation in the flight had been arranged to soften my position regarding Unions. This I would not do.

My attitude in class was often just as intransigent and hostile. In one class of about twelve students, seven of them got up and stomped out, largely because of my attitude.

On another occasion, one man became almost hysterical. He stood up screaming at the top of his voice. I had stated that I favored honesty and fair dealing. I expected each individual to earn his own way. I was opposed to theft of any description, including the legalized version of theft we call taxation. I viewed these remarks as equivalent to asserting that I was for virtue and against sin.

My enrollee, emotionally out of control, announced that I had helped him make up his mind. Anything I was for, he was against. Anything I was against, he was for. At this point, he ran from the room, packed, and left the campus. I never saw him again.

There was a humorous variation to this event in another session. During the summer months, we often had sudden downpours. Not infrequently, the rain was accompanied by hail. When a rain-hail deluge would arrive, the thunder of dancing pellets on the roof drowned out all talk and we had to wait until the storm passed. Many times, an electrical display and impressive rolls of thunder would accompany those storms.

One afternoon, a thunder-bumper was in full progress but the rain was relatively light. I kept on with my instruction in the face of one particularly querulous voice raised in opposition. This student sat in a rear seat and raised an objection to every point I tried to make. After my response, as I attempted to proceed, again he would interrupt.

The storm approached and strangely intruded. Every time my adversary tried to raise an objection, the thunder rumbled and growled and lightning flashed. When it stopped, he'd begin again only to be drowned out once more.

However, every time I got the floor, nature became still and every word of mine rang out. Then, as he tried to object, Thor's hammer would pound on the roof as though bidding him be quiet.

The storm had become the moderator of our debate and my opponent didn't have a chance. Finally, after at least five minutes of this phenomenon, he tied his handkerchief to a pencil and raised it above his head, waving It. "I surrender!" he shouted. "I surrender! I get the message."

With the passing of time, I became more and more engrossed

with teaching. I studied ways and means of saying what I wished to say in a manner calculated to engender cerebration rather than emotion. I discovered that my rigid attitude was the result of my insecurity on the platform. I had been so convinced that I didn't know how to teach that when I attempted it, I felt like a phony and, thus, tried to prevent anyone from discovering my weakness.

At last, working in front of a class became my greatest joy. It was only there that I experienced ease, calm, and certainty. Away from the classroom, I dashed about endlessly performing a thousand chores. But as class time arrived and I finally stepped in front of my students, I was happy. I no longer tried to pound my adversaries into submission. I was able to give them complete latitude in their expressions without feeling threatened by their views. What if they were right? My position was reasonable and valid. If not the *only* view, it was a logical and complete position. I was comfortable and my attitude changed.

Finally, I was able to believe in myself.

The strenuous nature of my many activities took their toll physically. Sometimes my back would "go out" and I'd hobble around on a cane, experiencing great pain. But nothing would keep me from my classes.

I had Link build a lectern that was just the right height so that I could support myself on it, letting my weight rest on my arms, with my legs dangling. He made it solid enough to support a person twice my weight.

Talking a full six hours per day for twelve days in a row drains one's energy. The human voice box isn't made for that kind of heavy usage. Again and again, I stood clinging for support, feeling blood run down my throat from the terrible exertion I demanded of my vocal chords. From mid-May into September, I talked at least 700 hours in class with only brief interruptions.

Outside of class, I spoke as little as possible. Except when raising money. All that I had and all that I was became concentrated in my efforts to teach, to communicate, to tell the truth as I saw it, before an ever growing number of people, young and old, who enrolled for one or more of our seasons.

My friends called me "enthusiastic" and "dedicated." My foes called me "crazy" and "fanatic." Whichever it was, the school at last became a success.

Chapter XCIX

The Trustees of Freedom School had two objectives that were introduced at each of our meetings. 1. The school must be put on a "pay as you go" financial footing as quickly as possible. Fund drives, on which we rolled for a good share of our revenue, were accepted as a necessary expedient, but only if viewed as a temporary measure.

2. I must begin attracting others who could be trained to pick up the reins if, for any reason, I should falter.

I sought to temporize in the first case. So long as our building program was underway, no conceivable enrollment would make it possible for income from students to cover full costs. With more housing and with a pair of classrooms, conceivably we could push our earned income upward.

In the second case, I tried to move at once. There were two young men who were among the more gifted students we had attracted. One was Butler Shaffer, a young attorney from Lincoln, Nebraska; the other was Seymour Leon from Chicago, Illinois.

To bring them on staff was desirable. But to do so meant an increase in payroll. I had managed to add Edy to the payroll, but Ruth and I were still dependent on income from the Gazette where we both worked. And as far as back pay was concerned, we were still in arrears. However, no one was pushing.

Before earned income could expand, we must acquire more in the way of housing. I anticipated that new staff people could live off campus.

With the help of both Link and Gene, I now designed a building that provided me with great satisfaction even in its planning stages. This was to be a three-story building built of whole logs. According to information I had at the time (which proved to be erroneous), no one had ever conceived of a building of whole logs which rose higher than two stories. The tendency for logs to roll under pressure had discouraged our pioneer forebears.

Link offered a remedy. We could build a large two-story building containing an auditorium with a balcony and a projection booth for moving pictures. This would take up the bulk of the first two floors.

In addition, there would be a furnace room and, beyond it, a library for our growing collection of fine books. This, too, would be two stories in height with the balcony, in this case, an entire second floor except for a central stairwell.

To make certain logs didn't roll, large vertical half-logs would be bolted to each horizontal log at ten-foot intervals throughout. This would certainly prevent any tendency to twist.

Once the large two-story base had been constructed, we would build a one-story cabin on top of it, utilizing the entire floor for housing. It would contain eight rooms and four full baths, allowing for occupancy of sixteen.

Additionally, we would construct another cabin matching Thunderbird Lodge, which would give us a total of twenty new berths. Combined with the three rooms open in Reno Sales Lodge (housing 6) and Thunderbird (housing 4) we'd have space for 26, plus staff.

Some of our good friends at J. I. Case Tractor Company gave us a bulldozer. We put it to work, gouging out the area just across the road from the girl's residence, which we now called "Columbine." The new building, when completed, we would name after Rose Wilder Lane in honor of her never-to-be-forgotten rescue of the school after its first year.

I was so happy about this building as it slowly rose that I told a reporter about it at the newspaper, and a story appeared. Construction was nearing completion when I received a telephone call from a man in Denver who said he was with the Architectural Board of Examiners. "Mr. LeFevre," he said, "According to the newspapers you are building a new school building a few miles north of Palmer Lake."

"That is correct," I assured him.

"I have checked our records thoroughly," he said, "and I cannot find your plan on file in this office."

"The reason is I haven't filed any plans with you," I told him.

"That is against the law," he advised. "A school building is a public building. Before it is built, we must approve of the plans. Safety requirements, you know. It appears that you are breaking the law."

"It's interesting you would say that," I said. (The truth was we had no blue prints whatever. Gene had sketched an ink drawing that was serving us well.) "I think you may be right. It's to be a school. It will be used as a school. However, I have a letter from the County Commissioners of Douglas County, which tells me that this place is a ranch. As a ranch, the County says that the new building is a ranch building."

"They can't do that." Horror was in his voice.

"I can appreciate your problem," I said. "But your argument is with the County, not with me. Actually, we haven't tried to conceal anything. We've built several school buildings here. We're planning on building more. But the County says we're a ranch. And that's the way it sits. So long as this is a ranch, we don't have to file plans with anyone."

"Well, we'll just see about that."

Before the day ended, a man showed up at the school. He looked at the construction, growled a number of things under his breath—he'd never seen whole log utilization before—and gave a parting shot to Gene who was on the site. "You don't seem to realize that I can order you to take this whole thing down."

"Sure you can," Gene said and kept right on with his work.

When I returned to the school later that day, Gene met me. "We may be in trouble," he said. "That inspector had blood in his eye. He threatened to force us to tear it all down."

"What do you think we ought to do, Gene?"

"Well, I don't know anything about it here in Colorado, but in Washington the State has more moxy than the County. And we don't have any plans. I think they can demand plans."

I shrugged. "We don't have blue prints. We don't need them."

"Back in Seattle, I know what I'd do. I'd draw up the blue prints and get an engineer friend of mine to stamp them. Then when they asked for the plans, I'd be ready."

"You're an engineer, Gene. Why don't you draw the up to specifications and stamp them yourself?"

"I'm licensed in the State of Washington. I don't have a Colorado stamp."

"By traveling east you lost your skills?"

"Just another little government racket, Bob. You know that."

"Then we've got to find an engineer in Colorado who has a stamp and will use it on our behalf."

Gene was thoughtful. "There is a guy down at Aircraft Mechanical. He just might do it."

"Let's check the law first," I suggested.

The statute covering the matter was easy to find. According to the wording, plans for a public building had to be approved, either by the Board of Architectural Examiners or by a licensed engineer.

The next day, Gene came to me again. "I've found a fellow in Colorado Springs who has a stamp. He's a good Joe. If you can slip him a couple of hundred, he'll stamp my blue prints when I draw them. It happen to know his family. But you'd have to grease his creases."

"Two hundred?"

"That should do it."

"I hate to put the burden on you, Gene. But can you burn some midnight oil and convert your line drawings to blue prints?"

"I'll handle it."

Professional competency was Gene's middle name.

I was slated for a trip out of town at this juncture and I advised the staff to cavil and delay if any inspector showed up. They were to let the official know that I never let the plans out of my keeping. He'd have to see me personally.

By the time I got back to Colorado, Gene had an impressive roll of paper done in the conventional blue. I had the foresight to take that roll to the office with me when I returned to my desk.

The moment nine o'clock came, I had a telephone call from Denver. The Board of Architectural Examiners was sending a man down to check on my blue prints. I'd better have them ready.

I advised that he'd best be prompt because I would leave the newspaper at eleven thirty. If he missed me, he'd have made his trip for nothing.

A few minutes before eleven o'clock, a large man with scowling visage stalked into my office and demanded to see the blue prints. I performed a brief pantomime in which I exhibited some confusion as to where I had left the plans. During this time, my visitor had difficulty in disguising the triumph he was about to have.

At last, I remembered and handed him the roll.

The inspector didn't spend a moment looking at the plans themselves. He simply unrolled to the first drawing and, there, winking up at him, was the engineer's stamp. Page two was similarly emblazoned. And so on through the pile.

With a muttered imprecation, he tossed the roll aside and strode out of the office. I never saw him again nor did I ever hear more from the outraged Architect. But I did hear indirectly.

The County went to bat to prove that Freedom School wasn't a school. The State argued that it was. The resulting battle between County and State took two years and resulted in a legal definition of what makes a school.

During that intervening time, we finished Rose Lane Hall, constructed the residence cabin, and built another residence building for a family on the shores of the creek. And then, in another triumph of design, we built a residence for Loy and me. Until then, Loy and I had been living in two-cramped basement rooms. Tommy's room didn't even have a window.

The new residence, which Loy and I occupied during the remainder of our stay on campus, took the shape of a hexagon, with central fireplace and umbrella designed ceiling, all of logs. Abutting the hexagon was a rectangle containing our bedroom, a garage, a furnace room and a small office for me.

We used the large nearly circular room for a student lounge and, thus, for entertainment. Additionally, it held a fine room and bath for Tom, and a splendid kitchen with an oven built into the reverse side of the fireplace chimney.

Loy must have the credit for this design. She is a whiz at interior decoration anyway but, in this case, she outdid herself. We called this new residence, "Falcon Lair," in recollection of our stay at Valentino's love nest in Beverly Hills. The place was artistic and, at the same time, practical. Indeed, Dr. and Mrs. Milton Friedman were so impressed with it that they copied down all measurements and informed us that they would build a duplicate. I understand that they did, although I have never seen it.

During an executive class in 1961, a man named Josh Greene was enrolled. He was an employee of the Deering-Milliken Company of South Carolina. Josh was an eager student and an apt pupil. He gained a great deal from the session and approached me when the two-week period ended.

"Bob," he said. "This is a course which Mr. Milliken, himself, should take."

I nodded agreement. We had received a $1,000 contribution through the mails from Roger Milliken. I was always interested in new enrollees who were able to pay their way. I knew nothing about the Milliken Company or Mr. Milliken, but Josh let me know that his employer was a very special person.

When Josh had provided me with additional information, I said, half in fun, "That's your job, Josh. You're supposed to return to your company and convince your boss to come out here."

"I know," he said. "I hope I can do it. Roger simply has to take this course." Josh took me seriously. But I had heard many promises before and put the entire matter from my mind.

The next year, Bill Grede sat in for one of my sessions. He was so enthusiastic about the material that he dug into his pocket and put up the necessary funds so that some nine of his good friends could come to the school with all costs, including transportation, covered.

We scheduled a special executive course of one week in April of 1963. In attendance were: the Executive VP of Alcoa, the Executive VP of the National Association of Manufacturers; Chairman of the Board of the Williamson Company of Cincinnati; President of the Falk Corporation of Milwaukee; President of Charleston Rubber of Charleston, S.C.; VP of the W. H. Brady Co. of Milwaukee; Executive VP of Perfex Corp., Milwaukee; and, VP and General Manager of Love Box Company of Wichita, Kansas. Also in attendance was Bob Welsh who had already launched his famous John Birch Society, Bill Grede sat in and we had a powerhouse.

By mutual consent, we kept Bob Welsh's attendance secret. I don't know whether Grede believed that his attendance would injure the Birch Society or that the Birch Society might injure the school. In any case, Welsh and I found common ground on most points, differing sharply and on the matter of what has been called the "conspiratorial theory." According to Welsh, the malaise creeping upon America was the result of a clandestine conspiracy. I had believed this myself at one time, but I had moved to the view that whether there was a conspiracy, the result would have been much the same. The American people were almost totally uninformed as to the nature of economics and government, and they were reacting according to human nature. The "sell-out" was occurring because people tend to follow every pied piper who offers them something for nothing.

On this point, Grede appeared to agree with both of us. He said during class that if we could manage to get the directors of the National Association of Manufacturers into one of my classes, then we could turn the country around and get it back on the track of fiscal responsibility and reality.

I applauded that observation, understandably, and suggested that Bill might undertake that task for me. He said he would try, but he was doubtful if his urgings would have the desired results.

Meanwhile, Josh Greene had done his homework. I received a telephone call one day from South Carolina. "Bob," Josh said after identifying himself, "I've been trying to get Mr. Milliken to take off the time to go out to Colorado for one of your courses. I've finally gotten him to agree to attend a session, provided you'll conduct it back here. Can you schedule a session in South Carolina?"

"Will Mr. Milliken attend the session in person if I come back?" I asked.

"Yes. He's agreed to that. However, he wants to know what you'll charge."

"Let's work it this way, Josh. Milliken w111 have to pay all my costs. Transportation, room and board, and the cost of books. He's to provide his own evaluation. After he's taken the course, he can pay me what he thinks it's worth. If he decides it's worthless he owes me nothing. I'll let him be the Judge."

"You want to do it that way?"

"Why not? What I really want is to get him into a class."

"Okay, Bob. I'll try to get it up. I'll get beck to you."

I explained the situation to Harry who gave me the necessary time away from my desk. Harry also decided he wanted me to serve as editor-in-chief of the newspaper. However, knowing how busy I was both with my editorial output and at the school, Harry said that I could hire an assistant to perform the actual task of editing. He wanted me to have the title. Along with the title would come a substantial increase in pay.

How could I say no? I accepted and hired a man to do the job. At the appointed time, I took off from the Denver Airport for my first session in the Deep South.

Mindful of the isolated character of the school campus and understanding my reasons for it, Josh arranged for my session with Roger to be in a splendid old hotel in Asheville, North Carolina. The Milliken Company was one of the leading textile producers in the country and it happened that none of those who would attend my course lived in Asheville.

I always preferred this arrangement. In order to achieve the intellectual intensity the course demanded, I wanted all attendees to break contact with their daily routines so they could give complete consideration to the ideas I planned to offer.

Before taking off, Josh explained that Mr. Milliken would be in attendance personally, together with a score of his top executives.

We had scheduled the session for a date after our summer schedule had been covered. An early winter storm was lashing the northern rim of states although we flew out of Denver under clear skies. My flight was scheduled to touch down in Chicago, where I would change planes for a flight to Atlanta. There, another change in planes would take me to Ashville.

Everything went well. I arrived in Ashville where Josh met the plane and drove me to the hotel. In the South, the weather was still mild.

To my great disappointment, Mr. Milliken failed to show. I conducted the session as I had promised. At its conclusion, the executives held a meeting during which they produced a letter they all signed, urging Mr. Mllliken to take the course.

One of the executives asked that a statement be put in the letter saying that if Mr. Milliken didn't sit in for a session, then he wasn't certain he wanted to keep working for the company. The information I offered had apparently made an impact, but not on Mr. Milliken.

After I returned to Colorado, Josh got me on the telephone again. He expressed disappointment that Mr. Milliken had not put in an appearance and explained how busy his boss was. I responded that a promise was a promise and I was gravely disappointed.

A few days later, Josh called me again. Through Josh, Mr. Milliken apologized for missing the session and agreed he was out of line. If I would return for another session, he would certainly attend the next time. On top of that, he wanted me to stage two more sessions, each one packed with his top men. I could be sure of his attendance at one of them.

Again, I managed to win time off by writing two more editorials in advance of publication date. Winter had come to the country. Instead of scheduling the session in Asheville, Mr. Milliken had reserved Yeaman's Hall, an exclusive Golf and Country Club in Charleston, South Carolina. There, the weather would surely be mild. I would stage two sessions back to back. Mr. Milliken would be on hand.

This time when I took off from Stapleton Field in Denver, a blizzard was in progress. We were able to land in Chicago as before, but by the time we had crossed the Midwestern tier of states, Chicago was socked in. All flights were being re-routed. My flight landed in Pittsburgh.

The landing was so late that the last plane for Atlanta had already flown. My best chance of getting to Atlanta, and then to Spartanburg, would be to return to Chicago on the following day. But the following day, I was scheduled to be opening my session in Yeaman's Mall.

In desperation, I approached a charter airline with a desk at the airport. Could I make arrangements to fly to Spartanburg, South Carolina?

After dickering on cost and lining up a pilot who was willing, I decided to charter despite cost and risk.

I had made a commitment. Perhaps it was my radio or my theatrical background. I believed the show must go on. I knew that Mr. Milliken would have taken a large number of his key people and he would have spent a lot of money getting them to Yeaman's Hall. He would probably be there himself. And what would happen if I didn't show up simply because the weather was rough? Milliken could miss a session but I could not. Business paid off on only one event. Results. Promises don't count.

I telephoned Josh to let him know that I would be landing in a small private plane and gave him the estimated time of arrival. Then, we took off from Pittsburgh. Visibility was only fair but we gained altitude and presently flew above the storm in the light of a three-quarter moon. Thus far, all was going well.

As we neared our destination, and the pilot started down through the overcast, the wings began to ice up. We had no de-icing equipment and had to regain altitude. We approached Spartanburg twice more only to ice-up and climb again.

With fuel running low, the pilot decided on one more try. Of course, I knew we would make it. The aviation industry has a perfect record in this department. Every plane that has ever taken off has come down. Somehow.

I don't know whether the chill had eased or whether rocking of the wings kept them from locking, but down we came for a good landing at about 2:00 a.m. I was met by a Milliken employee, whom I didn't know and who would have been delighted never to meet me, I am sure. Who wants to wait up at a deserted airport for a stranger who may not even show?

I was driven to the guesthouse on the Milliken property where I spent the rest of the night. The next morning I was chauffeured to Charleston and Yeaman's Hall.

My disappointment was large when, again, Mr. Mllliken failed to arrive. However, I staged the session as I had agreed.

My happiness was restored, however, when Roger Milliken, together with his cousin, Minot, from the New York office, showed up in time for my final seminar. Each of these two sessions at Yeaman's Hall contained about eighteen enrollees.

Roger was a joyful surprise. He was not at all the dour-faced man I had expected. He was younger than I, stood about two inches taller and had a crop of red hair. It was plain that the men who worked with him adored him and followed his lead in every detail.

In a room filled with brilliant men of high achievement, Roger stood out. That session for the Milliken Company proved to be one of the highlights of my career as an instructor. I pulled no punches and got along famously. However, there were several interesting exchanges.

Roger approached me in mid-week and said, "Bob, I'm going to have to be excused from tomorrow's classes. I'm very active in Republican politics, as you probably know, and there's an important meeting being held that I must attend."

"Well," I said, "I can't control you. But I won't excuse you. There's nothing going on at that meeting half as important as your attendance here. If you aren't in your seat when we convene in the morning, then you will be guilty of an unexcused absence."

Roger handled himself well. He looked at me quizzically and said, "Very well. If you won't excuse me, I'll be present." And he was!

At one point in class, a discussion of tariffs came up. Mr. Milliken was fairly well known for his support of tariffs to protect the textile business. I was asked what the libertarian position would be.

I stated flatly that tariffs were unwarranted. I gave my reasons, one by one. I could feel the atmosphere in the room grow tense. Free trade was an essential, I said. Every customer in the world should be free to buy the best product he could find at the most favorable price to him, anywhere in the world. Government interference at any point tended to protect the least efficient and punish the most efficient.

I could almost hear the air being sucked out of the room as the executives drew in their breaths and focused on Roger. Would he let my remarks pass without challenge?

When I finished my summation, Roger spoke up. He was sitting in the front and had to turn to face the balance of the class. "LeFevre is right," he said. The air escaping from eighteen sets of lungs sounded like a tire going flat all at once.

"If we can't make textiles on a competitive basis with the best in the world," Roger continued, "we're in the wrong business."

My esteem for Mr. Milliken zoomed. His observation not only required a dedication to truth, but also a large and generous point of view. If Roger was impressed by what I said, I was impressed with him.

When I finished the seminar, Roger asked if I'd mind flying with him in his private plane back to Spartanburg.

Mind? How often does one get to fly with the president of a major corporation in his private plane? Of course, I accepted.

Roger had a converted DC-3. The entire interior cabin was arranged like a living room with pivoting armchairs and all possible amenities. Minot and perhaps as many as six of the leading executives were also invited for the trip.

Roger and Minot sat together in the forward part of the cabin. As I was staring out the window at the scenery, Minot came back to my chair.

"Roger and I have been talking about your remuneration," Minot said. "Would you be willing to accept the sum in two checks rather than one?"

No amount was mentioned and my imagination was running rampant. I knew Roger had approved of what I had done. But how great was his approval? Would he give me $5,000 for my effort? That seemed a lot, but I hoped for something in that vicinity. I even let my hopes soar beyond. Was it possible that he could come up with $10,000?

I grinned at Minot. "It doesn't matter to me at all," I said. "The more checks the better."

He laughed. "Well, we've talked it over. We'd like to give you

$40,000 for your own personal use and another $60,000 as a contribution to the school. Would that be satisfactory?"

My dreams had not gone that far. I was overwhelmed.

"There is just one thing," I said. "I'm on salary with the newspaper so I'm being paid anyway. Would you mind making out both checks in favor of the school?"

"No. That can be arranged. Sure you don't want something for your own efforts?"

"I'm sure. We have this building program and it takes a lot of money. I can sure use it to help pay the bills at the school."

"We'll be drawing the $60,000 from one account and the $40,000 from another bank, if that's all right with you."

I was still stunned. "That's quite fine."

"And don't forget to send us a bill covering your expenses."

I had forgotten about that. "Bill? Oh, sure. Sure."

In Spartanburg, Roger insisted on taking me to his home. He lived modestly in a beautiful part of Spartanburg. His house was not ostentatious and his own offices were in a small annex he had added to the main building.

I met his beautiful and lovely wife and his children. I was in a state of exaltation and exhaustion. I have no recollection of how we spent the evening. I was treading on air at high altitude.

Back in Colorado, armed with a pair of checks of such gargantuan proportions, I was looked at with some awe by my staff. With the money we paid off the balance owing on the land and finished paying for Rose Lane Hall. The entire Milliken experience was one of the high lights of my life.

Chapter C

One of the events occurring in the country during the early '60's distressed me in a very personal way. I was running "The Freedom School." But now, in various parts of the nation, other Freedom Schools were being organized. They took the same name but operated in quite another fashion.

It was our position in Colorado, that man, as a free being, should be able to own his own property, manage it as he sees fit (provided he intruded on no one), but do so at his own expense.

The schools being organized in many places were put together by pressure groups with the idea of getting some new concessions from government. Many wanted new laws passed in their favor. Some wanted subsidies of one kind or another. Some sought gains for minority groups. But none calling itself a Freedom School stood up for freedom in the manner we did.

I was trying to understand and teach the meaning of freedom. Ours was an educational endeavor. But many a group using the same name was asking some kind of political privilege. Every now and again a letter would arrive, attacking me because of what people in other areas were doing.

More and more, we were called upon to explain and defend actions we had not taken and did not approve. We had made no effort to copyright the name. Our purpose was to operate without depending on government, and copyrighting is a tax-supported process. Further, had we attempted, we would have failed. A title cannot be copyrighted. No one person can own a word or any set of words. And rightly so! If words could be owned privately, any conversation would probably contain a property boundary violation. We could have, perhaps, obtained a trademark in which we used the term Freedom School either by spelling it in a unique way or by using specific type or some artistic logo exclusively our own. But this would not have prevented others from using the same words.

At one point, we actually brought in a team of analysts. We asked the experts to come up with an appropriate name for our efforts that would, in all probability, not be duplicated by others and would serve to identify our efforts. The suggestion was "Pine Tree College."

This suggestion came during the height of the campaign against us by the Colorado Springs radio station owned by Shel Singer. It was probably a good name for us, but I could just hear my adversaries singing the "They cut down the old pine tree..." dyed-in-heritage ballad. I didn't want to provide any more fodder for jeers than necessary.

Unofficially, we began to call ourselves "Rampart College," taking the name from the Rampart Range where we were located. However, our literature still bore the name, "Freedom School."

We did adopt the use of the term Pine Tree in conjunction with our publication efforts. We felt it necessary to communicate with our friends and well wishers on a regular basis. So, we launched first one format, and then another, trying to come up with a bi-monthly or monthly newsletter that would keep everyone informed. These various publications came out under the heading of Pine Tree Press.

We kept changing format because the Trustees urged us to make our efforts self-sustaining, dollar-wise. But no matter what the format chosen, our newsletter invariably lost money. The reason, of course, was that we not only mailed the publication to those who subscribed but also we used it as a major promotional piece.

Now, to further confuse the issue, a national magazine was launched calling itself *Ramparts*. We had no connection with it. In actuality, the magazine had a few articles in it that I was happy to see in print. But in the main, the slant of the publishers was anti-capitalist and hostile to private ownership of property and private enterprise.

The entire country seemed saturated with the belief that the government ought to own and manage the means of production and distribution. And that was the central theme of Karl Marx, which we saw as a colossal error. Most colleges and universities had been sponsoring and promoting this idea for decades.

In 1963, we determined to conduct a bold experiment. One of our problems related to our relatively short school year—May to September. Despite the cold and snows of winter, why not enroll a group of outstanding students for the entire winter season?

I could bring in some of the country's finest professors for lectures, and have in residence the economist who had done so much to awaken me to the virtue of private enterprise and private property—V. Orval Watts.

My organizational efforts succeeded and I lined up eleven of the finest professors. Dr. Watts consented to head the project, provided I could obtain an assistant for him. One of our outstanding students had been a young man named Bob Smith. He was hired as an assistant to Watts, who was named Dean.

This winter effort was costly. I traveled more than usual during the experiment, raising money to pay for it. We called the program a "Phrontistery" after the Greek word meaning, "a place for learning." (Or thinking.)

Thirteen students came to spend the winter with us, including two from Argentina. By now, we had attracted enrollees from England, France, Japan, India, Mexico and the Philippines.

But now, as I buzzed from place to place trying to raise funds, I ran into serious opposition. It became clear that the Freedom Schools and Ramparts Magazine were doing us no good. In vain did I deny any connection.

More and more businessmen were looking at me with a jaundiced eye. Most of those who had actually studied with me continued in support. But even among these stalwarts, I began to detect the gleam in the eye that indicated my bearer didn't believe my statements.

One firm, which shall remain nameless, gave me a run-around that became more or lese typical. At the outset I had obtained a small contribution with the assurance that when and if we ever attained tax exemption, there would be sizeable support. We won tax exemption.

The next time I called at the executive office of the firm, I was advised that they were impressed with the tax exemption, but it was clear that the school had no one on the faculty with the necessary credentials to do the bulk of the teaching. I was doing the teaching. And who, pray tell, was Bob LeFevre? When this lack was remedied we could count on a sizeable grant.

Now, with eleven Ph.D.s completely in charge of instruction, I approached the same firm. This time I was met with hostility. What about *Ramparts* and the spate of Freedom Schools? It was all well and good for me to deny a connection but, even if there was no overt tie-in, wasn't it true that the ideas I had been teaching had inspired those organizations?

I denied that we were that effective either for good or evil. But the "I don't believe you" gleam was there.

Also, the two themes launched in Trustees' meetings were trotted out in lieu of a contribution. The organization of the Freedom School (Rampart College) was not satisfactory. It looked to these businessmen like a one-man show. Who was my understudy? What effort had been made to assure continued existence of the school in the event that anything happened to me?

Besides, by now, with the kind of success the school had attained, we should be in the black. I countered that this was impossible while we were still putting up buildings. Well, if ever the school got into the black, they would give some big checks.

Obviously, I countered that if and when we were in the black, then I wouldn't be around asking for checks.

What was particularly hard to take was a letter arriving from one of the professors on Leonard Read's staff at the Foundation for Economic Education. This gentleman, whom I thought of as a good friend, railed at me. I was too extreme, he said. Further, he was going to write to every one of my donors and supporters and do his best to cut off all contributions to our efforts.

Let me recite one particular experience.

Through the kind offices of a man who had attended our sessions and was sold on the validity of our instruction, I was asked to stop at the headquarters of General Motors in Detroit. My friend would manage somehow to get me in to see the president of GM. Surely I could get some help from this source.

At the appointed time, I arrived at the big GM building and called on my former student, now an executive of the firm. He told me to wait and he'd got me in to the big man, if only for a few minutes.

I waited about half an hour.

Then, a fellow I didn't know came up to me and said, "Come with me." He wasn't friendly. I followed him.

He led me through some corridors and we entered a vacant boardroom. "Just wait here," he said, and left me.

I waited alone for another fifteen minutes. I sat in one of the chairs that circled the room, too much in awe to seat myself at the enormous board table.

Suddenly, two men stood beside me. It was although they had materialized from the Star Ship *Enterprise*. How they got there, I don't know. I hadn't seen them come in.

One of them was introduced as the President of GM, and there was a quick dead-fish handshake. I knew him from pictures I had seen. He was under great tension and extremely nervous.

Without waiting for me to say anything, the man I had come to see said: "Sorry I had to meet you this way. The place is crawling with IRS people and I don't dare have you come to my office. I can't afford to be seen with you. You're too extreme, LeFevre. I understand that you don't want government involved in business at all. God, that's pretty far out on the limb, isn't it?

"Our job is to make money for our stockholders. After all, this is a publicly held corporation. We'll make money any way we can, including government contracts. Sorry. I think you probably have some good ideas. But I have to think of the good of the whole corporation and I can't see our stockholders putting up anything for your efforts. Sorry."

Another limp handshake and the two men vanished through a rear door. I hadn't gotten beyond an incompleted sentence: "It's good of you to take the time..."

I am not suggesting that this treatment became general. But there was an increasing amount of it. The flow of dollars to the school was tapering off.

On the other side of the coin, Roger Milliken became more involved in our efforts. In 1965, he asked for nine classes exclusively for Milliken middle management personnel. In 1966, he asked for ten. We lengthened our school year to accommodate. Thanks to Milliken we now opened in mid-April and closed in mid-December.

All of these events in combination kept me moving at break neck speed.

In 1964, at last I was able to put Ruth Dazey on salary at the school. She continued working at the Gazette for awhile, holding down two paying jobs. But at least she no longer had to pay room and board for the privilege of living on campus.

By the time 1964 ended, I remained the only worker at Freedom School, still paying for that privilege. And, of course, I continued to provide room end board for three—Loy, Tommy and myself.

1965 proved to be a pivotal year. At our Trustees' meeting during the winter of 1964, we renamed the school officially. It became Rampart College.

The Trustees chose William Froh as president and I was named dean, in charge of instruction. Butler Shaffer and Sy Leon were hired as assistant instructors. And we began the year with high hopes. We had our first Milliken group in April and a good attendance up to June. On the 13th of that month we signed in a class of twelve, eight women and four men.

On the evening of June 15th, Loy complained she didn't feel well. I suggested that she'd been overworking. It was an easy diagnosis. Everyone present had been overworkir4g.

One of Loy's eyes was bloodshot and swollen. I presumed she had picked up an infection. The eye pained her a great deal and she felt so poorly that on the morning of June 16th, it seemed a good idea to get her medical attention. There was none in our vicinity,

That Wednesday morning was overcast. Loy and I drove into Colorado Springs together and I took her to Penrose Hospital, one of the finest in the country. We knew a number of doctors who practiced there and skilled assistance was available.

We commented on the clouds that darkened the eastern slopes of the Ramparts. They were a blue-black, sloped like folds of canvas and seemed only thirty or forty yards above the station wagon. "There's plenty of water up there," I said to Loy. "We're going to get a soaking."

Loy shrugged. "I really feel rotten. So, let it rain. Ida can handle everything. " Ida was Loy's helper in the kitchen—a big, competent woman.

"They'll probably swab out your eye," I said to her. "When you're ready, phone the paper. I can pick you up. But don't worry. You have a few items in your suitcase and can stay in town if need be. So, if they haven't finished with you by 11:30 don't give it another thought. Someone else can come in for you."

I dropped her off at Penrose and went to my editorial job. About 11:00, I phoned the hospital and learned to my surprise that she was quite ill and had been admitted. I dismissed the matter. She would have the finest of care and I had a class in session. I would eat lunch at noon on campus and convene my class at 1:00 p.m., as usual.

When I came out of the Gazette, the clouds were lower and looked dirtier. There was en eerie light over everything and no detectable wind. As I raced in the direction of the school, the first big drops came down to spatter against the windshield.

On campus, everything was in order. Ida stayed in a small room in our original building and served up a fine lunch. I advised her that she'd probably have to make dinner by herself. Loy and Ida shared the workload and Loy's absence created no real problem.

Just before one o'clock, I headed for Rose Lane Hall. Rain had started falling. There was an ominous feeling from the darkening sky, but thus far only a light sprinkle helped settle the dust.

We were accustomed to rain. In our two-storied classroom, complete with balcony, we were protected from the sound of the storm by the rooms above. I wasn't concerned with anything but the instruction. Rose Lane Hall had been well built. The huge logs that supported the auditorium ceiling weighed a ton apiece. We would be safe, no matter what.

As I proceeded with the Wednesday presentation, the storm struck. There were no windows but we could hear the distant roar of wind and falling water. I sensed that the storm was severe. But we were insulated and surely had no cause for alarm.

Three o'clock came and with it our fifteen minute, mid-afternoon break. Just as I announced the intermission, Dohn Lewis, clad in bright yellow rain gear, entered at balcony level.

He leaned over the railing dripping water on the desks below. "Bob, we need your help. Mud and water are coming into Reno Sales Lodge through the loading door. We're going to have to move our supplies or risk losing them. Can you give us a hand?"

"Sure thing," I said. Leaving my notebook on the podium I ran up the stairs to the balcony and joined Dohn.

One of the students sitting near the up-hill wall called after me, "Hey, Bob! Water and mud is oozing through the chinking on this side of the building."

"Why don't you take a seat on the other side of the classroom?" I called back. "The building is safe. Don't worry about it."

I opened the door to follow Dohn. It was only then that I realized the magnitude of the storm. The rain was coming down in torrents. We were under a Niagara. The road, which slanted past the huge side porch of the Lodge, was a river. The normal ruts had disappeared and in place of them were gullies too deep to estimate. The entire road was being washed away.

I dashed through the downpour, instantly soaked. I toiled up hill to Reno Sales Lodge, which had been constructed across the draw. Penny and their small son were in the main room, which was now being used as the school office. Tom was there as well, and Mohammet, the beautiful golden retriever owned by the Lewis'.

One glance and everything appeared in order.

"In there," Penny said, pointing to the connecting door, which led into the smaller room at the north end of the building. Dohn and I hurried into the storeroom where we kept our supplies of paper, publications and classroom materials.

Bill Froh and Ruth were there, doing their best to move heavy cartons away from the double door in that sidewall. The door was partly open. A mound of gravel had worked through the screen dove and was already a foot high on the hardwood floor. The building doors opened into the room, but the screen dove opened outward.

The problem was impossible to miss. The screen doors were no protection from the cascading water and mud sweeping down the hill outside. And the screen doors couldn't be moved. They were pinned tight by gravel and mud at least three feet deep. Someone had opened the inside doors, probably to get a look at the storm. Mud and gravel had caught between the screen and the solid doors. It cascaded into a huge mound inside the storeroom.

"Dohn," I shouted, "See if you can round up a shovel. We've got to move that gravel to get the door closed. Meanwhile, let's all move boxes away from the door. If we can't close it, we'll have to move everything into the office!"

Dohn left at a dead run. Bill, Ruth and I struggled with the cases.

Suddenly came the sound of a tremendous crack. It wasn't thunder. I straightened and looked into the office in time to see Penny, babe in arms, dash out the front door followed by Tom. Then, it was as if an explosion rocked the building. The uphill wall made of cinder block and reinforced steel gave way.

Roaring into the office came a landslide, filling the entire room with mud and granite, in a split second five feet deep. Our files and office machines were buried. Anyone remaining in that room would have been killed on the instant. We were in the smaller room and trapped.

Bill, Ruth and I looked at each other with stark fear. There was no chance of getting out the way we had come in. That room was full and the gravel was pouring into the storeroom from the inside door. And the gravel-buttressed screen doors would keep us from using the loading doors. There were no other exits and no windows.

Above the roar of the storm I heard Tom's voice. "Don't worry, Father. I'll get you out!"

In the drenching rain, Tom had climbed on top of the churning landslide now engulfing the building. He was on his knees at the top of the screens, scrabbling with teenage fingers at the barriers. How he found the strength, I'll never know. But that seventeen-year-old managed somehow to get a grip on the top crossbar of one of the screens. He pulled it outward and literally tore the door in half!

Somehow the three of us managed to crawl through that opening. We were safe.

Were we? I looked up the hill through the drenching rain. I could see what appeared to be a wall of gravel moving down the slope above us.

"The landslide is coming down the draw," I roared. "This whole building will probably go! Let's get the students!"

All of us raced back to Rose Lane Hall just below. In place of the road was a trench a foot deep, filled with swirling water and mud. If Reno Sales Lodge went out, Rose Lane Hall was next in line.

Inside the big building at balcony level, a scene of confusion met my eyes. Margie had marshaled what manpower among the students she could find. They had been working with her in the library, moving books from lower shelves. They were already too late in some cases. Four to five inches of slimy, oily mud lay over what had been a polished hardwood floor. Some of the books on the lower shelves had been immersed in slime as much as two inches. But she got them out with the help of many willing hands.

Mud and water was seeping through the cement chinking the length of the building. It was already about three inches deep on the classroom floor.

"Come on," I called from the balcony. "The lower floor of Reno Sales has gone. If the building goes, this one is next. We can't any of us stay here. There isn't time to get anything. It's a landslide! Come on!"

"Where to?" Someone shouted.

"Let's get into the dining room." I bellowed. "It's on the other side of the draw and is safer than this. Follow me."

As we crowded out into the rain, the havoc being wrought by the storm was instantly visible. I waded through the river that had been the road, and most of the students came with me. Three of the women were too frightened to trust themselves to that swollen torrent.

"Follow me," cried Tom. "I know how to do it. I'll get you across."

"Are you sure you know what you're doing, Son?" I called.

"Sure, Father! Come on!" He disappeared in the rain, leading the three women up hill past Reno Sales and toward the landslide.

All of us managed to get into the dining room, After a few minutes, Tom and his charges came down the hill through the clearing above the dining room. Everyone was soaked to the skin except Ida, who now joined us from her room. But we were all safe...at least for the moment.

The dining room had three large picture windows that looked up hill in the direction of the slipping, sliding disaster. Standing there watching, we saw huge boulders, in advance of the major slide, rolling and bouncing down the hill in our direction. Some of them were the size of dining room tables.

Suddenly Dohn said, "What about your folks?"

I had forgotten. Dad and his wife, Esther, whom he had married after breaking up with Mother, had moved to stay with us at the school. For awhile, they lived in a trailer because of our lack of space. But we had built a residence cabin on the banks of the creek and the two of them lived there, paying rent in support of our effort. They were in their seventies. From where we were, I had no way of knowing how they were faring. From the dining room, no part of the creek could be seen.

"Let me go get them, Bob," Dohn volunteered.

"Wait a minute," I counseled. "Most of the damage seems to be centralized right in this neighborhood." I was watching the water and mud flowing like a mighty river down the slope in our direction.

Even as I spoke, the roar of water on the roof changed into a more sinister sound. Great blankets of hail descended, drowning speech and leaving white pellets dancing outside amid the swirling deluge. Then, still looking uphill, I saw tall trees being uprooted and tossed about. The great forest bowed in our direction, pointing pine needled treetops at our temporary haven. It was as though a signpost was needed to show the tornado its route.

"Tom," I said, "Do you think you can get over to Falcon Lair?"

"Sure I can, Father. That's where I was when the storm started."

"I'm not even sure it's still there. But you can move faster than any of us. Get over there to see if the building is safe. Then get back here at once.

"Falcon Lair is in an entirely different location," I explained, "away from this draw altogether. That could be the one safe place at the school.

"We'll stay together right here until you get back, Tom." He needed no urging. Tom sped through the kitchen and out the back door.

"If Falcon Lair is okay," I said to Dohn, "then you can go to Dad and Esther and you'll have someplace to bring them. Okay?"

"What if Tom doesn't get back?"

"Let's give him a chance. He's already been a hero a couple of times today."

Suddenly the door burst open. In came Edith, Link, Gene, and a young man named Ray, who had been working with the horses under Link's supervision.

"I turned the horses loose," Link reported. "They know what to do in a storm. The creek's rising. They could get trapped in the barn if the meadow floods out."

"Good thinking," I said.

"The electricity's gone," Gene observed. "The phones are out. And without electric current the pumps don't work. So the plumbing won't work. Don't anyone use the john."

I shook my head. "I never saw a storm like this," I said. "How about it, Link? Do you remember anything this bad?"

"Some of the old timers say we get one like this about every hundred years. As far as I can figure, we got us a combination storm. Cloudburst, landslides, tornado, hail, and floods. It ain't friendly."

We all stood watching the effects of the storm. Outside the picture windows was a flagstone walk. The walk was filling with gravel, and those mighty boulders kept bounding down the slope. Thus far, they had all stopped short of the dining room. If one hit a windowpane, that would be the end of this refuge.

Ida had gone to her room and now came up to report that water was beginning to take over the lower floor of the building we were in. Outside, the mud and gravel piled up.

We could see Reno Sales Lodge. Despite the collapse of the uphill wall, the second floor—all of logs—held firm atop what was left of the first story. But it was directly in the path. The cascading rocks and mud had reached the eaves on the uphill side.

Tommy returned, proud of his speed record. "Falcon Lair's fine, Father. It's just raining and hailing over there. But there are some trees across the road. You'll have to climb over them."

Mud and gravel outside the dining room now lay at windowsill level. Then, it began to stack up against the glass. That meant it was three feet deep.

"I don't know how much pressure this glass will take," I said. "But I'm going to assume that this building will go, too. Dohn, see if you can help my folks over to the Lair."

"Yes, Sir," said Dohn, and dashed out the door.

"There goes my car," Bill Froh said.

"I don't see it," I said.

"I don't either. It was parked in front of Reno Sales. It just dropped into the ground."

"Holy cow!"

Another large boulder came leaping and rolling toward our window. "If that one crosses the road, it's time to head for the Lair," I said.

As though it had heard my observation, the chunk of granite did a parabola into the road, bounced to the near side and rolled to within three foot of where we stood. Only the thin pane of glass remained between it and us.

"Let's go," I said.

Together we trooped through the kitchen and out the back door. The weight of falling water was a physical burden as we hurried along the road, helping one another over the fallen timber.

As Falcon Lair finally loomed in front of us, it seemed the storm was less severe. We crowded onto the veranda that circled the building, and burst into the house. My dog, Princess, was happy to see us, and barked and danced in glee.

Tom asked, "Where's Mohammet?"

We all looked blank. Penny spoke. "Last I saw him, he was in Reno Sales. That was just before the wall caved in."

"If he was in there," I said, "he's probably done for. Thank God the rest of you got out."

"Everyone's here and everyone's safe," Bill Froh observed. "We have been pretty damn lucky. That's all I can say."

"Not quite," I reminded. "Dohn's gone after Dad and Esther. I hope he got to them in time. They must be scared out of their wits."

Everyone stood around thoroughly drenched, hair streaming with water. We looked as though we had swum the English Channel. The storm was subsiding.

"Everyone get out of his wet clothes," I called. "We can't stand around like this."

"We can't run around naked, either," one of women remarked.

"Then change into something."

"What something?"

"Sorry," I said. "I'm not thinking. Permission is granted. You can loot Loy's closets, you women. And I have some extra coveralls for at least some of the men."

"I'll get a fire going in the fireplace," Gene said. Presently, we had a fire roaring. It was the first sign of cheer we'd had.

"I' 11 get some buckets of water ready," Link observed. "There are three bathrooms in this building. I'll put a pail of water in each. The water will be muddy but don't worry. When you've used the john, pour in the bucket of water. The john will flush. Then go out and get another bucket for the next guy."

"How you going to fill the buckets?" I asked.

Link grinned. "The rain'll do it. So long as it lasts."

"And after that?"

I went out on the veranda accompanied by several others. From this splendid observation post, even though the gloom of storm was overall, we had good visibility across the meadow.

Our little creek had burst its banks. The meadow was under water. The creek had enlarged and was now a raging torrent about half a block in width. The giant hills on the north side, which carried the road back to the Counter's property, had been eaten away. Trees and slopes and road were gone. Naked cliffs of brown earth stood stark where ground cover and shrubs had once grown. Even as I watched, a huge section of earth loosened and slid into the surging flood. It was as though the land was made of brown sugar that melted away as we watched.

Cars parked in the meadow were up to their doors in water. No horses were to be seen. But where were Dad and Esther and Dohn?

After an hour of anxious waiting on our part, the trio arrived. The storm was retreating toward the east when my weary folks came reeling up the steps to the veranda. They were helped inside. They, too, were stripped of wet garments and clad in whatever was available, including blankets.

"We couldn't get up the front road," Dohn reported. "I had to take them across the meadow and up the back road. It has a more gradual ascent and it wasn't washed out. I think the worst is over."

Tom had a battery-powered radio and now reported that the storm had been enormous. Palmer Lake was isolated. So was Larkspur. Every creek had become a river. The mighty Platte flowing through Denver was over its banks. It carried furniture, buildings, and people adrift. Property damage was in the millions. No one was yet certain of injury or death, although there was an unconfirmed report that several persons had drowned.

We raided the pantry and Ida managed to put a ramshackle meal together. Some of the students brushed their teeth that night in soda water Loy had in the refrigerator. All our potable fluids were quickly used up.

I called everyone into the big hexagonal room with the fireplace and asked for their cooperation. I didn't want anyone to risk his person by going back to see how the other buildings had fared. I asked that they all spend the night at Falcon Lair. They could sleep in what beds we had—the elderly getting preference. Then on sofas and chairs, with the most hardy on the floor.

We had flashlights and candles. We had a warm fire that could be kept going all night. In the morning, with the storm out of the way, we'd decide what was best.

Bone weary and with aching heart I went to bed.

My beautiful school, for which I had labored so hard and long, was in shambles. I didn't want to know how bad it really was.

My wife lay in a hospital and I wasn't even able to telephone to find out how she was faring.

The reports on the radio had showed just how wide spread the damage had been. The Perry Park road, our only route in or out of town had been washed away. Bridges were gone. We were isolated and would have to survive as best we could, perhaps for days.

I had a score and more of persons on hand for whom I was responsible.

Somehow, I managed to fall asleep.

Chapter CI

Nearly everyone was up and stirring before I awoke from my troubled slumbers. One of the young ladies who had spent the night on the rug gave us a line I won't soon forget. "When I write to my mother," she announced, "she'll never believe I spent the night on the floor next to a college president." Bill Froh was pleased.

The staff had taken the initiative. Ida had disregarded my instructions about returning to the storm damaged area. She had spent the night in her own bed with water standing two to three inches deep under it. She had found the cooking range in working order. The gas line from the propane tank at the base of the hill had remained intact. Ida had a hot breakfast available for all.

Link and Tom had risen early. Link could find what he wanted in the woods, the way an Indian guide can trail a deer across a naked rock. He and Tom had gone up the slope to a position a few yards above Falcon Lair. "Dig there," he told Tom, pointing to the base of a Douglas fir. Tom had done so and almost at once struck fresh spring water. With a section of hose, Link piped that water into the house.

Back amid the ravages of the storm at Reno Sales Lodge, Link had repeated his woodcraft. Another shallow dig uncovered a second spring. Fresh, pure water was being fed to the kitchen by the force of gravity.

Then, Link started our generator. It, too, operated on propane gas. Once it began to hum, electricity was restored to refrigerators, freezers and one set of work-lights through the school. The whole place had been wired that way in the event of an emergency. Our generator was too small to operate everything, but at least it worked, despite the storm. We could get by, somehow, with food, water, and strategically placed electric lights.

When we had taken refuge at Falcon Lair, I had been fearful that the entire mountain was in motion and about to cascade on top of us. In actual fact, most of the damage had already occurred when we fled the dining room. Reno Sales was in shambles. Water damage was everywhere. Every roof had been hail-damaged and—except for Falcon Lair—every building had mud and gravel inside.

Dohn Lewis and Penny began the day in search of Mohammet. As they neared Reno Sales Lodge, they heard a whining from inside the building!

The room had six feet of gravel, but Dohn managed to climb in on top of it and locate the dog. He had been trapped by the rushing gravel, totally immobilized but otherwise unhurt. Dohn dug him out. Mohammet's first act was to grab a stick and try to get a game of "fetch" started. He took the whole experience as a lark.

Then, Dohn and Gene had grabbed shovels and gone off through the woods to construct a latrine. Although we had a trickle of water that could be used for drinking, there wasn't enough water to operate the plumbing. So a system was devised.

The building nearest the latrine was Falcon Lair. A bright red candle was stuck into a tin can and placed on the steps where it was readily visible. If a person wished seclusion, then he took the candle with him, night or day. A second person, noting the absence of the candle, knew that the latrine was "occupied." He (or she) waited until the candle was returned. It proved a most simple and practical means of maintaining individual segregation.

After breakfast, Link rounded up the horses by offering them fresh oats at the barn. The water in the meadow was subsiding and the whole place was a sea of stinking mud. Meanwhile, the creek was as broad as before. Gravel from higher elevations had filled the creek bottom forcing the run-off out of the stream's normal channel.

I gathered the students at Falcon Lair. The classroom was not usable. Neither was the library. I expressed chagrin over the fix we were in, but pleaded for everyone to remain calm. "Perry Park Road is washed out in three places," I was able to advise. "The bridge in Butler Canyon is gone. Please, try not to worry. We'll get you out of here at the earliest possible moment. Meanwhile, we have no telephone so we can't let anyone know that we have come through the storm with no injuries at all. Even Mohammet is safe. Actually, we've been lucky."

One of the students blurted: "Do we have to go?"

I was stunned. "Don't you want to go?"

There was a chorus of dissent. David Keeler, one of the students said, "You've been talking about the nature of contracts and the sanctity of boundaries. If you don't conduct the course aren't you in violation of our contract?"

"I guess I'm in error," I said. "I presumed you would welcome the chance to get away. And you're correct. I was offering to re-negotiate. We have no classroom. But it appears you can return to your rooms in Rose Lane Hall. Bathing facilities will be limited. The comforts and conveniences you are accustomed to won't be available. But if you can stand it here, I can sure stand and deliver the course."

I could see no single instance of reluctance or hesitancy. They wanted to stay.

"I won't have a blackboard to work with," I said. But all I need are my notebooks. My notebooks! My gosh. I left them on the podium in Rose Lane Hall. I have to have those."

"I'll get them for you," Walt Ryan said. "No problem. And maybe we can help clean up the place too. After all, we do have our mornings free."

"Where will you conduct the class?" Someone asked.

"Right here at the Lair. We'll hold it outside on the veranda or inside in the evenings, or if the weather goes bad again."

Walt immediately left and presently returned with my two thick, loose-leaf tomes. With those two volumes in my possession, I could conduct a seminar on a desert island.

It is fitting that this class, which lived through the disaster with us, receives special recognition. The eight women were:

Kathleen Cochran, Idaho Falls
Jeanne A. Doran, Los Angeles
Mrs. Ellagwen Green and her daughter, Linda, both of Dixon, Illinois
Mrs. Ann Hillwick, Yakima
Mrs. Floy Johnson, Klamath Falls
Mrs. Barbara Rankin, Yakima
Betty Wiebe, Beatrice, Nebraska

The four men were:

> Mark Ahern, Seattle
> Davis Keeler, Mt. Carmel, Illinois
> Alfred J. Love, Jr., Chicago
> Walter Ryan of Claremont, California

Without exception, this dauntless twelve set an example of fortitude, industry, and good humor that was an inspiration.

Link and Gene organized work brigades and everyone pitched in. I went around the property making a complete survey.

Reno Sales Lodge had been the principal target of the storm. The largest damage was to that building and the terrain immediately around it. It was a sad looking sight. Bill Froh's car was there. The rear end still clung to what was left of the roadway. But the front end pointed to the center of the earth and was out of sight. The ground had washed out from under the car, dropping it into vertical. At the other end of the lodge, another excavation had been created by erosion. It was fourteen feet deep.

Dohn Lewis appeared with a look of triumph on his face. "You're lucky, LeFevre," he said. "Here's your college!"

"What do you mean?"

"Look at this damage as opportunity," he suggested.

"Boy, will you be able to raise money!"

I was far from feeling such confidence. Nearly everything on the first floor of Reno Sales Lodge was ruined. Typewriters, office machines, files, all our records, promotional lists, books, and supplies of every sort. Just looking at the mess was heart-rending!

But then came a pleasant surprise. The log portion of Reno Sales Lodge, still inn position on the three standing walls below, hadn't budged. Indeed, we found it had been so firmly built that not so much as a door stuck. Dohn and Penny could move right back in.

I sought out Ruth. "Let's ready some telegrams," I said. "We'll have to notify the enrollees for the next class not to come. As soon as telephone service is restored, I'll ask you to get them out."

"Let's not be in a hurry, Bob. This is Thursday. We have more than a full week to get things straightened out. I don't think we'll have to cancel anything."

"Look at this mess," I said.

"No, look at the students," Ruth said. Six of them were in the classroom at that instant. Using plywood scoops and shovels, in bare feet and with jeans rolled up, the students were shoving water and mud out of the room. I took particular note of Ellagwen Green. Her father was the publisher of a daily newspaper. She had been raised with a societal position to maintain. She was refined and gentle, and always appeared in immaculate attire with her hair coifed and her nails buffed.

At the instant, she wore a man's shirt with one tail dangling and a pair of Tom's old trousers. Her hair was long and matted like remnants of old cordage. There was a smudge of dirt on one cheek and she had mud up to her knees and elbows. She was urging her daughter, Linda, to greater exertions, laughing and having a great time.

Ruth flashed me a smile. "Aren't they wonderful?"

"I never saw more beautiful women," I said, and meant it.

I had been feeling sorry for myself. I swallowed a lump. "If they can pitch in like that, we can whip this thing," I said.

"Then let's not talk of canceling."

"All right! Let's not talk. Let's all of us get busy."

I sought Link, "As soon as feasible," I told him, "get into town and hire extra help. We've got to shovel all the gravel out of Reno Sales. And I'll need clerks to go through our files, salvage everything that can be saved, making copies of things if necessary. Whatever it takes, let's put this place together. We plan to stay in operation."

Link grinned. "Sure thing, Bob. But we can't get into town yet."

Then, he winked. "Bill already said we'd stay a-running."

I had betrayed myself. I was president no longer, but I kept thinking and acting as if I was running everything. Link understood and he was amused. Link gave a shout and young Ray came trotting up.

"Jest figgered it out," Link said. "Go to the barn and saddle up my buckskin. I'm gonna send you into Palmer Lake. The road's out but the horse ain't skittish. He'll swim a crick with you on him if he has to."

Ray nodded and sped off toward the barn.

The students provided names and telephone numbers of relatives to be notified that they were safe and all was well. It would be up to Ray to send the messages. One message from me was for Harry Hoiles. I'd be at work again as soon as the roads were passable.

It took Ray the balance of the day to get into Palmer Lake, deliver the messages, and return. He reported that no one was worried about us, everyone being full of their own problems.

Palmer Lake was in the same fix we were. Fourteen inches of rain had fallen in about four hours. Property damage was extensive from Colorado Springs all the way to Denver. The government had declared the entire region a disaster area and the Feds were coming to offer help.

To make his trip, Ray had crossed three flooded stretches of highway where the road had been washed away. In Butler Canyon, with the bridge out, the water was deep enough for the horse to swim.

Link drove the bulldozer up to Reno Sales to begin putting the terrain back into conformity. He turned the operation of the equipment over to Ray, who moved it into the fourteen-foot drop where it disappeared from sight. Four days later we leased a second bulldozer to excavate the first.

It took three days for county road crews to repair Perry Park Road and nearly the same amount of time before telephone service was restored. At last, I was able to telephone the hospital and make arrangements for Loy's return. She had been seriously ill.

Indeed, we have conjectured many times that had we neglected taking her to the hospital on that fateful morning, she might have died. A tear duct was blocked and had become infected. A doctor had recommended a medication to which Loy was allergic. A tear duct sounds like a little thing, but an infection there could do irreparable damage without immediate treatment.

However, Loy was treated and bounced back swiftly. I think it is one of her great disappointments that in the critical moment when we were struggling against Jupiter Pluvius, she was in the hospital, isolated and alone. She was released from Penrose after two days and spent the balance of the week with Grace Froh, Bill's wife. We weren't able to use the telephone until Saturday. On Sunday, Bill borrowed Gene's truck, went to town, got a bath, and brought Loy home.

As quickly as possible we launched a fund drive to help pay for the repairs. At the same time, I found that our credit at the bank was excellent. The bank wanted to deal with me, however, and not Bill Froh. So I made the arrangements, even though I was supposed to limit my concerns to the academic side of our endeavors.

When it came to insurance, we had had fire, rain, windstorm, and hail coverage. The adjuster said, "Too bad lightning didn't set you on fire. You'd have gotten the full amount." As it was, we were able to collect between $3,000 and $4,000 for damage to the various roofs done by hail. It turned out that we were covered for whatever came from the sky or the air around us, but not from what came up from the ground.

Bill Froh did an excellent job. He made it possible for me to carry on with teaching and resume my post at the newspaper.

Our fund drive was relatively successful, but it didn't begin to cover costs. We had to bulldoze the entire creek bed and turn the flowing stream back into its banks. The supporting wall that had caved in, we replaced with re-enforced poured concrete—no more cinder blocks. Slowly through the ensuing days, the buildings were cleaned up, floors re-varnished, new supplies ordered, records salvaged. We managed it in two month's time and kept the school running throughout.

But nothing was ever quite the same again. Indeed, dating from the flood. it seemed that a whole series of events occurred which were the result of bad decisions or of poor execution.

One of the reasons Bill Froh had been put in charge of the school was to bring a better financial balance to our operations. Even I agreed that it was "too easy going." Bill knew how to "get tough." And, there is no doubt; our operation in some areas was wasteful and extravagant.

One of Bill's first actions was to decide we didn't need horses. They were a lot of work and brought us in no money whatever. By now, we had a string of 23 mounts. In summer, they grazed on our tall grass. But in the winter, we bought hay. And year around we had a bill for oats. Also, the tack needed constant attention and always some repair.

Furthermore, the horses were forever breaking through our front barbed wire fence where they roamed the beautiful adjacent meadow in which our neighbor, Bill Sorrell, tried to graze a few Angus. That's where the good grass was.

Before Bill decided to eliminate our equestrian program, and at my urgings, we made an offer to the Sorrells to buy that land—something in excess of 200 acres. With so many horses on hand, we had been compelled to buy hay year around. With the new meadow added to our 320 acres, we could cut down on summer hay costs.

This decision, one of many, must be classed as "penny-wise, dollar-foolish." The price for the land was reasonable enough, had we needed the land for purposes other than grazing. Our offer was accepted. Then, after joining those lovely, rolling meadows to what was already ours, the decision was made to get rid of the horses.

Bill had given the matter thought. One year, in an effort to make ends meet, we had tried to charge the students for using the horses.

We had no takers. The students loved to ride. But so thoroughly did everyone believe that education and all its amenities were "free" that few appeared willing to pay out of pocket.

Edith was on Bill's side, in respect to the horses. They brought in zero income and we had to shoe them each year, give them shots, tend for them if they were ill, feed them, and look after them. Keeping a string of horses is a bit like keeping a land yacht. You don't use it much. And its costs are such that if you have to ask about expenses, then you shouldn't have the yacht—or the horses. So, away they went. Only one or two were sold. Bill just gave them to anyone who was willing to accept.

We discovered belatedly that the horses had been a major attraction. Not that people came to stay with us because of the horses, They were "window dressing" in that sense. But they certainly did help make our campus appear desirable.

Then Bill began to clamp down on spending in various departments. He had a serious run-in with Loy. It was so serious that she never spoke to him again, nor about him to me without a snarl. He antagonized Dohn Lewis, Gene, and Link. Margie suggested that Bill was an ignoramus who should stay out of the library.

Even Ruth said she was having difficulty in working with him.

Our campus had been a happy one up until then. It had been impecunious, but joyful. Bill was following the instructions of the Trustees in a way that I couldn't manage. The wages we paid in each case were minimal. But as Bill clamped down everyone began thinking of his own well being and demands for more money became constant.

Just when it began I have no way of knowing. But now rumors and gossip about everything under the sun provided an undercurrent of unrest. Morale visibly declined.

The decision had been made to continue our single course in the subject of human liberty. But we were to convert into a graduate school that would offer Master's degrees in economics, history, philosophy, business management, and possibly psychology.

The reason for this shift appeared obvious to me. I had been the prime mover behind the decision. Up until this time, there had been no reason for students to come to our campus except as an adjunct to their vacations or to provide a completely different and unique experience. We awarded neither degrees nor credits.

Moreover, if we could bring to the campus some famous professors and make them a part of a regular faculty, we would be splendidly qualified to confer degrees or credits. We would have moved the school out of the woods into the mainstream of American education.

I had learned that very few people were interested in learning. They wanted credentials and the Freedom School, as such, didn't supply them. But as a graduate school, we would be meeting market demand. In a small way, of course, but still meeting it.

Surely, this would help provide cash flow income and perhaps assist in making Rampart College self-sustaining; this was the wish dearest to the hearts of the Trustees.

Bill cooperated completely with me. I began writing to various professors who might consider becoming a permanent part of our establishment. As I did so, it became evident that—with three or four people engaged in instruction at the same time—we needed a minimum of three or four additional classrooms. And we would need offices for the professors, even if they all lived off campus. This meant that we needed a new school building.

Gene sketched plans. We proposed a brand-new Reno Sales Lodge, renaming the reconstructed building at the top of the draw, Canyon Lodge.

Link selected a site for the new building at the one spot in the meadow that had been high enough to escape the creek overflow. Construction was begun.

By mail, I secured the services of two professors, putting both of them on five-year contracts. One of them was James Martin, Ph.D., who had been teaching at Deep Springs College. He was widely known as a revisionist historian. He agreed to head our History Department.

The other was Professor William Hutt, of the University of Capetown, South Africa. Hutt's essay in a book edited under the skillful eyes of Frederick von Hayek of Austria, and titled *Capitalism and the Historians* had been my first source of information concerning the good side of the Industrial Revolution.

Hutt had reached retirement age, but was willing to keep working. He would come to America to continue his endeavors as a supporter of private enterprise. He accepted the post of Chairmen of our Economics Department.

I asked them both to arrive as soon as their commitments made it possible so they could begin preparing the curricula we would need at graduate school level.

In further preparation for this conversion, launched a scholarly quarterly that was called the *Rampart Journal*.

Whatever minor economies Bill Froh may have achieved in his attempted streamlining, our spending increased rather than diminished.

I was sure we could manage. And the bank was giving us loans to make up for our shortfall whenever it occurred.

Chapter CII

In the early weeks of 1965, I received a letter from a reader who objected to one of my editorials. This event was not so unusual as to merit special attention, except for one thing. The letter was well written, the argument was logical, and the point of difference related to fundamental assumption.

The average letter from a disgruntled reader is emotional, and serves as an escape value far more frequently than it serves to advance logical discussion. This was an exception. Clearly, the author had a splendid vocabulary and was a woman. The letter was signed, Virginia.

I responded as I usually did. I published Virginia's letter along with my rebuttal. Shortly thereafter, I received a telephone call from the letter writer. The voice was fragile, and I pictured an old woman, or possibly someone of middle age with relatively weak vocal chords. Virginia wanted to come in so we could discuss the matter face to face.

With the pressure I was working under I was reluctant to make appointments. In this case, I did so since the woman agreed to come at my convenience and gave every evidence of being exceptionally intelligent.

My surprise can be appreciated when, at the appointed time, a diminutive schoolgirl of fourteen walked in and identified herself as the Virginia of our written exchange. She was a sophomore in high school, had long, dark hair, large brown eyes, and a look of eagerness. She really wanted to talk about ideas.

Recovering from my surprise, I went back over the subject of our discussion showing why I felt that her position, while derived logically, originated from what I judged to be a faulty premise. Virginia listened with intense interest.

When I finished, she said, "You are right. How stupid of me to make that error. Thank you for correcting me."

People who are willing to admit mistakes are rare. Fourteen-year-old people who will thank you for pointing out their mistakes are so rare as to be virtually non-existent.

I explained that her position was entirely logical and, except for her lack of experience, she would have reached the same conclusion I had reached and without my help. She didn't let herself off that easily, continuing to judge her reasoning powers in a harsh light.

There was something about Virginia that captivated me. I inquired into her background and learned that her father was dead. She had a married older sister and two brothers, one of whom was in trouble with the police. Virginia was candid almost to the point of creating embarrassment. She appeared to be without guile. She lived with her mother and grandmother about two miles from the heart of Colorado Springs. She had ridden her bicycle when she came in to see me.

From that time forward, I would hear from Virginia at intervals. I couldn't conceal my joy whenever she would phone or write. I had longed to have a daughter of my own. I fantasized that this was the kind of daughter I would have had, if I had had a daughter.

One weekend of exceptionally fine weather, Virginia appeared at the campus. She had taken it upon herself to ride twenty-six miles on her bike. The last four miles were on dusty, gravel roads and she was exhausted. She had neglected to let her mother know where she was going.

Loy and I prevailed upon her to telephone and to assure her parent that we would bring her home in the car. This we did after supper, tucking her bike into the rear of the station wagon.

I chided Virginia for undertaking that long a bike trip. I suggested that the next time she wanted to come out that she let me know. I'd be glad to let her ride with me.

So, in the early part of 1965, Virginia and I became good friends. She asked so many questions about the philosophy of freedom that I was enchanted. Nothing pleased me more than discussing this subject and Virginia made it easy for me to do so. I began calling her Gigi, and she called me "Papa." When I would get cross or become too blunt, she called me "Ogre."

Virginia reached my heart. She touched me in way no one had in a long time.

I do not mean to suggest that I stopped loving Loy for I did not. My feelings for Loy remained constant. But man is a complex creature. Although I am appalled to admit it, I actually loved this brilliant wisp of a girl. I was astonished at myself and I was outraged by feelings that welled up within me, beyond my ability to control.

I know that Virginia felt deep affection for me. It is also conceivable that she took advantage of it. She could twist me around to get my attention or almost anything she wanted. One way or another, I managed to crowd in as much time with her as possible, in the midst of my very pressing duties. If she maneuvered me, I readily forgave her. Our relationship made me happy. That was a great gift.

One of my dearest wishes was that she enroll in one of my courses. Our policy was to admit no one under the age of sixteen. So, Virginia was held at bay for two years. She finally did enroll for a course in 1966. She competed for a scholarship and readily achieved one. As I had anticipated, she did well during the course. When it came to comprehending concepts, ideas, and abstractions, she had few peers.

But there was a negative side to Virginia. She seemed to be totally impractical. I tried to teach her to drive a car. The attempt was futile. She knew what to do, but couldn't seem to coordinate her actions to what her brain told her.

She had no interest in learning or in doing anything domestic. She tried Loy's patience severely by her visible unwillingness to take an interest in cooking, serving a table, or helping with dishes. When virtually forced into such chores, she would either forget what she was doing, or perform so badly that it was easier to relieve her of the task than to insist. In a few instances, when I insisted, I was sorry for it afterwards.

During the difficult months of 1965 and 1966, Virginia was the one bright note in my life.

In 1965, following the flood, my father was stricken. He and Esther had to move into town so he could be close to a hospital for treatment. He had contracted "bone" cancer. X-rays revealed that his entire skeletal structure was riddled with malignancy. He was finally admitted to Eisenhower Hospital where he needed blood transfusions.

It is a sound policy, originated by the Red Cross, which encourages friends and relatives of those who receive blood transfusions to volunteer to replenish the stock of whole blood.

One day, I took the time to go to St. Francis Hospital, which was just across the street from the Gazette, so that I could help give back some of what my father had withdrawn.

After preparing me for the service, but before any blood was drawn, a doctor was called in. The medico checked my heart with his stethoscope, and then insisted on an EKG. I was informed that I was in no condition to donate blood and was urged to see my own doctor.

Further examination showed that my heartbeat had lost a great deal of vigor. I had developed something of a problem in one of the valves.

I laughingly explained this to one of my students, a life-long friend who happened to be in the insurance business. His name was Bud Reinhardt. He had, in fact, provided me with policies both for Loy and myself. He insisted that I consult one of the insurance company's doctors.

Bud, together with a couple of Trustees, descended on me. They demanded that I stop work at once and enter the hospital for what I believe is called a "by-pass" operation.

There was no doubt that I felt poorly. I was dragging myself around, but I didn't think I was that ill. Doggedly, I refused. The operation—which was called routine—would keep me off my feet from four to six weeks. In that length of time, without my efforts, the school would close. I knew it. Edith knew it. Ruth and Margie knew it. But I couldn't convince Bud. So, I simply became obdurate and refused to discuss it further.

I was still traveling widely in my efforts to raise money to pay for the repair of the campus. In one of these trips, I flew to Los Angeles where I hoped to enlist R.C. Hoiles into making a further donation. He had been very generous on one or two earlier occasions, and right now we really needed help.

On at least one prior trip, I had stayed as a houseguest with R.C. I made arrangements at this time to do so again. Mrs. Hoiles was a cripple, confined to a wheelchair. R.C. was in his late '80's, but still an omnivorous reader and physically active. He continued to dominate the newspaper chain he had forged.

The Senior Hoiles lived in a magnificent home and had domestic help, so my presence as a guest would not be a strain on them. Besides, I had become very fond of R.C. We had argued over many points, just as Harry and I had. These exchanges were always stimulating and I enjoyed them.

R.C. and I held to different views on the question of capital punishment. I believe we were in substantial agreement in all other areas. Harry had at one time shared R.C.'s position. Moreover, Harry had insisted that I be consistent in all my writings. It had taken me about two years, but I had finally convinced Harry that capital punishment and the doctrine of human liberty are at odds.

I arrived at the Hoiles' residence on Saturday and spent that night with them. I had arranged for a fund-raiser for Sunday evening, sponsored by some other students of mine, so I planned to be with the Hoiles only briefly.

On Sunday morning, we enjoyed a bountiful breakfast and as I followed R.C. toward his study where we had often discussed various ideas, he said, "Bob, we're having trouble with the water tank in one of the upstairs bathrooms. Do you know anything about those things?"

"Not much," I conceded. "But I've learned a few things. I've had to. Why don't I take a look?"

He nodded. I went upstairs to the troublesome piece of equipment and discovered the problem. There was no trick at all in finding the remedy. By bending the float rod slightly, I was able to reduce the level just enough to stop constant running. The chore completed, I returned to the study.

R.C. looked up from the paper and glared at me. "I'll bet you never held onto a steady job in your life," he said.

"What?" The observation was totally out out of context. Also it was untrue.

"I think you're a bum. You're no good, LeFevre. If I had my way, I'd fire you."

"Why, what do you mean?" I sputtered like a wet fuse. This made no sense.

R.C. launched into a tirade of bitter acrimony. I couldn't believe it. I finally said, "Is this some quaint way of thanking me for fixing your plumbing?"

He redoubled his attack, calling me every name he could put on his tongue. He repeated his earlier phrase, "If I had my way, I'd fire you. But Harry won't hear of it."

"If you're quite serious," I said, "why don't we talk to Harry? He always does what you want him to."

"Call him up, then."

A telephone was handy. I called Harry back in Colorado Springs. "Your father wants to fire me," I told him.

"Were you having a debate with him?" he asked.

"No. He just attacked me out of the clear blue.'

"Let me talk to him."

I handed R.C. the telephone and listened as he raved against me to his son. Finally, he said, "Here, Harry wants to talk to you." The instrument was returned to me.

"I'm sorry Dad feels the way he does," Harry said. "Of course I'm not going to fire you. Your job is safe as long as you want it."

"I really appreciate that, Harry," I said. "I don't know what has caused all this and I'm sorry about it."

"Forget it," he advised. "We'll talk about it come more when you get back."

I hung up.

"It's clear to me," I said, "that I am a most unwelcome guest. I'm sorry my presence here has upset you. But don't worry. I'll get out right away. Friends are coming to pick me up at eleven."

I went upstairs to my room and packed my few things, bringing my bags down as I returned.

I started out the front door and R.C. stopped me. "Where do you think you're going? Your friends aren't coming until eleven?"

"That's right. So, I'll just take my bags out to the curb and sit on them until my friends arrive. I certainly will not stay where I am so thoroughly detested. "

"Don't be a bigger fool than you already are," R.C. said. "What would the neighbors think if they saw you sitting at the curb?"

"They'd think that you threw me out," I suggested.

"I don't want them thinking that way."

"It's the truth, isn't it?"

"I haven't ordered you to leave. I'm now ordering you to stay here in the house until they come."

"R.C." I said. "I've always taken the position that the employer is right, even when I think he has made an error. I have conducted myself so that no criticism has ever come from me. I believe in free enterprise and I don't badmouth it or the people who say they are for it. Regardless of what you think of me, I shall continue to speak well of you."

"Humph," said R.C., and stalked back to his study.

I sought out Mrs. Hoiles, who had returned to her bed. I took her frail hand in mine. "Thank you for all your many kindnesses," I said to her. "It's doubtful that I'll ever see you again. R.C. has taken a violent dislike to me and everything about me. He's really cussed me out."

"I know," she nodded and smiled brightly. "He's like that sometimes. Please don't hold it against him. Once in a while, he's like this."

I shook my head. "I won't hold it against him. But at the same time, it is clear he wants nothing further to do with me. So, this is it."

"I understand," she said.

I went to the dining room and sat in a straight-backed chair until eleven o'clock when Dr. James Harris and his wife, Mary, arrived from Whittier. It was the last time I was ever inside the Hoiles' home in Santa Ana.

That particular trip to Santa Ana produced virtually no dollar return. I had been counting on substantial help from the Hoiles. But as I flew back to Colorado Springs I saw my position as editor with the Colorado Springs paper in a new light. Harry had assured me about my job. And he was a man of his word. I could keep working if I wished.

But I had done something that R.C. could not forgive. It wasn't my position in respect to capital punishment. I couldn't believe our differences to be of such magnitude as to convert me into an evil genius in his mind. Indeed, R.C. loved a debate as much as anyone could. He didn't like to lose and he lost infrequently. Indeed, although I was sure of my position, R.C. clung to his.

Of course, since I never had an opportunity to discuss the matter further with him, I cannot be sure. But I now saw what I believed to be the crucial factor in his wrath toward me. My influence with Harry had come between him and a son whom he dearly loved.

R.C. was a genius in two fields. He was a shrewd businessman. Additionally, he was an uncompromising champion of human liberty. His elder son, Clarence, had exhibited the same type of shrewd business judgment, but when it came to doctrine, Clarence could take it or leave it alone.

Harry, on the other hand, displayed the dual qualities of his father. He, too, was an excellent businessman. In addition, Harry was an idealist who was quite capable of holding to the cause of liberty even when dollar income might suffer. Harry had demonstrated that by keeping me in his employ when I had been the star of "Editor on the Spot."

When it came to establishing ultimate priorities, both Clarence and Harry followed the lead of R.C. I am, perhaps, making more of their differences than is warranted. But my influence with Clarence was virtually non-existent. So far as Harry was concerned, he and I had debated virtually every shade and nuance of freedom, each of us gaining points and losing points until we stood together. That was R.C.'s problem. It was named Bob LeFevre. His resentment of my close affinity to Harry had probably smoldered beneath the surface for some time. He had given no indication of this until that fateful Sunday morning, when the dam of his emotions had given way.

As I studied my own situation, it dawned on me that I would be doing Harry and the newspaper a disservice if I continued as editor. I would be driving a wedge between father and son, for Harry would never go back on his word, and R.C. would never change his view of me.

Back at my desk at the *Gazette*, I gave a month's notice. It had to be that, or I would become a perpetual bone of contention within the Hoiles family.

Harry asked me to reconsider. He assured me that he didn't mind debating with his father or standing between me and his dad. I told Harry that the day he could assure me that I would not become a source of friction between him and his father, on that day I'd be delighted to return to his employ.

That day never arrived.

R.C. died in 1970 at the age of 91. His devoted wife outlived him by only a week. I was able to attend the funeral for Mrs. Hoiles, but I was conducting a seminar at the time of R.C.'s passing.

Returning to 1965, when I left the *Gazette*, new financial strains were placed upon our tiny, formative Rampart College. Not only was I unable to make my monthly payments to the school, but it also became necessary for me to receive a wage from the school.

I hoped that by giving all my time to the school—and now that I had some thoroughly qualified professors on the faculty—we could handle the burden of the increased outflow of dollars.

Actually, deep down, I was aware that support was dwindling. But my credit at the bank was tops. And there was just a possibility that I could find new support. With the school now in the mainstream of education, perhaps enrollment would increase, both in numbers and in dollar amounts, so that we could weather the storm.

There was one very healthy sign. The powerful Milliken organization increased its patronage of my services by one seminar in 1966. And there were businessmen who had promised substantial help if and when we conferred degrees; that is, if and when we had qualified professors in residence. Maybe, just maybe, I could pull it out.

There was one other chore I could perform. I asked Bill Froh for his resignation, and he cooperated. In my judgment, Bill had done a good job. I think the Trustees agreed. But in the judgment of virtually all others, Bill was getting zero in the way of cooperation. However, saving the salary paid to him offset my own entrance as a paid employee to a large degree.

Meanwhile, our new Reno Sales Lodge was completed. We were ready to begin our operations as a graduate school.

Chapter CIII

One avenue of financial salvation was made available. A loan officer at the First National Bank, where Rampart College had its various accounts, recommended the procedure. Why not make application to the government for emergency funds? They had been made available to those in the "disaster area," which certainly included the school.

Out of hand, I turned down the recommendation. But because of the magnitude of our difficulties, I felt that I should place the final decision on the shoulders of the Trustees. I had so often been proud of them. I was really curious to learn what they would say. Never was I more delighted with one of their decisions.

We had taken a firm position against government involvement in private enterprise. Rampart College was private in every sense of the word. We would not even accept enrollments from students who had secured government loans. We wanted no government money whatever. After all, there is no such thing as "government" money. Everything the government has in its hands, it takes from taxpayers' pockets.

The Trustees stood fire. One more private college (with government help) wasn't that important. What was meaningful was our position. We would hold to the free market and live or die with it. Our survival wasn't the important thing. Our integrity was. There was no dissenting voice. If we went under, then we would sink with all flags flying. We would be mealy-mouthed hypocrites if we preached one thing, yet clandestinely practiced something else.

And so the die was cast.

In 1967, Milliken requested that I conduct the sessions for their middle management trainees and executives on the East Coast, rather than in Colorado. It didn't require a degree in math to discern that it would be considerably less expensive to fly one person (me) to and from the East Coast, than to send anywhere from sixteen to twenty-six people from the East Coast to Colorado.

Knowing my preference for an isolated location, Milliken arranged for sessions to be conducted at the Mimosa Inn, located at Tryon, North Carolina, less than an hour's driving time from his headquarters in Spartanburg, South Carolina.

I consented and made arrangements for Sy Leon and Butler Shaffer to carry a good deal of the teaching load at the school so I could be free to handle the Tryon seminars.

At the outset, this appeared to be fortuitous. We could run a full schedule of sessions in Colorado with Tryon serving as an auxiliary campus for the Milliken group.

A Milliken seminar was a one-week affair in which the instructor lectured from eight in the morning until nine at night for five days in a row, plus a two-hour "get acquainted" session the evening prior to the opening. The firm wanted about fourteen such seminars in 1967. On campus, we planned four one-week executive sessions plus seven two-week sessions and two weeklong workshops.

Additionally, we organized a thirteen-week (one night a week) seminar to be held in Colorado Springs which would cover much the same material offered in an executive seminar.

While we carried on with our traditional classes, Professors Hutt and Martin were setting up their curricula and we were promoting the enrollments of qualified students for the opening of our graduate school, now slated for Spring of 1968.

I conducted the first two Milliken sessions at Tryon. In the midst of the second, a completely unforeseen blow fell. The Milliken Company was undertaking a basic reorganization that involved an expansion through purchasing a chain of textile mills. The decision was made to cancel the balance of the Freedom School seminars scheduled for that year.

I asked for an audience with Roger and he generously provided the time. I explained the disaster such a loss of income would mean to us at this particular time. I have never found Roger Milliken to be other than magnanimous and understanding. Even though our agreement was entirely verbal and not legally binding, Roger agreed to pay Rampart College the full tuition he would have paid had we conducted the courses.

That decision made it possible for us to continue operations during the scheduled school year. Without that income, we would have been forced to close at once.

However, two other events intruded. Our regular enrollment fell off. For the full year, we obtained only 82 students. This reduced attendance in two sessions to four each and gave us several with an enrollment of six or eight. During 1967, I spent a great deal of my time (which was now all mine) in an effort to raise funds. But many a businessman who had been on very friendly terms now turned a deaf ear.

I was fortunate, at one point, in being able to secure the interest of a foundation and also of a wealthy family who considered a splendid endowment for our efforts.

Along with declining enrollment and dwindling dollar support, I traveled more extensively than ever. It may have been an error to ask Bill Froh to serve as president, due to the antagonism he generated. It may have been another error to dispense with his services when we did. The school was left to fend for itself virtually without a decision-maker in attendance.

Indeed, I began to wonder if I could make a valid decision about anything. My heart was giving me a few scares. I was physically exhausted. But I believed in the fundamental integrity of the staff and faculty. Certainly, I knew that Butler and Sy understood the philosophy and were able and ardent instructors. Things should have gone well. At least, in theory, that was true. Instead, my constant absences served to engender further gossip and intrigue.

There were a number of little things that happened, each of which made an impact far beyond its intrinsic merit. Let me provide just one example.

The wealthy family I had interested in the school told me that sometime during the summer they would visit the campus to see how things were progressing. If they liked what they saw, we could count on "substantial" dollar support.

One of our students, desirous of flaunting any and all authority, decided that he would show everyone just how independent he could be. He obtained a black flag—that of anarchy—and ran it up our flagpole along with the American flag. He was aided and abetted by a staff member who shall remain unidentified at this juncture.

With that black banner fluttering from the pole, who should appear on campus but the senior members of the family considering an endowment. They took one look at the black flag, turned their limousine around, and disappeared in a cloud of dust. They wouldn't even respond to my letters.

This was, of course, during that portion of the 60's when students around the nation were exhibiting this same license as freedom. It was not the kind of behavior that we taught or recommended. Indeed, I had already published my position in respect to anarchy, which appeared under the title: *Autarchy versus Anarchy*.

The irony of this event came home when the staff member responsible for the black flag demanded a raise on the grounds that he had exhibited exactly the right amount of defiance to authority.

The final and crushing blow came when the bank called me in. My line of credit was at an end, they informed me. In 1968, I would have to begin the process of reducing the debt. And there would be no new money whatever.

We had long ago finished paying for the original purchase and the bank had taken a first mortgage on the property as security. Unless I began making repayment, the bank would, in 1968, begin foreclosure proceedings. We owed better than $500,000 and had additional obligations relating to contracts and various accounts, which pushed total debts up to something near $700,000.

Meanwhile, another event helped to bring things into crisis. My two professors, Hutt and Martin, were at odds. Each had full latitude to teach his own discipline as he would. I had counted on my own ability to persuade them to a position more closely in harmony with my own beliefs and to each other. One way or another, and despite rumors to the contrary, no effort was ever made to gag them or to insist on any particular "line." It was understood that I would teach what I believed to be true; they were at liberty to do the same.

I thoroughly detest and reject the idea that an instructor can be pressured into offering ideas that he thinks false. Any professor, who would permit this to happen to him, as I see it, would lack integrity.

But now Professor Hutt approached me and asked to be released from his contract. He couldn't abide Martin and the ideas I expressed made him "greatly uneasy." Indeed, his position was that if he stayed on at Rampart his own reputation would suffer. He wanted out.

His contract was lucrative, but he would forego it totally. Please, would I let him go? There was no question of Hutt's integrity. Nor had I ever sought to bind him. I immediately released him. A sizeable obligation vanished.

Now, I made a colossal error. From remarks I had heard (I am ashamed to say that I had succumbed to some of the gossip in circulation), I had concluded that Martin felt the same way. He and I had a personality conflict probably based on our respective chemistries. Indeed, some of my staff had reported that Martin was very unhappy and would jump at a chance to get away.

So, I called him into my office and released him from his contract, too. I didn't discuss it with him and, thereby, leaped into the fire out of a sizzling pan.

Martin stalked from the office. A day later, I received a letter in which he informed me that he was prepared to hire legal representation and that no matter how hard I tried, he was going to hold me to the contract. Only one year of the five-year term had run. I had four more years in which I would pay his full salary plus provide him with housing. Any failure on my part and he'd see me in court!

Martin had been among those most ardent in insisting that government was totally unnecessary. But not if he needed it in dealing with me.

I told him that financial reverses made it necessary for me to close the school. It didn't matter. School closed or no, I personally owed him the money and he would be after me from that time on until he got every dime coming to him.

At the end of the school year in 1967, we thinned out the staff to the degree possible. Except for my four angels, and my son, everyone seemed angry with me. Even Tom looked at me as if I were a stranger; Loy and I were sniping at each other; and, although loyal, Margie, Ruth and Edy were shaking their heads.

Up to this time, we had received about a dozen reservations for enrollment in the graduate school. I was compelled to write to cancel those reservations. But now I received hostile letters from many one-time well wishers. Dr. Rothbard, an economist I greatly admired, wrote that I had no "right" to close the school.

I responded that I'd keep it open if I could, and then went on to explain friction that had developed between Martin and me. Rothbard counseled me never to voice criticism of anyone who believed in liberty. He would never do it, he assured me. It was important that all good libertarians present a front of solidarity to the rest of the world. I thought the advice sound, and still believe it to be so.

We issued a prospectus for 1968, intending to hold classes to the degree possible. Meanwhile, I sought out the real estate firm that had sold us the property originally, and listed it for sale with them.

We struggled through the winter of '67-'68 and managed to secure something of an enrollment for the seminars. But the bloom had gone.

I had only two sources of comfort during this trying time. My dog, Vesta, and Virginia. The latter was a frequent visitor at the school who wanted to talk with me about ideas. The former didn't have to discuss anything, and was content if I patted her head or tweaked an ear.

The foundation I had managed to interest in our efforts now demanded a return of the money not yet expended. Their contribution had been earmarked for library expansion. At the recommendations of Hutt and Martin, we had been adding to our books. We had kept a careful accounting, of course, and were able to send back a check in the full amount still on hand.

Fortunately, Milliken came back on line and booked a few seminars. But instead of a dozen or more, the number was reduced to six. It appeared that we'd have difficulty staying open for the full school year of 1968.

Then, suddenly, we got a break. The real estate firm found us a buyer. The Mennonites had been seeking a property that they could use for an educational endeavor. They had already made a tentative offer on a piece of land at the head of Ute Pass. The realtor showed them what we had, and they decided in favor of our campus rather than the rival parcel.

I was able to prove to the bank that we had a sale pending and, in consequence, they did not foreclose. They waited for the deal to come to fruition with the understanding that our entire debt would be paid. Indeed, we insisted on all cash. The Mennonites, as it happened, wanted an all cash purchase! They had the money.

We signed the papers, and completed the transaction, granting possession at the end of 1968. Thus, we paid all our obligations in full and still had a considerable sum left over. We went back over the books to make certain that everything had been handled. The only unpaid obligations related to our original group and the unrecompensed labor they had performed for years. With approval from the Trustees, each of us was paid in full.

Now, what would I do?

Clearly, there were two courses of action open. I could close the school. The sums of money remaining could be dispensed as follows: 1. I would have to pay Dr. Martin for the full term of his contract in advance. It was the only remaining obligation. With whatever sums left I could make a contribution to some other tax-exempt organization, such as Leonard Read's Foundation or the new organization started by Dr. Harper, the "Institute for Humane Studies."

The other option was to relocate the school and continue operations. In that case, I would pay Dr. Martin on a monthly basis during the unexpired period of his contract. Instead of giving away whatever assets remained, they would be retained for the continuing endeavor at the new location.

I favored closing. I was half-sick and had little inclination toward work. I had labored night and day from 1954, when I first joined the *Gazette*, up to the end of 1968. During that time, I had never managed more than a week or so of "free time." And such weeks came possibly once every other year. I had neglected family, friends, health, and everything else. What I needed was about six months of total inactivity.

But several factors militated against shutting down. First, no one wants to quit, particularly under fire. Secondly, I could see small reason for rewarding Dr. Martin with a large cash outlay. Thirdly, I was feeling rather badly used by both Read and Harper, although I still leaned in their direction on the basis of doctrine.

Now came another reason. It came in the person of Sy Leon. Speaking on behalf of my girls and his wife, Riqui, he wanted to continue. Why shouldn't we move to a more favorable location? Colorado was "equally-inaccessible" to all. Studies showed that, as things now stood, our largest market would be in the Los Angeles area.

Another factor was in our favor. At the end of 1968, Milliken has asked for classes in 1969. That would mean some income. If we had a new location, those classes could continue and we could organize new ones in addition.

If we operated carefully and on a small scale, we could make it work.

Still on the horns of a dilemma, I boarded a plane for Los Angeles to see what I could find in the way of a new site for the college. If we found a location in Southern California, I would close our present Board of Trustees and keep only those who lived nearby.

A key man in respect to relocation was one of our Trustees, Chuck

Estes, from the Los Angeles area. I learned from him the enormous gap between Colorado and California real estate prices. When I went out to look at possible location, the California realtors laughed at me. I still had a sum of six figures with which to work. To me, that was impressive. They thought I was being funny.

I located a possible site. It consisted of a large residence in the midst of an abandoned orange grove of eight acres. Price? $800,000. We had just sold 526 acres complete with twelve buildings for a comparable sum. But there was something else to think about.

In Colorado, payments on mortgages were made once a year. In California, with monthly payments staring at us for a balance of say, S700,000, I couldn't be certain of lasting more than thirty days. Besides, we'd have all the costs of moving, all the legal work of reorganization, and a completely undeveloped market. What staggered me was Estes' observation that the price was a snap. That parcel would go fast, he assured me.

Then I located something else—a lovely residence in Arcadia, situated on two acres of land. I took Chuck to see it. He judged it to be a "steal" at something close to S65,000. The broker was entirely honest end candid. If I had any notion of getting it re-zoned for school use, I was wasting my time. Zoning rules in Arcadia were strictly enforced.

I took that advice with a grain of salt. I'd had experience with zoning in Colorado and knew that the principal function of most zoning boards is to arrange for variations. So, I didn't let the R-1 classification stop me.

The house, itself, was huge (7,200 square feet of floor space) and in A-1 condition. Loy and I could occupy the premises. As soon as feasible, we could use one, two or even three rooms for classrooms or meeting rooms. Clara Baldwin, oldest daughter of the famous Lucky Baldwin, had erected the building. It was Lucky who originally owned most of what is now Arcadia and who gave us the Santa Anita Race Track, named after his youngest daughter—the pride of his paternity.

Having had loads of experience with large homes, the place seemed ideal.

In the name of Rampart College, I made an offer that was accepted. The plan was that Sy and Riqui, my three women, Loy, and I would go. All other members of our Colorado operation were dropped.

Then, Virginia wanted to come, too. Her mother was entirely willing. So Loy and I became, in name at least, Virginia's foster parents. One additional event sheds light on our situation.

Earlier, we had taken Tom out of public school and enrolled him in a private school called Fountain Valley. He had completed high school and had gone on to Denver University, a private institution where he also took up residence.

Things did not go well for Tom at the university. Every campus was, by this time, infested with young people who were "living it up" and acting defiantly in regards to any kind of authority. One of Tom's roommates came from a wealthy family that catered to his every whim, and Tom came under his influence to some degree. I am happy to say that the influence was far less than it might have been.

Also, at this time, America was at war in Southeast Asia and the draft had been reinstated. Tom approached me for advice as to what he should do. I gave him the best counsel I could.

"The government," I said to Tom, "is an agency of legalized force. It has exhibited skill and efficiency in only one area— that of collecting whatever it wants from the populace. There are three things government traditionally takes away from the people over whom it exercises coercion. It takes their money and we call it 'taxation.' It takes their property and we call it 'eminent domain.' Or, it takes them as people. We call this a 'draft.'

"As you know, I disagree with the government's power to do these thing. But I concede. The government is lot bigger than I am and I have never found a way of successfully preventing the government from getting what it wants.

"The government takes my money. It is a tax. I disagree with its power to do this; but I do not question the reality of that power. So, despite the fact that I disagree, I pay.

"Fortunately, at the moment, the government doesn't want any land or other property I have. If it did, it would file an action against me and would take what it wants. Of course, it would pay me. But it decides how much I am to be paid, and then taxes me and everyone else to make up the sum.

"You might look at this as another form of tax to be paid in a person's right to own, but nonetheless, a tax.

"In your case, the government has decided that it wants you. What recourse do you have? First, you can flee to another country. If you do, you are paying the tax in lost opportunity and possibly lost citizenship. Or, you could become a fugitive and live clandestinely. That, too, pays the tax. You would live like a hunted criminal constantly looking over your shoulder. That is, as I see it, a rather high tax.

"Thirdly, you can let the government do as it pleases with you. That, too, pays the tax. Fortunately, the government does give you a small "out." You could declare yourself to be a "conscientious objector." As I understand it, and the rules change all the time, your claim might be disallowed. If past experience gives any clues here, you would probably still be drafted. You would merely be permanently assigned to every kind of dirty job the military can dream up, but you would not be assigned to a combat outfit.

"Or, the government gives you the 'opportunity' of 'volunteering' (under duress, of course) for one or another branch of the services.

"In short, Tom, the government has levied a tax against you which it insists that you pay by services rendered. It gives you a few choices about what kind of service, but you will either pay by fleeing or you will pay by choosing your service. Failing any of these, the government will simply kidnap you (legally, of course) and put you wherever it pleases.

"Now, it is the task of a prudent man to pay no more tax than necessary. Pay you will! I'm sorry. I have no method in mind where you can avoid or evade payment. You'll pay. And it is your judgment that must prevail, not mine. Whatever your decision, you will have to live with it.

"If you expatriate yourself, that is the cost you will pay. If you become a fugitive, then you pay that cost. If you take C.O. status and succeed in it, you'll pay that way. And if you 'volunteer' or not, you'll pay that way. Pay you will.

"My advice to you, and the only advice I can offer is this. Think through your options, and then take whatever course of action is the least costly. To you, of course."

Tom listened carefully and made up him mind. He enlisted in the Coast Guard, a non-combatant branch of the service. So, he was at sea on the icebreaker, Glacier, at the time of our move to California. He had been living away from home ever since 1965,

Right after Thanksgiving, in 1968, Loy, Virginia and I left the school during a heavy snowstorm. Sy, Riqui and the three girls remained to supervise the shipment of school supplies and the surrender of the property to the Mennonites.

We took possession of the Arcadia property in the name of the college. Before the year ended, the other five people remaining on staff showed up in Southern California. Our new epoch began.

The story of this new beginning is quickly told. Months before our actual departure from the Rampart campus, Sy and I flew to Los Angeles together. Our plan was to find a temporary headquarters for the school until such time as a re-zoning could take place in Arcadia.

Harry Hoiles was still the publisher of the Gazette in Colorado Springs. But his brother, Clarence, was helpful to me and suggested a rental in Santa Ana, not far from the Santa Ana Register where he and R.C. operated the flagship newspaper of the growing chain.

We obtained the major portion of the top floor of the First Western Bank building at Fourth and Main Streets in Santa Ana on a five-year lease. Prior to our arrival, the bank agreed to remodel that floor to our liking, and it did so.

Sy arrived just before Christmas and we went to the bank to take possession. The bank insisted on a six-year lease. The reason given was that the remodeling had been more costly than anticipated and it would take six years, rather than five, for the investment to pay off.

I had explained to Sy that he would be managing everything. I would agree to teach, or write, but beyond that I didn't want to be active. Now, our shipment of furniture and school equipment and records, including a 10,000-volume library were in transit.

My oldest son, Bob Jr., had, in the meanwhile, married, had three children, and was second in command at Lyons Van and Storage. So, I had arranged with his firm to handle the move for us.

Also, my second son, Dave, had married and had two children. Both sons from my first marriage were living in California and it appeared that, at last, we would all be in the same state. However, about the time we moved to California, Dave and his family moved to Colorado and took up residence in Lakewood, a suburb of Denver.

Prior to our move, Bob Jr. had advised that I should have a place to unload our shipment. If the storage company had to hold it, costs mounted very quickly on a daily basis.

Thus, when the bank demanded we sign on for an extra year, our shipment was already on the way. Since our survival in the new location was problematical and we had no assurance of being able to last more than a year, the added year on the lease seemed trivial. With only a modest protest, I signed the six-year commitment as the President of Rampart College.

Then, the bank wanted someone to co-sign the lease for added assurance. Curiously, the bank was quite willing to accept my signature as a private citizen to back up my signature as President. While I had been paid back wages, much of that money had gone into furnishings for the new house the college had purchased in Arcadia, so I had very little in the way of this world's goods with which to act as anyone's guarantor. Anyway, I signed again, backing up my own signature with a second signature.

I protested this and accused the bank official of sharp practice. I got a shrug in response. I could take it or leave it. I "took it."

It didn't take long to discover that any hope of re-zoning in Arcadia was illusory. The realtor had represented the situation honestly and completely. I had deceived myself.

Now Rampart College owned a residential property and leased its own headquarters. This meant that we had to operate without a campus.

Our overhead in Santa Ana was only a trifle of what it had been in Colorado. But our income was greatly reduced as well. From the beginning we bit into the reserve we had acquired from the sale of the Colorado campus.

I was on salary and I paid a substantial rental fee for occupying school property in Arcadia. The income from Milliken classes, conducted in the east, all went to the school. Sy went to work to organize local classes and, in my judgment, did an outstanding job.

We held two or three seminars in our offices in the bank building, but this site was not suited to the type of seminar that had gained us so much recognition. To offset this, Sy organized a pair of seminars that we conducted on the island of Catalina.

Then, reaching out ever further, he organized others at an inn on Carmel Valley Road outside of Salinas in central California. These took on some of the character of what we had achieved in Colorado. However, they barely paid for themselves.

We decided to conduct classes by mail and I wrote two home study courses: *Fundamentals of Liberty* and *Raising Children for Fun and Profit*. We obtained a few mail order students, but hardly enough to make the effort worthwhile. Much later, my course *Fundamentals of Liberty* was used by Robert Ringer as the basis for a book which he made into a national best seller called, *Rebuilding the American Dream*.

We produced a pair of 16mm color films in which I provided brief exposure to a pair of ideas fundamental to an understanding of liberty. It was Sy's idea that rental of these films would bring in much support and great rental fees. They didn't.

Then, I put some fifty thirty-minute lectures on tape cassettes that we offered for sale. Dollar-wise, they cost more to produce than they brought in.

Sy came up with the idea for a really popular magazine that would sound the clarion note of freedom. We spared no expense on the two issues we managed. And they were beautiful publications. However, they failed to take hold and, again, we faced dollar losses.

Sy proved to be a marvelous PR man and he knew how to travel first cabin. We spent a great deal of money trying to find our niche. Nothing jelled.

The truth underlying all these efforts was that I was ill. The loss I experienced as a result of the Colorado experience had wounded me deeply. I tried to hide my feelings and to carry on as though nothing had gone wrong. But I was heartsick and weary. There is no question that I became testy and difficult.

Sy knew me well. Indeed, we were very close and I trusted him completely. But he began to argue with me and show up weaknesses in my presentations. I'm sure he did it with the best of intentions. He so much as told me that I was mentally ill and needed outside help.

The friction between us mounted. The only place where I obtained any surcease from continuing pressure was back in South Carolina. I had moved my headquarters for the Milliken classes to the Holiday Inn at Greenwood, some sixty-five miles south of Spartanburg.

Meanwhile, I did my best to encourage Sy as a teacher. He was excellent on the platform. But teaching is a demanding task and Sy invariably refused. It seemed to me that if Sy would attempt to conduct classes in Santa Ana while I continued putting them on in South Carolina, we could turn things around. But Sy detested any kind of rigorous schedule and always found some reason to avoid teaching.

Finally, I prevailed on him on one point. I pressured him to organize the League of Non-Voters. He demurred at this, too, because of all the time and energy it would involve. However, he finally did make that move and, thereby, won personal recognition by providing a useful vehicle in which I refused to participate.

At last, the bad feelings between Sy and me reached a breaking point. I would either have to fire him or let him take over completely. I considered both avenues.

We had finally paid off Dr. Martin. The only on-going obligation related to the house in Arcadia and the bank lease. So, we sold the house (at a profit) and used that money to continue operations of the school.

At last, I made a final decision. Sy had done a wonderful job as a PR man. To fire him seemed unfair and unjust. But we were not getting along. And there was no question about it. I was worn out and needed a rest. Sy was right on that score.

I resigned from Rampart College. Rather than drop the seminars for Milliken, which Sy wouldn't consider conducting, I decided to keep on with them for awhile. But I turned the college and all its remaining assets over to Sy, and he became President.

The lease at the bank building had two more years to run. I promised Sy that I would help him pay his rent for one of those years. By that time, he should be on his feet enough to handle the final year.

As things finally worked out, he apparently wasn't able to. Faced with a lawsuit, I paid off the bank in full.

Sy was able to work out what I was told was a most lucrative arrangement with Harry Browne. Browne had produced a couple of best selling books and was well known nationally. At the end, Sy closed the school and the adventure begun so many years before came to an end.

Epilogue

I have been most fortunate. I've been able to tell my story and, at the same time, continue to live beyond it. It is a bit like attending one's own funeral in a conscious state and, thus, being able to judge the true character of one's friends and relatives. In the course of reciting the principal events of a full and adventurous life, I have been able to see and even to make allowances for my various adversaries. Indeed, I have been careful to set forth their actions in the most kindly and forgiving light.

I have not been motivated toward tolerance because of a particularly benign state of mind. Rather, I have been able to see that my foes may have had valid grounds. I do not believe that I have always been heroic or above reproach. I had made many errors.

Strangely, I first decided to write my biography when I had gained sufficient insight into my own character to be able to set down my mistakes. I went through a period where I detested myself because of them. With the perspective of time, I found that I wasn't always the charming, likable, innocent fellow I confidently hoped others would see when they looked at me.

But that phase went into eclipse and I discovered a new detachment—a way of looking at myself and what I had done *sans* self-adoration, and yet without anger or remorse over my periodic displays of bad judgment. It was then that I decided on the working title for this effort: "Beyond Malice."

This is, so far as I can presently discern, the great attainment of age. It is the ability to make peace not only with the world, but also with one's self. A person must forgive the shortcomings of others and be able to forgive himself as well. It is only when the desire to make atonement (or to force others to make it) vanishes, that mature judgment knocks.

Children invariably want to "get even." "Even" does not exist in reality. What you or I may want and what you or I may get will never coincide. Adults do not waste time with futilities.

What have I learned as a result of my experiences?

I have learned that man-made government is man's great enemy. Further, my own experiences with the Freedom School, and then with Rampart College demonstrates that a man-made government is not necessary. There, in those beautiful foothills of the Rampart Range in Colorado, we lived without government "protection" and "services" to the degree possible at this time. "Degree possible" denotes my own limited ability to create conditions outside and separated from government at any and all levels. Doubtless, others will come along having more ability who will be able to move further in this direction than I can.

The new frontier, waiting to be conquered by man isn't a continent, or even the vast reaches of space. Were a new location to be found—were it possible to achieve colonization of some planet other than Earth—a flight to take up residence would be an escape, a way of temporizing with the real frontier.

Today's frontier challenge comes from the mind.

It is absurd to suppose that all will see this, or prepare to cope with it. Nor is it necessary. No frontier has ever demanded that everyone cross the barriers. Nor has there ever been a guarantee that those who do cross it will find paradise. Indeed, there is no guarantee whatever. Doubtless many wrong avenues will be followed. Predictably, some persons will fail and even die in making the attempt.

But the future of our species beckons in that direction. Human beings are going to have to learn to live in a society that is *not* ruled by man-made government. This was not always true, but it is true now. Relocating with the same philosophic baggage in tow will produce the same errors we are struggling with now.

At this juncture, the argument of the unthinking invariably surfaces. "Every human being is capable of performing evil deeds," it will be said. And this is true.

"We cannot afford the evil that human beings are capable of inflicting on their fellows." This also is true.

"It follows, therefore," say my opponents, "That we must have a government capable of restraining those who would perform these evil deeds." Then in a burst of generous condescension, my adversaries exclaim: "You would probably be correct, LeFevre, if men would somehow behave themselves properly. But they don't. Clearly, if men were good, government could be abandoned. But human nature won't change. And, therefore, we must have a government to impose by force upon all, so that those evil doers are captured and punished, either on a local scale or world-wide."

I believe I have stated the position of my adversaries fairly. There is invariably the same oversight. If we have a government, it will be human beings who will be hired to restrain the evil in others. Who are these persons who will be hired, either by popularity contests or by direct application? They will be just as human and as much disposed toward evil as those to be restrained.

If people are capable of committing evil deeds, then the people occupying the offices of government will be cut from the same cloth. They are evildoers, too. There is not a single shred of evidence that they will be otherwise.

If men are capable of committing evil actions, granting them power over others makes evil actions certain. But there is a difference. When men in government commit an evil act, they are legally shielded from the consequence of the act. If ordinary people, endowed with neither rights nor powers over our fellows, began to behave on a daily basis the way the people in government behave, then the world would be in flames. We would have a reign of terror in which ordinary people went from house to house, took what they wanted, and proclaimed that their "need" justified their performance.

As a matter of fact, that is what we are beginning to experience, and we call it "terrorism." But all that is happening is that small groups of persons—noting what governments have done since they were devised—have set themselves up to emulate their political masters.

The frontier of the mind is a frontier that decries terrorism from all persons, not merely from those without legal protection for the violence they inflict.

If a band of armed men with the latest devices for mass murder raid an opposing country, we wait to learn who sent them. If they are the minions of some state, we applaud their bravery. If they are acting independently of government, we call them terrorists.

But if we care to be honest, it is the nature of an act that makes it one of terror, not the name of the sponsor.

There was a time in man's history when such actions may have been necessary and even fruitful. When man lived in a state of barbarism, governments were the barbaric answer to every problem. Kill or be killed, was the rule.

This was at a time when the best techniques for murder centered on the athlete. They benefited the man strong enough to wield a sword and skillful enough to shoot an arrow, or even a bullet. The people who risked life and limb in these contests was limited by the size of the armies of the respective combatants.

That age has passed. Our technologies have marched in the direction of peace, while our politicians continue to gird for war. Now we have the equivalent of death rays (the laser) and an explosive potential so vast that we talk calmly of wiping out a hundred or more cities at a time.

Our athletes today train for football, basketball, and other spectator sports. And mean little men cower in bunkers far underground, pushing buttons. The same motivation grips them that mastered Ghengis Khan or Torquemada.

"We are the 'good guys'!" they proclaim. "Those other guys are 'bad'. For the triumph of 'good' we must kill them or they will surely kill us!"

Or, they say: "We must teach them our catechism so they see the world and Creation as we do. Since our way is good and all others evil, we are doing 'good' if we inflict our wills upon them before they inflict their wills upon us."

Then a further and presumably conclusive argument is offered. "We know that those other guys are bad because of what they have done. We are merely evening the score!"

Will the government that has never cast a stone please stand up to be identified?

I have spent my life as a crusader. I love my country, which love begot my efforts when I saw what I took to be an alien philosophy encroaching on the concepts set forth in the Declaration of Independence. I am still enlisted in that crusade.

But as I labored to restore the dream of freedom and independence of our ancestors, I realized that the American government *in its actions*, was as much an enemy of freedom and independence as any other government on earth.

In the name of freedom, it enslaved us and made us dependent upon it. In the name of protection, it committed such actions of intervention and violence throughout the world that other people see it as a danger of vast proportions, thus increasing the risk we all face. To cloak its behavior in benign garb, it performed various acts of alleged generosity; it used the money it had wrested from the toiling, perspiring workers by force. It punished success and rewarded failure.

There is something else I learned as well. Freedom cannot be imposed; it must be earned. It will not arrive with the blare of trumpets and the sound of marching boots. I cannot make you free, much as we both might approve.

Real freedom will come quietly when the idea of liberty so dominates the informed mind that the individual blessed with those thoughts begins to act in accordance with the principles of "live and let live."

The merit of human existence is found in human variation, not in cloning. The thrill of achievement comes because an individual learns to excel, not because he blanks out his individuality and makes himself part and party of the group.

This means that, in a total sense, we will *never* have a free society. We will, instead, have free individuals who strive within a culture where non-freedom continues to lurk. It is our own nature, as human beings, which we must conquer, not the nature of others. The job must be performed one by one.

Why do I see a free society *in a total sense* as an impossibility? Because we were not all born at the same moment and will not all live in the same way with the same values. Some of us are younger and some older than others. Some of us have had more experience. We are not all endowed with equal potential for wisdom or restraint.

Freedom is not a goal that can be achieved; it is the necessary means to all other goals.

In the final analysis, all governments consist of human beings. We have nothing but people with which to work. To imagine that human beings calling themselves "government" are endowed with the ability to achieve goals which persons outside of government could not achieve, is to ascribe mystical or diving powers to government.

Where is the evidence to sustain such a conclusion?

I am told that government is necessary for us to have highways and roads.

Governments do not built roads using equipment, natural resources, and manufactured products. Government does not provide any of these things.

I am told that government provides the money with which to pay for the people and the equipment and the products used.

But the government has no money of its own. All that it has it wrests from those who earn money by productive effort. If this were not true, government would immediately halt all taxation. If government halted all taxation, then it would cease to exist.

In short, people provide roads. In the interest of justice and fair play, those who use the roads should pay for them and those who do not use the roads should not be required to pay for them.

I am told that we must have government in order to adjudicate disputes.

Government does not adjudicate anything. People do all the adjudicating that is done.

There are only four possible outcomes of every dispute. You win; you lose; you compromise; or, you keep disputing. There are no other possibilities. It does not require a black robe or a high bench to discern the reality of disputes or their settlement.

Disputes will have to be adjudicated. Government is not needed—people are. A judgment is as good as the wisdom within it. The black robe cloaks the lack of wisdom.

I am told we must have government in order to protect society. I marvel at the "protection" government provides. There is hardly a spot on earth that hasn't been torn up and damaged by war—a government exclusive—or by roving bands of terrorists who make their own private wars as they emulate governments, or seek to set up one of their own.

I do not see government protection. Each government treats certain other governments with favoritism, thereby awakening the cupidity of some and the envy of others. Government converts the world into an armed camp, in which human beings stand guard so that other human beings won't attack. But the only reason for wanting to attack is the existence of the other government in the first place.

When war comes, people are drafted and shot at in order to protect the government that created the tensions that led to war.

Government cannot even protect its own politicians.

Two recent Presidents escaped assassination attempts, not because they were well protected, but because their assailants were inept.

The last time a President was assassinated, it occurred in broad daylight on a busy street in front of crowds of people. The government investigation created a continuing dispute as to how many people tried to kill President Kennedy, which one did kill him, and why.

Meanwhile, a man was arrested and accused of the crime. While the alleged villain was in a police building, surrounded by government protection, he was gunned down in front of a national television audience. We call this protection?

A policeman is only an armed guard. An armed guard is as effective as his skills make possible; whether he was hired by the government or not has little to do with those skills.

In short, whatever protection is possible can be and has been provided by people. Government has merely provided a mystique. It suggests that by granting a group of persons a license to steal, beat up, and murder others, society will be protected.

The final argument is that if the laws are stern enough—if the police are granted total power, are armed, and stationed at frequent intervals on the street—then crime will cease. Particularly if the courts back up the police in their accusations.

Were such a procedure to be followed, freedom would cease and every urban center would be no more than a prison. But even this would not stop crime. In support of that last conclusion, might I suggest that an examination of the incidence of crime occurring inside prisons be undertaken. There, in a confined area, with armed guards in sight of everyone, we have one of the largest and most persistent recurrences of every crime known to man.

I could go on with one illustration after another; but cataloguing governmental failures is not necessary. The reality we confront as a result of human nature stands starkly before us all.

There are three points that must be looked at now. Each stands in the way of our maximizing human well being. They may even stand in the way of human survival.

One is human gullibility. What we want is a world in which crime never appears. That is as impossible to achieve as a totally free society. It will never occur. A few moments serious reflection should show that there would always be someone who is angry, maladjusted, emotionally upset, or sadistic. Some of those persons will, at the same time, be cunning and clever. Crimes will occur.

But we are gullible. When a politician announces that he will achieve what we want if we grant him more power, we grant him that power. He will not achieve it, because such an achievement is contrary to the reality with which we must deal.

But our gullibility, our belief in centralized power, now administers the *coup de gras* to our reason. If we shift the problem to the shoulders of government, then we can shift responsibility. And that is what we want. We can put the problem out of our minds. When a crime occurs, it is now the other fellows' fault. So we authorize the government to commit crimes which, were we to do them, we would be criminals ourselves. So we change the meaning of words. A crime committed against a criminal is no longer a crime.

The second point we must consider has an equally fallacious base. It is the assumption that, to improve human well being, we must all act together. Nothing could be further from the truth.

First of all, we will never all act together. That is contrary to human nature. If human history tells us anything, it tells us that human beings do not agree. There are half a dozen major religions in the world and at least half a hundred interpretations of those religions.

There are scores of philosophies and thousands of explanations of practically everything.

Human beings do not yet universally agree that there is a right or a wrong, that two and two add up to four, that the world is round, or that human beings cannot fly.

I have met thousands of human beings. I have never yet met a man totally capable of handling his own affairs. We all make mistakes. Our species falls far short of the perfection of which we like to dream.

But I have reached one conclusion that has to stand. While no human being can manage his own affairs perfectly, he will handle the affairs of others with less effectiveness than he handles his own. Most believe the contrary, demonstrating that we believe according to our fantasies. not according to reality.

And now the third point.

Like children, we want to "even the score." We want vengeance and retaliation. We want restitution from, and punishment inflicted upon the wrong doer.

That is the glowing ember of hate that keeps governments alive.

To achieve vengeance, retaliation, to command restitution, and to punish others demands the ability to injure human beings.

My opponents at this point can be heard on every hand. "Why do you stand up for the criminal, LeFevre?" is the roar of protest. "Don't you think he deserves to be injured? Look at what he did!"

I carry no brief in favor of the criminal. That is why I carry no brief in defense of those in government. Setting a thief to catch a thief doubles the amount of loot stolen.

"But look at all the evil deeds that have been committed!" I am urged; "Do you want those villains to 'got away with it?'"

My answer is: "They already got away with it or they would not be criminals."

Nor am I comforted by those who say to me: "You're right, LeFevre. And government is wrong. So we will set up private agencies of retaliation and restitution (which will be called 'protection companies'.) Then, when we go after the criminals and force them to repay or we will imprison or kill them, we will be doing 'good' since people will voluntarily pay for our services. Taxation can be dispensed with."

Any agency that carries out the public will to commit violent acts upon other human beings—whether authorized by legal *federal* or by sponsors putting up the funds—is, by its actions, a form of government.

Government is nothing more than a group of people who sell vengeance and retribution to the inhabitants of a limited geographic area at prices made possible by force (either monopolistic or competitive) and charged by those who carry the guns.

So the cry continues: "Let us even the score. Then, we can have peace."

Let us see about, "evening the score."

The United States was, to a large degree, wrested from the prior inhabitants by force, trickery, or both. To "even the score," this land must be returned to its former owners.

I do not condone what happened and I cannot deny it. But the fact is that those persons performing the trickery and imposing the force are all dead. The wrongs perpetrated *cannot* be made right. Many of us who live here now are the descendants of some of those persons. Many others are not. But long before the first European settlement appeared on these shores, those holding the terrain stole the same resources from each other.

If we are to be fair and honest, the effort to "even the score" must go beyond returning the land. Those of us here have produced nearly everything we have from this same land. Since the land must be restored, it follows that all that has been gained through it must also be returned to the original owners.

That would mean that every non-Indian in America must be pauperized. Surely, you would not want to see the thief gain at the expense of those he has wronged?

Such a procedure is clearly absurd. We don't know precisely who was wronged, or how much and how many have gained thereby. What is done is done, however wrongly.

Consider some of our more current exploits. Consider the bombs we have dropped in Europe, Japan, Korea, and Vietnam. That has to be made right, too. Whatever was taken must be restored.

It is impossible.

How about the state of Israel? It was wrested from the Palestinians with the concurrence of certain modern governments including our own. Why? The claim was that it had originally been the land of the Israeli. True enough. After they had wrested it from the Caananites. And before that? The Caananites were taking it from each other.

The human race, through its various governments, is facing its past and endeavoring to make the past less bloody than it has been. To do so, we must shed more blood. Our present is filled with gore and our future has become problematical.

The amount of human life and treasure expended on taking care of the past is destroying the present and putting the human future into eclipse. All in the name of "getting even."

Goethe was never more wise than when he said: "Let the dead past bury its dead."

When I recite these facts to those who listen, many respond: "You may be right, LeFerve. Peace is better than war. As soon as I got my vengeance, my restitution, whatever is coming to me or mine, we can stop."

On that basis, governments will never stop. Their furnaces are fired by human hatred and the lust for vengeance—the desire to "got even." This is the human malady. It is the father of terrorism and the mother of the modern state.

War is the luxury of barbarism, a luxury that civilized life cannot afford. It comes down to you and me in a very personal way. Have you ever been wronged? I have. Indeed, if you have managed to absorb much of the foregoing, you have the story of some of the times I have experienced injury at the hands of others.

I am told constantly that the desire for vengeance is an unavoidable characteristic of our kind. It has become a characteristic, but it is not inevitable. Infants are not born with a thirst for vengeance. They learn it. Let them be taught something else.

The truth—and I have tried to tell it—is that I, too, have wronged others. I haven't intended to. Nonetheless, it has happened.

If we care to be honest, few of us can claim no wrongdoing. Presuming, of course, that we have matured enough to attend school.

I find that I an ignorant in many ways. But I do have some competence. I have the ability to develop skills and to earn a living. I am capable of earning enough so that my family and I can eat with some regularity.

I have not done this perfectly, as a reading of my story demonstrates. But I have been skillful enough to feed myself and my loved ones fairly well.

There is no way that I have the ability or skills to feed society. I'm not that effective. Neither are you.

Further, I have been able to earn enough to clothe myself and my loved ones (not always as we might have wished), but I've done a fair job, despite my mistakes.

But, I'll tell you what I can't do. I haven't the skills or abilities to clothe society. Neither do you. You may be able to do a better job than I've done. It may be that some of you have fallen short, in which case my compassion goes to you.

But you can't clothe society, either.

And the same can be said of housing. Like me, you can do a fair job. Sometimes you may find shelter in a hovel, a cave, or under a bench. And possibly you've done well enough to live in a mansion with every comfort and convenience. But there is no way that anyone can house society to its satisfaction.

The same is true of protection. Efforts to food, clothe, house, and protect society are exercises in futility. And when government is called upon to do those things, government can't do it either. What it does is wage financial war upon the productive and pass inadequate funds over to those less productive (for whatever reason), while keeping the lion's share to "administer" the "program."

The net result is injury to the poor by helping to create gullibility, dependency, and injury to those less poor by making them more poor.

Is the human situation hopeless? Yes, it is, if we continue to depend on government. But that is something we don't have to do.

For example, there is one crime I can absolutely prevent from occurring. My own.

I cannot prevent you from committing a crime, if you make up your mind to do it. The government cannot prevent it, either. But I can see to it that I don't commit a wrongful act.

I might add that this is no easy task. I am as prone to anger as any. I cry out against inflicted pain and injustice. I know and understand the emotion that can engulf anyone and make him yearn to inflict an injury on another person.

Also, if I have injured another inadvertently, I can come forward and try to make things right. It isn't easy. But it can be done.

Sooner or later, we must reach the conclusion that government is obsolescent, if not already obsolete. Will everyone agree? Of course not. You cannot control what others may think, and neither can I.

But you can make a beginning. You can decide to support yourself and to provide your own food, clothing, and shelter. Yes, even to provide your own protection, as a result of your own efforts. You cannot do it perfectly because you and I are not perfect. But you can be effective to a large degree.

Some will do a better job than anything I could possibly achieve. Some may not do as well. But you'll do a better job of it when you believe in yourself than when you become dependent on politicians and expect them to do it for you.

How can one individual assist in maximizing human well being by advancing the cause of liberty? His first task is to learn his true nature.

1. Each of us has the ability to think and act as he pleases.

2. Each of us controls his own energy. We do it wisely or foolishly, but we do it individually. We may act on the advice or the command of others. Or we may decide not to. Our own energies remain under our individual command and control.

3. It follows that I cannot make you free; I can earn my own freedom by controlling myself instead of trying to control others.

4. What steps to I take when I wish to be free?

5. I free myself from dependency on others when that dependency is created or maintained by force. Since there is no way that I can survive without the help of others, I will always be dependent to some degree. But I can depend upon the voluntary support others provide when they willingly buy my goods or my services. If I have to compel them to buy my goods or services—either directly at the point of a gun, or indirectly through governmental avenues—then I am acting in a way that is counter-productive and anti-freedom.

6. Having recognized this point, I break off all relations with government.

a. I will make no contribution to any political campaign or political party.

b. I will endorse no issue and no candidate.

c. I will not vote.

d. I will de-register and refuse to participate in government-sponsored proceedings of any sort.

e. I will not run for office, nor hold a political job even if asked.

f. I will patronize those persons and firms that have the least to do with government.

g. If a firm or individual is heavily subsidized by the government, I will have nothing to do with it; it is an arm of the State.

h. I will not ask for government help, guidance, advice, money, or emolument of any kind.

i. I will accept no government check for Social Security, welfare, injury, pension, or for any difficulty I may be in. I will solve my own problems.

j. I will set my own standards in such a way that I impose on no one.

k. I will injure no one for any reason.

l. I will be as generous and helpful to others as my ability makes possible.

m. I will live up to every contractual agreement I voluntarily enter into.

n. I will, therefore, take great care to only enter into those agreements that are worthy of fulfillment.

o. I will be true to the highest and best within me, committing no act of theft, dishonesty, or violence against any other human whatsoever.

The foregoing are the rules. How many will follow them? Predictably, very few. That is why human society is in such upheaval. What I have set forth isn't popular.

But it is factual and in harmony with the reality that is man.

The fact that I do not participate in government at any level and in any way does not cause the government to cease to exist. Should you reason your way through the human morass and decide to emulate the non-participation procedure, government will surely continue.

That, in itself, should cause rejoicing. The recommendations I have set forth provide a method that will be as gradual as the dawn of intellectual integrity. That is as it should be. Any other procedure will contain a reaction, a backlash that can destroy any temporary gains.

By employing the method of logic and learning, no one is coerced into accepting an unwelcome or a misunderstood objective. He advances toward freedom and a free society exactly at the speed and to the degree that he is prepared for it. That is the only way it can be done. It will not be popular because we have been nurtured on the hopes of panaceas and quick political solutions. But it is the only way that will never have to be repeated.

Today the world is sick with the greatest social disease of all. It isn't herpes or syphilis. It is, in fact, a pagan faith in the State. Around the world, terrorists are operating under the noses of various governments, often aided and abetted by those same governments.

We will move *toward* a free society, one by one. We will never achieve a free society in the sense that we can finalize the process. The price of freedom is eternal effort aimed at achieving self-control and self-mastery. We do not achieve this by controlling others. We move toward achievement when we learn to control and govern ourselves. Freedom is self-control, not license to impose on others.

It has taken me a lifetime to learn this. I am grateful that I have lived. I am even grateful that I have made mistakes, yet continued to live so that I could learn more. Man learns by trial and error. Few of us learn much of anything by success.

I am also grateful that some across this great country of America agree with at least some of my conclusions. They are out there now, quietly minding their own business, improving their own performance, raising their own standards, and willfully imposing on none.

At the moment, man knows too much and understands too little of what he knows. But the answer you seek for is in yourself. There is no logical "other place" for it to be.